PIONEER BATTALIONS IN THE GREAT WAR

PIONEER BATTALIONS IN THE GREAT WAR

Organized and Intelligent Labour

by

K.W. MITCHINSON

LEO COOPER
LONDON

First published in Great Britain in 1997 by
LEO COOPER
an imprint of
Pen & Sword Books Ltd
47 Church Street
Barnsley
South Yorkshire
S70 2AS

© K.W Mitchinson 1997
ISBN 0 85052 566 7

Typeset by Phoenix Typesetting, Ilkley, West Yorkshire.

Printed in England by Redwood Books, Trowbridge,
Wiltshire

CONTENTS

Acknowledgements vii

Introduction ix

Foreword xv

1. Converting and Creating 1
2. Blooding the Innocents 26
3. The Chosen Few 54
4. Pioneering on the Somme: The Opening Phase 69
5. Pioneering on the Somme: Grinding On 90
6. All Aboard the Trench Line Special 110
7. "Build their Dugouts, Make their Roads" 121
8. Working in Partnership 146
9. A Race Apart? 166
10. In Search of Skills 191
11. Pioneering in Retreat 219
12. Converting and Countering 244
13. Pioneering through Others' Eyes 266

Postscript 287

Appendix I   Casualties 290
Appendix II   Establishment 299
Appendix III   Battalion synopses 301
Appendix IV   Examples of pioneering work 317
Sources 324
General Index 325
Index to Arms, Formations and Units 327

ACKNOWLEDGEMENTS

Many people and institutions have helped with the production of this book and their assistance is here gratefully acknowledged. In particular, Dr. Gwyn Bayliss, Rod Sudderby, Ian Carter and the staffs in the Departments of Printed Books, Documents and Photographs of the Imperial War Museum have, as usual, been of immense help. Permission to use the documentary and photographic collections held by the Museum and from those of the Public Record Office, the Light Infantry archives and the DLI Museum, has been granted by the Trustees of those bodies. Peter Liddle granted permission to use the papers of the Liddle Collection housed in the University of Leeds. My thanks too, to his staff who displayed great tolerance and understanding. Many regimental museums kindly responded to my enquiries regarding extant sources. Particular thanks are due to Colonel Cowley of the Light Infantry Office, Pontefract, Captain Bob Bonner, the Manchester Regiment and Steve Shannon of the DLI Museum. My appreciation too to the staff of the many libraries and archives who showed such patience and energy in pursuit of my enquiries. Numerous individuals have provided either help, encouragement or both, and several have allowed me access to documents in their personal possession. These include Dr. Roger Anderson, David Barlow, Nigel Cave, Michael A.Cooper and Sue Latimer. Finally, special thanks to JB.

ABBREVIATIONS

ACI	Army Council Instruction
C.E.	Chief Engineer
C.O.	Commanding officer
CRA	Commander Royal Artillery
CRE	Commander Royal Engineers
CSM	Company sergeant-major
CCS	Casualty clearing station
DCM	Distinguished Conduct Medal
GOC	General officer commanding
G.S.	General service (wagon)
M.C.	Military Cross
MID	Mention in despatches
M.M.	Military Medal
M.O.	Medical officer
O.C.	Officer commanding
OTC	Officer training corps
R.E.	Royal Engineers
RQMS	Regimental quartermaster-sergeant
RSM	Regimental sergeant-major
W.D.	War Diary
W.O.	War Office

NOTE: The designation of battalions throughout follows that of the *Official History*. Thus the 9th Battalion, The Border Regiment becomes 9/Border. Similarly, regimental spellings also follow Edmonds, James and *Soldiers Died*.

INTRODUCTION

When the nations of Europe marched to war in August 1914, few on either side believed that it would last long. Modern technology, and the perceived superiority of one nation's will over another, caused many to feel that the troops would be home before the end of the year. Previous wars involving Great Powers had indeed been fairly brief affairs. Despite the experience gained in the Russo-Japanese and Balkan Wars, some observers continued to argue that where large armies had the space to deploy and manoeuvre, modern artillery would not sufficiently dominate the battlefield to prevent an early decision. Some of the more perceptive realized that, short of a collapse of morale on one side, recent technological developments made the idea of a war of movement somewhat anachronistic.

The German assault upon France through Belgium and Luxembourg did almost bring a swift conclusion to the war. Fortunately for the Allies the Russian army in the east diverted significant German forces from their western offensive. As the BEF concentrated its divisions near the Franco-Belgian border, determined Belgian resistance at Namur and Liege further slowed the German advance. It was halted at the Marne in September, and later thrusts were repulsed at Ypres in October and November. With the failure to break the French within Schlieffen's designated six weeks, and the coming of winter, the two sides paused and began to dig.

Meanwhile, Britain had become one huge recruiting camp. The small professional regular army was to be supplemented by an expanded Territorial Force and a massive new organization, known familiarly as Kitchener's New Armies. As it would take months (if not years) to house, equip and train this new force, more regular battalions were recalled from their Empire postings. Territorial units were either shipped out to replace them or, alternatively, to take their place alongside the regulars in the trenches abroad. For trenches was the word that was already beginning to dominate, at least temporarily, the minds of those who conducted the war. The war of movement had given way to a war of stalemate in which the exhausted armies glared and fired at each other from a rapidly growing system of trenches and breastworks. These hastily dug excavations were separated from each other by stretches of increasingly broken and disputed ground. The most pressing requirement for those occupying the trenches and manning the guns behind, was that the earthworks offer some protection from the shells which were daily directed against them. In the eyes of the Allied commanders these were never meant to be permanent constructions, but soon it became evident that the Royal Engineers and the infantry alone could not be expected to fight as well as maintain the burgeoning number of trenches and gun emplacements. Furthermore, the camps and railways under construction to accommodate and supply the growing armies were also absorbing an ever-increasing amount of the scarce resources of available manpower.

In November 1914 the War Office began to consider how this dilemma could be solved. Its solution, announced to the GOCs commanding the various army groups in early December, was to create and post a Pioneer battalion to each division of the New Armies then forming in the U.K.[1]

From the outset these new units were designed to be equipped and trained as conventional infantry. The difference was that they were intended to be more closely affiliated to the divisional Royal Engineers than with the brigades of infantry. Consequently they were to be provided with a selection of technical stores, and would be given special training in entrenching, road-making, demolition and other work which could generally come under the description of 'pioneering'. Because it was envisaged that these units would spend much of their time digging, they were ordered to ensure that at least 50% of their strength should be composed of men who were used to working with pick and shovel. The other 50% had to possess a recognized trade. The skills decreed as appropriate ranged from joiners, masons and bricklayers to those found in any of the metal trades. Yet, because these units would be used at the front, even the skilled men were to be instructed in trench digging.[2]

This decision was later confirmed, and in early January an Army Council Instruction[3] expounded a little further on the duties the new units would be expected to perform. In addition to road making, demolition and entrenching, battalions were to be trained sufficiently to undertake technical work on railway embankments, to be able to construct wire obstacles and to bridge and to fell trees. The technical instruction was intended to take place at the same time as battalions continued with their more conventional infantry training. The War Office asserted that as trained men became available an engineer officer and NCO would be attached to every unit. The role of these new units was defined as one of fighting infantry, capable of providing 'organized and intelligent labour' for engineering operations.

Commanders of New Army divisions were instructed to ascertain which battalions under their command would be best suited for conversion to Pioneers. In a statement which showed a fine disregard of the motives behind many men's enlistment in the Kitchener battalions, the War Office announced that if a man in one of the selected battalions did not possess the qualifications for a Pioneer, he could be transferred to another battalion and replaced by a volunteer from a different unit. If a division found that none of its battalions was suitable for conversion, it could receive one from another division which contained more than one unit which fulfilled the requirements. In such instances, the loss of a battalion would be made up by one posted to it from army troops.[4] The War Office decided that serving officers with some knowledge and experience of field engineering would be most suitable to command the units. To supplement what would be an obvious shortage of regular officers, men who in their civilian careers had been in engineering or similar professions would be recruited to the units or, if necessary, transferred from battalions in which they were already serving. Finally, it was declared that men in these new units would wear a distinguishing badge (the crossed rifle and pickaxe was designed later), and that apart from officers, all ranks would receive 2d a day more than corresponding ranks in the infantry. In addition, they would, as men in any infantry unit, be eligible for proficiency pay.[5]

In making this decision the War Office was following a system which had been introduced to the Indian Army in the early years of the century. Kitchener, who was a Royal Engineer, is usually given the credit for allocating a Pioneer battalion to each of the Indian divisions, and he was certainly intimately involved in the decision to do the same with the New Armies. Although Pioneer battalions as such had never before existed in the British Army, troops who fulfilled what would later become recognized as pioneering work had featured in previous wars. Edward III had some with him during his campaigns of the Hundred Years War and pioneer contingents were present with some artillery and infantry units during the seventeenth and eighteenth centuries. In 1750 there was a suggestion that a Corps of Pioneers should be created, but nothing came of it. A hundred years later an Army Works Corps was sent to the Crimea but following adverse reports on the drinking habits of its men, it was quickly disbanded and the idea abandoned.[6] It is sometimes difficult to distinguish such groups of men from what were later to evolve into the Corps of Engineers; but with the creation of Pioneer battalions, the administration and organization of the two arms were to become distinct and partially independent.

In the hectic days of late 1914, when the regulars and the Territorials overseas were clamouring for more guns, shells and supplies, the organization and equipment of the New Armies remained in a state verging on anarchy. The question of kitting out and accommodating a few battalions of Pioneers was not at first seen as an additional problem. After all, the units were already in existence and thus, apart from the supposed additional R.E. tools with which they were to be supplied, did not create any extra problems for the Quartermaster-General. They would simply have to take their turns along with every other unit. What was of more immediate concern was to ensure that sufficient units were nominated for conversion and that they contained the required proportion of skilled to unskilled men. For the time being they could continue to drill, parade and dig with whatever uniforms, rifles and tools they had so far been able to accumulate.

NOTES

1. W.O.162/3 3/12/14 20/Gen.No./3593 (A.G.1)
2. In late December it was decided that each battalion should have: 16 carpenters and joiners, 16 blacksmiths, 16 masons and bricklayers, 8 tinsmiths and 4 engine drivers and fitters. These 60 tradesmen were to be distributed equally among the four companies. In addition, other men with the same trade were to be included, if possible, up to 50% of total establishment. (ACI 282 of 1914)
3. ACI 27 of 1915 L.20/Gen.No./3593, (M.T.2)
4. W.O.162/3 op.cit.
5. ibid.
6. Elliott, E.R., *The Royal Pioneers, 1945-1993*, (SPA, 1993) p.9-11

FOREWORD

by General Sir Hugh Beach, GBE KCB MC

When the Armistice which ended the First World War was signed in November 1918, every British division serving on the Western, Southern and Balkan fronts had its own pioneer battalion, as did the Australian divisions, the New Zealand division and the Canadian Army Corps. Nearly 80,000 men were serving in these units. So far as the British army was concerned some 68 battalions, all of them belonging to infantry regiments bearing famous names (and including one regiment of Foot Guards) served during the war as pioneer battalions, some throughout the war. It is a strange anomaly that up to now no book has been written about these battalions and even in the regimental histories of their parent regiments they have received scant notice. This oversight is totally undeserved. The present book undertakes the heroic task of chronicling the activities of these units, from their painful creation through to their final disbandment, in a way which goes far towards setting right the neglect of the past 80 years.

Towards the end of 1914 the onset of trench warfare on the Western Front had created a huge demand for manpower with a basic training as infantry but with special skills and aptitude for earthwork. Half were expected to be men used to working with pick and shovel, the other half to possess recognised artisan trades. Pioneer battalions were to be strong units numerically, 24 officers and 860 men being a typical establishment. They were to work for the most part in detachments, responding to the instructions of the Commanders Royal Engineers of each

xv

division. Their special skills were recognised by a rate of pay 2d a day more than their infantry equivalents (though substantially less then the Royal Engineers) and they were supposed to receive special training to match, though not all did. The jobs they did were legion. Those foreseen by the original Army Council Instruction were ambitious enough, including road making, demolition, entrenching, bridging, tree felling, the construction of wire obstacles and work on railway embankments. In practice the pioneers concentrated, as they were asked to do, upon the domestic economy of trench life: shoring, revetting, the building of dugouts, overhead cover and shell-proofing, sapping, mining, building trackways for men, mules, guns and ultimately armoured vehicles, tunnelling and the rendering habitable of flooded shellholes in seas of mud. Although living conditions and the incidence of casualties were less severe in Pioneer battalions than in normal infantry battalions they were at times horrific enough. And by 1918 some Pioneer units were fighting on the front line: one battalion sustained 50 percent casualties in a week and was rewarded with one VC, one DSO, four MCs, one DCM and nine MMs.

Their story is told here in as much detail as space allows, with punctilious accuracy and spiced with a wealth of human touches. It is a story of enormous effort and heroism, told in a cool understated tone of voice which makes the tale only more poignant. At the end of the First World War all the Pioneer battalions were disbanded or changed back to normal infantry. In the Second World War the Pioneer Corps had to be re-created, on a vastly larger scale and remained in the order of battle till the 1990s. Now it has been merged into the Logistic Corps and only one pioneer regiment remains. It can look back on a proud history which this book goes a long way towards documenting and substantiating.

Chapter 1

CONVERTING & CREATING

The decision to create Pioneer battalions came after the first three of Kitchener's New Armies had, on paper, been formed. These formations were still a long way from being ready to go overseas to fight, and providing them with Pioneer units was a relatively simple job. Five divisions of the First New Army (9th–14th Divisions) had a battalion nominated from within the existing formation – the exception being the 9th (Scottish) Division which had the 9/Seaforth Highlanders, probably a K3 unit, attached to it. The six divisions of the Second New Army (15th–20th Divisions) and the six of the Third (21st–26th Divisions) similarly had one battalion from within its own ranks converted to fulfil the role of Pioneers. Kitchener's original Fourth New Army was broken up in April 1915 to provide drafts, and was initially replaced by the battalions which had been raised by the efforts of local recruiting committees from cities, towns, organizations and even individuals. These divisions (30th–35th) were supplied with battalions which had been raised locally either specifically as Pioneers, or which had been converted fairly early in their history. The Fifth New Army (36th–41st Divisions) had its Pioneer battalions supplied in the same way. During the course of the war two New Army divisions were to lose their original Pioneer battalion and have it replaced by another.

With the exception of the 49th Division, those first line Territorial divisions which went to France all received Territorial Force units to serve as Pioneers. Similarly, apart from

1

the 59th Division, which eventually had a Kitchener battalion posted to it, and the 60th which had a locally raised Pioneer unit, the second line Territorial divisions which fought in Europe also had T.F. battalions as Pioneers.

The Guards Division supplied a Guards battalion to serve as its Pioneers and the 63rd (Royal Naval) Division had a locally raised Pioneer unit posted to it in June 1916. The 74th and 75th Divisions, which served in Egypt, and the T.F. divisions which went to India and Palestine (43rd, 44th, 45th, 53rd and 54th) were not allocated Pioneers. Finally, when the eleven regular divisions formed in 1914 and 1915 were given Pioneers, they were originally serviced by two T.F., two locally raised battalions converted to Pioneers and seven battalions specifically created as Pioneer units.

Of the sixty-eight battalions that served officially as Pioneers, twenty-five were converted during their training period in Britain. Only one of these was a Territorial unit, the remainder being New Army battalions. When the men enlisted in their chosen, or sometimes allocated battalion, they of course had no suspicion that they would be switched from the role for which they had joined up to one which was to involve more physical labouring than actual fighting. Many New Army battalions were a cross-section of society and in them might be found men of many different occupations, trades and classes. The initial 100,000 recruits tended to come principally from the commercial classes, but the subsequent enlistments came from not only the clerks, but also in increasing numbers from the working and labouring classes. It was largely from these later units that the Pioneer battalions were eventually to be selected.

The divisional history of the 23rd Division states that a 'census' of trades and skills possessed by the men was undertaken within divisions to discover which of their battalions would be best suited to conversion.[1] This appears to be the only surviving published reference to any such formal investigation. How extensive they were is open to speculation, but as the War Office directive required them to conduct such an exercise, most divisions probably did go through some sort of assessment process. In some divisions, especially those where men from the commercial classes were brigaded with recruits from mining districts, the task would not have been particularly difficult. The overwhelming number of the chosen battalions was selected simply because they contained in their ranks a large number of pitmen. The 12/KOYLI was a natural choice. The West Yorkshire Coal Owners' Association decided to raise a complete battalion and equip it at its own expense. It contained at least 300 men from the Featherstone district, most of whom were colliers from the pits owned by the Charlesworth family. The remainder were also mainly miners from other pits in the West Riding and were later described as 'hard sons of toil'.[2] Similarly, the two battalions of the South Wales Borderers which became Pioneers in early 1915 also contained large numbers of miners. The 5/SWB was said to contain a higher proportion of men schooled in mining and engineering than any other battalion in the division. It was this factor, combined with its expertise at erecting huts at Parkhouse, which decided the authorities on its selection.[3] Its sister battalion the 6th, was also apparently selected because the 'high percentage of miners in its ranks naturally marked it out'.[4] The 7/Yorks & Lancs was composed 'at first almost exclusively of miners',[5] while the 11/DLI. was composed 'largely'- (one source claims it was 95%)[7] of colliers. From the other end of the country and a different sort of miner, the Territorials of the 5/DCLI were chosen to become Pioneers because so many of them were used to manual work. In the 10th (Irish) Division the 5/Royal Irish Regiment was picked because, as one source suggests, the 'majority' of its men were either miners or artificers.[8]

Many of the men in the 11/South Lancs were also undoubtedly miners and it is probable that a large proportion within the ranks of the 11/King's Liverpool came from the mining districts of West Lancashire. The 9/Gordon Highlanders was created from an amalgamation of surplus personnel from the 8th Battalion and a large draft from the depot.[9] Given the recruitment area of the regiment it would seem likely that when it was decided to select a Pioneer battalion for the 15th Division, the Gordons were an obvious choice. Another obvious choice for conversion was the 17/Northumberland Fusiliers. Following an approach by the Army Council to the company management, this unit was raised by the North-Eastern Railway as a means by which the employees could serve together with their friends and workmates. When the idea was first mooted the company issued a circular to its employees promising that any worker who enlisted could be assured that adequate provision for his wife and children would be made, that his job would be kept open and that his pension contributions would be kept up by the company. On this assurance nearly 3,000 men responded, and the battalion was filled within a few days.[10] In January 1915 the War Office decided that this battalion of railmen would make an ideal Pioneer unit. This decision was later supported by its historian, who also claimed that it contained an 'unusually high number' of skilled men.[11]

While it is easy to see why these several units were selected for conversion to Pioneers, it is more difficult to understand why, other than by positive discrimination, the 11/Hampshire was chosen. This battalion was originally a K2 unit and had been posted to Dublin in 1914. Its geographical proximity to the 16th (Irish) Division probably secured its conversion, and until the division was broken up in 1918 it remained the only English battalion in the Irish Division. Neither does there appear to have been any obvious reason why the 6/East Yorkshire was selected in the 11th Division. This was a division composed very largely of northern units and there were battalions coming from more obviously mining areas than East Yorkshire. The decision may have been made because the battalion was reputed to have a high proportion of Section D men of the Army Reserve in its ranks.[12] Because these men were assumed to be slightly older than the usual recruit, it was perhaps thought they would be better suited to Pioneer work rather than as conventional infantry. The case of the 9/Border battalion serving in the 22nd Division, is similar to that of the East Yorks. This division contained several units that were likely to have had a larger proportion of miners within their ranks. There were men from the coalfields of Workington and Whitehaven serving with the battalion, but according to the regimental history, the Borderers were actually chosen because they had acquired 'such a good reputation for good trench

4

work'[13] rather than because they contained more miners than any other battalion. Although his battalion did contain miners, Second Lieutenant Dillon of the 14/N.F. thought his unit was selected for conversion because it was 'the worst in the brigade'. He claimed that the reason for this unhappy state of affairs was 'partly the kindly but ineffectual management of our C.O. and partly because we had a number of technicians amongst the miners'. Ultimately Dillon was not too disappointed as he later acknowledged that the decision to create Pioneer battalions was 'one of those War Office crazes which did much to let me continue to exist'.[14]

Despite the divisional history's claim that a census was conducted, in divisions such as the 23rd it was possibly a case of simply appointing a surplus battalion to become the divisional Pioneers. This division was comprised of K3 units and had assembled at Aldershot in late 1914. One brigade contained four battalions from the North-East and another, four from Yorkshire. The third brigade, the 70th contained two Yorks & Lancs battalions and one each from the KOYLI and the Notts & Derby. A thirteenth battalion, the 9/South Staffs, had been attached to the division as army troops. It seems likely that with the possible exception of the 11/West Yorks, which was raised at York, any of the battalions in the division would have been suited to conversion. Whether any real census into the make up of the battalions was carried out is unknown, but the South Staffs was the one selected. It was the only unbrigaded unit and the authorities would have been loath to take a battalion from the reasonably homogenous 68th or 69th Brigades and have it replaced by one from a different part of the country. The units of the 70th Brigade were a little more disparate, but as they had already spent some time as a brigade it was probably considered preferable to keep them together. Having recruited from the towns and villages of the Staffordshire coalfield, the 9th Battalion would have been a rational and perfectly adequate choice.

There is very little published or extant material to indicate how the men themselves felt about their unexpected transition from infantry to Pioneers. There is sure to have been some disappointment, especially as neither the men nor the authorities had much idea about what the function of the Pioneers would be. On the other hand, some units must have felt an element of satisfaction at having been picked out from the other units because it was felt they had something special to offer. When the C.O. of the 18/Northumberland Fusiliers explained to his men that the War Office wanted two of the Fusilier battalions to become Pioneers, and that the 18th was to be one of them, apparently only two men objected. The first did so on the grounds that this new task should deserve a higher grade of pay, and withdrew his objection when it was announced that Pioneers would receive two pence a day extra, while the other objected on principle, 'being always against every proposal made by anyone above him'.(16) Many of the men were miners, used to hard digging, while those who were were not, rapidly 'did their best to master the art of handling the pick and shovel'. William Jaeger, a bugler with the 11/King's Liverpool, also thought the increase in pay of two pence a day did much to assuage any resentment at being converted.

The company magazine of the North-Eastern Railway, from which the 17/N.F. had been raised, told its workers that it was a 'signal honour in being selected as a 'pioneer' battalion from among the vast number of battalions . . . It is not likely', it declared, 'that the honour will be largely shared'. Like most people at the time the writer of the article had little idea of what the word 'pioneer' meant. He prudently decided that the significance of the battalion having been allotted as 'divisional' rather than 'brigade' troops, was a difference that would 'be best appreciated by those with a knowledge of military affairs'.(17) Although he had no knowledge of the work the men would be undertaking, he was on firmer ground when he suggested that it seemed 'improbable that such a valuable body of technical men will be doomed to spend long periods in the trenches'.(18) Similarly, Lt. Capper of the 8/Sussex remembered that when they were told the battalion was being converted, 'we took it as a compliment'. Capper believed that the battalion's 'advanced state of training' convinced the authorities of its suitability, but he did concede that because he and his companions saw little or nothing of the other battalions of 54th Brigade, 'we were hardly in a position to judge'.[19] The men of the 5/Royal Irish Regiment possibly thought they were in for an easy time when they were told they were to be converted. Initially they believed their new role was to become simply the division's odd-job men and provide a guard for divisional HQ.[20]

It was clear that given the anticipated expansion of the BEF and the disruption that converting existing battalions caused to their divisions, another means of raising sufficient Pioneer units would have to be broached. The War Office decided therefore, that future divisions should include battalions specifically raised and recruited as Pioneers.

As the consequence of this decision the new Fourth of Kitchener's New Armies was created by local recruiting committees in towns and cities up and down the country. In order to provide the new divisions with Pioneer battalions, several companies and organizations were encouraged by the War Office to raise units specifically for that role. The great recruitment campaigns to create what were known as the Pals battalions were already beginning to sweep the country and in huge displays of patriotic sentiment, men in their thousands queued to enlist. Twelve battalions of Pioneers were recruited during these heady months of late 1914 and early 1915.

Three of these units came from the Middlesex Regiment and were known as the 1st, 2nd and 3rd Public Works Battalions. There were certainly many manual workers from the various London boroughs within their ranks, but because they were raised by John Ward, the 'Miner's M.P.', the battalions also attracted a large number of miners from the Staffordshire coalfield. Another unit raised specifically as Pioneers was the British Empire League Battalion, more correctly known as the 20/KRRC. However, the unit which believed it was the first to enlist men for the particular role of Pioneers was the 19/Welch. The battalion was formed in February 1915 largely of men from Glamorgan; it was brought up to strength by drafts from other battalions of the 38th Division.[21] In September 1915 one of its sister battalions, the 23rd, was raised at Porthcawl as a Pioneer unit.

7

Another such battalion was the 1/12 Loyal North Lancs. This unit began enlisting recruits in August 1915 and by the beginning of September had taken 800 men. By March 1916 it was declared ready to go overseas and was subsequently sent down to join the 60th (London) Division at Warminster. The divisional commander, Major-General E.S.Bulfin, found himself in command of a mixed bag of troops. He recorded his surprise at the obvious intelligence of the bulk of the infantry, who came from Territorial battalions of the London Regiment. He considered these educated men to be very different from the regulars with whom he had spent his army career. The Londoners were also very different from the men of the Pioneers whom he described as a 'hard-bitten, thirsty lot of Lancashire miners'. Bulfin was in fact probably more at home with this type of man and was deeply impressed by their proficiency with a spade. He later described this prowess as 'a perfect revelation'.[22]

Two other battalions raised specifically as Pioneers came from areas of the country where a large proportion of the men were used to hard manual work. The War Office approached the County Durham Recruiting Committee in August 1915 with a view to recruiting a Pioneer battalion and a similar approach was made to its counterpart in Worcester. The consequence was the creation of the 14/Worcester, raised initially at his own expense by Colonel Sir Harry Webb, and the 22/DLI. Both areas could supply men with the necessary physique and skills, yet because so many suitable men had already enlisted in other battalions both units took several months to reach establishment. The raisers of the 22/DLI claimed that recruitment was 'handicapped' by the Derby Scheme,[23] but the Severn Valley Pioneers, as the 14/Worcester were known, continued to recruit well over establishment. At one point it was reported to have over one hundred surplus subalterns. Consequently, when in June 1916 instructions arrived ordering the battalion to France, there was 'keen competition' among the personnel to ensure they were chosen for embarkation.[24]

There was also a number of Durham miners within the ranks of the original members of the 20/KRRC. This battalion was raised at the suggestion of Freeman Murray, the secretary of the

British Empire League. When recruiting began in September 1915 Murray's son was appointed its C.O. and, like the 22/DLI, the unit found recruits initially hard to come by. Only 100 had enlisted by the middle of October but by the end of the following month its strength had risen to 800. Most of the men came from East London, especially the Woolwich area, so the unit was sure to contain a large proportion of manual labourers as well as some artisans from around the shipyards of the Thames. However, among the later enlistments were the miners from the North-East and some men from Somerset. The battalion history implies that these men deliberately joined this unit, knowing of course that it was a Pioneer battalion,[25] and so we may assume they believed they had the required skills or expertise. The skills which were evidently lacking were those of a culinary kind. Because the battalion had been so comfortably billeted in London, the cooks were unable to practise or develop their art. Unfortunately, when the battalion removed to Wellingborough, their inadequacies and lack of experience became all too apparent.[26]

It was all very well for the War Office to decide that certain New Army battalions should be converted to Pioneers, but it was a different matter to provide them with adequate equipment and trained personnel to instruct them in their new role. Some battalions such as the 8/Welch, were fortunate in having officers with some pioneering experience attached to them from their early days. Other battalions relied upon old soldiers, who returned to the Colours and often to their former regiments, to instruct recruits in the rudiments of army life. Although these men had no knowledge of pioneering work and their words of command were often even obsolete, they provided the newly appointed officers with a wealth of experience and support. Yet even the 'old sweats' were in short supply. In the 19/Northumberland Fusiliers the 'sprinkling' of former soldiers was supplemented by what were described as the 'ambitious' amongst the newly enlisted men.[27]

Some battalions were fortunate enough to acquire a good deal of their equipment within a reasonably short time. The pressure on the authorities to supply the New Armies seemed overwhelming but the 12/Yorkshire 'received practically everything . . . in a very short time'.[28] The 19/Lancashire Fusiliers, which had not yet in fact been designated a Pioneer battalion, also received its clothing and equipment 'within a month of its birth'.[29] The historian of the 12/Yorks put the rapidity of their equipping down to the fact that the battalion was raised 'somewhat later' than the majority of the New Army battalions.[30] The 17/Northumberland Fusiliers, which began recruiting at the same time as the second line Territorial battalions, was 'completely equipped' within eighty days.[31] By contrast, the 14/N.F. received no uniforms for months. One of its junior officers later recalled that those men whose landladies were not kind enough to patch their trousers were frequently seen with shirt tales flapping in the breeze.[32] The 17th Battalion was helped immeasurably when the stores department of the North-Eastern Railway offered immediate payment to any manufacturer who could supply the necessary uniforms and equipment.[33] The battalion was lucky as not all of the equipment arriving at the mushrooming camps was of the correct or regulation type. Most of the few rifles which were obtained were obsolete patterns and the scarlet and blue militia tunics, complete with full dress peaked caps and civilian overcoats, gave observers of the erstwhile miners of the 7/Yorks & Lancs the 'impression of a battalion of chauffeurs'.[34] The 9/Gordon Highlanders was offered non-Gordon tartan kilts but instead opted to wear drab until they could be supplied with tartan of their own. Among the battalion's first acquisitions were six bicycles, probably not the most important equipment for a unit of would-be Pioneers.[35]

Other military and non-military items were sometimes provided by the various battalions' 'raisers'. For example the West Yorkshire Coal Owners' Association is reported to have spent £10,000 on equipping the 12/KOYLI. A good deal of this money was spent on supplying the battalion's camp at Farnley Hall with electric light, cladded huts and mains water.[36] The historian of the 18/Northumberland Fusiliers gave fulsome praise to its sponsors, the Military Committee of Newcastle and Gateshead Chamber of Commerce, for the comforts provided to the troops while in training. Neither did this flow of provisions necessarily dry up once the battalion had gone overseas. The Mayor of Oldham wrote to the C.O. of the 24/Manchester in 1917 asking what the the town could send to improve the facilities for its battalion. After consultation the colonel requested a gramophone, records and 1,000 spare needles. Some weeks later these all duly arrived at battalion HQ.[37] Similarly, the NER sent each of its men in the 17/N.F. one hundred cigarettes at Christmas 1917, while the sponsors of the 18/N.F. despatched red and white roses for the men to wear on St. George's Day 1916. The High Sheriff of Monmouth donated £150 to provide a magnificent Christmas dinner for the men of the 1st Battalion in 1917,[38] while, perhaps as an expression of sympathy with its recent conversion to Pioneers, the Corporation of the City of Glasgow supplied the pipes, drums, dirks, sporrans and uniforms to equip fully a band for the 16/HLI.[39]

The War Office struggled to provide sufficient accommodation, equipment and uniforms throughout the summer, autumn and winter of 1914–15. About the only thing of which it was not short was men. Many of those battalions which were to be converted to Pioneers in early 1915 had reached full strength within a matter of days. Yet in some, men continued to be accepted.[40] This not only exacerbated the problems of supplying them with the essentials, but could also create ill-feeling when the units were posted overseas. Furthermore, once a unit had been selected to become a Pioneer battalion it sometimes involved a significant percentage of its original members being transferred from a battalion in which the man had probably specifically chosen to enlist, to a unit which he perhaps had chosen not to join.

It was suggested earlier that divisions might not have taken the strictures about the relative proportion of men used to manual labour too seriously. It could be that in some cases the order was simply ignored or a report submitted which claimed the correct proportions already existed. This might well have been the case for those battalions recruited from mining areas but even so the 8/Welch recorded that it had to exchange 'four or five officers and 150 men' who did not have a recognized trade with those

11

that did from other battalions within the 13th Division.[41] The majority of the intake appear to have come from the King's Own Royal Lancaster Regiment. This substitution represented about 15% of its existing strength. If the entries in a log covering the early months of the 9/Gordon's existence were made in the correct chronological sequence, and the various statements suggest that they were, the trades of the men were only surveyed some two weeks after the battalion had been converted. The first indication that it was to be withdrawn from 44th Brigade came in a War Office letter which informed the C.O. that the word 'Pioneer' would be added to the name of the unit and that the battalion was to be reorganized immediately. At some leisure, the men were then quizzed about their civilian occupations. Of the 1,106 men on the nominal roll there were only 199 who were deemed unsuitable for work as Pioneers and recommended for transfer. Of the remainder, 437 or 48%, were described as 'pick and shovel workers', 233 as 'miscellaneous and fit for retention', but only 220 or 24%, were men with recognized trades. The battalion thus fell some distance short of the prescribed requirements.[42]

The history of the Yorkshire Regiment states that once it had been converted its 12th battalion, which was 'unofficially' a Pals battalion, deliberately recruited men from the skilled artisan class. However it makes no mention of it having to get rid of any of its original members.[43] The 19/Welch was certainly brought up to strength in April 1915 by an influx of men from the 123rd and 151st Field Companies, R.E.[44] Coming from the Engineers, these men were supposedly skilled tradesmen; their new battalion is the only one definitely known to have received a draft of such soldiers during their time in training.

The Coldstream Guards seem not to have bothered to discover whether men going into the newly-created Guards Pioneer Battalion possessed the particular skills, or in the specified proportions. Orders to form a Pioneer battalion from the 4th(Reserve) Battalion arrived at Windsor in July 1915. The C.O. of the new battalion met with his counterpart of the reserve battalion to decide upon who should be appointed to the staff of the Pioneer unit and which senior NCOs should be transferred from the reserve battalion. It was agreed that the proportion of 'old soldiers' to recruits in the new unit should be approximately 200 to 800[45] but there is no mention of any discussion concerning civilian trades or specialities. Once selected, the men were allocated to companies and then sent on leave. Within 13 days the entire battalion, including the transport, was fully equipped and ready to leave for France. It embarked on 15 August 1915, its name having been changed to the 4th Battalion Coldstream Guards (Pioneers).

The Guards were an exception, but whether they had been converted since formation or raised specifically as a Pioneer unit, most of the battalions suffered the same frustrations and experiences when trying to reach some sort of fitness for overseas duty. The essential difficulty was trying to get information as to what their future role might be. The C.O. of the 12/KOYLI apparently 'sought authoritative advice on the subject, but he sought in vain'.[46] His solution was to acquire as much information as possible on the battles then raging in France and Belgium and by questioning anyone home on leave or with wounds about the conditions and types of warfare they might expect to encounter. With so many shortages, especially perhaps in R.E. officers who might have been able to point C.O.s in the right direction, it was left pretty much to the battalion to train in whatever way it thought best. This allowed room for a great degree of initiative. When 2Lt. Dillon, an eighteen year old youth, was confronted by 200 hard-bitten miners from the Morpeth area he bought the War Office manual called Infantry Training from a station bookstall and began drilling them.[47] Examples such as these are legion. Anyone with a particular speciality that was thought might be eventually useful was engaged as an instructor – William Jaeger remembered attending knot-tying classes.[48] Several battalions seem to have made an attempt to practise bridging, but most of the time not spent on drill was used for digging practise. Many young officers from non-industrial backgrounds were astounded at the rate at which their men could move earth, shore it up and dispose of the spoil.[49]

It was easier to find non-commissioned men who possessed

skills which might prove useful to them as Pioneers than it was to find the officers to command them. Because Pioneers were a new concept in the British Army any potential C.O. who possessed a combination of technical and military experience generally came from the Pioneer battalions of the Indian Army. Where possible these officers were appointed to command the new battalions, but such men were few and far between. Most units, like their counterparts in the infantry, were commanded in the early weeks by 'dug outs' – officers recalled from the retired list – or by leading figures in the community from which they were raised. Some of the 'dug outs' were former Indian Army infantry or cavalry officers, men well past their prime but eager to do their bit. The 8/Sussex had such a man appointed to command it. Owing to an old injury, Colonel Sutton could not sit on a horse. Instead of leading the marching column on horse-back, Sutton gamely marched at the head. He kept to the side of the road and each of the platoons gradually overtook him. When the whole battalion was in front of him he called a halt, and struggled back to the head.[50]

Lt.Col. Morley was appointed to command the 14/N.F. and, although like Sutton a 'kind and easy man', he had 'no idea how to train a unit'. It apparently 'never occurred to him to have classes for his officers to teach them the elements of their duties'.[51] Most of the C.O.s who led the units soon after formation were replaced when their commands left for overseas duty. Some of the new commanders were not much younger or fitter than those they replaced. Several of them, for example Lt.Col. Heale of the 14/N.F. and formerly of the 121st Indian Pioneers, died within months of taking up their commands. Those original commanders who did manage to go abroad with their units also tended not to last long. The demands of active service generally proved too wearing for these elderly warriors, and they returned home. Once they had served a few months abroad second in commands were sometimes promoted to take command of another battalion of Pioneers.[52]

An exception to this was Colonel Trower of the South Wales Borderers. Trower had only just missed the engagement at Rorke's Drift, and in 1914 was appointed to raise and command the 5th Battalion. He remained with it on active service until well into his '60s. This represented admirable continuity of service, but Trower was not an engineer and throughout the war, Pioneer battalions could often have a colonel with no pioneering or engineering experience posted as its C.O. By the same token, a former C.O. or second in command of a Pioneer unit was equally likely to be sent to command an infantry battalion.[53] Because the C.O. only had limited control over the day to day work of his battalion, this seemingly illogical means of appointment probably did not greatly affect the efficiency of the unit as far as its pioneering duties were concerned. He was more of an administrative and organizational figurehead than a decider of destinies. However, the appointment of a non-Pioneer C.O. might explain why so many battalions spent most of their time out at rest training for other than pioneering tasks. There were many retired colonels and majors who, whether suitable to command Pioneer battalions or not, made themselves available should their country need them. It was generally assumed that younger men would be promoted to replace most of them once the initial work of raising the battalions was complete. The difficulty for the time being was for their battalions to acquire sufficient suitable junior officers to get them into a preliminary state of efficiency.

Pioneer battalions suffered from the same shortage of officers as did the remainder of the New Armies. But what added to the difficulties confronting those units raised or converted to Pioneers was not only did they require a full complement of officers, they also wanted those whose civilian skills would be relevant to their anticipated military role. It is known that various divisions were searched for officers with engineering, scientific and mining skills and that when discovered, these officers were often transferred from their original battalion to the one selected to become the divisional Pioneers. The 7/York & Lancs had at least nine such officers posted or transferred to it as it trained in England,[54] while several officers with no engineering background were posted away from the 14/N.F. and replaced by those who had.[55] On the other hand, because they had by chance been commissioned into battalions that were later

15

converted, some Pioneer battalions were already well supplied with officers possessing engineering skills. This was especially true of battalions which came from traditional mining areas. Besides the three members of the Charlesworth dynasty who joined the 12/KOYLI, there are also many other instances where the sons of the local coal or engineering barons enlisted in their local regiment. Incidental references give illustrations of many such young men joining a wide selection of battalions. These references frequently describe the officers, usually when they became casualties, as 'a professional engineer' or 'a mining engineer'.

A fairly typical example of such was Robert Kershaw. He had served in his school OTC, enlisted as a private in the Argyll & Sutherland Highlanders in August 1914 and was then recommended for a commission. Because he had worked in a large engineering workshop, when commissioned he joined the 9/Gordon Highlanders.[56] Even the 20/KRRC, which was not one of the battalions most obviously composed of former miners, apparently had at least two officers in each company with engineering experience.[57] Of the original officers of the 17/N.F., eight were definitely described as 'engineer', while several others are listed as NER inspectors and apprentices. Only seven of the thirty had not served at least in their school officer training corps, and four had fought in the South African War.[58] Other young men came from more unlikely backgrounds and were possibly more typical of the great majority of junior officers. Cecil Hall from decidedly non-industrial Purley, had attended the City of London School and spent three years in the Honourable Artillery Company. He was employed by a bank and left the HAC in order to spend more of his non-working hours with a medical mission helping the poor in Bermondsey. When war broke out he was commissioned into the Leicestershire Regiment and then transferred to the 22/DLI.[59]

It is evident that when they went overseas some battalions lost one or two of their officers fairly early on to specialist schools of instruction or to the R.E. There are several instances too of battalions still in England acquiring the services of men with engineering backgrounds who had come home from France for a commission. These individuals would provide their new units not only with technical expertise but also knowledge of the sort of work and the conditions in which it had to be done when the battalion went overseas. One such example was 2Lt. Simpson of the 26/Middlesex. He had gone to France with the 5/North Staffs, was wounded and on recovery, was commissioned into the 25/Middlesex. Appalled at what he considered to be wide-spread corruption in billeting money at Cambridge, and at the prospect of going to Siberia, he requested and was granted a transfer to the 26th.[60]

When considering the numbers involved and the massive growth of the New Armies, it is perhaps inevitable to discover that some officers were considered inadequate to the task. It should however be remembered that what might have seemed to one C.O. or staff officer a perfectly efficient and adequate set of officers might to another individual appear to be nothing but a group of incompetent bunglers. One example will suffice to show some of the problems faced by members of the regular army when training the men of the Kitchener units.

One of the Public Works Pioneers battalions, the 18/Middlesex, was raised in January 1915. When Captain C.H.Wolff, a staff captain with the 33rd Division inspected the battalion in April 1915, he reported that the 'officers and men were very untrained' and that the officers 'did not know the correct words of command'. Furthermore he declared, 'the C.O. states that there is a good deal of drunkeness in the regiment'.[61] The C.O. and his second in command, both of whom apparently frightened the life out of the junior officers, were regular soldiers. One young subaltern later wrote of how depressing and confusing it was to serve under them.[62] When the battalion went overseas two junior officers were, for unspecified reasons, returned to England, another was soon put under arrest for disobeying orders and a fourth was sent home having been 'unfavourably reported on'.[63] Whether the officers of the battalion were as bad as their superiors believed, or wanted to believe them to be, can hardly be determined at this distance. There are other instances of slackness reported in the War Diary, but when 2Lt. Lester joined the battalion in July 1916 he found everyone, except the C.O. and his second in command, to be helpful, charming and on top of their jobs.

Keen and efficient as the majority of junior offciers probably were, many of them were generally as inexperienced in the ways and methods of the army as the men they commanded. Although a good proportion of them were straight from school they had somehow to acquire and demonstrate their authority over the very often older and more worldly-wise volunteers. The great majority of the men were of course totally unfamiliar with the procedure of army discipline. The idea for example that going absent without leave constituted a grave military offence, was to many 'almost an absurdity'.[64] In only two months of 1915 six men of the 14/N.F., then at Halton Park, lost up to five days' pay for going absent on different occasions.[65] The regimental history of the 20/KRRC admits that the 'formal discipline of the battalion was a little rough to begin with', but that in time it 'vastly improved and became extremely good'.[66] In battalions with large numbers of miners or tradesmen with strong union traditions, the men would have been used to taking concerted and collective action against authority. Officers thus had to tread warily when dealing with offences; the method employed in the 5/SWB was to attempt to keep punishments to 'a necessary minimum' and set the right example themselves.[67] This method probably worked and was no doubt used extensively within many battalions for dealing with the more common offences. Regimental histories can hardly be expected to dwell on the more unpleasant or less honourable aspects of their battalions' training periods, although occasionally they can be a little more candid. The historian of the 18/N.F. admitted that, 'There may have been a better behaved battalion in the Army; if there was, its men were 'plaster saints' . . . . our conscience, however, pricks us as regards absence without leave in the early days when our homes were near and we had not long donned khaki'.[68] The more common type of history stresses how well the men did conduct themselves in their unfamiliar role.

The sudden appearance of a group of men in an area un-accustomed to either soldiery or citizens from other parts of the country, sometimes caused alarm amongst the locals. When the 9/Gordon Highlanders arrived in tranquil Haslemere it was reported initially to have been received with 'misgivings' by the inhabitants of Hampshire. The apprehension soon gave way to a willingness to feed and accommodate the citizen army.[69] Similarly when a very wet and bedraggled half battalion of Yorkshire miners arrived in leafy Wareham, the locals quickly overcame their surprise and concern, loaned the soaked troops some of their own clothing and helped to provide accommodation.[70] However, keen as the men were to learn their new trade, they could not be expected to ignore all of the hardships the army put their way. One of the soldiers' greatest grouches was the allocation of leave. When the men of the 7/Yorks & Lancs felt their allocation was not what it might have been, they made their grievances known. Other battalions of the 17th Division had been enjoying a fairly liberal ration of leave but between Christmas 1914 and July 1915, the men of the Yorks & Lancs had only been granted it for special circumstances. The subject was 'a sore which became more and more aggravated' until the arrival of orders for France finally brought it to a head. The colonel petitioned the divisional commander, who announced that he was prepared to grant 48 hours leave to 25% of the men. Priority however, he declared, should go to those married men who could pay their own fare![71] The men of the 14/N.F. did a little better than those of the York & Lancs. When the battalion was warned for France at short notice, all men who had not yet been granted leave were immediately awarded 48 hours.[72]

As the somewhat necessarily improvised training in the U.K. progressed, and the inevitable departure for overseas active service drew nearer, yet more problems arose to further compound the difficulties of officers in trying to build *esprit* and improve efficiency. A considerable percentage of those who had enlisted in August and September falsified their ages and during the rigours of the ensuing winter, their health began to let them down. There is also some evidence to suggest that men who were not in the best of health specifically enlisted in Pioneer battalions because they believed the medical was not as rigorous as that for the infantry. Amongst other occasional references, a letter of Pte. R.J. Bevington, then serving in France with the Honourable Artillery Company, mentions that, 'volunteers being asked for, Basil joined the Pioneers . . . men with bad feet had first refusal as they do not sit in the trenches'.[73] There is no extant official record to prove that Pioneer battalions did deliberately accept men of a lower medical category than the infantry, but that they did suffer from a large number of men who were not up to the required medical standard is apparent.

'Many' of those who ended up in the 12/KOYLI were described as being 'by no means young', with 'more than a few' having reached their half-century.[74] This meant that when the final medical was given to the men before embarkation, large numbers were declared to be unfit and were consequently retained at home. This caused disruption and disorganization for their places had to be filled by men from different units who possibly did not possess the same skill or trade as those they replaced. Transfers on a large scale were not so damaging if they occurred early on. For example, the 5/DCLI, lost 'large numbers'[75] in September 1914. Neither need it have affected morale too deeply if the numbers were made up from men serving in the battalion's depot company or if the new men possessed suitable skills. The 19/Welch for example, would appear to have had little difficulty in absorbing its drafts from the 123rd and 151st Field Companies R.E. in April 1915.

Postings or withdrawals of men could cause significant disruption if the battalion had already welded itself into something of a homogenous unit. One unit which suffered in this manner was the 18/Northumberland Fusiliers. Just as it was ready to embark for France the battalion had to lose nearly 90 men, roughly 10% of its strength. The men involved were miners and skilled engineers who, it had been decided, were essential to the munitions industry and would have to return to civilian service. Although they came from the reserve company, the men who replaced them were not thought to be 'fully trained'.[76] The battalion complained long and hard about the effect their loss would have on its efficiency, but the protests were to no avail. The nominal roll of another battalion of the Northumberlands, the 17th, shows that no fewer than 380 of its original recruits were transferred out before embarkation.[77]

Those battalions of the First, Second and Third New Armies which were converted to the Pioneer role in the U.K. usually went with their divisions to France. The great majority of these battalions were still serving alongside the units with which their divisions had originally formed. Many of these divisions had a regional title reflecting the area from which most of the troops were recruited. For those battalions which had been created as Pioneers there was usually no such divisional link to their home area. They were allocated to divisions as and when they were considered to be sufficiently trained and equipped for overseas service.[78]

Despite all the problems they had experienced in getting themselves trained and equipped, there was still an immense enthusiasm and confidence within both the converted and the specifically raised units. They were now embarking upon the task for which they had enlisted. The hardships, disruption and disappointments of training were now forgotten. They were going to cross the Channel, assault the German positions and sweep on to Berlin. Lt. Robert Kershaw of the 9/Gordon Highlanders looked forward to his departure and on receipt of orders wrote excitedly to his parents:

> Thank heaven the tedious time is over. Thursday will be the happiest day of my life . . . I am chosen at last to fight for my country, my whole and only one ambition in life. Pray nightly that I may catch a column of Germans with one of the machine guns at close quarters.[79]

The exuberance of Kershaw and thousands of others like him, masked their inexperience. The infantry, artillery engineers, pioneers, ambulance units and all the other divisional troops, might well have felt they knew their jobs and what was to be expected of them. Unknown to the men in those units, many of their superiors did not share that confidence.

NOTES

1. Sandilands, H.R. *The 23rd Division, 1914-19,* (Blackwood, 1925) p.13
2. England, Capt. R.E. *A brief History of the 12/KOYLI,* (Wakefield, n.d.) p.20
3. Atkinson, C.T. *The History of the South Wales Borderers,* (London, 1931) p.62
4. ibid. p.65
5. Gilvary, Capt. M.T. *The History of the 7th (S) Battalion, the York & Lancs (P),* (Talbot Press, 1925) p.5
6. Inglefield, V.E. *The History of the Twentieth (Light) Division,* (Nisbet, 1921) p.3
7. Unpublished diary of 11/DLI, attached to W.D.
8. Cooper, B. *The 10th (Irish) Division in Gallipoli,* (Jenkins, 1918) p.206
9. Falls, C. *The Gordon Highlanders in the First World War,* Vol.II (Aberdeen U.P. n.d.) p.53
10. Shakespear, J. *A Record of the 17th and 32nd Battalions,* N.F.(NER) Pioneers, (Newcastle, 1926) p.1
11. ibid. p.11
12. Wyrall, E. *The East Yorkshire Regiment in the Great War,* (Harrison, 1928) p.22
13. Wylly, H.C. *The Border Regiment in the Great War,* (Gale & Polden, 1921) p.28
14. Dillon, N.M. papers. (Liddle Collection)
15. Shakespear, *J. Historical Records of the 18th (S) Battalion, N.F. (Pioneers),* (Newcastle, 1920) p.9
16. Jaeger, W. papers. (Liddle Collection)
17. *North-Eastern Railway Magazine,* 1915. p.8-9
18. ibid.
19. Capper, D.J. papers. (Liddle Collection)
20. Cooper, op.cit. p.206
21. Marden, T.O. *The History of the Welch Regiment, Part III* (Cardiff, 1932) p.286
22. Dalbiac, P.H. *The History of the 60th Division,* (Allen & Unwin, 1927)
23. Ward, S.G. *The Story of the Durham Light Infantry,* p.330
24. Stacke, H.F. *The Worcestershire Regiment in the Great War,* (Cheshire & Sons, 1929) p.46
25. Turbeville, A.S. *A Short History of the 20th Bn KRRC,* (Hull, 1923) p.2-3
26. ibid. p.4

27. Cooke, C.H. *Historical Records of the 19th (S) Bn. N.F. (Pioneers),* (Newcastle, 1920) p.2
28. Wylly, H.C. *The Yorkshire Regiment,* (No publisher, n.d.) p.349
29. Latter, J.C. *The History of the Lancashire Fusiliers,* (Gale & Polden, 1949) p.99
30. Wylly, *Yorkshire Regt.,* op.cit. p.349
31. Shakespear, *17th N.F.* op.cit. p.6
32. Dillon, op.cit.
33. *NER Magazine,* 1915 p.6
34. Gilvary, op.cit. p.4
35. Falls, C. op.cit. p.53. When the battalion was supplied with a limited quantity of English pattern trousers, one member apparently declared that he had 'come down to be a Gordon Highlander, not a postman'. The unit had to wait until late February 1915 before it could hold its first parade fully kitted out as a Highland regiment.(W.O.95.5460)
36. England, op.cit. p.19
37. Mitchinson, K.W. & McInnes, I. *Cotton Town Comrades,* (Bayonet Press, 1993) p.102
38. War Diary
39. War Diary
40. A W.O. directive of 2 December 1914 ordered that each locally raised battalion must recruit up to 1,350 all ranks. The extra 250 were to be organized as a 5th(Depot) Company. Then, not later than two months before the battalion was likely to go overseas, a 6th Company would be formed. (W.O.162/3)
41. Marden, op.cit. p.283
42. The skilled men can be loosely grouped as: 28 used to working with wood, 35 from the building trades and 157 from the metal trades. There were also 17 sailors, all of whom were retained. (W.O.95.5460)
43. Wylly, op.cit. p.349
44. Marden, op.cit. p.286
45. War Diary
46. England, op.cit. Appendix III p.135
47. Dillon, op.cit.
48. Jaeger, op.cit. Following the death of one of its members, the 11/King's underwent a rapid course in how to conduct a military funeral. Sgt. Jones was thrown from a pony trap in Farnham and killed.
49. Dillon, op.cit.
50. Capper, op.cit.
51. Dillon, op.cit.
52. Among other examples, in 1916, Major R. Stephenson of the 18/N.F. was appointed C.O. of the 9/S.Staffs and Major C.H. Gascoigne

became C.O. of the 14/Worcester. In 1917 Major G. Brown became C.O. of the 11/King's having been 2 i.c. of the 10/DCLI.

53. Examples include: Major P. Wilson, who left the 9/DLI to take command of the 2/4th Dukes, Lt.Col. Stewart of the 14/N.F. became C.O. of the 6/Leicester and Lt.Col. Grant-Dalton left the 19/Welch to become O.C. 2/West Yorks.

54. Gilvary, op.cit. p.5

55. Dillon, op.cit. Three weeks after it was converted, the 9/Gordon Highlanders had three junior officers attached to it from other regiments. These men were described as 'engineers' who would 'help in training, with a view to them eventually being absorbed in the battalion'. (W.O.95.5460)

56. Kershaw, K.R. papers. (Liddle Collection)

57. Turbeville, op.cit. p.3

58. *NER Magazine,* 1915 p.30

59. Hall, C.C. papers. (Liddle Collection)

60. On the strength of the fact that he had been a bomber with the North Staffs, his colonel told Simpson to give a demonstration of firing an explosive charge. The young man had no idea of what he was supposed to do, but went ahead as the rest of the battalion and various staff waited expectantly. He blew the charge on a field in Tring: 'The noise was deafening; windows were heard to be crashing in houses quite some distance away, and the hole made by the explosion would have taken a good sized bus'. On joining the 26/Middlesex, he found a 'host' of friends who had served with him in the North Staffs. (Liddle Collection)

61. Wolff, C.H. diary. (Dept. of Documents, IWM)

62. Lester, Lt.Col. R.M. *The Years that changed the World,* (Unpublished, Dept.of Docs. IWM)

63. War Diary

64. Shakespear, op.cit.

65. War Diary

66. Turbeville, op.cit. p.142

67. Atkinson, op.cit. p.59

68. Shakespear. op.cit. p.96

69. Falls, op.cit. p.53. The battalion's officers were similarly apprehensive some days later on pay night. A 'certain liveliness in the lines and a good deal of difficulty' in getting the lights put out was reported. With a note of some relief, the adjutant noted that the men were 'only jovial and not insubordinate'. The battalion subsequently formed a branch of the Army Temperance Association, which boasted 300 members. (W.O.95.5460)

70. Atteridge, A. *History of the 17th (Northern) Division*, (Maclehose, 1929) p.12
71. Gilvary, op.cit. p.7
72. War Diary
73. Bevington, R. papers. (Liddle Collection)
74. England, op.cit. p.21
75. Wyrall, op.cit. p.79
76. Figures computed from the nominal roll given in Shakespear, 18/N.F. op.cit.
77. Shakespear, 17/N.F. op.cit. Over 120 men of the 9/Gordon Highlanders were posted away some time before the battalion left for France. (W.O.95.5460)
78. Before going overseas, many infantry and Pioneer battalions often spent time on coast defence. If a Pioneer battalion had already been allocated to a division, the time spent in training depended on when the rest of the division was sent abroad. The 5/Northants, for example, spent some eight months with the 12th Division 'strenuously engaged in battle training and engineering work'. The Northamptonshire Regiment, Regimental Committee, (Gale & Polden, 1932) p.276. Alternatively, Pioneers such as the 10/DCLI which had not already been earmarked for a specific division, could remain on or near the coast until such time as its future had been decided.
79. Kershaw, op.cit.

Chapter 2

BLOODING THE INNOCENTS

The story of how units received orders for mobilization and transport overseas has often been told. The experience of one battalion is very similar to that of another. The arrival of orders, the hectic recall of absent men, the issue of new, often unfamiliar equipment, the frantic collection of animals and vehicles and the one hundred and other impediments that would always arise at the last moment were experienced by most units. Orderly rooms issued screeds of orders, NCOs harrassed, cajoled, encouraged or bullied their men to collect equipment, leave unnecessary belongings and parade at the given time. Officers arranged their kit with the help of batmen and tried to ensure their platoons were keeping to the allotted timescale and procedures. It was dramatic, exciting and sometimes orderly. Usually it worked, and the men paraded for the station and left whatever camp they had been occupying with an air of expectation, anticipation and perhaps foreboding. The mobilization of Pioneer battalions differed very little from those of ordinary infantry. A look at how one such unit received its orders and proceeded abroad will suffice for most.

In March 1916 the 11th Battalion of the Leicestershire Regiment was stationed in the city of Leicester. The unit had been raised during the previous autumn by the mayor and local recruiting committee specifically as a Pioneer unit. Its familiar name was the Midland Pioneers.[1] On 3 March a confidential letter from the War Office, coming via Northern Command, arrived at battalion HQ. Even though the battalion was without rifles, machine guns or ammunition, the letter ordered immediate mobilization. The following day the adjutant hastily indented for vehicles, animals, harnesses and various other necessary articles. Unfortunately, half the battalion had just been vaccinated and was thus suffering from painful after-effects, while the other half was bracing itself to undergo the same discomfort. Not one of the four companies had a captain in command and the unit was short of eight subalterns. Furthermore, so the adjutant informed Northern Command, when the transport animals and vehicles arrived none of the men in the transport section claimed to have had any experience or training in how to handle them.

On 13 March the battalion paraded to hear that it was officially under orders to mobilize. The orderly room was informed that now the 11th was about to go overseas, a 12th Battalion would be formed later from the men who did not go with the 11th. Before the order had been executed, Lt.Col. Burton of the 2/Middlesex arrived to take command of the, as yet, non-existent 12th Battalion. The colonel then discovered that the GOC of the 19th Reserve Infantry Brigade, of which his battalion was supposed to be a unit, had arrived to inspect the battalion. In an effort to rectify this embarrassing situation it was decided to hand over to Burton the 11th's depot companies so that he could at least demonstrate there were some men under his command.

Four days later 64 mules arrived for the 11th from the remount depot. As there was no central area where they could be stabled, the animals were dispersed to various locations scattered about the city. Meanwhile, more, largely unspecified articles continued to shower upon the quartermaster's stores. The C.O. wrote again to Northern Command, this time requesting that all the NCOs currently away on courses should be allowed to return to the battalion. These men were subsequently returned. On 18 March three officers who were unfit for overseas duties joined the 12th Battalion, thus compounding the C.O.'s problems of officer shortage. The requested harnesses eventually arrived and all surplus clothing and equipment was withdrawn from the men. These items were then handed over to the 12th Battalion. To fill the newly-made space within their packs, the men of the 11th Battalion were issued with clasp knives, field dressings, gas helmets and several other pieces of previously unknown equipment. The required number of NCOs was then secured by promoting a total of 90 NCOs or privates by at least one rank. These helped to replace 21 NCOs and five privates who had been posted to the 12th Battalion. Four Army Supply Corps drivers reported from Lichfield and, along with various transport vehicles, a dozen officers' chargers arrived. Unfortunately, there were almost as many chargers as there were officers, To bring the officers up to establishment a lieutenant of the RAMC reported to take up duty and, on the day before the battalion was given a civic send off by the mayor and people of Leicester, three company commanders, two lieutenants and seven second lieutenants arrived to take up their posts. These officers hardly had time to look at their companies and platoons, let alone discover anything about their state of training or preparedness for war, before the battalion entrained for Southampton.

It was 0230 hours on a cold March night that the men climbed aboard the trains at Leicester and began a long and fairly uncomfortable journey to the south coast. On arrival at Southampton one of the newly-arrived lieutenants was promptly admitted to Netley hospital for an undisclosed ailment, followed next day by two privates who fell out during a route march. On 26 March the battalion embarked upon three vessels for transport to France. HMT *Marquerite* promptly put back into harbour because the weather was considered too bad for her to attempt the crossing. While seeking safety in Southampton Water she managed to foul her anchor; this further delayed her eventual departure. Next, the HMT *Rossetti* decided the weather was too rough for her, and also put back. This left the *Pancras* to steam across the Channel and reach Le Havre alone. Three days later the other two ships braved the crossing and the battalion was at last re-united.

Helped by four attached musketry instructors the Midland Pioneers spent the first three weeks of their service in France training. D Company spent much of its time receiving instruction on field work, and at least one of the transport men was sent away to Abbeville to attend a cold shoeing course. However, if the officers imagined that they could have a few uninterrupted weeks of training and getting to know their men, they were to be disappointed. Within the space of few days one man was sent away, mentally deranged, two were admitted to the Field Ambulance with gonorrhoea, two went to hospital with cerebral meningitis, 29 were struck off strength with undiagnosed illness and a constant stream of men, including the RSM, disappeared to the Field Ambulance for a few days at a time with sickness. Over a dozen others were sent into quarantine after having developed German measles and one young man was returned to the base as under age. Finally, as this initial period of overseas duty was coming towards a close, one of the privates who had recently been promoted acting lance corporal was, for some undisclosed misdemeanour, deprived of his stripe.

The experience of the 11/Leicester was by no means unique. Battalions up and down the country faced similar problems and suffered in the same manner. 2Lt. Capper of the 8/Sussex, recalled the somewhat dubious honour of having to awaken his reputedly intemperate transport officer in the middle of the night to inform him that a consignment of mules was awaiting his immediate collection at Colchester station.[2] The excitement generated by the move overseas could also pose unexpected problems. The officers of the 9/South Staffs had a difficult time preventing their men from wandering around the docks at Southampton in preference to sleep.[3]

In France the port of arrival for most battalions was Le Havre. After disembarkation men faced a stiff march up a steep hill to the rest camp. The 11/DLI had an unfortunate experience within only a few hours of landing. Formed up in column of fours the battalion, no doubt anxious to impress any observing French civilians or military personnel, marched towards the camp. As the leading files stepped onto a bridge over a river, hurtling towards them came two draught horses pulling a driverless wagon. The astounded column broke ranks and as the wagon tore past, pressed themselves desperately against the bridge abutments. No-one was hurt but one man's rifle ended up in the river below. The subsequent court of inquiry solemnly pronounced that the 'public' should pay for its replacement.

Many men's reminiscences of their early weeks in France embrace the train journey from the coast to the division's or battalion's assembly area. For 2Lt. Capper this at least brought relief from the 'endless hanging about and boredom' of his first twenty-four hours overseas.[3] The 11/Hants, Pioneers to the 16th Division, landed at Le Havre in December 1915 and soon clambered aboard waiting French railway trucks. Thirty-six men crushed into each wagon, the only lighting in them supplied by some very gloomy hand-held oil lamps. The train lurched and bumped off into the night only to come to frequent juddering halts for no obviously apparent reason. During the odyssey the men received no hot water for brewing up and the horses remained unwatered for 25 hours. Every now and again boxes of rations would be flung into the trucks, but with no means of heating the stew the men ended the journey thoroughly stiff, fed up and hungry. The 9/Border suffered similar trials during its journey from Le Havre to Amiens. With all lights prohibited the battalion entrained in pitch darkness. Confusion reigned as men attempted to sort themselves into their cattle wagons, and in the difficulties one man dropped his rifle from the train. To heighten further the battalion's embarrassment, soon after its arrival at Longeau Sgt. Potts managed to lose the bolt of his rifle.[7] In view of the unprecedented wastage the Great War was to generate, these two incidents might seem trivial. But to a new battalion just embarking for overseas duty and thus anxious to avoid underlining their inexperience, they appeared devastating.

Because they at least travelled with their weapons, the Hants and the Borderers were a little better off than the Pioneers of the British Empire League. The unfortunate men of the 20/KRRC were ordered to hand in their rifles before embarking for France in March 1916. Anticipating that the obsolete rifles they handed in would be replaced by new Lee Enfields, the battalion sailed to France without arms. Passage across the Channel was a disconcerting prelude to its eventual concentration. One half of the battalion embarked upon the already mentioned *Marquerite* and the other on the *Rossetti*. Having poked her bow into a rolling

Solent this last named vessel soon returned to Southampton, followed shortly after by the equally dubious *Marquerite*. The *Rossetti* tried again the the next morning and once more decided discretion was the better part of valour. Meanwhile, those who had suffered on board the *Marquerite* were eventually disembarked and two days later sailed on a more stalwart vessel. When both halves finally assembled the battalion was sent up to the Ypres sector. To its profound anger, rumours abounded throughout the Salient that this new battalion was composed entirely of conscientious objectors. It was nine embarrassing days later that the battalion was finally issued with rifles.[4]

The amount of training battalions could do once near the front depended upon the sort of sector they were posted to or whether their division, when they joined it, was in the line or out at rest. The majority of Pioneer units began their overseas service in the region to the south-west of Armentieres. After the Battles of Neuve Chapelle, Festubert and Aubers the area became a relatively quiet one. Owing to the nature of the land, and the attentions of the German gunners, the breastworks and trenches in the sector required constant repair. Pioneers thus obtained early experience in this work and also in methods of pumping and drainage. It also gave them the opportunity to conduct various experiments in how they should approach their work.

The 5/Northants for example, discovered that where the German trenches were close to its working site, it was preferable to use rolls of French wire intermingled with barbed wire stapled to the ground. This cut down on the noise made by working parties. The 9/South Staffs tried various systems of making brushwood hurdles – a job to which most Pioneers were put in their early days abroad – before deciding that the best method was to use pairs and insist upon a minimum of one-and-a-half hurdles per man per day. The battalion also experimented with sandbagging and concluded that it was unsatisfactory to lay them in the manner obviously preferred by units which had originally built the breastworks. The Staffs decided they should instead be laid with the 'same care and attention as a bricklayer does to bonding'. Whenever possible C.O.s took the opportunity of allowing their men to practise their soldiering as well as

31

pioneering skills. While out at rest in September 1915 the 4/Coldstream Guards were ordered to fire ten rounds rapid wearing gas helmets in addition to its usual routine of drill, musketry and bombing. Route marches were frequently done to harden feet, build *esprit* or simply to fill time. On one such occasion in early 1916 the 9/North Staffs were passed by General Haig's staff car. If not sufficiently impressed at being so close to their Commander-in-Chief, the men were amazed to see Haig get out of his car and take the salute as the battalion marched past. The 22/DLI used some of its marches as an opportunity to experiment with cooking over open fires, while the 9/Seaforth Highlanders, obviously deciding against combining the two skills, attended lectures on cooking and wiled away other potential training time in harvesting with local farmers.

In addition to the problems of acclimatizing to the new surroundings and the excitement of actually being overseas, the troops had also to absorb, or at least give the impression of absorbing, volumes of daily orders. These covered a multitude of aspects of service life. They could include warnings that 'under no circumstances' should heavy draught horses be trotted rather than walked, that troops should not attempt to sell clothing or food to local civilians, that they should be alert for enemy spies wearing British and French uniforms, they were not to allow animals to wander near railway lines, were to be wary of 3/4 inch steel spikes contaminating bags of oats and were not to be seen wandering about in rest areas with dirty boots and long hair. Pioneering or fighting must have seemed at times more simple than being at rest.

The early experiences of a battalion overseas are usually well recorded in War Diaries and regimental histories. The novelty of the experience, the lack of casualties or other notable events allowed the intelligence officer or the adjutant to note the battalion's activity in some detail. Occasionally, the diarist will even note the casualties sustained before they sailed.[5] The 14/N.F.'s diary recorded the loss of two officers and 40 other ranks to hospital soon after its arrival, while that of the 22/DLI noted that Captain Hurford, one of the company commanders, broke his leg in a riding accident almost immediately after the unit landed

32

on the coast.[6] Pte. Irwin of the same battalion was sent away to hospital after having broken his leg while detraining at the base camp and Pte. Cowie of the 18/N.F. lost one of his legs as he sat dangling them in the open door of a railway truck. The luckless Cowie was the battalion's first recorded casualty. Another early officer casualty was Lt. Stoward of the 10/DCLI. While watching men unload timber from a G.S. wagon, a piece fell onto Stoward's head and he was sent off to No.6 Field Ambulance. Like the 11/Leicester, the 5/DCLI also experienced an outbreak of German measles immediately upon its arrival in France. A regular flow of Cornishmen went off to hospital during June and July 1916. In addition to the numerous evacuees suffering from gonorrhoea, lumbago and scarlet fever, Pte. Avery was admitted to the 105th Field Ambulance 'on account of his teeth'.

While many battalions had men admitted to hospital or declared to be unfit for duty soon after their arrival,[7] others were lucky enough not to lose them until they went into the line. Occasionally the casualty noted in the War Diary was not necessarily a member of the battalion. For example, while cleaning his rifle a member of the 18/Middlesex accidentally shot and killed the French owner of his newly-occupied billet. Once in the forward zone, War Diaries generally continue to record the casualties until such time as they became so numerous that an entry for each individual was no longer considered worthwhile. Two exceptions to this practice are the diaries of the two Pioneer battalions of the South Wales Borderers. Throughout the war they continue to record not only deaths, but also the names of the wounded. During the tumultuous days of March and April 1918 writing up the diary in such detail must have taken a considerable amount of time.

Some diaries not only record the names and regimental numbers of the casualties but also note the circumstances in which the men were killed or wounded. For example, the 14/N.F. noted that 'Sappers' Tulip and Wales were killed by British 5.9" shells falling short, while Sgt. Pickering was wounded by a battalion sentry who fired upon the NCO as he returned from No Man's Land with his working party. Another two men of the battalion were killed and two wounded during a Mills bomb demonstration. Accidents at bombing demonstrations were fairly common, the 5/SWB having lost Captain Lewis and Pte. Dart during such an occasion at Merville. This battalion had already lost one man in somewhat strange circumstances. At noon on 20 July 1915 the battalion had arrived at St. Omer: ten minutes later, Pte. Lewis was reported to have accidentally drowned in the canal 'when not responsible for his actions'. In similar fashion, the cap of Pte. Bedding of the 5/Northants was found alongside the canal at Arques and his body was discovered a week later. Another man who for some undisclosed reason found being overseas too much of a strain was Pte. Prior of the 9/South Staffs. After less than a month in France, Prior shot himself.[8] Sometimes, the War Diary goes into some detail about the character of the casualty. The writer for the NER Pioneers recorded that when Sgt. Syd Morris was killed, the unit lost 'one of the whitest men we had in the battalion'; later Pte. Gent, 'another fine lad', was also killed. Other equally personal comments appear in several diaries. When Sgt. Lester and Cpl. Mitchell were transferred from the 9/South Staffs to 112th Brigade's Machine Gun Company, the diarist noted that the men were both 'excellent NCOs'. Finally, there are also instances of awards of compassionate leave; only one month after its arrival the 11/DLI allowed the McLean brothers to return to England to visit their dying father. The War Diary can also record matters which although not of immediate concern to the battalion's working habits were considered important to its morale. One such example is found in the diary of the 4/Coldstream Guards. On 28 October 1915 the King was supposed to inspect the battalion, but the visit, for some at the time unknown reason, was cancelled. The following day the diary noted that the cancellation was a consequence of the king having been thrown from his horse, the reception given the sovereign by his cheering troops having caused his horse to rear. On 30 October, no doubt with a true sense of loyal relief, the diarist noted that,'the King's condition is improving and no complications have arisen'.

Moving towards the front was also an experience generally well recorded by Pioneer battalions. The 7/York & Lancs was surprised to be transported from the rear by a fleet of London buses, complete with posters and discarded tickets from their last journey in the capital. On arrival at billets, battalions could hope to spend a few days settling in and undertaking some training before moving up to the line. The quality of the billets they inherited was commonly recorded in the diaries. Troops quitting billets were supposed to ensure that they were clean enough for the arriving battalion to occupy without extra work. This was not always the case, as the 18/Middlesex found when arriving at Gorre. The billets were described as 'very dirty and in bad condition'. The 9/Seaforth Highlanders were surprised to find quantities of rifles, equipment and small arms ammunition lying around when it took over billets at Fort Rouge in May 1915, while the 16/Royal Irish Rifles were appalled to witness their first camp at Raincheval. The area lay in a hollow which the autumn rains had turned into little better than a swamp. The sanitation facilities, or lack of them, were described as being in a 'shocking state'.[9]

Experiences such as these could sometimes cause the diarists to include a pointed statement or two aimed at the staff. In the expectation of being comfortably housed on arrival, the 14/N.F. endured a wet and dreary march to Hazebrouck. It was met by Major Pack-Beresford, who told the battalion that it would find billets not in Hazebrouck, but in Hondeghem. Observing the somewhat disgruntled aspect of the battalion on receipt of this information, the major innocently enquired why the unit's billeting officer had not been sent ahead 'as ordered'. Rather succinctly, the diary noted, 'The order was never received'. At the end of the next day's march it arrived at a field which, it was informed, was to be its billet for the night. The men had no blankets and there were no tents. It was a cold but dry night, so the other officers were a little puzzled next morning to hear one company commander complaining of heavy rain during the night. The confusion was settled later when another officer, who had been sleeping in the same furrow as the company commander, explained that the cold had effected his bladder. Not bothering to get up in the dark, he had turned over, unbuttoned and 'simply let fly'.[10]

Another battalion of the Northumberland Fusiliers, the 18th, also suffered from what was either a lack of proper staff work or a failure to fulfil orders. When A Company moved to Abbeville it was 'detained for several hours without any shelter, in heavy rain'. This less than satisfactory affair was subsequently 'brought to the notice of GOC 34th Division', although what, if any, action divisional HQ took remains unrecorded. What might elicit even more angry protestation was the experience of battalions once they came within range of the German guns. It was normal practice for infantry battalions to have some period of trench acclimatization; they were put into the line for a day or two beside a more experienced battalion who would show them the ropes. After a period, the unit would then be expected to be able to hold its own sector of line. This practice was also fairly common among Pioneer units although at least one battalion was not so fortunate.

On 11 February 1916, a month after having landed in France, the 18/N.F. was sent into the front area and began its pioneering duties. The War Diary believed the circumstances in which it took up its responsibilities were less than satisfactory:

A, C and D Companies, without any preparatory attachment, ... [were] expected to take over the duties of the companies they relieved. [9/South Staffs]. Men who had never been under fire were expected to work under shell fire by day and rifle and machine gun fire by night. This appears to me a serious mistake. The men rose to the occasion and did extremely well, but Pioneer work in the trenches is not a simple job and requires learning and I am sure it would be advantageous to let a company of the new battalion work with a company of the battalion in the line for a few days, before taking over the work entirely.

This was by no means a unique experience but, unlike the unfortunate Fusiliers, most battalions did have the opportunity to enjoy a period of acclimatization. The diarist of the 16/Royal Irish Rifles had clearly expected that his battalion would be thrown in at the deep end as he recorded with some relief that they were first to be attached to the 8/Royal Scots. The Scots were he noted, 'fortunately then in the first line putting up barbed wire in front of our fire trenches'.

36

Two companies of the 19/N.F. were luckier than those of its sister battalion as they were attached to the 5/SWB; the other two companies worked for a time with the 19/Welch.[11] Four officers and 16 other ranks of the Fusiliers also apparently spent time with the 4/Coldstream Guards. The Guards had previously been instructing a company of the 19/Welch. The 5/SWB had been attached to the Indian Meerut and Lahore Divisions for Pioneer training, while its machine gun section received instruction from the Dehra Dun Brigade. Similarly, the men of the 13/Gloucester were attached to Field Companies of the R.E. and the 18/Middlesex before they undertook their full responsibilities. Being attached to the R.E. for training had obvious advantages. In his War Diary the C.O. of the 20/KRRC remarked upon the 'helpful suggestions and supervision' made by the R.E. officers. Battalion specialists could also receive instruction from other units, although the snipers of the 9/South Staffs were probably particularly fortunate in being allowed to practise their trade in the front trenches working alongside the line holding units. Battalions which were converted to Pioneers somewhat late in their military careers were usually given some sort of instruction in their new role. Companies of the 7/N.F. were detailed in R.E. working parties for instruction and the officers and NCOs of the 4/South Lancs were sent on short courses to give them some idea of their new duties. However not all such battalions were so well served. The 24/Manchester, for example, was given no instruction and really only first learned of its duties when its companies were attached to the R.E. Field Companies two days before 1 July 1916.

Most Pioneer battalions could reckon on being at the front either under instruction, or in some cases doing the job on their own, within two weeks of leaving the U.K. Sometimes, one or more companies would be detached almost immediately on arrival and might stay away from the remainder of the battalion for up to a week or two. The four companies of the 9/South Staffs were split up within a few days of arriving at the front, and remained as virtually independent groups for several months. Some of its platoons occupied defended posts under their own commander while others were engaged on field works. One officer, who clearly took a technical interest in his work, noted at some length incidents he observed and projects completed. After a shell had struck a dugout he described the nature of the explosion as very 'interesting'. On studying the wrecked dugout he noted that the shell had gone through two sandbags, two inches of timber and four feet of earth before exploding and causing a crater some four feet in diameter. On another occasion he drew a sketch elevation in the War Diary of a strengthened barn, complete with explanation of the effects of enemy shell fire upon it. One platoon of the 8/Sussex also spent a period away on detachment soon after it arrived in France. It was sent to prepare Hondecourt Chateau as a suitable lodgement for its divisional staff – a task which allowed the men to temporarily luxuriate in soft beds and enjoy the pleasures of a large house. Experiences such as this persuaded the junior officer in charge of the detachment that, 'the picture of 'Tommy' as a humorous, carefree and optimistic chap, with a sardonic sense of humour, was not in any way overdrawn or idealized in those days'. He did concede that it was possibly 'over sentimentalized' by the popular press of the day but that nevertheless, in those pre-Somme days, it was a convincing portrayal.[12]

The 7/DLI, converted to Pioneers from within their own division while overseas in 1915, needed some of the 'old Bill' phlegm when it surveyed its new camp in November 1915, Sorely missing the intimate contact it had enjoyed with the battalions of its former brigade one of its diarists wrote:

> Canada Huts lay, one might almost say floated, between Ouderdom and Dickebusch, and was separated from Dickebusch Huts by only a few acres of liquid mud, which, if anything was more prohibitive of intercourse between the battalion and its old comrades in the 6th, 8th and 9th Battalions, than a barbed wire fence could have been.[13]

The elderly Colonel Vaux, habitually wearing an oilskin coat, matching hat and carrying a long pole, 'as though out for otters', was frequently seen wandering about the camp superintending improvements. The chronicler later noted that if any man within the battalion had assumed becoming a Pioneer was a 'cushy' job, they were soon disillusioned. A member was apparently over-heard one night on the Menin Road to remark in a tone of disgust 'DLI! **** engineers and navvies'.[14] The 11/King's also had an unsettling introduction to the front, in its case only a week after landing. On the battalion's first night up, four men were wounded by shrapnel. Although this was hardly a significant loss it was sufficient for the worried C.O. to order that companies should be set to work the following day in a less exposed area.

In contrast, the 8/Royal Scots had a rather more gentle intro-duction to its new role of Pioneers. The battalion had been in France since November 1914 and became Pioneers to the 51st Division in August 1915. The men began work on the Bouzincourt – Albert –Aveluy line, daily leaving billets at 0800, starting work at about 0900, enjoyed their haversack ration between 1130 and 1230 and finished work at 1500. When they returned to billets they could partake of the comforts of the dry canteen, run under the supervision of the chaplain and which 'quickly proved to be very popular', or, if it was their turn, have a bath in the bath house the battalion had itself constructed. Every member of the battalion had a bed, again built by the men themselves, and each week of December saw two officers and 32 men away on home leave. To cap it all the battalion football team crushed the North Irish Horse 13-1 in the semi-final of the divisional cup, before next defeating the Cyclist Company 7-1 in the final. This was clearly the sort of agreeable introduction to work expected by the 10/DCLI. After only two weeks in France an indignant adjutant complained to his diary that: 'Although we were informed that Sundays would be given to us as holidays, we carried out the same work as on the day previously'.

These early experiences overseas helped to identify the strengths and weaknesses of battalions and as they were usually in a quiet sector, helped to build battalion morale. Besides the lessons to be learnt on practical field engineering, some units discovered difficulties in the general operation of the system and suggested alterations. Perhaps the unit most critical of the existing practices was the 18/N.F. In typically forthright tone the War Diary records:

The Battalion has now been in the front area over eight weeks. The experience gained shows the great importance of all ranks, especially officers, having a thorough training in Military Engineering. I consider that the allowance of money and material given in Engineering is quite insufficient. A definite course should be drawn up and care taken that it is gone through carefully. During the month [March 1916] Second Lieutenants have been sent to this Battalion, neither of whom has any experience in Pioneer work, while officers trained with this Battalion in England have been sent to other Battalions. This system seems entirely wrong.

The C.O. had very firm ideas about how his battalion should be run and the methods employed to make it work efficiently. He demanded that each of his company commanders regularly complete forms stating how many man hours were required for a particular job and warned that each company should have another task elsewhere in the line in case enemy shelling inhibited work on the first. 'It should', he thundered, 'never be necessary to march a working party home'.

As they found their feet and discovered the range and variety of tasks allotted to them, casualties in these early days overseas were generally light. A few men might be wounded and the occasional man might be killed by a shell. Unless they were wiring in No Man's Land, in 1915 Pioneers rarely ran the risk of being killed by rifle or machine gun fire. Some men were killed or injured working in quarries or in tunnelling activities, but battalions lost most of their men through sickness or incapacity brought on by the conditions in which they worked. Sometimes these could amount to a significant proportion of battalion strength. Although it had no fatalities from enemy action and only eight men wounded, in October, November and December 1915 the 5/Black Watch lost 128 men to hospital.[15] The 4/Coldstream was losing an average of just under three men a day to hospital during September, October and November 1915 in addition to an unknown number who were excused duty or on light fatigues. In the 9/South Staffs about one sixth of the men who reported sick in January 1916 were excused duty completely, about a third were put on light work and the rest were on 'medicine and duty'. Even allowing for a percentage of malingerers, the sizeable number in the last group – usually around 150 a month – would mean that a reasonable proportion of the battalion was not feeling particularly healthy. Strength could also be reduced for other reasons. Territorial battalions lost a steady trickle of time expired men. They were sent down to the base and home; if they re-enlisted they qualified for a month's leave in the U.K. The 5/Black Watch lost a dozen men in this manner in October 1915 alone. Even as far into the war as the summer and autumn of 1916, the 6/Argyll & Sutherland Highlanders were sending two or three men a month back to the base as under age.

Men away on courses and on leave further reduced numbers available for working on the myriad tasks being allotted to Pioneers. There are scores of examples of officers and men of Pioneer battalions being sent on machine gun, bombing, signalling, and occasionally, engineering or field work courses. A battalion could easily have at least ten men away at any one time on such detachments. Leave allocation is a little more difficult to determine as many War Diaries do not give much information about the numbers of other ranks away with passes. The 8/Royal Scots thought the weekly December allocation of two officers and 32 men was 'most satisfactory'. This had increased from two and 14 respectively in October. Although leave could still on occasions be closed, allocations across the BEF were normally increased during winter months, and by 1 January 1916 the same battalion noted that all men who had served overseas for 12 months had been home on leave.[16]

Unless they had taken part in one of the major battles of 1915, fatalities in most Pioneer units were fairly light. A typical example is that of the 11/DLI. It landed in France on 21 July 1915 and between then and its arrival at the Citadel on 15 July 1916, it had sustained one officer and 33 other ranks killed, with three officers and 153 men wounded. Similarly, the 17/N.F. had lost under a dozen battle casualties in its first two months overseas, but had suffered 'a steady reduction' of strength owing to sickness.[17] Other battalions were equally lucky to escape with such low casualties figures. During April 1916 the 11/Hants had

41

only two men accidently wounded, two who died from gas poisoning and another temporarily gassed. The writer of the 23rd Division's history recalled a story in March 1916 when a company of the 9/South Staffs moved up to the line:

> These innocent 'braves' marched gaily into Calonne [near Vimy] in column of fours, followed by their transport. Presumably this event occurred at the German observer's dinner hour. Otherwise it is certain that, though the steaming cooker which accompanied them might have induced the Germans to think the railhead had been moved forward, a shortage of Pioneers in the division would have been the inevitable consequence.[18]

Like their comrades in other Pioneer battalions, the thoughful amongst the men of the DLI and the Northumberland Fusiliers realized that once the authorities decided the battalion and the division in which it served were capable of undertaking offensive operations, they could anticipate a much higher rate of loss.

*   *   *

In the early months of their overseas experience the New Army divisions, and the regulars and Territorials who had preceded them abroad, had of necessity been obliged to do their carrying and digging themselves. The R.E. Field Companies attached to each division had undertaken the more specialized work, but the bulk of the labouring had to be done by the infantry. This was not an arrangement particularly favoured by either side and even when a Pioneer battalion was allocated to a division already in France or Belgium, or indeed when a complete New Army division arrived in France, there was no immediate relief from the labouring tasks for the infantry. When the Pioneers did begin work and when the new divisions had undergone their trench acclimatization, the infantry were still to be called upon to perform the jobs that many might have assumed would be done by the Pioneers.[19]

The relationship between the Pioneers and the Commander Royal Engineers, under whose authority and supervision they generally came, is looked at elsewhere. At times this relationship was difficult and, on occasions, even acrimonious. The men

42

themselves were largely unaffected by any resentment or difficulties which might have developed between their own officers and the R.E. Working parties remained very largely under the control of their own officers, and when the job was completed, or day dawned, the men returned to their own, rather than R.E. camps. Because much of the Pioneers' work had to be done nocturnally, some of the daylight hours in camp could be spent in training. It has already been noted that when out at rest the opportunity was taken to give the men training in both conventional soldiering and pioneering projects. Important as both aspects were, the overwhelming evidence suggests that the emphasis was put on the former rather than the latter. It was during such a rest period that the 20/KRRC became 'knit together as a happy family'.[20] The reason given by the chronicler for undertaking infantry rather than pioneering training was because the battalion had had so little opportunity to practise these tasks while in England. Of course, a considerable time was still spent digging and wiring, but the Rifles were certainly not alone in stressing the need for musketry etc. The daily training schedule for the 9/South Staffs in April 1916 included one hour's running drill, three hour's platoon and company drill, handling arms, wood fighting, judging distances, fire control, bayonet fighting and P.T. As an apparent concession to its role as Pioneers, afternoons were occupied in route marches, with short breaks to practise loading and unloading tools from G.S. wagons. Six months after its conversion to Pioneers the 9/DLI seemed reluctant to abandon its role of fighting infantry. While at rest the battalion organized 16 competitions, ranging from musketry to signalling and bugle sounding. Only part of one competition had any direct link to pioneering skills; this entailed 'the preparation of some simple defensive work in Field Engineering'.[21]

The 4/Coldstream Guards had several sessions of wiring practise supervised by an officer of the R.E., but the 18/Middlesex, like many other battalions, felt that its training in December 1915 was 'hampered by most of the country being under water'. Officers were sometimes sent away for a day's course on aspects of pioneering work; several subalterns of the 9/North Staffs, for example, went to La Canche in April 1916 to attend lectures on 'The repair and maintenance of roads'. Yet while they were at rest, and in theory undergoing training, few battalions were left to enjoy their time without interference from authority. They were frequently despatched on carrying duties or sent to build or improve nearby camps. One of the reasons why the Oldham Comrades were chosen to become Pioneers to the 7th Division was said to be because of the quality of the ablution benches and latrines they had laboured to build during their early weeks in France.

In more distant theatres of war Pioneers tended to be thrown into the fighting a little earlier than their comrades in France. This was often a result of heavy losses among the infantry and the need to keep the line manned. The 5/Royal Irish Regiment, Pioneers to the 10th Division, landed at Suvla Bay on 7 August and within a few days were line holding. The battalion suffered 156 casualties on 16 August alone. It experienced a quieter time after it was withdrawn and moved to Salonika; there it could settle down to more conventional pioneering duties. It laid out camps, made roads, dug wells and arranged water supplies, carried ammunition and, in a display of Allied cooperation, had attached to it 500 men of the Greek Labour Corps.

The 6/East Yorks, Pioneers to the 11th Division, also landed at Suvla on 7 August and had an even more bloody time than the 5/Royal Irish. Having been equipped with what one officer described as a 'marvellous uniform' consisting of pith helmet, Indian khaki and shorts, the battalion had arrived at Mundros in advance of several other units of its division. When the division landed at Suvla the Yorkshiremen attacked Scimitar Hill. The general attack failed and the Pioneers were ordered to withdraw. Exhausted from their effort one company and HQ details were next ordered to attack the vital position of Tekke Tepe. The attack was made and 'this little party of East Yorkshiremen had achieved the brilliant feat of reaching a position farther east on the heights above Suvla than any other British troops'.[22] Unfortunately, it was indeed a 'little' party. Fewer than 30 men had reached the top of the hill and were surrounded. The C.O. saw no alternative other than to surrender. On attempting to do this Colonel Moore was run through by a Turkish bayonet and died. Written less than ten years after the event, the regimental history described this 'foul murder of a British officer, a prisoner of war, [as] another instance of the treacherous nature of the Turkish soldiery'.[23] Meanwhile the other three companies of the battalion advanced up the hill, but being met by severe rifle fire the attack withered away. The two days of 8-9 August cost the battalion 350 casualties, of whom 211 were missing. Despite the arrival of some reinforcements brought up from Imbros, by 22 August the battalion numbered only some four officers and under 300 men. Further reinforcements arrived in September. One officer who came with this draft was typical of the young subalterns who had been itching for overseas service. Wyn Adams, who came from prosperous Richmond in Surrey, had champed at the bit while stationed at Harrogate with a reserve battalion of the East Yorks. In a series of letters to his aunt, which clearly reflected his frustration at remaining at home, he declared he found Harrogate 'horrid' and was relieved not to be sent to France with a draft as he wanted to get to the Dardanelles with his own lot because 'it's warmer'. Within four weeks of arriving on the peninsula he was writing to his aunt asking for chocolates, cigarettes, a great coat, and hoping for a blighty.[24]

The East Yorks were evacuated from Gallipoli and sent to Alexandria, but instead of following the 5/Royal Irish to Salonika, in July 1916 it returned to Europe. Going in the opposite direction, and after having spent less than two months in France, the 9/Border left Marseilles in late October 1915 for 'an unknown destination'. While steaming through the Mediterranean the battalion was kept constantly on the alert, wearing life belts and practising emergency procedures. To pass the time a 'really stiff' on board obstacle course was devised by the Royal Navy, and the men were declared to be 'excellent and all very cheery and pleased with life'. The 'unknown destination' turned out to be Alexandria. Speculation on their future employment was quashed when instead of disembarking (the officers did manage a quick tour of the town), the ship turned around and again headed out to sea. Four days later the battalion disembarked at Salonika and marched to a bare hillside designated as their 'camp'. Several long nights of chilling rain followed, and with no protection and with bread described as a 'luxury', the men endured a depressing introductory period. A regular post did begin but the men could do little training as they were confined to the enclosed hillside. By the end of the month snow began to fall. Lt. Col. Cooke, a retired Indian Army officer believed his men 'stood the exposure splendidly . . . the health and cheeriness generally of all ranks during a very trying experience was marvellous and surpassed all that could have been expected'. Quite remarkably there were reported to be no cases of frostbite and only seven went to hospital. The battalion eventually settled into a routine of road making, improving camps, bridging and quarrying.

Like the 6/East Yorks, the 8/Welch had also fought in Gallipoli and sustained heavy casualties. In the few months it spent on the peninsula, 176 of its men were either killed or died. In January 1916 it was withdrawn, and by March the battalion had arrived at Basra. It remained in Mesopotamia, enduring the privations of the terrible terrain and climate, until February 1919. With temperatures reaching 126 degrees in the shade, the men had to dig, wire and march across endless expanses of rocky wasteland and build roads through the inhospitable mountain ranges. There were occasional outbreaks of cholera, but the chief killer was sun stroke. During the summer months of 1916 an average of two men a day died from it and the average daily sick parade amounted to 28 men. By August only 383 men of the battalion were deemed fit to undertake a march, On top of the dangers of disease, heat and the Turk, there were the added problems created by marauding Arab tribesmen. Besides those who were killed in action or died of wounds, an additional 116 men died from other causes during the ill-fated Mesopotamian campaign.

In France, other Pioneer battalions were also fighting but without suffering the same sort of losses as those which had served in the East. The 5/Northants spent some time in the spring of 1916 in the Loos area. The battalion was actively involved in the crater fighting near the Hohenzollern Redoubt and on two occasions repulsed German counter-attacks; the colonel received a complimentary letter from the divisional commander thanking him for the work done by his battalion. The 11/Hants was also involved in the Loos sector and, during a period on loan to the 47th Division, dashed forward to consolidate the new crater when a mine was blown near the Double Crassier. The 18/Middlesex had what was described as a 'stiff fight'[25] in May 1916 when the enemy blew several large mines in the Duck's Bill area near Annequin. Its No.16 Platoon held the line for one-and-a-half hours until it was reinforced, losing seven killed and 22 wounded in the process. This successful engagement did something to redeem the rather low morale within the battalion. In addition to some unsatisfactory events which dogged the battalion in its early months overseas, the intelligence officer had written a critical account of an incident a few weeks earlier. On this occasion a party of men was clearing a drain known as the Suez Canal when, 'There was a needless scare due to a want of discipline and power of command . . . resulting in a number of men leaving the drain . . . and retiring several hundred yards'. The 12/Notts & Derby, with rather more success, was thrown into the front line almost as soon as it arrived. The battalion manned trenches in reserve to 71st Brigade and was then ordered to attack. It reached its objective but was forced to retire when the 71st and 72nd Brigades were compelled to withdraw. It then succeeded in holding the former German front line before being relieved by the Guards. The GOC 24th Division sent the unit a wire congratulating it on its work.

The 4/Coldstream Guards also fought around the Duck's Bill and lost two men drowned – Privates Regg and Williamson – in the flooded crater in February 1916. The 8/Royal Scots was in another mined area close to Arras in March. Here, near the Labyrinth it frequently unearthed long-dead French and German bodies and won praise for the 'ease and rapidity'[26] with which it could erect wire entanglements around the mine craters that littered the area.

A little later in the year, and very soon after its arrival in the Laventie area, the 5/DCLI was working furiously for its comrades of the 61st Division. One chronicler wrote that 'from every part of the Divisional front the 1/5 DCLI would be seen like ants for ever busy in repairing, constructing and carrying'.[27]

The troops of the 9/Seaforth Highlanders were involved in the Battle of Loos, digging communication trenches to the Hohenzollern Redoubt and frequently having to drop their tools and repulse bombing attacks by the enemy. On 27 September A Company was ordered forward to Support Trench, but found its way blocked by the 2/East Surreys. The Surreys 'began to retire in disorder and we endeavoured to rally them.' The brigadier declared that this 'fine example shown by the men of the Pioneers eventually had the effect of some order being attained'. The historian of the 9th Division called them 'a shining example of pluck and endurance' and recalled that 'they were as notable for their fighting as for the value and quality of their work'.[28] After the battle had died down parties of the 14/N.F. were sent out to bury the dead. They came across scores of bodies lying in neat rows before the German wire. Dillon remembered his men initially thinking the corpses were merely sleepers. Once they had steeled themselves to do the job, their apprehension dissipated and Dillon's men ended up by bowling a head down the line of corpses to see which trunk it fitted.[29]

The 9/Gordon Highlanders was also heavily engaged in the Battle of Loos. Lieutenant Robert Kershaw was thrilled at the prospect of further fighting, having already written home that 'we have to dig ourselves in in a pretty exposed spot, but I don't doubt we shall have some great fun'. During the battle two platoons were ordered to go up with the assaulting battalions and the C.O. picked Kershaw's as one of those to go. He later explained: 'I could see it would have broken his heart if I had not sent him for one. He thanked me with all his heart when I told him I had selected his platoon'.[30] Kershaw and his men stormed the German line but he was killed while attempting to gain further ground. Two nights later four men volunteered to go out and bring in his body for burial in Quality Street Cemetery. Kershaw was only one of 75 fatalities sustained by the battalion during the battle; another ten succumbed to wounds in the immediate aftermath.

Among other Pioneers who found themselves acting as fighting troops within a few days of arriving in the front area were the 7/York & Lancs and the 11/DLI. Two signallers of the

York & Lancs won praise, and one the DCM, from their division for keeping an advanced signal station operating during the German gas attack on Ypres in December. The whole battalion was reported in the War Diary to be 'cheerful and interested in this new form of aggression', and while digging on the Bluff in February 1916 one company was used to repulse another German attack. For a period of six weeks in the aftermath of Loos the Durhams were attached to 60th Brigade and served as front line troops. In contrast, and once it had lived down the embarrassment of having no weapons, the 20/KRRC by its own admission had a fairly easy breaking in. Its first jobs in what was for the time a pretty quiet area were draining and helping to build a light railway north of Ypres. Perhaps the most notable achievement during this period was that the battalion defeated the 1/Grenadier Guards at football.

The Rifles was one of the several battalions whose early experiences suggested that the BEF remained somewhat vague as to the attachment of the arriving units. When it landed in France the battalion expected to be attached to the 6th Division. On arrival at Winnezeele it learned that it was instead to go to the 20th, and then finally ended up in the 3rd. The battalion's historian recorded that this posting to a regular division was looked upon as a 'conspicuous honour', although, as he later wrote, 'it was to prove as exacting as it was conspicuous'.[31] One unit referred to itself as 'nobody's child',[32] while another regimental history noted the strange life of a Pioneer battalion and the difficulties such an existence had for both the historian and the unit:

> The 12th was now the Pioneer battalion of the 40th Division, but their history is not easy to trace since they belonged to no particular brigade in the division, and were from time to time attached or temporarily transferred to other divisions or areas, where work of the kind for which the Battalion had received special training happened to be most urgently required.[33]

One battalion which did not have the same gentle acclimatization as that enjoyed by the 20/KRRC at Winnezeele was the

18/N.F. It found itself frequently detached from its own division and sent on what one of its officers called 'John the Baptist expeditions'.[34] This meant the men were sent hither and thither to get things ready; he later concluded that a battalion attached to a strange division 'does not have a very rosy time. It has to fight for everything it wants, from baths to beer'.[35] On one occasion a working party was caught by a trench mortar or some other 'vile machine'. When the debris had stopped falling and the smoke cleared, the remains of Pte. Blackshaw, 'mutilated past removal' were discovered. Later in the day those of Privates Dufour and French were also found and buried alongside what little remained of Blackshaw. The battalion was trying to dig Russian saps under No Man's Land in front of La Boisselle, but the work was hampered when the artillery discovered that the unit contained a large number of skilled miners. The Pioneer C.O. was then pestered continually to allow the gunners to use his men to dig observation posts and gun pits. When the attack took place on 1 July the Russian saps were not used, but the C.O. nearly came to grief himself when he put a foot through one.[36]

One company of the 18/N.F. was detailed to hold the line from the opening of the bombardment until the infantry went over the top on 1 July. The company manned the Glory Hole, and although it had never before been used for this purpose, five of its men won Military Medals during the period. Like many others, this battalion was preparing itself and the ground for the expected British offensive on the Somme. Apart from one division, whose Pioneer battalion was still on its way towards the front, all divisions which would take part in the offensive had their Pioneer units already attached. During the summer of 1915 and again in the spring of 1916 the War Office had been trying to ensure that enough infantry battalions serving in France had either already been converted or were in the process of doing so, to furnish all divisions with a Pioneer unit. The process of conversion had caused considerable anguish for several battalions with a deserved reputation as fighting infantry. These now faced the prospect of fulfilling a role about which they had little knowledge or, it could be assumed, little appetite. As soon as divisional orders for the offensive were drawn up and circulated,

50

their men would know that they were unlikely to take a leading role in the coming attack. However, those men in battalions which had been raised as Pioneers or those converted early in their existence knew, like their comrades in the other divisional formations, that their hastily acquired skills and their efficiency might well prove crucial to the overall success of the operation.

NOTES

1. Unless otherwise stated, the following detail comes from battalion War Diaries. PRO references for War Diaries are given in Appendix III. See Appendix II for mobilized strengths.
2. Capper, op.cit.
3. ibid.
4. Turbeville, op.cit. p.8 The adjutant complained bitterly to the W.D. about this humiliation. After having explained how musketry training was 'rendered difficult owing to an entire absence of musketry instruction appliances', he went on:'The somewhat exceptional circumstances under which the unit arrived at a danger zone to work, should have influenced the home authorities to see that rifles were provided for the battalion on its arrival at such a destination'.
5. For example: Pte. Debney of the 5/Northants was accidently shot while the battalion was still in Folkestone and Pte. Nicholls of the 5/DCLI was left behind with German measles.
6. Major T.G. Davidson of the battalion thought that Hurford's accident 'did not distress us greatly for though an amusing man, he was difficult to take quite seriously'. (Davidson's papers, DLI Museum)
7. Soon after its arrival the 18/Middlesex ascertained that 297 of its men were over 40. Of these 58 were declared to be fit for base duty only. A few days later, another 45 were deemed unsuitable for front line duty. This removed a tenth of its strength and when the replacements arrived, a mixture of men from Staffordshire, Lancashire, East Anglia and London, nearly a quarter of them were declared unfit for service.
8. Pte. Haining of the 9/Seaforth was mentioned in his battalion's War Diary for bravery when saving the life of a French boy who had fallen into a canal at Busnes in June 1915.
9. Poor billets were not only an overseas phenomenon. When the 9/Gordon moved into huts at Perham Down vacated by the 8/Welch, they were described as being in a 'most filthy and disgusting condition; the blankets were issued covered with vermin and were refused'. (W.D.)

51

10. Dillon, op.cit.
11. Several other battalions, such as the 12/Yorks, had their companies instructed by two different divisions simultaneously.
12. Capper, op.cit.
13. Unpublished typescript history of the 7/DLI. (DLI Museum)
14 ibid.
15. Two men of the Black Watch died in hospital during this period: one from frostbite and the other, Pte. Thomson, from epilepsy.
16. To allow for travelling time home, in December 1915 leave for men to Scotland was increased to nine days. When leave re-opened in March following a break, the battalion's weekly allocation was reduced to two officers and eight other ranks.
17. Shakespear, op.cit. p.27. The 11/King's lost several men to hospital when a party tried to dig out some men of another battalion who had been buried by rubble from the cathedral in Ypres. The first rescue party then had to be freed by a second after it too had fallen victim to the collapsing building.
18. Sandilands, op.cit. p.39
19. The CRE 37th Division complained that:'The infantry have worked very badly on night shifts and their hours have been too short'. (W.D.) The C.O. of the 9/Gordon Highlanders also thought:'The system of infantry parties under R.E. supervision being used to mark out tracks with posts did not answer well', and suggested that the task should be done by Pioneers. (W.D.)
20. Turbeville, op.cit.
21. 9th Bn. DLI *Handbook,* published in August 1918. (Newcastle Local Studies Library)
22. Wyrall, op.cit. p.103
23. ibid, p.104
24. Adams, W. papers. (Liddle Collection)
25. Wyrall, E. *The Diehards in the Great War, 1914-19,* (London, 1926–30) p.241
26. Ewing, J. *The Royal Scots, 1914-19,* p.256
27. Matthews, E.C. *With the Cornwall Territorials on the Western Front. Being the History of the 5th Battalion DCLI in the Great War,* (Cambridge, 1921) p.4
28. Ewing, J. *The History of the 9th (Scottish) Division 1914–19,* (Murray, 1920) p.48
29. Dillon, op.cit.
30. Kershaw, op.cit. The W.D. noted that G Company went into the battle with 203 O.R. It came out with 88, a casualty rate of 57%

31. Turbeville, op.cit. p.13 The battalion did spend some time working for the 6th Division, but was not its official Pioneer unit.
32. Walsh, Capt. St.G. papers. (Oldham Local Studies Library)
33. Wylly, op.cit. p.350. In its early months overseas, the 12/Yorks even became part of the Loos garrison in conjunction with corps cyclists. This duty involved manning six keeps in addition to their normal duties.
34. Shakespear, op.cit. p.33
35. ibid.
36. ibid, p.38

Chapter 3

THE CHOSEN FEW

It might be imagined that when a battalion already serving overseas was informed it had been selected for conversion to a Pioneer unit, there was some initial disquiet and reluctance to accept its new role. After all, the men of the New Armies and the Territorials who had opted for foreign service had enlisted to fight the Germans and hurl the invader from the soils of France and Belgium. They had spent their time in England training for the role of attacking infantry, imagining glorious charges across the green sward of No Man's Land and advancing remorselessly upon the seat of the evil Kaiser. Now the prospect of following tamely in the wake of their former brigade comrades, putting out fields of barbed wire, digging new trenches and strong points and merely carrying forward the paraphenalia of war, seemed far removed from their initial dreams. Of course, those units which had specifically been raised as Pioneers did not have to undergo this apparent humiliation, but for the enthusiastic enlistments of 1914 and early 1915 it was to come as a rude shock.

Once the decision had been made to provide each division with some sort of Pioneer unit the essential problem was how to appoint such units (and initially there was no certainty that they would be actual *battalions*) to those divisions already overseas. The decision to appoint a Pioneer battalion to every division had been made sufficiently early for the New Armies to have one selected before they went abroad. The difficulty came when deciding how Pioneers should be appointed to the regular and the Territorial divisions already on the continent. Many

Territorial battalions had gone to France independently rather than with their division. Once in France they were attached to regular divisions, the result being that infantry brigades were increased from their usual four, to five and sometimes even six battalions. When the New Armies began arriving in France it was decided that the Territorial battalions – several of whom had been overseas since November 1914 –should be removed from their host regular divisions, withdrawn from the line and be reformed into their original Territorial divisional formations. These pre-war formations had of course been created from battalions with close regional connections. When reassembled they too would then need to have a Pioneer battalion selected, preferably, from within their own ranks. It was originally thought that the regular divisions would have Service battalions of the New Armies appointed to fulfil the role for them. In the face of opposition and some criticism from senior officers, the War Office was to change its mind several times before the eleven regular divisions did finally receive their allocation.

Within First and Second Army there was a great deal of discussion as to how the decisions should be made and then which battalions should be chosen. A intriguing batch of memoranda and correspondence between GHQ, the commander of Second Army, General Plumer, and his three corps commanders shows how the problem was addressed between July and September 1915.[1] It is unclear how much sustained interest Lord Kitchener kept in the issue of Pioneers once the concept had been agreed, but the Great Man had already expressed his views on the matter of those to be converted with a member of Sir John French's staff. The final decision about which battalions would be selected did, however, rest with the commanders in the field.[2] At first General Plumer was not convinced that each division should actually have a battalion specifically designated as Pioneers. He circulated his three subordinates requesting their opinions and comments on his initial thoughts. He suggested that the skills of the numerous engineers, artisans and mechanics found within the ranks of the New Armies and the Territorials could be utilized by putting them to work under the supervision of R.E. On occasions, he thought, they could even be allowed to work independently on such projects as revetting, splinter-proofing dugouts and so on. At this stage the commander was thinking of perhaps forming 'something approaching a Pioneer Corps', which would be placed at the disposal of the CRE of corps, or divisional and brigade commanders. Alternatively, he suggested existing Field Companies could have sections composed of skilled men attached to them and which might even be used as eventual reinforcements to those companies. He made it clear, however, that these groups should not be used as labour companies to relieve the infantry of the unskilled labour which they would ordinarily be called upon to perform.

Within a few days of this memo (8 July) Plumer informed his subordinates that it had been decided that all divisions within II, V and VI Corps should, like the 9th, 12th and 14th New Army divisions already within the corps, have a Pioneer *battalion*. He suggested that suitable units could be found from within the 'spare' Territorial battalions attached to the brigades. The commander of V Corps, Lieutenant-General Allenby, replied that given its area of recruitment – the coal fields of West Lancashire – the obvious choice within the regular 3rd Division was the 4/South Lancs. The question of providing the 46th (North Midland) Territorial Division with Pioneers was more of a problem. If, he explained, one battalion was taken from the 3rd Division and sent to the 46th one of the regular brigades would thus be reduced to its four original battalions. Moreover, he thought, it was unlikely that another suitable battalion in addition to the 4/South Lancs could be found from within the 3rd Division. The only possibilities among its attached T.F. units were the Honourable Artillery Company and the Liverpool Scottish – both of which were battalions of clerks rather than skilled men. The solution, he suggested, was to increase the Field Companies of the 46th Division by the addition of at least two sections, each of one officer and 50 men. These men would be drawn from those already with the division, or by drafts from Rouen. By this means at least 300 skilled officers and men would be added to the existing strength of the Field Companies and, furthermore, get around GHQ's stipulation that new units could not be created. He was supported in this proposal by the GOC

46th Division who, not surprisingly, was reluctant to have one of his brigades reduced to three battalions in order to create one of Pioneers.[3]

The commander of the 5th Division, Major-General Kavanagh, did not support the suggestion but did believe that an increase in the strength of the Field Companies was desirable. However this should not, he thought, be done at the expense of the infantry battalions. The only way which he would support the proposal was if the strength of the infantry was increased to compensate for the loss of men to the R.E. Furthermore, he added, each battalion had already formed its own Pioneer detachment and these men should on no account be taken from their units. The commanders of VI and II Corps, Lieutenant-Generals Keir and Fergusson, were also experiencing difficulties in selecting suitable battalions. None of the three T.F. units in the 5th Division was accustomed to manual work and the two in the 6th Division were recruited from London and consisted of clerks and shop-keepers rather than artisans. Having gone to France as a complete unit in April 1915 the 49th (West Riding) Division did not contain any 'spare' battalions and would thus have to have one posted to it. In the 4th Division, of the limited options available, the 7/Argyll & Sutherland Highlanders appeared to be the most suitable choice. As an alternative the divisional commander requested that the 2/Monmouth which owing to severe losses had been removed from the division and amalgamated with its 1st and 3rd Battalions, should be returned. The battalion he wrote, was 'most suitable for this purpose, and were used a good deal for this class of work while with the division'.

When attempting to find a suitable battalion divisional commanders were asked to discover whether any C.O. might be willing to offer his battalion for conversion to Pioneers. Unfortunately, the GOC of II Corps reported that only one battalion under his command was prepared to volunteer. This battalion was the 8/DLI which certainly would have been acceptable, but like the GOC 5th Division, Lieutenant-General Fergusson thought the Monmouth battalions would be better suited. He suggested that the three units should resume their individual identity, be withdrawn from the 28th Division, where the amalgamated unit was presently posted, and become the corps three Pioneer battalions. The problem was, he acknowledged, that the scheme was apparently 'repugnant' to each of the three Monmouth battalions. Moreover he questioned the advisability or benefit to a division of having a T.F. Pioneer battalion labelled as such against its wishes and which had not been specifically recruited for that purpose. It was for that reason he declared, that he was only submitting the name of the 8/DLI and hoped that two battalions would be sent from elsewhere to fulfil the role in his other divisions.

In an effort to facilitate and speed on the deliberations the Chief of the General Staff sent a memo to General Plumer addressing the question of the Territorial Force battalions then under his command. There were, he explained, 23 T.F. battalions 'spare' and available for conversion, and only 19 were required to provide each regular and T.F. division with Pioneers. The selection of battalions would require 'careful consideration, after examination of the class of men and the area of recruiting'. When New Army battalions were transferred as Pioneers to regular divisions their place in their former division, he continued, might be taken by T.F. battalions until such a time as another Service battalion became available. It appears from this suggestion that one of the principal concepts behind the T.F. – its territorial identity – was considered expendable and that units could be used to plug whatever gap or perform any function that the army considered necessary. With an almost cavalier approach to the importance of regimental *esprit*, and indeed to the existing conditions of service, the Chief of Staff declared that T.F. units selected for conversion would have to undergo certain personnel changes in order to provide them with the sufficient percentage of carpenters and blacksmiths, etc. Showing a more compassionate attitude towards his T.F. battalions, General Plumer did not agree with the idea of selecting an existing battalion and calling it Pioneers, preferring instead the idea that divisional commanders should be allowed to build up a Pioneer unit. Such a formation should, he suggested, begin with a small establishment and then be gradually expanded by the transfer of officers and men from battalions within their divisions. Unfortunately for the future status of several T.F. units, Plumer's advice was not heeded.

In another attempt to speed up the process, two days after the first memo the War Office sent another to Second Army. This contained a list of regiments which had provided Pioneer battalions to the First, Second and Third New Armies, and an incorrect list of those which had not but which might contain a unit suitable for conversion.[4] Second Army meanwhile had also been trying to move the process forward. Plumer informed the GOC II Corps that his suggestion of the 8/DLI as Pioneers for the Northumbrian Division was unacceptable. Because the battalion was considered to be too weak, the corps commander was requested to nominate another that night. (21 July) A flurry of telegrams continued for the next few hours and continued well into the small hours of the following morning. Lieutenant-General Fergusson urgently requested that the decision for the 50th Division be postponed until its understrength battalions had been reinforced. If he was forced to chose before drafts arrived, he said he would select the 6/DLI. GHQ replied that this unit was also too weak and wanted another nomination with a strength of between 700-800 men. The only battalion with such a high establishment was the 9/DLI, but it had not yet been asked whether it was prepared to accept the new role. General Plumer was under intense pressure from GHQ for a decision and reported upwards that although it was of the required strength the 9/DLI had not volunteered for conversion. With a strength of well over 900 the 9/DLI actually exceeded GHQ's requirements, and was consequently deemed to be *too* strong. If an immediate decision was required, and even though it too had not yet volunteered, the 7th rather than the 9/DLI was considered to be a better choice.

GHQ had already decided that the 8/Notts & Derby and the 6/Duke of Wellington's should become Pioneers to their respective divisions, the 46th and 49th, and it now also approved the appointment of the 7/DLI for its own 50th Division. This latter division possessed two battalions too many so it was decided to allow the 5/Border to remain with it and post away the other

59

T.F. unit, the 5/Loyal North Lancs. This was a relatively simple decision but the question of which battalions should replace the Territorials from Newark and Skipton in their respective infantry brigades once again caused a rapid exchange of messages. GHQ suggested that the 1/16th London and the 4/Gordon Highlanders should be sent to the 49th and 46th Divisions. This proposal caused dismay at corps level. The commanders considered that the introduction of these two T.F. battalions into T.F. divisions from a very different regional background negated the Territorial principle and would consequently be resented by all. An alternative solution was suggested by the GOC VI Corps. Lieutenant-General Keir believed that if the West Riding Territorial Association was informed of the problem, it would either be able to raise a Pioneer battalion from its own recruiting area or, alternatively, provide another unit to replace the 6/Dukes.

Another argument against withdrawing T.F. battalions from their existing divisions was the fact that many of them had built up very good relationships with the regulars in their brigades. This relationship had often been forged in the heat of battle, particularly the Second Battle of Ypres and had, in the view of at least one corps commander, produced 'excellent results'. The regulars had developed a huge respect for many of the T.F. battalions and were equally reluctant to lose the comradeship of their 'Saturday afternoon soldiers'.

However, GHQ was clearly becoming annoyed at the prevarication and demanded decisions. Second Army told II Corps that two of its brigades which currently had six battalions each would have to lose at least three T.F. units. Various names were bandied about and the 1st and 3rd Monmouth, which had resumed their individual identities, were transferred from 84th Brigade. When the 46th Division's O.C. learnt that he was receiving the 1/Monmouth, he immediately petitioned that *it* should become the Pioneers and thus allow the 8/Notts & Derby to remain with 139th Brigade. A similar request was made by the GOC West Riding Division when he was informed that the 3/Monmouth would be posted to his command. Both commanders opposed the idea of splitting a brigade to find a Pioneer battalion only to have it replaced in its former brigade by a battalion of Monmouths. Furthermore, given their recruitment areas of Newport, Pontypool and Abergavenny, the Monmouths were obvious choices for conversion. One source states simply that the 2/Monmouth was 'specially adept in the use of pick and shovel',[5] and, despite its losses at Second Ypres, still retained over 500 men from its original area of recruitment. The 1st and 3rd Battalions were also still composed of men from the regiment's traditional areas, but in comparison to the units in their new divisions both battalions were still very much under strength. This provided the divisional commanders with a convincing argument. They insisted that if a full strength brigade relieved one of much weaker composition in the line, huge problems with regard to deployment, distribution and boundaries would follow. Given the weakened state of the Monmouth battalions they, argued, confusion would be the inevitable result.

General Plumer acceded to his commanders' requests and then wrote a long justification to GHQ in the anticipation of discontent, if not outright rejection:

> When the 46th and 49th Divisions were told to nominate battalions for conversion they had practically no alternative but to nominate the strongest battalions in the brigades. One cannot therefore be surprised that when these Divisions received their additional battalions, they should have taken the opportunity to urge at once that the original composition of their brigades on a Territorial basis should not be altered . . . It is only on paper that a battalion can be suddenly made into a Pioneer battalion by the stroke of a pen. If the men were really pioneers there would be a strong argument for adhering to the previous choice, but they are not.[6]

Several other points were made with equal force and having been presented with what amounted to a *fait accompli*, GHQ agreed to the proposals and the necessary transfers and conversions went ahead. General Bulfin called together the officers of the 1/Monmouth to 'express (his) regret' at their departure from his division. He told them that they had experienced a 'rough time' and showered praise upon them and their battalion. He concluded by stating that he hoped it would 'continue to make history' in its new division.[7] Bulfin was followed by the commander of the 84th Brigade, who talked of the battalion's 'splendid and distinguished conduct'.[8] However, whether it was a slip of the tongue, an incomprehension of the way by which Pioneer battalions were to be grouped, or simply because he had been misinformed about the battalion's future, he despatched it while assuring its officers that he confidently expected the unit to continue its 'brilliant career in [its] new brigade'. When it departed for the 29th Division the 2nd Battalion apparently consoled itself with the thought that 'sooner or later they would have the chance of getting their own back from the Boche'.[9] To the 49th Division the 3rd Battalion took not only a fine fighting record but, more importantly for its intended role, extensive tunnelling experience gained on the infamous Hill 60.

Several battalions in Second Army had thus come close to becoming Pioneers and others had become so against their will. The whole process had taken less than six weeks and had been concluded during what was, fortunately, a fairly quiet time as far as fighting was concerned. Similar activity was going on in First Army and it is worth looking at a few examples from there to complete the picture of these initial stages of conversion.

The 4/Royal Welch Fusiliers had served in France with the 1st Division since December 1914. In August 1915 it was informed that it was to be removed from the regular division and posted instead to the 47th (London) Division. Being a T.F. formation it was, of course, a prime candidate for conversion and although it had already suffered considerable casualties the fact that 'almost all the then remaining warrant officers, NCOs and men were skilled miners no doubt largely weighed with those who decided the change'.[10] One source claims that, 'the excellence of the pioneer work . . . testified to the wisdom of the Higher Command in their selection'.[11] This is a rare instance of the authorities receiving some congratulation upon achieving a correct decision and could be contrasted with the views no doubt expressed by the officers of the London Rifle Brigade when they were told that the battalion was to begin pioneer training. This class-conscious battalion, composed almost exclusively of young middle-class office clerks, enjoyed an extremely prestigious position among other Territorial units. It suffered huge casualties during Second Ypres and when eventually withdrawn from the line its men were dispersed over most of northern France. For some weeks they performed multifarious tasks at the BEF's numerous rail heads. It was not a function the battalion enjoyed and so it was horrified to learn that the army was thinking of making this employment permanent. Fortunately, after representation by important friends in high places, authority changed its mind. The battalion was brought up to strength from its own third line unit and remained as fighting infantry.[12]

A Territorial battalion of the Scottish Rifles, the 1/6th, began training as a Pioneer unit in early 1916. Its men, recruited from the coal fields and ship yards of Hamilton, spent some time under instruction from, among others, the 18/Middlesex. After several weeks of digging and wiring the authorities changed their minds and the unit returned to its former occupation of fighting infantry. A few months earlier in August 1915, a Territorial unit of the King's Liverpool regiment, the 7th Battalion, also received word that it was to be converted.[13] In a letter home, Private Marriot described a visit by a divisional staff officer who enquired into the civilian occupations of the officers and men:

> . . . finding that most of us were skilled or intelligent labourers, carpenters, engineers, fitters, etc., it was decided we should become a pioneer regiment . . . So we have been taken off trench work and have ever since been going through a course of instruction . . . Today we have been finding the tensile strength of timber by means of algebra!!! Every division is doing the same, even one of the Guards regiments has been taken for it, and all Kitchener's men have properly trained Pioneer battalions. It is not in Divisional orders yet, but I am pretty sure that our appointment will follow in due course'.[14]

Many people might have disagreed with Marriot's assertion that the Pioneer battalions in Kitchener's armies were 'properly trained', but like the fear among the LRB, the speculation proved unwarranted and the 7/King's remained as infantry for the rest of the war.[15]

The Territorials knew it was inconceivable that a regular battalion within the regular divisions would be converted. Not surprisingly therefore, several battalions expected to become the unit selected within their division. The fact that there were more T.F. battalions attached to divisions than would be required to bring divisions up to the new establishment was some comfort, but the fear that they would be selected would account for the alarm in the LRB even before the actual instruction to begin pioneer training arrived from 4th Division HQ. Even if the order was written so as to make it seem almost an honour to be chosen, the Territorials did not like the conversion. Some T.F. officers might not have been quite so disappointed at the switch if their battalion had been allowed to remain with the regular divisions. They had shared the glory with the regular soldiers in halting the German attack at Ypres and could perhaps, even as Pioneers, look forward to continuing this close bond which had developed between them. As the 5/Cheshire, serving with the 5th Division, had actually indented for tools and taken up its new role, it was reasonably confident that it would remain with the division. Unfortunately GHQ then decided that T.F. battalions should not become Pioneer units in regular divisions. The Cheshires were retained by the 5th Division for only a few more weeks before they were sent to become Pioneers to the newly reconstituted 56th (London) Division. Had they known that the LRB by virtue of its status within the London Regiment had managed to avoid becoming Pioneers, the Cheshires might have been justifiably aggrieved to learn that they were now being posted to the division in which the LRB served. Not only were they deprived of the comradeship of the regulars, they were also posted to a division whose battalions came from a very different region of the country.

The 8/Royal Scots had originally been earmarked as Pioneers for the 7th Division. A T.F. battalion from Haddington, it had been with the division since November 1914. It began Pioneer training in August of the following year, working daily under R.E. supervision. However, when GHQ stipulated T.F. units shoud not be Pioneers to regulars the battalion was sent to fulfil the same function for the 51st (Highland) Division. Similarly another Scottish T.F. unit, the 5/Black Watch, had also begun Pioneer training in a regular division. The battalion had served with the 8th Division since November 1914 and, like the 8/Royal Scots, had practised wiring for some weeks. In October 1915 it was inspected by the Brigadier-General of 24th Brigade who told the men they were becoming divisional troops and would be made into a Pioneer battalion. At the time, the unit was very under strength – numbering only some 513 other ranks – but it remained as Pioneers until it again reverted to infantry in January 1916. It too was sent to the 51st Division.

With the exception of some regular divisions the appointment of Pioneers to divisions then in France or Belgium was almost complete by early 1916. However, there were still some decisions to be made as the original composition of certain divisions had altered. In these instances it is harder to see how the authorities decided upon which battalions to choose for conversion. For example, in January 1916 the 91st Brigade had been transferred *en masse* from the 30th Division to the 7th Division. This was part of the plan to stiffen the New Army divisions with a brigade of regulars; consequently 21st Brigade was posted to the 30th Division in exchange. The staff of the 7th Division thus had four New Army battalions from which to choose when it was ordered to select a Pioneer battalion. All four battalions were units of the Manchester Regiment and all were 'Pals' battalions. They had similar backgrounds and were composed of men from factory, mill and office. As there was nothing to chose between them, and none of the four would be anywhere near fulfilling the skills and trade requirements laid down by the War Office directive, the staff decided to pick the Oldham Comrades as the Pioneer battalion. How the decision was actually made is unrecorded – it might have been the simple expedient of sticking a pin or, more likely, the 24th was chosen because it had the lowest seniority of the Manchester battalions in the brigade.

Another fairly obvious choice for conversion was the 19/Lancashire Fusiliers. The battalion's nucleus had been created from a group of men who had missed the train carrying the 16th Battalion away from Salford station.[16] Within the new battalion was a company of Eccles Pals and another full company from the mining town of Swinton. The unit had lost heavily on 1 July 1916 and in subsequent operations around Ovillers but there would still have been enough former miners from the East Lancashire coalfield to justify turning it into a battalion of Pioneers. In late July, GHQ of the 49th Division was informed that owing to the difficulty of finding drafts for all three Monmouth battalions, the 3rd Battalion, then serving with the West Riding Division, was to be disbanded. The Fusiliers, who were at the time GHQ Troops, would be despatched to replace the Monmouths when the division decided it could accept them.[17]

Pioneers of a more ephemeral nature were appointed by the 1st Cavalry Division. The precise history of this battalion is a little unclear as it has no mention in either James or Becke, and it is possible that not all of its War Diary has survived. The 8/Royal Scots claim to have been relieved by an unnamed Cavalry Pioneer battalion at Courcelette in December 1916, but the 1st Cavalry Division's Pioneers seem not to have been formed until early January 1917. It was composed of platoons drawn from the XI Hussars and the 2nd and 5th Dragoon Guards. There is no evidence to confirm or deny whether the men chosen either possessed a trade or were used to manual labour. The battalion was probably disbanded for almost a month, and then reassembled at Hesdin in May with a strength of 25 officers and 789 other ranks. It moved to Roclincourt where it constructed camps for two more cavalry Pioneer battalions. These came from the 2nd and 9th Cavalry Brigades and included both Hussars and Yeomanry. The three battalions were under the overall command of Brigadier-General Beale-Browne, while the original unit, now apparently known as the 1st Cavalry Division Digging Party, was commanded by a captain. There is no War Diary from June until September but entries reappear for October while it worked with the 183rd Tunnelling Company near Ypres. After this, there are no further references. One of its two sister battalions, the 9th Cavalry Brigade Pioneer Battalion, existed from May until July and had a strength of 20 officers and 597 other ranks. There is no trace of the War Diary of the other battalion.[18]

The conversion of the 19/L.F. and the subsequent disbanding of the 3/Monmouth took place some weeks after the Somme offensive had opened. By that time, in addition to performing their more anticipated duties, existing Pioneer battalions had been engaged in several bouts of ferocious fighting. In order to understand and illustrate how the Pioneers contributed to the British attempts to dislodge the Germans from their deep defences sprawling along the ridges of the Somme chalklands, it will be useful to look in some detail at how Pioneers were used by their respective divisions and whether they achieved or completed the objectives and tasks asked of them.

NOTES

1. The bundle of documents is classified as W.O.158.293, 'The Formation of Pioneer Corps and other units'. (Second Army HQ, July-September 1915)
2. A letter (17/7/15) from General Lambton to Lt.Col.FitzGerald of the W.O. in response to a discussion Lambton had had with Kitchener: 'I have given Lord K's views on the question [of Pioneers] to the C-in-C and to the Chief of the General Staff, and the matter is being gone into at once'. (Kitchener Papers, PRO 30/57/50 WA/111)
3. The GOC 46th Division also pointed out that another advantage of his proposal was that each new section would only require one extra lorry, one water cart and one cooker.
4. The War Office list incorrectly asserted that among those regiments which had not already furnished a Pioneer battalion were the KOYLI and the North Staffordshire. Both these regiments had, by July 1915, provided such battalions.
5. Brett, G.A. *The 1/2 Monmouth Battalion,* (Pontypool, 1933) p.50
6. From Second Army to Brigadier-General Whigham, GHQ. 8 September 1915
7. War Diary
8. ibid.
9. Brett, op.cit. p.51
10. Maude, A.H. *The 47th (London) Division 1914-19,* (Amalgamated Press, 1922) p.37
11. ibid.

12. See Mitchinson, K.W. Gentlemen & Officers, (IWM, 1995) for a discussion on the attempt to convert the London Rifle Brigade.

13. At the time, the 7/King's was serving with the regular 2nd Division.

14. Marriott, S.C. papers. (Liddle Collection).

15. Another factor bearing upon the possible conversion of the 7/King's was the pressure exerted on Sir John French by Kitchener to reconstitute the London and West Lancashire Territorial Divisions. The 7/King's was a member of the pre-war division. French was still resisting the pressure when sacked in December 1915. The 55th was eventually reconstituted in January 1916, and the 56th during the following month. (Kitchener Papers, PRO 30/57/50 WA/118)

16. Latter, J.C. *The History of the Lancashire Fusiliers*, p.99

17. The 19/L.F. arrived at their new division in the early hours of 7 August. (W.O.95.2766, GHQ 49th Division). The 3/Monmouth sent 200 men to its 2nd Battalion and another 252 to the 9th Entrenching Bn. Most of these were posted to either the 9/Welch or the 9/Welch Fusiliers in September. *On the Western Front with the 1/3rd Monmouth*, (No name or date)

18. In *The History of the Eleventh Hussars*, (London, 1936), L.R.Lumley writes of the Cavalry Pioneer Battalion being formed from drafts arriving from the Cavalry Depot during Third Ypres. The formation was: 'A change from inaction and the work was cheerfully done in the hope that it would be a small contribution to help the infantry'. (p.275) Members of the regiment were certainly working as Pioneers some months before Lumley appears to have acknowledged them.

Chapter 4

PIONEERING ON THE SOMME: THE OPENING PHASE

In subsequent decades the experience of the Somme was to burn itself deep into the British psyche. What had been intended as an offensive to open the road to victory turned into a bloody slogging match of attrition. Kitchener's armies, so full of enthusiasm and confidence in their ability to seize the torch from the exhausted regulars and ridiculed Territorials, hurled themselves against the formidable German defences which dominated the heights between the Somme and the Ancre. Tactics for both the infantry and artillery had been devised to allow for their inexperience. Assaulting brigades were to advance in waves, supported by the divisional Field Companies of R.E. Attached either to these companies, or directly to the brigades, were the Pioneers. Several of these units had even less experience of active service than the Pals and other Service battalions that were to advance upon the German trenches on 1 July 1916.

The infantry tactics employed on 1 July were an acknowledgement that General Rawlinson, commanding Fourth Army, had little confidence in the skills or expertise of the New Armies. The assaulting brigades had spent time during the previous weeks practising their attacks over mock-ups of the German positions. Once the artillery barrage lifted onto the German second line, wave after wave of British troops with rifles at the port, would advance across No Man's Land at walking pace. The concept of the attack was not for the infantry to have to fight for the trenches, but merely to occupy them after the artillery had killed or demented the defenders. By the frequent

69

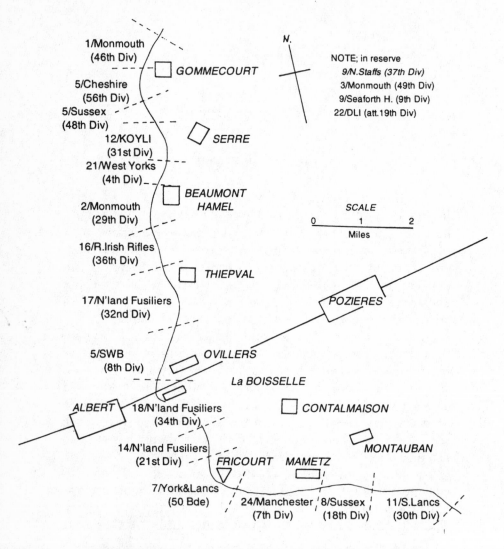

1/Monmouth
(46th Div)

GOMMECOURT

5/Cheshire
(56th Div)

5/Sussex
(48th Div)

12/KOYLI
(31st Div)

SERRE

21/West Yorks
(4th Div)

BEAUMONT
HAMEL

2/Monmouth
(29th Div)

16/R.Irish Rifles
(36th Div)

THIEPVAL

17/N'land Fusiliers
(32nd Div)

POZIERES

5/SWB
(8th Div)

OVILLERS

La BOISSELLE

ALBERT

18/N'land Fusiliers
(34th Div)

CONTALMAISON

14/N'land Fusiliers
(21st Div)

FRICOURT   MAMETZ

MONTAUBAN

7/York&Lancs
(50 Bde)

24/Manchester   8/Sussex   11/S.Lancs
(7th Div)   (18th Div)   (30th Div)

N.

NOTE; in reserve
9/N.Staffs (37th Div)
3/Monmouth (49th Div)
9/Seaforth H. (9th Div)
22/DLI (att.19th Div)

SCALE
0   1   2
Miles

DEPLOYMENT OF PIONEER BATTALIONS; 1ST JULY 1916

exhortations of senior commanders, brigades had been lulled into the expectation that their role would be easily accomplished. They knew what they had to do and, although some were clearly sceptical about the claims of the staff, they had executed the moves several times on the training grounds. What few, if any, of the individual battalions had done however, was to work out in detail how they were supposed to cooperate with the Pioneers and the divisional R.E.

There is little surviving evidence to indicate that there was regular close coordination between the infantry and the Pioneers within a division. This might suggest that the brigades were not much concerned about the nature of their technical support. They knew their job and assumed that those behind would know theirs and do it accordingly. And that was probably the essential aspect of the issue. The infantry would not consider it part of their task to delve too deeply into the affairs of the supporting troops. Although there is an almost total absence of recorded meetings between the officers of the infantry battalions and those of the R.E. and Pioneers attached to them, there are sure to have been unrecorded ones. Decisions had to be made about where ammunition should be dumped, communication trenches dug or where strong points should be built. The principal decisions were taken by the brigade staffs in consultation with the CRE. They agreed about what the supporting arms were expected to do and how those expectations would be met. Nevertheless, given the time many of the units had served together, there must have been a substantial amount of discussion between the officers of the infantry and their counterparts in the Pioneers. One Pioneer officer, Lt. Capper of the 8/Sussex, is known to have had good, close working relations with a battalion in his division.[1] His platoon was to be attached to a company of the 6/Northants for the attack. Capper already knew the company commander and platoon officers, and had several preliminary discussions with them to analyse maps and photographs and to examine how they should cooperate when the time came.

Of the seventeen Pioneer battalions which were to take part in or act as reserve during the attack of 1 July, six had served

71

with the same division for between 15 and 18 months. These were some of the battalions which had been raised as New Army infantry but were later chosen to be converted to Pioneers from within the division in which they already served. Another three had served with their division for over a year. The social and working relationship built up between the officers of these battalions and their former comrades in the infantry, both during their training in the U.K. and their service abroad, was certain to have improved the overall morale and efficiency of their divisions. Furthermore, twelve of the Pioneer battalions had crossed to France during 1915; six of these, as well as the 2/Monmouth which had been over since 1914, had actually served as fighting infantry. They had taken part in battles such as Second Ypres before being converted in the summer of 1915. Although they were subsequently sent to divisions other than those in which they had fought, the receiving divisions would have known of their deeds and reputation and thus surely received them as seasoned campaigners. Several of these units could claim to have had more active fighting experience than the divisions which they joined. Even those battalions which were posted to experienced divisions a few months before the battle would bring with them expertise which could be used with benefit.

The fighting skills of the 2/Monmouth were amply demonstrated at Ypres in early 1915. Following its period as line of communication troops in May 1916 it was posted as Pioneers to the regular 29th Division. The battle experienced 5/Cheshire was sent to the currently reforming 56th (London) Division some five months before the battle opened. The 24/Manchester remained with the same division to which it had been transferred in January 1916, but was not converted until two months before the offensive began. Although these three battalions had all therefore gained battle or trench holding experience, their time as Pioneers was somewhat limited. Other battalions which were to participate on 1 July and which had not spent as much time in France were the 18/N.F. and the 12/KOYLI. The former had been with its division since its formation, but had only arrived in France in January 1916. The 12/KOYLI, which had arrived in France in March 1916 after pioneering in the different terrain of the Egyptian desert, was also a well tried unit and had been a member of the 31st Division for just under a year.

Only two Pioneer battalions which were to take part in the opening of the offensive could be described as novice units. Both the 22/DLI and the 21/West Yorks had only arrived in France in June 1916, and both came without a division. The Durhams were so new to overseas service that when they moved up to Albert on 1 July the men had not even been issued with steel helmets. The battalion was temporarily attached to the 19th Division until 2 July, when it was next posted to the 8th Division. The 21/West Yorks was also sent to a regular division, the 4th. The battalion had only left Skipton on 14 June. It managed subsequently to fit in a few days' trench acclimatization before being sent out into No Man's Land on 1 July to bury the morning's dead. This task was later described by one of its officers as 'a very trying experience for a battalion just out from England'.[2]

Although none of the battalions which took part in the opening phases had actually served as Pioneers during a set piece battle, there is no evidence to suggest that they were not as confident about the outcome as the infantry. They could anticipate that the brigades would occupy the German trenches and hand them over to the Pioneers and R.E. for reconstruction. Several units are known to have practised their tasks on mock-up trenches shortly before the attack, but even those which had not been allowed the time to indulge in such activities would have considered they knew enough about digging to complete their tasks successfully. None of the battalions was anticipating that it would have to do much more than dig and carry, although some platoons in some units were allocated more specific tasks to fulfil. Preparations had been going on for months and as the day of the attack approached morale remained high. The consensus was that once the infantry went over the Pioneers would execute both the general and the more specific jobs with a minimum of fuss and delay. Because this was to be the biggest battle yet undertaken by a combination of regular, Territorial and New Army divisions, it is worth looking in some detail at the preparations made by the various Pioneer battalions.[3]

An initial meeting of company commanders to discuss the forthcoming attack was convened by the C.O. of the 14/N.F. at Meaulte on 8 June. The C.O. passed on the orders he had received from the CRE and told his company commanders that they would take their orders directly from the R.E. officer attached to each company. While the orderly room wrestled with the attack's administrative demands, the companies continued their work on existing projects. Two companies were completing rooms in the Queen's Redoubt and some hospital dugouts, while the remaining two were engaged in digging communication trenches or working on a road between Carcaillot Farm and Becordel. During the night of 23-24 June 648 men were employed on opening up nearly 2,000 yards of fire and communication trench from what had been concealed saps – a task for which the battalion received a congratulatory wire from Division. This job entailed a substantial amount of work in an area only some 100 yards from the enemy trenches. The Fusiliers were helped by 26 sappers, but each man working on a fire trench still had to take down three yards of roof, one foot thick, before then squaring it up and revetting. For work on the stretches of communication trench, two men had to take down four yards of roof, each of which was two feet thick. The work had been calculated to require between four and four and a half hours – an estimation which proved accurate. After successfully completing this task the companies went back to carrying, completing dugouts and trench maintenance. The company commanders were briefed on what was expected of their commands on 1 July: opening up more underground saps, making strong points, marking out tracks for the artillery and transport in preparation for cutting through banks and filling in trenches and ditches.

Their colleagues in the 18/N.F. were also heavily engaged in digging. Between 10 May and 23 June the battalion laid over 2,000 yards of trench tramway, dug gun pits, dugouts and observation posts for three batteries of French 75s, repaired substantial lengths of communication trenches, constructed 18 medium trench mortar emplacements, including their necessary saps and ammunition stores and began building emplacements for four heavy trench mortars. Only two of these were completed, but they alone required the removal by hand of nearly 300 tons of spoil. Once the attack began, the 17/N.F. were, like the 18th, ordered to complete artillery and infantry tracks over the British trenches, open up Russian saps and reconnoitre routes for wheeled traffic. The troops, like most men of Pioneer units, were ordered to carry 120 rounds, two sand-bags tucked in the belt, a 1lb tin of bully beef, biscuits, wire cutters and two Mills bombs. Before they advanced companies were ordered to ensure all spare tools and stores, such as brooms, zinc water buckets, wash basins, portable food cupboards and other such nefarious items, had been handed in to the quarter-master. Once they had gone over the men were warned that they were not permitted to bring back wounded or collect souvenirs. Finally, a battle surplus of five officers and 24 men was ordered to remain at the transport lines. One somewhat disconcerting aspect of all this pre-battle preparation was the appearance on 30 June of a draft of 65 men. Although this procedure became common once the battle had begun, these newcomers were about to be thrown into the cauldron only hours after they had arrived at their battalion. The 14th Battalion had also received a draft of 50 men, but that had been much earlier in the month. They had had three weeks to get acclimatized and absorbed by their companies.

A great deal of digging had also been done by the two battal-ions of Pioneers serving with Third Army. The task of the 46th and 56th Divisions was to launch a diversionary attack on the German stronghold of Gommecourt. This village, which lay at the northern end of the battlefield, was surrounded by trenches and dugouts of immense strength. The 5/Cheshire had already dug an advanced British front system in May which substantially lessened the distance between the British and German lines. Helped by the infantry who provided covering and digging parties, nearly 3,000 yards of fire trench and 1,500 yards of communication trenches had been excavated during the course of three nights. On the left of the London division, the 1/Monmouth of the 46th Division had also been busy. The Welshmen had begun digging four Russian saps in June, working in trenches around Foncquevillers which were knee deep in mud. By the last week in June the trenches were thigh deep in water, but the digging continued at a rate of about 20 feet per day on each of the four saps. Working in such filth made the mens' clothing deteriorate to an appalling extent, but they laboured on in the dreadful conditions knowing that unless the saps were dug the infantry would find the task of crossing No Man's Land that much more difficult.

To the south of Gommecourt the British line was held by the 48th Division. There was to be no attack in this sector, but that did not excuse the 5/Sussex, the division's Pioneers, from working as hard as any. Its colonel reported that his men were often working up to 14 hours a day, wet through and with no means to dry out, and most of the time under fire. Every available man including signallers, Lewis gunners, batmen and other details, was called upon to do his share with the spade. On 1 July the battalion was pulled back to Mailly-Maillet and reassembled for the first time since 23 August 1915.

On both banks of the Ancre Pioneers could be seen working alongside their comrades of the infantry until the final hours before the attack began. The 2/Monmouth helped the regulars and Newfoundlanders of the 29th Division replenish advanced bomb stores and carried R.E. tools up to the front trenches.[4] Platoons of the Monmouths were to go over in the rear of the infantry waves and help to consolidate the fortified village of Beaumont Hamel. Only some 200 of the men had been issued with steel helmets – the remainder being told to collect them from the dead and wounded as they advanced.[5] On the southern bank of the river, and opposite the formidable Schwaben Redoubt which crested the Thiepval ridge, the 16/Royal Irish Rifles had also been carrying and digging. The battalion had only moved up to Thiepval Wood in late May and at once began to carry gas cylinders, dig assembly trenches and erect shelters in the front area. Enemy shells rained down upon the wood during the period, but casualties remained light. On the evening of 30 June the adjutant reported with some satisfaction that all the work allotted the battalion had been completed.

Of the Service Pioneer battalions which would be in action

that day, the 24/Manchester had been in France the longest. It was also the unit which had spent the least time as Pioneers. The battalion assembled at Grovetown, received its instructions and prepared for battle. Two companies were to be attached to Field Companies, another would open up communication trenches and saps, while the fourth remained in reserve. After moving forward from Minden Post they were to put Mametz village into a state of defence and make Bunny Wood into a strong point. The troops were to advance with picks and shovels slung on their backs, so making it easier for them to fire their rifles. However, lest the Oldhamers thought they might be able to take part in the fighting, a particular order warned them that:

'It is to be distinctly understood by all ranks that Pioneers are not to take part in the offensive but only act on the defensive if ordered by an officer or senior NCO on the spot. Their work is the most important, i.e. consolidation of captured positions'.

To a battalion which had been only recently converted from infantry, the authorities seemed anxious to devalue its whole reason for being in France.

When the attack began most Pioneer companies were ordered to assemble at a map reference, with the attached R.E., and wait for the brigade staff's order to advance. They would then proceed to carry forward the stores and begin their allocated digging. Battalion orders generally warned them against expecting a specific length of waiting time, of the necessity of moving in small groups, what equipment to take with them and to keep under cover as much as possible. Careful procedures were laid down about how and which dumps should be emptied first and then how a relay system would operate to replenish them. Situation reports were to be sent back at least every half hour and units were instructed to 'hold at all costs' any position on which they were working. In contrast to the order issued to the Oldhamers, some battalions were warned that they might have to forsake their pick for their rifle. They were told to be wary of mobile German machine gunners resembling stretcher bearers and of orders to 'Retire'. Anyone hearing such a shout was to ignore it 'entirely, no matter from whom they hear it'. Any food or water found in the German trenches was to be avoided in case it had been deliberately contaminated. One of the stranger instructions circulating in some battalions was a warning to officers against taking large sums of public money into action.

To the men, the planning seemed meticulous; it remained only for the signal to advance for the smooth machine to slip into gear. During the Great War troops were rarely informed of the intricate details of their tasks; they assumed officers and senior NCOs had sufficient knowledge of the plan and objective. There is some evidence however to suggest that in this campaign, some officers were not entirely sure of what their precise role was supposed to be: Dillon, of the 14/N.F. claimed that when he advanced, he had 'not much idea of what he was meant to do',[6] while years later, Davidson of the 22/DLI, made an even stranger claim. Despite the fact that he had been with the battalion as a company commander since April, Davidson recorded his surprise at discovering that in the advance, 'it seemed likely we should be employed under the R.E. in reconstructing trenches'. He makes no mention of the fact that his battalion was a Pioneer unit, and a few days after the battle opened again expressed his surprise when, 'it became evident that we were not to be employed in the main assault'.[7] In contrast, the preparations made by a neighbouring battalion seem to have been far more explicit. The 8/Sussex specified that all officer and NCO platoon commanders would be given maps showing the German trenches and that all parties must be familiar with the compass bearings of the sites where they were supposed to be working.

As 'Z' Day approached it became clear that in some sectors the German wire had not been sufficiently broken by the bombardment to allow the infantry access to the enemy trenches. The attack was postponed for two days, and the waiting continued. It also gave some commanders the opportunity to press their Pioneers to greater efforts. Opposite Gommecourt the GOC 46th Division decided that the 1/Monmouth should continue work on the four saps and extend them by means of an open trench to within 100 yards of the German lines during the night preceding the assault. The problem was how to evacuate the Monmouths without impeding the infantry moving up through the trenches for the attack. In an attempt to resolve the dilemma the C.O and the brigadier of 137th Brigade held a hastily convened meeting. It was suggested that the Monmouths should stay in the trenches until the infantry attacked and go over with them. However, then came the news that the advance was to begin at 0730. If the saps were opened out during the night and the men remained in them they would be exposed to over three hours of daylight and observation by the Germans looking down on the straight trenches and their huddled men. It was decided that the saps should be opened during darkness and the men withdrawn as the infantry prepared to move up. In the neighbouring 139th Brigade sector it was agreed that the Monmouths should remain in the saps during the night and open them up as the infantry began to cross No Man's Land.

On the right of the Monmouths and facing the southern flank of Gommecourt Wood, the 5/Cheshire did not have saps to worry about; here it was hoped that the advanced front line would allow the attacking troops to get across No Man's Land without heavy losses. Consequently, three companies of the Cheshires had been detailed to go over with the third wave. Once in the German lines they were to construct strong points, consolidate a particularly formidable German position known as the Quadrilateral, remove enemy barricades, bridge trenches and put up sign boards. To help clear the way for the infantry, Bangalore torpedoes were to be exploded under the German wire a few hours before Zero.

Bangalores were also to be used on the 34th Division's front. A subaltern of the R.E. led a party of 19 sappers and 20 infantry from Keats Redoubt at 0100 and, although he failed to explode them at the intended objective, destroyed some knife rests and their attached wire.[8] The 18/N.F. appear not to have been involved in this operation, but a party under the command of Lt. Parkinson was out at night in No Man's Land digging a trench mortar emplacement. It also had one platoon assembled in the sap under No Man's Land. For safety reasons the group was to be withdrawn to the British end of the tunnel when the

Lochnagar mine was fired. It would then return to the far end, open up the sap and join with other platoons to dig a communication trench three feet deep. The eight saps coming under the responsibility of the 8/Sussex were to be blown five minutes before Zero. Three of these contained a flammenwerfer which would be used to assist the advance of the infantry. The Sussex would then continue the saps across the remainder of No Man's Land and convert them into communication trenches.

The British bombardment intensified as Zero approached. Once at their assembly positions there was little for the men of the infantry or Pioneers to do until the whistles blew and the barrage moved onto the next line. The C.O. of the 16/Royal Irish Rifles decided that the Germans probably knew the time of the attack and so moved his men forward an hour before schedule. When the Rifles arrived at Lancashire Dump the Germans shelled the area so ferociously that the battalion was forced to shelter in slit trenches reconnoitred by several officers the previous day. From these positions the battalion witnessed the attack of its division towards the Schwaben Redoubt. In the words of its C.O., 'Ulster charged . . . .and no-one faltered'. Their actual view of the attack was badly obscured by the dust, smoke and flame which enveloped the heaving crest. After observing the opening minutes of their comrades' attack, the Rifles shouldered their burdens and advanced towards the former British front line. Just to the north of the river the 2/Monmouth were also trying to get forward. Hampered by crowds of returning wounded coming down the trenches, the Monmouths advanced towards what had already become a disaster. The troops of the 29th Division were cut down in swathes as they crossed No Man's Land. The helmetless Monmouths struggled against the flow of wounded as best they could, and were soon detailed to begin digging a communication trench from the Ancre towards the Redan ridge.

To the north of the 29th Division, the 31st met with similar disastrous results in its attack against Serre. The Pals from Sheffield and Barnsley had barely struggled from their own trenches before annihilating fire erupted from the German lines. Single companies of the 12/KOYLI attached to each brigade

1. A regular feature of a Pioneer's life was road clearing. Men using scoops to sweep mud from a road near St. Julien during Third Ypres. (IWM Q6057)

2. In the absence of scoops, brooms and squeegees were used to clear liquid mud from a plank road near Ypres in January 1918. (IWM Q8400)

3. Pioneers of the 11/Liverpool enjoying an alfresco meal in exposed conditions near Ypres in December 1917. Note the regimental badge on some helmets (IWM Q8441)

4. Men of the 22/Durham Light Infantry Pioneer battalion pose for the camera during a break from their labours near Maurepas in December 1916. (IWM Q4628)

35. A combined working party of 2/Monmouth, RE and TMB personnel repairing a plank road near Hooge during the breakout from the Salient in October 1918. The party are building up the side of a mine crater before laying the road on the top of the bulwark. (IWM Q11774)

36. Typical of the many plank roads laid across the slough beneath the Passchendaele Ridge. This photo shows men of an Australian Pioneer battalion laying a road near Chateau Wood in September 1917. (IWM E800)

7. The continual need for trench boarding meant that carrying parties of infantry, RE and Pioneers were in constant demand. Here Lancashire Fusiliers carry the cumbersome boards across the ineluctable terrain of the Pilckem ridge in October 1917. (IWM Q6049)

8. Light railways were pushed across captured ground as soon as prevailing conditions allowed. Pioneers were frequently employed in laying and running such lines. This track was constructed near Feuchy during the Arras offensive of 1917. (IWM Q5248)

were to dig communication trenches across to the former German lines. Orders before the attack had ranged from instructing the Yorkshiremen how to fold their cardigans, to how to disable captured German field guns. Neither of these were of much use to the battalion now as it was ordered to take over the British front line. As one writer recorded: 'As an effective fighting unit, the 31st Division had ceased to exist'.[9] It was Corporal William Townsend's 24th birthday. A miner from Pontefract, Townsend had enlisted in the Coal Owners' battalion and was now told to 'grab a rifle and hold the line'; being more familiar with a pick or shovel, he later claimed that he had not much idea how to use it. Manning a position in front of the British line Townsend was immediately shot in the head and later captured.[10] His surviving comrades did what they could for the British wounded who lay close to their own lines and held the front trenches until relieved the following day.

The line between the 31st and 56th Divisions was the area held by the 48th. The 5/Sussex had been withdrawn to the rear as corps reserve, and as it was not ordered up it sustained no fatalities. It was, however, a different tale either side of their divisional boundaries. The 12/KOYLI ended the day having sustained about 185 casualties, 38 of which were fatalities.[11] On the Sussex's other flank the 5/Cheshire had a similar total of 180 casualties, of whom 47 died. The Cheshires had suffered badly, like the rest of their division. The London brigades fought their way into the German lines but during the course of the day were gradually forced back by Germans bombing down the communication trenches towards them. One platoon of the Cheshires tried to carry bombs through the curtain of impenetrable fire falling on No Man's Land, and lost 23 men in the process. Another company began work consolidating the civilian cemetery in Gommecourt, while a third succeeded in destroying a barricade on the Hebuterne-Gommecourt road. Officers were knocked over, troops lost direction, trenches were full of wounded Londoners, and German snipers picked off any who showed himself above the wreckage of the ruined German positions. As the enemy's bombing attacks increased in frequency and intensity, and as their own supplies became exhausted, there was nothing more the survivors could do. The order of 'every man for himself' was sent to as many of the isolated groups as could be located. During the short period of darkness Londoners and Cheshires made their way back across the devastated zone to the relative safety of their own trenches. The report of the division's CRE[12] later praised the cooperation between the Engineers, and in particular the London Scottish, but made no mention of the part played by the Pioneers.[13]

To the north of Gommecourt Wood the North Midlanders of the 46th Division fared even worse. During the night the Monmouths had managed to extend two saps by a further 60 yards, but the party working on No.3 had suffered from heavy fire and those who were supposed to work on sap No.4 could not even reach their position. Deep mud and congestion in the approach trenches meant that this sap remained far short of its intended length. Nevertheless, in the early hours the companies moved up and prepared to follow the infantry. They waited in the reserve trenches for the order to proceed, but the infantry attack was such a calamity that 'the necessity for their doing so never arose'. Suffering from enemy retaliation, the Monmouths remained in the area until it became clear their services would not be required; they returned to their camp at Pommiers at 2100 having lost two officers and nearly 100 other ranks. These casualties were light compared to those of the Staffordshires and Sherwood Foresters of the attacking brigades but to the Pioneers, it meant the loss of several more of the original battalion who had been out with it since early 1915.

The most successful advances had taken place along the southern shoulder of the German line. Running almost West-East from Fricourt to where the British forces joined the French at Maricourt, it was assailed by three British divisions. The 7th attacked towards Mametz and succeeded in storming and securing the front positions. The 24/Manchester followed in the wake of the infantry and began erecting and building strong points; the saps under No Man's Land were opened up and became communication trenches across to Bulgar Point and Mametz Trench. The work proceeded with minimum fuss and with fairly limited interference from the Germans. The brigades appreciated the work of the R.E. and Pioneers, and the Engineers in turn acknowledged the assistance given them by the Oldhamers. Even the *Times* reported that the battalion's work was 'worthy of the highest praise'. The attack had gone so well that only one of the Comrades had been killed, although another two would later die of wounds received that day. Not surprisingly, one of the battalion wrote home in almost euphoric tone shortly after the battle:

> The noise of the bombardment was simply terrific. It was Hell absolutely . . . I thought at one time that the Germans would be blown back straight to Berlin. I've seen hundreds of prisoners. What a dirty cut throat lot they were. It made one feel that you could load your rifle and let them have it and feel no pity for them. The majority were old chaps. One greasy dirty old chap being at least 60 if he was a day. They seemed pleased to be captured and said that our bombardment had been simply awful. You see, they don't like the medicine we are doling out to them now. It is alright when they are at it but when they meet British soldiers man to man they invariably throw their hands up and cry for mercy. They give very little trouble when captured. They have more sense. We have just arrived in rest billets for a short time. It feels nice to be quiet I can tell you.[14]

The troops of the 7th Division could feel justifiably proud of what they had achieved; so too could those of the 18th and 30th Divisions. On the right of the British line the 11/South Lancs followed the brigades across towards the brickstack of Montauban and immediately began consolidating. No Man's Land was wider here than in several other parts of the line so supplies had to be taken greater distances. The South Lancs carried and successfully dug four communication trenches, losing 21 dead during the day. On their left, a company of the 8/Sussex witnessed the attack by the 8/East Surrey commence with the kicking of footballs into No Man's Land, and then turned to its own duties.[15]

Several platoons of the Sussex went over with the attacking brigades and were to be relieved by the remaining platoons once the initial objectives had been achieved. Two platoons became entangled in the fighting, helping the infantry to take a position known as the Loop. Strong points were consolidated and the saps were opened and available for traffic by 1600. Work was carried on by reliefs around the clock; two saps were turned into traversed trenches and new trenches started to link across to the captured positions. For this and the work it was to complete later on the Thiepval ridge, the division in which the Sussex fought gained a reputation as one of the most dependable and formidable in the BEF.

It was in the centre and north of Fourth Army's attack that the greatest calamities took place. The 21st Division went over just north of Fricourt and met with heavy opposition. The Pioneers of the 14/N.F. had the greatest difficulty even crossing their own trenches, but made their way across No Man's Land in the wake of the infantry. Weighed down with tools, progress was slow. One company became hopelessly mixed up with two battalions of the KOYLI and it took some determined work by officers to disentangle the parties and organize the erection of wire and the consolidation of Round Wood. Another company became mixed up with the 15/Royal Scots of the neighbouring division, while members of C Company lost touch not only with each other but also most of the Field Company to which it was attached. The fourth company was the last to move forward and encountered crowds of troops coming the wrong way down an 'up' communication trench. The infantry who had managed to penetrate the German lines held on in some places, but the Pioneers of B Company eventually ran out of wire and returned to their own lines completely exhausted.

It was the same story of chaos and confusion just to the north of the 14th, where its sister battalion the 18th supported the 34th Division. Lieutenant Nixon's platoon in the tunnel discovered that instead of the supposed two feet of earth covering, there were in fact twelve. The men had begun digging with bayonets at midnight and an hour after the explosion of the Lochnagar had broken through to the surface. Telephone cables were immediately passed through the opening. By 1000 a hole large enough for men to pass had been excavated. As soon as it was opened, the work of the Pioneers was hampered by wounded men seeking refuge and carrying parties trying to get up. C Company in the Glory Hole had played a part by lighting smoke candles when the attack began and stood by awaiting further orders. The company which was supposed to send men to dig the communication trench had been prevented from getting forward on schedule by returning wounded clogging the trenches. Its officers tried to take them over the top, but shell fire drove them back into the shelter of the rapidly deteriorating trenches. When it did struggle into the front system and began digging, persistent shelling and machine gun fire frustrated its progress. D Company was ordered to carry bombs across to the crater; a task completed and repeated several times during the next few hours. A Company was told to assist the 10/Lincoln in a bombing attack on the strong point known as the Heligoland, but as the Lincolns emerged from their trenches they were swept away by machine gun fire; the Fusiliers stayed where they were. A further bombing attack planned for the afternoon was similarly countermanded. In view of the carnage all around them, the two Fusilier battalions had been remarkably lucky. Their fatalities for the day amounted to only 17.

To the north of the Albert-Bapaume road the 8th Division attacked up Mash Valley. The division had not yet received its allocated battalion of Pioneers, the 22/DLI, and instead had attached to it the experienced 5/SWB borrowed from the 19th Division. This division was in reserve and did not get its own Pioneers back until the 22/DLI became officially attached to the 8th Division on 2 July. The attack, across a very wide No Man's Land and against German positions which could enfilade the advancing troops, withered and died. The Welshmen were not sent across to reinforce what had rapidly disintegrated into a total failure, and remained in their assembly positions.

The other Pioneer battalion of Northumberland Fusiliers in action that day was the 17th. Its division attacked the Leipzig Salient and the southern part of the Thiepval ridge. As the attacking troops were swept away or pinned down in No Man's Land, initial success soon turned to failure. Like the Borderers to their south, the Fusiliers could do little except take what shelter they could from the enemy retaliation. They suffered casualties, including four dead, but the plans for reconnoitring and constructing artillery and infantry tracks as far as Mouquet Farm were necessarily abandoned for the time being. Its mauled division was withdrawn from the line, but the Pioneers were attached to Field Companies and the 12th and 25th Divisions. They were to remain working in the sector for a further two weeks.

As darkness fell, the tracks and trenches leading to and from the lines remained choked with returned wounded, exhausted survivors and fresh troops moving up to relieve them. For the Pioneers though, there was little respite. The 17/N.F. were not the only Pioneer battalion to be retained when its division was withdrawn. The British trenches had been so badly knocked about by the German guns, and what few gains had been made in the enemy lines had to be consolidated, that the Pioneers worked feverishly to wire, carry and dig. With a message of encouragement from the legendary Tom Bridges still ringing in their ears the troops of 22/DLI moved up to join their division and spent much of the time burying and carrying R.E. stores to a dump in La Boisselle. The 16/Royal Irish Rifles began digging a trench across towards the Schwaben, where elements of the Ulster Division were still holding out. Amidst a scene that was 'beyond description', one company commander helped to re-organize the British positions in front of Thiepval Wood. One company carrying bombs passed through the curtain of fire three times, and lost 36 of the 73 men who attempted the journey. For three nights the battalion tried to dig across No Man's Land for the 49th Division. Its positions in Aveluy and Thiepval Woods were under constant bombardment, and besides digging, it also strove to keep the tramway working. When it was promised the help of another battalion of Pioneers (probably the 3/Monmouth) to assist with the communication trenches, its diarist claimed, 'it did not materialize except for a few minutes'. After the fourth successive night of work, and with the troops 'much exhausted', its colonel went to brigade HQ and succeeded in securing a night off.

In the Fonquevillers sector, the Pioneers of the 9/North Staffs were ordered up to relieve the 1/Monmouth. On approaching Bienvillers the battalion found the village so full of troops belonging to the 46th Division, that the order was countermanded and the Staffords returned to Berles. The Monmouths remained working until 4 July when they eventually took over the billets vacated by the 9/North Staffs. This battalion had since been ordered to join the 34th Division near Becourt. The mauled brigades of this division had been withdrawn on the night of 3–4 July, but the 18/N.F. stayed in the line to carry and bury around Scots Redoubt. The remnant of the division was split up, with two brigades being posted to the 37th Division. The Pioneers were 'disgusted' to learn that they too were to be detached from their division; they believed that a loosely worded message caused an administrative error which, in turn, led to its departure from the division. The 9/North Staffs arrived to relieve the angry Fusiliers on the night of 6–7 July. Despite leaving behind the personnel which had formed the divisional salvage company, the Northumbrians marched away with a strength which amounted to a little under the combined total of two of its division's brigades.

The 17/N.F. had been withdrawn from its temporary attachment to two other divisions on 4–5 July. Its historian later remarked that it always considered itself to be a 'lucky' battalion and cited several instances as examples:[16] One company had only just left Authuille when the Germans began shelling it (causing 60 casualties to the incoming unit), and 15 minutes after the HQ of another company left its dugout the shelter was smashed by an incoming shell. The battalion which took over from the North-Eastern Pioneers, the 6/SWB, lost 80 men when moving up to complete the relief. After winning praise for bringing in the wounded of the 8th and 34th Divisions, the 5/SWB returned to its own division, the 19th, and began working alongside the 9/North Staffs near La Boisselle. The 24/Manchester remained in the Mametz area converting strong points and trenches around Pommiers Redoubt until 5 July. Companies of the 8/Sussex continued to widen and deepen the ends of the saps which passed under the former No Man's Land, while others worked on Montauban Alley and Caterpillar Trench. On 8 July the bulk of the battalion was pulled back to rest at Grovetown.

Despite the disaster which had befallen Fourth Army, the offensive was to be continued. Because the main successes had been achieved in the southern sector, it was here that the principal assaults were to be maintained. Pressure would also be kept on the centre and northern zones, in particular towards the Pozieres and Thiepval ridges. There was never a significant pause in the fighting, but certain attacks attracted more prominence than others. For the Pioneers, the preparation for the coming assaults had to be coordinated with the necessary work of repairing the damaged British trenches and ensuring that the captured positions were wired, converted and kept supplied. The men of the Pioneers who had been withdrawn could look upon their peformance since 1 July with some satisfaction. With the exception of those units whose infantry had failed to get across to the German lines, the Pioneers had done all that had been asked of them. In those sectors where the attack had failed, there was nothing the Pioneers could do. If the infantry could not clear the way to allow the work of consolidation to begin, the Pioneers were doomed to remain in their own trenches until ordered to carry across whatever could be taken through the wall of exploding steel. Several companies had attempted to do this, and suffered accordingly. In the sectors where the infantry had taken the German trenches the Pioneers extended the saps and dug communication trenches despite the enemy counter-bombardment. Overall, their losses had been light; a total of 187 dead or about 1% of the day's fatalities, and probably fewer than 600 wounded. But, if the men had not realized it before, the fact that the majority of them had stayed working in the forward zone for several days after their divisions had gone was an ominous indication. They could anticipate further and more frequent attachments to other divisions and continued labour in the front areas. Casualties might never reflect the losses sustained by the infantry, but to be exposed to the dangers for longer periods and with fewer opportunities for rest and recuperation was suggestion enough that being a Pioneer was not a sinecure.

NOTES

1. Capper, op.cit.
2. Wyrall, E. *The West Yorkshire Regiment in the Great War,* (Bodley Head, n.d.) p.215
3. Unless otherwise stated, the detail comes from battalion War Diaries.
4. The increase in the amount of R.E. stores issued by C.E. Fourth Army in the build up to the offensive is clear from the following table: (W.O.95.451)

	March 1916	June 1916
Coils of plain barbed wire	220	2,700
Picks	3,200	66,000
Shovels	7,200	74,000
Coils of barbed wire	12,000	52,000

5. Brett, A. op.cit. p.55
6. Dillon, op.cit.
7. Davidson, Major T.G. Unpublished memoir in DLI Museum.
8. *W.O.95.2444* (W.D. of CRE 34th Division).
9. England, op.cit p.47
10. Collection of photos and papers in the Light Infantry Archive, Pontefract.
11. Casualties have been computed from the lists of *Soldiers Died*, War Diaries, regimental and battalion histories.
12. W.O.95.2939
13. In his book, *The First Day of the Somme,* (Allen Lane, 1971) p.171-2, Martin Middlebrook recounts the experiences of 2Lt. Arthur of the 5/Cheshire.
14. Mitchinson, K.W. and McInnes, I., op.cit p.71
15. Capper, op.cit.
16. Shakespear, op.cit. p.38

Chapter 5

PIONEERING ON THE SOMME: GRINDING ON

Besides the digging and wiring, two of the most frequent tasks which fell on the Pioneers during the early days of the Somme campaign were to act as stretcher bearers and bury the dead. Mention of the work done by the 21/West Yorks has already been made, but it was only one of several units which were detailed to undertake this grisly task. When clearing the bodies of the London Scottish who fell in front of Gommecourt, a Pioneer officer of the Middlesex Regiment thought it was a 'horrible sensation to realize that the soft masses under one's feet were the bodies of one's own countrymen'.[1] In a letter to his sister a private of the 9/North Staffs, whose brother had been killed shortly before, wrote that burying was 'an awful job and every one I buried, I thought of our dear brother; and when we were identifying them the photo they had in their pockets of wives and children made me think what a shock it must be to those at home'.[2] Days after the attack, wounded were still being discovered and brought back to the British trenches. Men of the 5/SWB were particularly active in La Boisselle area, four bearers in particular being praised by their officer for the work they performed.[3] This was in addition to the battalion's bombers playing a leading part in an attack near the village on 3 July. Before it was withdrawn the battalion received another order of the day from the seemingly indestructable Lt.Col. Trower. The C.O. wrote: 'Whilst all will join in deploring the loss of many gallant comrades, all will rejoice that so many of our original number are left to stand shoulder to shoulder in danger and recreation'.

The 19/N.F. was brought down from the Arras area and attached to the 29th Division near Beaumont Hamel. Here it worked alongside the Pioneers of the 29th and 48th Divisions in digging fire trenches and bringing in the dead from No Man's Land. On 6 July its working parties managed to bring in four wounded who had been lying out since 1 July. The battalion was withdrawn to Acheux Wood two days later and then, still detached from its own division, was sent to perform heavy work in and around Carnoy. One company of the 9/North Staffs worked nearby collecting the dead of the 34th and 21st Divisions, while others worked on a tramway extension up Sausage Valley. All the battalion's machine guns and their crews were in the forward area with the infantry near Gordon Dump. They remained working and burying in and around the front lines for almost three weeks. By the time it was pulled out the battalion had lost nearly 60 killed and wounded. When the 22/DLI was finally withdrawn after several days collecting dead near Ovillers, 'numbers' of men were described as showing 'acute distress'.[4] A short spell of rest at Amiens appears to have restored their nerves and morale.

Meanwhile the work of carrying and consolidation continued. The 7/York & Lancs was among the first units to build a log and sleeper road in the forward area. (Owing to a shortage of timber at the front, these did not become commonplace until mid-September). Using three-inch thick planks, the Pioneers built a road through Fricourt village to its wood beyond between 4–6 July. It was substantial enough to allow heavy howitzers to be hauled into newly dug positions in the wood. When the road was complete and the advance continued, the battalion laboured to transform a former German communication trench from Montauban towards Longueval into 'York & Lancs Alley' – a 'comparatively safe road to the front'.[5] A little to the north the 5/Northants was busy realigning enemy trenches near the Albert-Bapaume road and lining dugouts with metal frames.

The next major offensive was to take place on 14 July, but

before the attack on the German second line could go ahead, Mametz and Trones Woods had to be cleared. Trones involved bitter fighting, with Pioneers responsible for digging trenches up towards the German positions and then carrying bombs into the wood. Mametz was to be the bloody initiation of Lloyd George's 'Welsh army' – the 38th Division. The division's Pioneers, the 19/Welch, were to have two companies attached to each of the attacking brigades and dig communication trenches from Caterpillar Wood to the captured ground. Three platoons of B Company followed the 14/Welch into the wood and successfully consolidated what little ground had been secured. As the other battalions tried to fight their way further into the dense undergrowth, the Pioneers became heavily involved in the fighting. Two platoons of C Company were prevented from leaving their own positions owing to the intense enemy fire that was brought to bear on the Welsh trenches. German resistance in the wood remained ferocious and on 10 July a platoon of Pioneers was ordered to create a diversion by attacking it from a different angle. The men were cut down almost as they clambered from their own trenches. Several platoons were continuously employed bringing up rations and supplies from Minden Post, while others were still trying to dig trenches across the open ground to the edge of the wood. Most of the men were fighting and carrying in the incessant bombardments or machine gun fire, without rest or respite, for nearly 48 hours. When the shattered Welsh battalions were withdrawn, the Pioneers left too. In three days the 19th had lost 35 dead and over 100 wounded.

The capture of Mametz Wood meant that a night attack on the second line could proceed. The assault was a remarkable success, and in the wake of the 7th Division the 24/Manchester moved up to build strong points in the ruined village of Bazentin-le-Petit. While working at their tasks the C.O. of a nearby battalion sent an urgent request for help to stem a German counter-attack. Two platoons of the Manchesters rallied to its help and having piled their tools, beat off the enemy attack with rifle fire. One officer and five other ranks were killed and over 40 wounded. The success of that day also presented the British with the opportunity to seize High Wood. Unfortunately, the chance was not taken, and instead of taking this dominating feature in one day, its eventual capture was to result in some of the heaviest fighting and casualties of the campaign. Many divisions were thrown against the resolute German defenders before the 47th Division, with the 4/RWF as Pioneers, secured its tortured trunks. In the days preceding this success the 18/Middlesex had been heavily involved in trying to dig a trench from Crucifix Corner across nearly 1,200 yards of open, shell-swept land to the wood. An observer of their efforts, who described them rather simply as 'navvies in civilian life', wrote: 'They worked as though they were opening up Piccadilly, and took as little notice of German shell fire as they would have done of the London traffic'.[6] Two platoons were suddenly called upon by an officer of the RWF to advance into the wood and repel a German counter-attack at the point of the bayonet. After a confused engagement the Pioneers returned to their spades and completed 1,150 yards of trench in fewer than 40 hours.

High Alley, as the trench became known, later became the responsibility of the 8/Royal Scots. Another Scottish Pioneer battalion, the 9/Seaforth, was also engaged in the same sector. The battalion supported the South Africans during their attack on Delville Wood and under a severe bombardment recon-noitred potential positions for future strong points. Another detachment was responsible for ensuring supplies of water to its 9th Division. When the storage tanks were punctured by shell fire, the platoon officer borrowed some canvas ones from the cavalry and kept the queue of waiting water carts supplied. Other regular divisions were also in action near Delville Wood. The 10/DCLI of the 2nd Division went to work in the evil place on 26 July but was withdrawn when its division attempted another attack. In the evening, 600 Cornwalls carried up stores to the forward positions. As they stumbled between the blasted trees they came under fire from a German area shoot; one company alone lost 11 killed and 18 wounded. The following day, while again carrying up supplies, the O.C. of the 2/South Staffs called upon several platoons to help in repelling a German counter-attack.

Longueval village finally fell to the 5th Division, in which another Highland battalion, the 6/Argyll, served as Pioneers. When the Somme campaign opened the battalion was at rest. It received a large draft of just under 300 men on 1 July, and was fortunate to enjoy two weeks' company and pioneer training before it moved to Fricourt. It helped in the capture of Longueval and lost 13 dead and just under 100 wounded. It also lost nearly a dozen men to munitions production at home and another four who were returned to base as under age. The battalion spent some time consolidating what little remained of the village before returning to rest. The training programme prepared for the unit included a period described somewhat vaguely as 'night pioneer training'.

August started quietly enough for the third of the Highland Pioneer units, the 9/Gordon Highlanders. The battalion spent a day hay-making with French farmers near Beaumetz, but as the Somme campaign ground on, this rural idyl could not last for ever. By the second week of the month two platoons were trying to open a communication trench across what had been No Man's Land with Bangalore torpedoes. One writer later wistfully reflected such activity was 'certainly safer than attacking as the infantry did, but not attractive'.[7] These weapons had an unfortunate habit of exploding prematurely and when one did, a sergeant won the M.M. for bringing in a man wounded by the explosion. Another example of extreme bravery shown by a Pioneer was that demonstrated by Pte. Nolan of the 9/South Staffs. A company of the battalion had been digging saps with the purpose of connecting them to those of the 34th Division. Nolan and four companions crawled out from their work to reconnoitre a nearby enemy trench. Having established it was still in enemy occupation, they returned to collect bombs and secured permission to go out again. With the other Pioneers acting as carriers, Nolan ran along the German parapet for about 20 yards, bombing as he went. One enemy machine gun team turned and ran, pursued by Nolan who hurled bombs at its retreating figures. He then returned for the gun, took it back to the British trenches and resumed his work of attempting to link up with the 34th.

After its virtual annihilation at La Boisselle, and its loss of two

94

brigades to another division, the 34th Division had been reunited in early August. Members of the 18/N.F. who acted as the divisional salvage company had stayed in the front area even though the battalion and its division had been withdrawn. This small group of men, sometimes with parties of infantry, yeomanry and cyclists temporarily attached for work, collected an amazing assortment of abandoned equipment. They worked with such enthusiasm that brassards were issued to prevent them being arrested as looters. The company was responsible for sorting through unclaimed packs as well as collecting and despatching to base anything that could be regarded as useful. It cooked salved rations on salved field cookers and in July collected, among other things, 12,998 rifles, 51 machine guns and 12 trench mortars. On one occasion it had everything required to kit out an entire battalion except for clothing, iron rations and gas helmets. As a diarist wrote, although such work 'brought but little glory . . . [it] resulted in a great saving of public money'.[8]

One company of another Fusilier battalion, the 14th, was employed making a track for stretcher bearers alongside the light railway under construction through Delville Wood. Possession of the wood had been ferociously contested and apart from uprooted and dismembered stumps, little of it remained. However, as a route towards the front it was still regularly bombarded by the Germans. Enemy guns would throw an intense barrage on a particular zone for 15 –30 minutes, before moving on to another. The Fusiliers were caught in one of these area shoots and cowered among the roots and fallen timbers as the shells shrieked around them. One of its officers later thought that the task entrusted to them had been 'useless . . . and I suspect only put in hand to employ us'.[9] That particular piece of criticism sounds somewhat harsh, as duckboard and corduroy tracks were always needed by the infantry and their animals. Even in the chaos and confusion of the Somme fighting, it is unlikely that a company of men would have been sent to work so near to the front merely to stop them from sitting around in their muddy holes a few hundred yards to the rear. As the battle dragged on and the gains remained minimal, frustration, disappointment and a belief that the staff did not know what it was doing, were sentiments widespread among the enduring soldiery.

One Pioneer battalion which, like many others, suffered from break downs in communications, confused orders and aborted tasks, was the 12/Notts & Derby. Having spent several months in the Neuve Eglise sector, the battalion and its division arrived on the Somme. It bivouacked at the sprawling and muddy camp known as the Citadel, by that time about two miles behind the front. It began work immediately, one company coming under the orders of the CRA to prepare gun pits, while the remainder were occupied in digging dugouts, shelter trenches and signal stations in Bernafay Wood. The men worked continually from 2-17 August, when its division attacked Guillemont. Because the attack failed to retain its objectives the battalion, which had moved up to follow the infantry across, hung around the forward area awaiting further orders. On the following day the infantry tried again and, once more, the Pioneers moved up to support. One company dug a communication trench of 270 yards to a depth of 4' 6", and was subsequently shifted to another job. This was the repeated story of several days. The Pioneers would remain in the forward zone, waiting either for the order to move up if the infantry had been successful, or to move on to other tasks if they had not. It is not surprising they knew little of what was going on for any reports brought back by runners from the attacking troops were directed to infantry and brigade HQs rather than to the Pioneers. The death of officers, NCOs and runners meant that situation reports were often not written or carried; at times commanders were in complete ignorance of how the infantry was faring amid the shells and mud only a few hundred yards in front of their position. It was no good ordering the Pioneers to leave their shell holes and advance if there was nothing to consolidate. On occasions the Notts & Derby were ordered to dig a trench or connect up shell holes in advance of what had been the British jumping off line and leave covering parties until relieved by the infantry.

On 21 August, after nearly three weeks of work at the front, the battalion, with its men 'absolutely played out', moved back to the Citadel. In appalling conditions and still within range of

German medium guns it suffered periodic inspections and drill for another four days. It spent a further two nights huddled under ground sheets against the pouring rain, and eventually on 27 August moved into huts at Heilly. Here in relative comfort, it had the chance to see if the Pioneers were to share in the glory of the alleged victory by watching the recently released official film *The Battle of the Somme*.[10] The respite was short-lived for on 30 August the battalion once more moved up towards the line and began working at Fricourt and Pommiers Redoubt.

The guns hauled up the plank road laid by the 7/York & Lancs to Fricourt Wood were in almost constant action on counter-battery work or laying barrages for the infantry. Consequently, the German artillery frequently searched the wood with shells and gas. It was to this unhealthy spot that the 24/Manchester moved in mid-August. Working parties went out towards the spot on a map which had once represented the village of Guinchy. Their main task was to dig assembly trenches, but often all they could do was seek what little shelter they could while German shells fell about them. Promised covering parties often failed to materialize and sometimes, finding themselves as the front line troops, the Manchesters had to abandon their digging and, as they had done at Bazentin, repulse German counter-attacks with rifle fire. Division after division was hurled against Guinchy until on 30 August the 7th Division was ordered to take its turn in the inferno. The attack was postponed for a few days, but the Pioneers remained digging in the front trenches. They learned that the attack would be attempted on 3 September and that they were to dig new communication trenches once the infantry had gone across. The importance of the work was underlined in the orders:

> It is only by means of these that the wounded can be evacuated, stores and ammunition brought up and touch kept with our front line companies. We must therefore complete the work at all costs.

The attack, like so many before, failed. Having lost nine dead and 51 wounded, and with the situation described as 'obscured', the Oldham Comrades made their weary way back to Fricourt Wood.

The Comrades returned to work the following day and began digging a cable trench running from Pommiers Redoubt to Longueval – some 5,000 yards. To protect the telephone cable the trench was dug to a depth of six feet. On the day it was completed orders were received that the division would be leaving the Somme and go to the quieter zone of Second Army. Another regular division, the 3rd, had already left Fourth Army. General Rawlinson sent it on its way with a message which 'greatly regretted' its departure – a regret that was not shared by the division itself. Although he was not to receive the same opprobrium as that reserved for General Gough and his Fifth Army staff at Ypres a year later, Rawlinson and Fourth Army staff were disliked by many under their command. Soldiers at the front blamed the carnage in which they were immersed on those who they perceived were most immediately responsible. Although despised by most, politicians, war profiteers and the censored newspapers were too far removed from the troops, and consequently were difficult to target directly. The work of the staff and their directives, on the other hand, were all around them. Because they were responsible for where the assaults should take place and for who should make them, it was to them that the accusing finger was directed. Staff officers were ridiculed for their immaculate uniforms, their assumed life of comfort in the rear and resented for the disruption they could cause in the trenches when gathering intelligence; paradoxically, they were also criticised for not spending sufficient time in the front lines to experience the prevailing conditions for themselves.

Despite the widespread contemporary antipathy, post-war publications of battalion histories usually ignore or skate over the often poor relations between staff and fighting troops. However, there are exceptions. In a rare example of condemnation, an officer of the 20/KRRC pulled no punches in his criticism of the handling by Rawlinson and his staff of the September attacks on Guinchy and Guillement:

Although it seemed transparently obvious to troops on the spot, it took a long time for the Higher Command to recognize, and battalions were allotted tasks too heavy for divisions. In these futile and costly operations, doomed in the nature of the case to failure, the 3rd Division was sacrificed, and its Pioneers were repeatedly brought forward into its most obnoxious assembly positions in order to consolidate enemy lines which were not captured.[11]

The Pioneers of another regular division, the 5th, could also complain with some justification of the work they had been doing in an adjoining area. The 6/Argyll had lost 12 killed and 111 wounded when trying to support the division's attack near Morval. Whether its earlier 'night pioneer training' was of much assistance to the battalion as it dug and wired amidst the stinking shell holes and obliterated trenches is unrecorded.

Another of the regular divisions had, until September, enjoyed a reasonably quiet time. The 4th Division, with its newly appointed Pioneer battalion the 21/West Yorks, had spent part of July, all of August and most of September further north. At the end of September the luck of the Wool Textile Pioneers seemed to be holding because, although far from safe, most of the battalion was working on the railway at Plateau Station near Bray. The 14/N.F. too had been fairly fortunate. Despite the incident in Delville Wood, losses had been light and most of August had been spent doing routine work near Arras. Drafts brought it back to strength and it moved south to the Somme in September. Its work was constantly interrupted by the seemingly incessant rain and the constant shelling, but it left Dernancourt for Vermelles in early October with a far from insubstantial strength of 24 officers and 724 other ranks.

September saw the first offensive use of tanks. Few in number and in many people's eyes used prematurely, they did have some success at Courcelette. To the Pioneers the tanks meant even more work. New roads had to be laid or existing ones improved and camouflage positions made at their assembly areas. One officer and 58 men of the 5/SWB known as the 'Tank Section', were detailed to accompany the monsters along the roads as they waddled towards the front; another twelve men having gone on ahead to lay the tapes the tanks were to follow. There was no such novel work for the Pioneers of the 19/Middlesex – merely the unrelieved stress and strain of working at the front. As they laboured in the mud and destruction that once was Delville Wood their adjutant, formerly one of the most diligent and lengthy of diarists, lost his enthusiasm for recording the intricate day-to-day detail of his companions' work; the physical and mental difficulties he faced when compiling the diary is apparent in the increasingly cursory and succinct entries.

It was not only the shelling, which heaved and punctured the earth in which they worked, that caused mounting Pioneer casualties. The featureless, void landscape necessitated the accurate use of the compass. In later years several Pioneer officers remarked that the only reliable method of laying tapes for nocturnal digging was to go during daylight and take bearings. During one night reconnaissance two officers of the 11/Hants heard movement in front and challenged the dim silhouettes. A voice replied, 'We are the other platoon'. The officers advanced, only to be fired upon by a German patrol. Captain Cade was killed immediately and Lt. Hazard tumbled, wounded, into a shell hole.[12] The following day, as its division assembled for an attack, the battalion became the garrison of the shattered remains of Guillemont. Two companies of the Hampshires were to go over with the Irish brigades, but as they rose from their shell holes they were met with such concentrated fire that the attempt to consolidate withered away. Thirty-two Hampshires were killed that day. Apart from 1 July, this was the highest single day's loss of any Pioneer unit during the campaign.

Assaults on the shell-blasted Thiepval ridge continued throughout August and into September. Numerous divisions and their Pioneers attempted its capture, and eventually towards the end of the month the 18th Division succeeded. The 8/Sussex sweated away at the roads and tracks leading to the assembly trenches and tried to connect the shell holes into something resembling a line. Companies worked in reliefs, with one of the four always available in case of emergency. Once the brooding Schwaben Redoubt had been taken, the Sussex moved in to clear the dugouts and dig covered communication trenches up to it from Thiepval Wood. To the north-east, a stained patch of pulverized mud that had once been the German stronghold of Mouquet Farm was finally taken. The 6/East Yorks followed so close behind the infantry that a platoon began consolidating the position even before the enemy had been cleared from the cellars. In a bid to get to work, the platoon commander ordered his own men into the attack. After four hours of hurling grenades and smoke bombs down the warren of tunnels beneath the farm, one officer and 35 German defenders surrendered. The Pioneers lost 24 killed and 52 wounded that day, but earned three M.C.s, one DCM and five M.M.s during the month.

The fall of Guinchy and Delville Wood persuaded the commanders that success could still be achieved. The Germans were, so it was claimed, approaching the end and one or two more pushes would see their morale collapse. The Germans were certainly suffering, but there was little real evidence to fuel any optimism of capitulation. Nevertheless, the Guards Division was brought in to spearhead the attack towards the next ruined village, Les Boeufs. The 4/Coldstream had been preparing the ground and working around Trones Wood since the middle of the month. Knott Trench had been extended towards the infamous Waterlot Farm and tracks snaking around the shell holes and across ruined trenches had been laid and maintained. On 15 September a battle surplus of three officers and 149 men (including the transport) was withdrawn and the rest of the battalion moved up. Its task in the coming attack was to keep communications open by repairing tracks behind the jumping off lines. Unlike the rest of the division, most of which was cut down by enemy machine guns firing from the Quadrilateral, casualties among the Pioneers were not heavy. Three days later 50 men were detailed to clear the battlefield, burying 437 of their comrades in the process. Among those collected was the second in command of the regiment's 3rd Battalion. The kits of the dead were catalogued, labelled and sent to the rear. There were to be another two weeks of demoralizing and dangerous work before the task of maintenance was handed over to the 5/Cheshire whose division, the 56th, had worked its way up through Leuze and Bouleaux Woods. The exhausted Guardsmen made their way back across the shelled wilderness to Mericourt station, hoping for swift evacuation and rest. Instead, they hung around for four 'long and tedious hours' until a train eventually arrived to carry them away.

The Coldstream were pulled out several days after their division had already disappeared for rest and rebuilding. In comparison to some Pioneer battalions, the 4/Coldstream had spent a relatively short period in the line. Other units were less fortunate. As August turned to September, and the supposed summer into official autumn, several battalions appear to have virtually lived in the forward area. The long period of work might have been punctuated by the odd day spent a few miles to the rear, where there was a chance of a change of clothes and a bath, but these were often irregularly spaced. Alternatively, one company in turn might be given a day off, although whether a day spent in a rain-soaked shell hole still within range of the German guns was much more appealing than a day at work, might be debatable. The 22/DLI spent such a period near Waterlot Farm. It was supposed to go over with the infantry of its division, and although the attack was cancelled, the DLI were retained in the front area and suffered heavily from enemy shelling. Twenty-four were killed and over 30 wounded. In addition to these casualties, one man accidentally shot himself in the foot while cleaning his rifle and another died of asphyxiation while sleeping in an unventilated bivouac. When, after three dreadful weeks the battalion was finally relieved, the troops were so weary that the shambling withdrawal was nicknamed the 'Retreat to Meaulte'.[13] The 5/Northants stayed on for a further ten days after its division had been pulled out following the failure of the October attacks. Similarly, while its division was elsewhere, two companies of the 13/Gloucester tried several times to dig a trench beyond the ruins of the Schwaben Redoubt. These attempts resulted in a 'total failure as points could not be located, shell fire was very heavy and the state of the ground made any digging impossible'. During the month the battalion lost nearly 20 dead and over 40 wounded.

The fortunes of the 18/Middlesex also took a further turn for the worse during the misery of September and October. On its way back to the Somme a substantial number of men had fallen out of the marching column and an officers' conference was later held to discuss the disgrace. The C.O. decided the men concerned should be punished by extra drill in full marching order. Three weeks later, more problems arose. The adjutant's 'want of appreciation' of the importance of a divisional order caused 'serious inconvenience' to the transport – an embarrassing 'miscarriage' being only narrowly averted. Then came the 'regrettable incident' mentioned earlier, concerning a number of drunken soldiers and the subsequent criticism of the investigating officer. When the battalion began work, things did not much improve. Platoons were often involved in carrying supplies to the front trenches. Slipping and groping their burdened way along the treacherous duckboards, they were in constant danger of disappearing into the slimy blackness of the adjoining shell holes. Lt. Davies tried gumboots and became very annoyed when the boots failed to gain a grip and he ended up staggering about 'like a drunk'[14] in front of his platoon. One working party was supposed to rendezvous with an officer of 11th Field Company, but in the inky blackness, and after having splashed about for two hours in water three feet deep, the attempt was abandoned and the troops returned to camp. On another nocturnal task one platoon came across members of an infantry carrying party up to their waists in mud. It took 100 men of the Middlesex four hours to free the trapped men. The battle against the elements, compounded by the distance the troops trudged each night and by their own shells falling short, ensured the battalion's casualty list rose remorselessly. As a working party slipped and staggered between its camp at Montauban and its work near Les Boeufs, a British shell fell among it and killed almost a dozen men. Morale sank still lower when the second in command tore a strip off a subaltern in front of his platoon and when one of the battalion's more colourful and durable characters was wounded and evacuated. One night in October Sgt. Wilkinson, an ex-regular of indeterminate age but certainly in his fifties, was hit in the back by shrapnel. He would not allow the stretcher bearers to carry him away until he had spent a full two minutes

103

telling the Germans what he thought of them. His platoon officer recalled later: 'The men just stood in silent wonderment at his remarkable swear vocabulary'.[15] After losing several more men during a bombardment in December, the battalion received orders that it was to be relieved. With hopes for what would be their first genuine rest for nearly five months and of spending Christmas out of the line, the battalion began the slog to the rear. As they made their way along the duckboard tracks the order was countermanded and the battalion was instructed to about turn and recommence work. Its one compensation was that it was allowed to switch camps; it took up residence in some improved accommodation at Pommiers Redoubt.

Similar stories of unremitting work and strain could be repeated for other battalions some of which, during what was to become the final assaults of the campaign, were later acknowledged in the *Official History*. For example, after having spent some time working on battle HQs and dressing stations in the White City, a company of the 8/Royal Scots and a party from the 2/2nd Highland Field Company began digging New Munich Trench in preparation for their division's next attack. The 10/DCLI sent two platoons to consolidate a position won by its division on 13 November near the Ancre, while nearby, the 13/Gloucester was striving to make the Hamel-St.Pierre Divion road fit for limbered traffic. Two platoons were also extending an infantry track beyond what had been the former German front line. The 5/SWB were busy consolidating the German positions captured near Grandcourt and, like the Gloucesters, worked under continual shell and machine gun fire. Just below them in the Ancre valley, the Severn Valley Pioneers were labouring to improve Station Alley and helping the 13/KRRC and the HAC to secure the eastern edge of Beaucourt. Despite the mud and growing despondency, November also saw some success further north. The 12/KOYLI, once again back in the sector where it had fought on 1 July, was congratulated by one of the division's brigadiers for the work it did in bringing in wounded once the wreckage of Serre had finally fallen.[16] But the month also witnessed some of the most savage disappointments. Some of the most ferocious fighting took place for the ancient burial mound known as the Butte de Warlincourt. The 50th Division was launched several times against this shell-drenched hump of contaminated soil. After its earlier successful attack against Prue Trench and the Starfish Line, the division had been withdrawn. Its Pioneers, the 7/DLI, were not so lucky and remained working until the division re-appeared for the forthcoming attack. On 5 November seven platoons of the 7th tried to reinforce its 9th Battalion, then attempting to maintain its tenuous grip on the Butte. Several times the Pioneers struggled from their brimming shell holes, but on each occasion were driven back by heavy fire.

The weather had become the deciding factor in the Somme campaign. The battlefield, drenched by chilling rain, deteriorated into a landscape of mud and desolation. In this abysmal creation the cold, exhausted troops sought what little shelter their scrapes and shell holes proffered. The period of set-piece assaults was, for the moment over, but the work of survival continued and local attacks against objectives shrouded in snow or swallowed by mud were still attempted. The 2/Monmouth was one of several Pioneer battalions mentioned for its work during these attacks. When its division advanced towards Le Transloy, the consolidation of the captured ground was described as a 'remarkable feat'. The ground was frozen to a depth of 18 inches but under searching fire, the Monmouths hacked at it with such determination that a line was dug in 20 minutes.[17] The bulk of the work that winter however, was the unceasing demands of the infantry for dugouts, passable roads and tracks and trench maintenance. Working parties were constantly seen bowed low with equipment or shovelling mud from tracks into sumps and ditches. In such conditions the numbers of men despatched to hospital or suffering from ailments brought about by the unfriendly elements rose alarmingly. The diarist of the 11/DLI complained that after jobs which included burying putrid German corpses near Combles and 'owing to the long journey to and from work under bad weather conditions, long hours of work and the bad condition of bivouacs, the men appear to be run down and are in real need of a rest'. The 7/York & Lancs was in such a bad way that it was lent men from several battalions to keep it up to a reasonable working strength; of these, the 'great majority' were of such 'poor physique that they soon succumbed to the toil . . . . and dribbled off to hospital'.[18] The Oldham Comrades too, suffered from a constant haemorrhage of men. In mid-January, the adjutant wrote:

> During the whole of this month owing [1] to the large numbers of sick, mainly sore feet due to the constant marching through the mud and [2] to the large number of men detached for various duties, e.g. burying cables for Corps Signals, Forward Water Supply, unloading party at Beaussart railhead, tramway maintenance etc., the number of men available for ordinary work has been very small.

It is difficult to be precise about working or battalion strengths in the winter of 1916-17. War Diaries often record the arrival of drafts, but unlike entries later in the war, they only infrequently mention total strengths. From the few references we do have, the average strength of a Pioneer battalion at that time was somewhere around 700. Once the transport, HQ details, men away on courses and leave and those excused duty are taken into account, the nightly working strength was probably about 500. In some corps and divisions, Pioneer strength was thought to be so low and the work in progress so demanding, that the infantry, itself woefully below establishment, was plundered for men to work alongside the Pioneers. A Pioneer Group was formed in XIV Corps in October and in the 46th Division, a Divisional Provisional Pioneer Battalion was created some time later with four officers from the 1/Monmouth as its company commanders. In the 8th Division a composite battalion of 600 men was created in December. This unit was commanded by an officer from the Pioneer battalion, the 22/DLI, and spent much of its time on road maintenance in Maurepas Ravine and making trench boards. Other sections erected wire in front of the British outposts and revetted the front trenches.[19]

Nor was it only men that could be in short supply. War Diaries often complain of inadequate supplies of timber and metal for shoring and lining trenches and dugouts. This was perhaps a mixed blessing. If the materials were not forthcoming, the excavations were liable to cave in and work would have to begin again; on the other hand, there was nothing more difficult than humping timber props and expanded metal frames in a saturnine night up winding and clogged communication trenches towards the front.

Trench work in such frightening conditions required endurance of the highest degree. It continued without remission throughout the winter snows and thaws and on into the spring rains. In 1917 great battles were to be fought elsewhere and, following the enemy retreat to its new lines of prepared defences, the Somme battlefields became the rear area for divisions at the front. Hutted camps appeared in what a few months before had been areas of the bitterest fighting and the roads, now safe from all save the heaviest German shells, groaned with traffic bearing loads for the front. The task of maintaining them passed from the Pioneers to the non-combatant units, although the Engineers retained overall responsibility. The Pioneers and the Field Companies moved forward with their divisions to take up familiar tasks in new surroundings. Fuelled by reports in the newspapers, some observers commented that the retreat to the Hindenburg Line marked a serious depletion in German strength and an acknowledgement that she had been mortally wounded by the attrition on the Somme. Perhaps some troops at the front did believe such propaganda, but it is difficult not to assume that when a Pioneer officer such as Captain Alfred Baer, who had seen action in the Dardanelles and France, wrote home from his hospital bed that the 'Germans are at the end of their tether', there is more than just a touch of sardonic humour in the letter.[20] Clearly though, the full horror of the campaign had not touched all of Britain's soldiery. When the 7/DLI came out after a particular gruelling and filthy period of work in March 1917, a soldier of the 59th Division newly arrived from Ireland, remarked with some shock to a weary and unkept Durham that life too in the 'Emerald isle' was pretty grim: 'They throw bottles at you there!', he declared.[21]

As the Pioneers and their divisions moved across the area laid waste by the retreating Germans, new skills were acquired. Booby traps, delayed action mines and a hundred other evils to kill, maim or inconvenience the incautious Tommy had to be neutralized. R.E. and Pioneers swarmed around the new positions, dismantling, disconnecting, rebuilding and, inevitably, laying tracks across the vacated wilderness of ruined trenches and discarded equipment. Armchair observers of large scale maps could advance their pins and believe final victory was in sight; troops in the field could not allow themselves the luxury of illusion. Guns were still firing across the trenches on the Somme as Third Army began preparations for a new offensive. Pioneers and R.E. would be found plenty of work in the months to come. Like those spent on the Somme, they would be arduous and the work unglamourous. The contribution they would make to the preparations and continuance of the coming offensive would help to decide its success or failure. Most of the jobs they performed were repetitive and monotonous, with circumstances affording little opportunity to devise new working practices or develop other than the basic skills required of them. Yet, at times, units were expected to undertake less mundane and less dangerous tasks. The protracted violence of the Somme proved that Pioneers had become an essential and integral part of the BEF. Against the background of lessons learned from the campaign and how these could be applied during the four major offensives of 1917, it is worth looking at the general characteristics of Pioneer battalions and at the specialities sometimes expected of them.

NOTES

1. Lester, op.cit.
2. Mellors, P. papers. (Liddle Collection)
3. Croft, W.D. papers. (Liddle Collection)
4. Davidson, op.cit.
5. Atteridge, op.cit. p.156
6. Quoted in *Official History, 1916 Vol 2*. p.111 FN.
7. Falls, op.cit. p.95-6
8. Shakespear, J. *The Thirty-Four Division*, 1915-19, (Witherby, 1921) p.302

9. Dillon, op.cit.
10. The 24/Manchester is featured briefly in the film. The battalion is seen assembling at Minden Post preparatory to moving up.
11. Turbeville, op.cit. p.25
12. Lt. Hazard was found by Cpl. Snelling, who then went to get assistance. A small party spent some time trying to recover Cade's body, but abandoned the attempt.
13. Davidson, op.cit.
14. Lester, op.cit.
15. ibid.
16. The battalion was awarded two M.C.s and five M.M.s for its work.
17. Gillon, S. *The Story of the 29th Division*, (Nelson, 1925) p.92
18. Gilvary, op.cit. p.31
19. In March 1917 two nocturnal parties went out to wire and dig near Maurepas Ravine. 2Lt. Summerscales led the second party, which was carrying the screw pickets, and was later posted as missing. A court of enquiry concluded that he must have fallen into German hands. When the Germans retired to the Hindenburg line, the grave of an officer was exhumed by the British and the remains were identified as those of Summerscales. (W.O.95.1966) Davidson, who was in charge of the other working party, went to look for Summerscales, but gave up after a German patrol passed within a yard of him. (Davidson, op.cit.)
20. Baer, A. papers. (Dept. of Documents, IWM)
21. Unpublished history of 7/DLI, op.cit.

Chapter 6

ALL ABOARD THE TRENCH LINE SPECIAL

Although the Somme had achieved little in terms of territorial gains, it had provided the General Staff with some essential and valuable lessons. It is not the place here to discuss whether the lessons were sufficiently taken on board by those who planned the infantry and artillery tactics of forthcoming battles. What is of relevance to this study is to attempt to discover whether the divisional staffs and the BEF as a whole had benefited from the experience of the Somme in respect of how they used their Pioneer battalions.

Several of the second line divisions of the Territorial Force only crossed the Channel and took the field in early 1917. Despite being sent to spend their early weeks of trench acclimatization in the freezing and flooded wastes of the Somme, some of them arrived in France without a Pioneer battalion. These divisions would take their share in the coming battles, but the great majority of those divisions which fought the battles of 1917 had previously fought on the Somme and already had Pioneer battalions attached to them. As we have seen, during the campaign they had been used in a variety of means; from carriers of supplies, diggers of trenches and wirers of positions, to fighting troops. Although their casualties had not been as high as those of the infantry, several battalions had lost significant numbers of men.[1] Over the winter they were brought up to what, for the rest of the war, would be considered 'establishment' and, like the rest of the BEF, waited with some trepidation, to discover what the new year would bring.

110

The next major British offensive was not to begin until Easter 1917, but the demands of trench warfare ensured that the tasks of the Pioneers remained unrelenting. Throughout the early months of 1917 working parties helped their comrades in the infantry to wire, carry and dig. Dugouts were constructed, camps in the rear made more comfortable, gun pits dug for the artillery, and a thousand and one other jobs done in an attempt to make the life of the front line soldier a little more safe and tolerable. One of the tasks which befell an increasing number of Pioneers during 1917 was working on railways. It is not surprising to see the 17/N.F. spending a great deal of its time in such occupation, but a good percentage of Pioneer battalions spent at least some of the year assisting specialized railway troops or R.E. in laying track or preparing the ground over which the track was to pass. This was not a completely new task, for platoons of some Pioneer units had already spent a proportion of their time working on tramways and railways. What was new was the *number* of units that would be involved. As early as August 1915 one platoon of the 5/Northants had laid a 3'6" gauge tramway in a trench near Houplines, and 40 men of the 18/Middlesex with 'railway experience' spent some time as a ballast party on a decauville track in Trones Wood.[2] In April 1916 XVII Corps had even created a Railway Company from its Pioneer battalions; each unit contributed about three officers and 120 other ranks. The XIII Corps had been running a smaller Tramway Company with a party of the 9/Seaforth Highlanders on permanent attachment since January 1916.

The preparations required for the offensive on the Somme had necessitated a hugely increased railway capacity. Railheads were extended and miles of additional track and sidings laid to carry men and supplies to the front. Two and a half companies of the 16/Royal Irish Rifles were employed in building a 17 mile long broad gauge line from Candas to Acheux within weeks of their arrival. The battalion laid track at the unprecedented rate of about 1,100 yards of steel a day. Several of its officers, presumably those with the necessary experience, were even allocated specific engineering rather than mere supervisory tasks. The final spike was driven in mid-February but the companies continued

to work on sidings and stations until May.[3] The overall responsibility for the construction and then running of the railways fell
to the R.E., who, as the months passed, became stretched to the
limits of manpower. The demands became so great that in a
report of August 1916[4] the Chief Engineer of XVII Corps
suggested that the existing corps Railway Company should be
extended. He claimed that to keep a 60-centimetre light line
running to serve his three divisions required 25 other ranks from
Army Troops Companies, 60 ASC men and eight tractor drivers
as well as the ten officers and 360 men from the Pioneer battalions within the corps. The line concerned connected two points
on the broad gauge, was about 50 kms in length and in places
ran to within 600 yards of the front trenches. Because there were
so many other demands upon the Pioneers, normally only two
battalions were able to furnish their quota of men. He recommended that the present unsatisfactory state of affairs should be
improved by creating a permanent unit of R.E. personnel,
supplemented by a more regular supply of Pioneer detachments.
The army knew things had to be placed on a more efficient
footing and decided to create new organizations designed to ease
the burden on the R.E.

Perhaps the most obvious option for the staff was to convert
the men of the NER, now in uniform under the guise of the
17/N.F. into railway troops. The battalion's historian believed
simply that, 'no better selection could have been made'.[5] A
quick look at the skills possessed by the men is enough to
confirm that belief. Although by the time the battalion was
converted some of the originals had been killed or wounded,
casualties had been fairly light. Furthermore, as some of the
replacements had come from the battalion's own training
battalion the 32/N.F., they possessed skills similar to the originals. Of the 1000 plus men who embarked for France,[6] 308
were described as 'Engineer'. These men worked in the
company's different engineering departments and would have
been either skilled or men who were certainly used to wielding
a pick and shovel. They are distinct from the largest proportion
of the men whose civilian job was simply described as
'Operating', presumably the drivers, firemen, guards, signalmen

112

9. Pioneers and RE used a variety of means to transport tools and stores. These mules are equipped with saddles designed to carry two dozen shovels. Aveluy Wood, September 1916. (IWM Q1338)

10. A soldier (left) wearing an empty Yukon pack, a common piece of equipment for Pioneers, passing wounded on hand pushed bogies near Messines in May 1917. Bedraggled camouflage screening hangs from trackside posts. (IWM Q5839)

11. Signallers of the 5/Northants operating an electric daylight lamp near Feuchy during the Battle of Arras. Note the improvised mounting. (IWM Q5257)

12. The machine gun section of the 11/Leicestershire holding a captured German trench at Ribecourt on the opening day of the Battle of Cambrai. (IWM Q6279)

13. Constructing and erecting trench bridges were frequent tasks for Pioneer battalions. This is a standard trench bridge crossing former German trenches at Gommecourt. (IWM Q4906)

14. Pioneers of the 10/DCLI constructing a pontoon bridge over the canalised River Scheldt in October 1918. A German prisoner (left) is conversing with a British officer. (IWM Q11435)

15. Pioneers of the 11/DLI on a light railway at Elverdinghe on the opening day of Third Ypres. (IWM Q2641)

16. After a gruelling period on the Somme, the concert party of the 11/DLI posed for this picture at Picquigny in October 1916. Captain G. S. Fillingham (*Sitting centre*) was posted from the regular 2/DLI. He recalled: 'A typical pioneer job was this – be present under shell fire all day in support of the main attack. Then move forward and grab ground and dig trenches in so called no man's land under enemy fire at night. Go back before day break, sleep and start all over again. Casualties no object'.
(Michael A Cooper/DLI Museum)

etc. There were nine men who had worked in the company's hotels – perhaps later to become officers' servants or company cooks – solicitors, policemen and scores of porters, booking clerks and office workers. It is difficult to imagine a group of men better suited to building and running a railway than these men from the East coast and it shows that, on occasions, the army was capable of fitting men with specialist skills to specialist employment.

The 17/N.F. worked on the construction of the line between Mesnil station and Aveluy crossroads and on converting the Beausart – Aveluy line from metre to standard gauge. The battalion also worked on the extension of this line to Mouquet Farm. Its work was much admired and appreciated, so much so that rumours began sweeping through the ranks that it was to be downgraded into a Labour Battalion. There was some understandable resentment over this rumour, but things were sorted out when it was announced it would be officially converted to a Railway Pioneer Battalion. In keeping with its new title the unit spent two months in early 1917 employed in constructing light railway workshops at Thiennes. This involved building huge sheds of 75,000 square feet and thousands of yards of sidings.

Light railways rapidly proved to be an essential means by which supplies could be brought from the railhead towards the front. Such lines could sometimes be built in dead ground to within a few hundred yards of the front trenches. If local circumstances permitted, manually operated tramways could then be laid to take the supplies closer still to the front trenches. The artillery would often take advantage of a light railway as a means of bringing up shells and spares; on occasions though, gunners seemed not to have appreciated its existence:

> Although our line was primarily made for the benefit of the gunners, we were by no means popular with them; in fact, many of them were very rude to us, declaring that our wretched little railway attracted the Boche's shells to their positions.[7]

Although there is an instance of at least one Pioneer battalion laying and maintaining tracks with wooden rails,[8] the standard

War Office track for these lines was of steel rails weighing either 16lbs or 20lbs per yard. They were joined by a bar fish-plate with four fish-bolts and supported by steel sleepers to which the rails were clipped. A lighter 9lbs track was used for short, isolated lines and battery feeders.[9] It was probably such a line that the 8/Royal Scots relaid near Pozieres Dump in January 1917 and then by means of two branch lines extended it to nearby artillery batteries. The most common tractor used on the standard track was the 20 h.p. Simplex, which was capable of pulling between six and eight loaded three ton trucks.

By the middle of the Somme campaign it had become evident that pressure upon the Pioneers and R.E. to build and run the railways was causing them both severe problems. The issue was raised in the autumn at a senior officers' conference held at Fourth Army's infantry school.[10] There was a suggestion that the Pioneers should establish a school in which they would train infantry in how to build light railways. The proponents argued that if sufficient infantry became skilled in the right techniques, fewer demands would be made upon the Pioneers and Engineers. Fourth Army staff counselled caution over the matter, declaring that there were already so many schools running that it was proving very difficult to find the necessary staff to act as instructors. Moreover it was thought that the infantry 'already had more to learn than they have time for' and that battalions would probably not be able to spare the men to attend courses even if they were established. The staff sought to shift the responsibility somewhat by stating that if there was thought to be sufficient demand for more schools, they should be organized on a divisional, rather than on an army or corps basis. The idea of creating a Pioneer-run school for railway building was thus shelved, although the Engineers continued to train its personnel involved in railway construction. In an attempt to improve the position further, several Army Tramways and Foreways Companies were formed by the R.E. in March 1917. These companies salved rolling stock and ruined line and laid new track for divisions and batteries. Pioneers were frequently called upon to assist the one hundred men of such units; three companies of the 2/Monmouth for example, spent some days helping

114

No.3 Company build a divisional spur in November 1917.

The creation of these units did help the flow of supplies, but they were not the great panacea. Because they could not operate railways and tramways alone, the R.E. still required a massive input of Pioneer or infantry labour. The C.E. of IX Corps wrote a stinging criticism of how the preparations for the extension of tramlines during the Messines offensive had been hamstrung by other demands upon the Pioneers who had been detailed to assist in the construction.[11] He complained that although the 16/Royal Irish Rifles had, in theory, been made available ten days before the attack for special training on rapid track laying, little time had in practice been allowed as the battalion was continually being called upon to carry. He recommended that if the special training necessary for rapid laying could not be included in Pioneers' regular training programmes, a battalion must have at least one week of uninterrupted practise. He asserted that all Pioneer officers should be sufficiently trained to set out and lay a tramline from a working plan, and insisted that over wet ground 800 men must be available if the anticipated target of laying one mile of track every six hours was to be achieved. As plans to continue the offensive developed, the C.E. concluded that demands made upon Pioneers were hardly likely to diminish.

During the Third Battle of Ypres tramways and light railways were pushed across the disputed zones from several lines operating behind what had been the British front on 31 July. The 17th and 18/N.F., 8/Royal Scots, 6/East Yorks, 13/Gloucester and 5/Sussex were among the Pioneer battalions involved in building and running the light railways for XVIII Corps in July 1917. These battalions tended to do the technical work while the attached Labour Companies, the 172nd, 49th and 148th, did the manual work in the rear areas. The 18/N.F. was organized into two shifts, and each shift into a number of gangs. In effect it was the gang rather than the platoon which became the unit of employment. Gangs were formed of men drawn from all four companies, so giving each a cross-section of skills and expertise. Gangs could thus work independently and were self-sufficient in skills. By contrast, the 22/DLI seems to have been organized slightly differently. It decided to send the whole of C Company to the Light Railway Training Camp near Poperinghe so that it became the specialized railway company within the battalion. The company then worked with the 7th Canadian Labour Company near Ypres, before next going a little south to join the 8th Canadian Railway troops in Ploegsteert Wood. The other three companies meanwhile remained on more conventional pioneering duties. The 12/KOYLI and A Company of the 4/South Lancs were also heavily involved in light railway work near Ypres, while the 19/Lancashire Fusiliers worked with the 2nd Battalion Canadian Railway Troops on the light line running from Wieltje to Bridge House. Parties of the 12/KOYLI had earlier acquired useful experience in working tramways when it operated a line during the depths of a Somme winter.

Whether building tramways, light, medium or standard gauge railways, the major problem facing the men in the Ypres area was the nature of the ground. In the rear areas too, shelling had done much to destroy the drainage systems and even if the water was still retained within the dykes, there were so many ditches crossing the fields that the tracks had to be laid on numerous bridges and rafts of brushwood. The 8/Royal Scots was employed on bridging the Steenbeke as well as working on the medium gauge line from Morteldje Dump through Kitchener Wood and a light railway from Morteldje to the Langemarck road. When Third Ypres opened the 7/York & Lancs was only supposed to be assisting the railway engineers, but within three weeks, apart from the final surveying details, the battalion was in sole charge of all work in the forward area. The battalion claimed it would have done this job as well had it possessed the necessary instruments.[12] The York & Lancs had already been involved in the huge building project of what became known as the Great Midland Railway. This was a broad gauge line running from near Peselhoek to the Yser Canal and was later extended for a further 1,000 yards to the east of the canal. Among the many other obstacles to be overcome, one company had to construct a timber pile bridge with a span of 120 feet over the canal. It seems reasonable to assume that even with the help of the R.E., unless a good proportion of the Pioneers had some

116

civilian experience in railway or heavy manual work, the project was unlikely to have been completed on schedule.

The experience of railway building in Flanders inspired one of the officers of the 17/N.F. to write a thick tome covering the surveying, construction and maintenance of light railways. It contains a mass of statistics and tables relating to how embankments, culverts, cuttings, bridges etc should be built, dug or reinforced. It appears to have been required reading for the officers and NCOs of at least one company of the battalion for a note inside it requested that it should be perused, signed and returned to D Company's orderly room. Its format and mass of statistics hardly makes for easy reading, a fact perhaps confirmed by those who claimed to have read it. Only two of the company's second lieutenants acknowledged receipt of the book, both indicating that they read it on the same day. Of the ten sergeants who were supposed to study it, only five did so – four of those doing so on the same day. The CSM was apparently either too busy to bother with it, or so put off by the intensity of the text that he baulked from the attempt. One of its few coherent sections is the Introduction. In this, Captain Garvie sums up the intention behind the book and the principle problem of building railways in Belgium:

> Instructions contained herein, have for their object, saving time by avoiding delays, standardizing the work and beating the Bosche . . . .The three main principles of railroading in Flanders are, drainage, more drainage, and still more drainage.[13]

After five months building the Great Midland Railway the 17/N.F. ceased to be officially Railway Pioneers and rejoined its own division. Having survived the rumours that it might be converted into a Labour unit, there was subsequent disquiet at a comment alleged to have been made by the divisional commander. Having watched the battalion on parade soon after its return, he apparently remarked that he had 'never seen a finer collection of men in France'. He then went on to praise the work the battalion had done on the railway, stressing that it was both essential and important, before finishing on an ominous note: 'I feel it is a pity that such a fine battalion should be on Pioneer work and therefore lost as a fighting unit'. To the suspicious men of the battalion this sounded as if they would be converted to conventional infantry and ordered 'over the bags'.[14]

There were also rumours passing among the men of the 7/York & Lancs. From mid-October 1917 the War Diary recorded between ten and twenty casualties a day while it ran the railway in the forward zone. There are no records of any drafts to replace the losses and in November, battalion HQ was asked for its views on a proposal that the unit should be converted to Light Railway Troops. If the conversion went ahead, it would mean more tools, equipment and the posting of some technical personnel. The C.O. replied by stating that he would not object to the proposal providing that the battalion could remain intact, keep its name and that the addition of technical personnel would not prejudice the promotion or position of the existing staff. Despite this positive response, the army staff obviously changed its mind and the battalion heard no more of the proposal.[15]

Like many pioneering duties, railway work was relatively safe and at times enjoyable. The losses of the 7/York & Lancs were excessive – the 17/N.F., for example, lost only seven killed and 62 wounded in five months of working in the Salient.[16] The 20/KRRC spent a very happy time with Canadian Railway Troops in 1917, its historian noting that 'most of us would have been well content to remain permanently working with the Canadians on this pleasant job'. The battalion's own division apparently missed its Pioneers for when the unit returned, the divisional band welcomed them back to camp. Railway work was also generally fairly undramatic, although on occasions, men could be killed in accidents and collisions.[17] Furthermore, if the enemy had good observation over the British areas tracks and dumps were regularly targeted. Engineers or Pioneers were usually called up to repair the damage and if the opportunity presented itself, Pioneers seized the chance to prove that they were not merely labourers. Shortly before the Battle of Messines opened for example, about twenty yards of a light railway near the Bois Carré were blown up. A corporal and ten men of the

6/East Yorks spent eight hours in the semi-darkness of a June night pushing up 15 truck loads of rails and sleepers to the gap. They next unloaded and repaired the damage – all within 400 feet of the enemy line.[18]

Endurance and courage of a different sort was required for railway work in Mesopotamia. The 8/Welch spent most of June and July 1917 pulling up one railway and rebuilding it else-where. The battalion was split into its four companies, with two pulling up the light railway line between Sindiyeh and Kifu, the third loading the rails and sleepers onto a river steamer while the fourth unloaded and relaid the track. The intention was to link this new line with the Baghdad – Samarrah broad gauge track at Sumaikchah station. In Flanders, their fellow Pioneers had mud and German shells to contend with; in the desert, the 8/Welch had heat, hostile Arabs and Turks and the desolate, ferocious terrain.

NOTES

1. Appendix I lists the total fatalities of all Pioneer battalions.
2. Unless otherwise stated, the detail comes from battalion War Diaries.
3. Although in the rear area, such work was not without its dangers: In January 1916 the Rifles lost two killed and 18 wounded when a train running over unballasted track was derailed.
4. War Diary of CRE Third Army, W.O.95.383
5. Shakespear, op.cit. p.49
6. Figures are taken from a nominal roll printed in the battalion history.
7. Shakespear, *18/Northumberland Fusiliers,* op.cit. p.69
8. Owing to a shortage of bolts in December 1916, the 12/KOYLI had not been able to replace wooden rails with steel ones. (W.D.)
9. A wide variety of track was used by the different armies, but the BEF usually, although not exclusively, used two weights – 9lbs and 16lbs. The decauville track had to be of the latter kind.
10. Report of Senior Officers' Conference, (Fourth Army, No.34/66). Crouch papers. (DLI Museum)
11. Report of C.E. IX Corps. Quoted in Addison, G. *The Work of the R.E. in the European War.* (Mackay, 1926) p.206
12. Gilvary, op.cit. p.59 Although the battalion was never officially converted to a Railway Construction unit, it did spend several days training in the means of laying light railways before it began work in

the Salient. The value of light railways for the evacuation of wounded was expressed in a letter from the Surgeon-General to the battalion. He stressed how the 'regular and methodical' evacuation of train loads of between 60 and 100 prevented the CCCs from being 'embarrassed' by having large numbers dumped upon them at one time. (W.D.)

13. Papers of Capt. Garvie. (Dept. of Documents, IWM)
14. Shakespear, op.cit. p.72
15. Gilvary, op.cit. p.63
16. Several of the the 17/N.F. fatalities from this period are buried in Buffs Road Cemetery.
17 In October 1917, L/Sgt. H. Lawrence of the 4/Coldstream Guards was killed in an accident involving a decauville locomotive.
18. Wyrall, op.cit. p.230

Chapter 7

"BUILD THEIR DUGOUTS, MAKE THEIR ROADS"

(Unknown Pioneer, 21/West Yorks)

Far away from the broiling heat and dust of the desert, in early 1917 at least one Pioneer battalion commander decided that he would have to instigate changes if his unit was to improve performance. When several officers of the 18/N.F. went to reconnoitre the trenches of what was to them a new sector, they found themselves in difficulty because not one possessed a map. Partly as a consequence of this mishap, and equally importantly as a consequence of the confusion the battalion experienced in the maze of trenches near Becourt on 1 July, the C.O. decided that from then on, one man per section would be 'systematically instructed in the divisional front line system'. Improving performance was to be a major consideration throughout the BEF in 1917. As far as the Pioneers were concerned the year would see the creation of the Pioneer school at Rouen and mass influxes of men transferred from the Royal Engineers. Meanwhile, preparations for Third Army's offensive at Arras went on in the caves deep beneath the ancient city and in the fields and woods of the rear areas.

The attack by Third Army was designed to coincide with an offensive by the French further south. The German defences to the east and south of the city had been sited with the expected thoroughness and care. Infantry assaults would attempt to push the enemy from the ridges overlooking the increasingly battered city. As usual, supplementary orders began to appear and training, when duty in the trenches permitted, became more

121

intensive. The Somme campaign had bogged down amid ever deteriorating battlefield conditions which at times had made communications impossible. For the forthcoming battle, greater care would be taken during the preparatory stages to ensure that the lack of adequate and passable roads and tracks would not again frustrate the work of the infantry and artillery.

The men of the 7/DLI quickly realized they were being used differently when the Arras campaign commenced. The confident expectation of a return to open warfare meant that the battalion was instructed not to follow behind the waves of attacking infantry in the normal manner, but to open up and maintain the tracks and roads leading to the front. The conditions under which the battalion laboured was later to be described as 'infinitely better'[1] than on the Somme, although the work was similarly unremitting. In some ways the work it did was not particularly different from that performed by at least sections of the battalion in earlier battles; road making had always, of course, been an essential part of the Pioneer's repertoire. But at Arras, it was the amount of time that the battalion was to spend on this task, at the expense of other equally familiar roles, that was to be different. The 7th Division also decided that it would not push its R.E. and Pioneers forward too soon after the infantry had gone over. Elements would certainly be kept back to clear roads servicing the front, but sections of both Engineers and Pioneers were expected to move across No Man's Land and lay tracks during the night following the attack.

A formidable amount of work had to be undertaken before the battle officially opened. Hampered by snow and frost the Pioneer battalion of the 1st Cavalry Division had begun work in January on double tracking the railway running from St. Pol towards Arras. By April it was attached to the Canadian Corps, employed in consolidating craters on Vimy ridge and helping to maintain a nearby light railway. Shortly after, the battalion moved closer to Arras and became attached to the 5th Division. It worked on trenches close to the sector where the 9th Division was preparing for its part in the offensive. The work done by the 9/Seaforth Highlanders and the R.E. Field Companies of the Scottish Division is fairly typical of that detailed to a division in

122

the run up to the battle. In the space of about two months the units dug or cleared 9,400 yards of trench; laid or cleared 12,000 yards of road; laid or repaired 3,800 yards of tramway; dug 14 observation posts, ten heavy trench mortar emplacements with at least ten feet of cover and 38 emplacements capable of with-standing hits by 4.7" shells; provided storage facilities for an additional 1,500 gallons of water; laid 2,000 yards of pipe, built three brigade HQ and one telephone exchange; strutted or improved 89 caves and dugouts and erected 4,013 bunks.[2] Most of this work was done during weather which alternated between heavy frosts, driving snow and rapid, trench-collapsing thaws.

Other battle orders followed familiar patterns. The 12/KOYLI were informed that the word 'Retire' was no longer part of the BEF's military language and that anyone using it should be considered an enemy. The 18/N.F. were warned that any soldier found with a self-inflicted wound would be arrested and a report containing the names of any witnesses to the act would be sent down the line with him. The 24/Manchester was cheerfully warned that any man who surrendered to the enemy without good reason would be tried after the war and shot. As Z Day approached specified battle surpluses were ordered and R.E. stores, ammunition, food and the other necessities of war, were organized for carriage to the front. Trench mortar sites were dug and new communication trenches, bomb stores, aid posts and dugouts excavated. Meanwhile, field guns and howitzers pounded the German lines, while gas barrages drenched their rear areas and front emplacements. After a short delay caused by a blizzard, the infantry went over. Several divisions reached their first objective, but during the course of the next days, as in previous battles, the attacks were frustrated by a combination of poor weather and tenacious German resistance.

Pioneers stuck to their tasks as the fortunes of battle eddied around them. One platoon of the 9/Seaforth, which had worked without rest for nearly 18 hours on an artillery track, reported with some relief that their new box respirators had proved 'most effective'.[3] The 9/North Staffs made roads near Tilloy passable for field guns and were next shifted to work on trenches and infantry tracks when the attack in front of them faltered. Later, a composite company of one platoon from each company took over the line and sent out patrols to link up with the 63rd Division. Among other jobs, the 6/Argyll spent five nights wiring in the open, while the 7/York & Lancs worked for over three weeks repairing trenches and making Feuchy into a 'tidy ruin'. During a later attack the 9/North Staffs followed directly behind the 13/Rifle Brigade and connected up shell holes to form the new front line. The Pioneers used their rifles and Lewis guns on the German lines, eliciting what was described as a 'feeble' response from the enemy even when the Staffords had their heads clearly above the parapet. About 40 Germans – some unwounded and of 'good physique' – surrendered to the Pioneers. The area over which the battle swayed was undermined by an extensive network of caves and as German positions fell, Pioneers and R.E. were sent forward to clear the underground works of booby traps and debris. Essential as these tasks were, the 'most important work' during this period was according to one R.E. officer with perhaps a degree of self interest, 'undoubtedly the repair and maintenance of roads'.[4] He explained that between 40 and 50 craters were filled in or bridged in about 35 miles of road and concluded that: 'It would have been quite impossible to keep pace with the advance had not most of the R.E. and Pioneers been available for this work'.

Again, casualties among Pioneer units, although substantial, were not severe. One of the 9/North Staffs thought that his battalion had 'caught it pretty heavy for Pioneers', believing that it had lost four officers and about 60 men.[5] The War Diary gives three officers and ten other ranks killed, with over 100 wounded and 11 missing. The final figure of killed and died of wounds amounted to three officers and 32 men. A diarist of the 5/Northants thought their casualties were 'more serious than usual',[6] with over 50 killed, whereas the 6/Argyll had only ten killed and 22 wounded. Because it spent much of its time working on roads behind the lines, the 7/DLI lost only eight dead while the 7/York & Lancs, labouring nearer the front, lost 29 killed or died of wounds.

Further down the Hindenburg Line British divisions were battering away at the the German stronghold of Bullecourt. The village itself, earlier the scene of a disastrous attack by the Australians, was nothing but an obliterated ruin of shattered farms and cottages. Beneath the rubble, in the cellars and across the surrounding fields, lay a formidable line of German defences. As the troops fought their way across the fields and into the outskirts of the village, communication trenches were dug to provide cover for relieving troops. The 24/Manchester was ordered to dig such a trench, known as Bullecourt Avenue, from the Ecoust St.Mein – Noreuil road north through the railway embankment and on to the slowly advancing British front lines. In view of the chaotic situation, the exact position of the respective front lines then being unknown, the Manchester's C.O. insisted that a qualification be added to the CRE's original instruction. The rider ordered that: 'The Battalion is not to be sacrificed. If the shelling is too bad, you will return to camp'. Over the next few weeks the trench was dug and maintained by the Pioneers who stayed in long after their division had been withdrawn. By the time the battalion was itself taken out, 18 of its men were dead and 75 had been evacuated down the line. On one night alone 109 had been affected by a gas barrage, but prompt action in donning respirators meant that only six were actually evacuated. The majority of the others remained at work. In recognition of the extremely unpleasant weeks spent in the area, the *Official History* noted the work done by the 24th on Bullecourt Avenue: 'But for this piece of work, which was carried out with magnificient courage, it would have been impossible to keep the troops in the village supplied with small arms ammunition and grenades'.[7]

While the Oldham Comrades and other Pioneer battalions worked among the shell holes and ruined trenches of the Arras sector, preparations were in train for what was to be the most meticulously planned offensive yet attempted. Before trying to throw the Germans from the high ground to the east of Ypres, the southern shoulder of the Salient had first to be secured. This necessitated seizing the Messines ridge – a low but significant hump of land stretching from just south of Ypres to Ploegsteert. Months of work had resulted in the excavation of deep mines, now primed and ready with thousands of pounds of explosive concealed within their galleries. Pioneers had been heavily involved in helping R.E. and infantry dig the passages and distribute the spoil. When the mines were blown on 7 June 1917 one observing Pioneer of the 19/Middlesex described the scene as 'the most wonderful sight of my life . . . It was a great but terrible sight and it seemed as though Hell had been let loose'.[8]

The effect of the mines upon the German defenders was devastating. Many were simply blown to oblivion, while those who survived were so dazed they offered little resistance to the advancing British and Dominion troops. The principal task of the Pioneers was to clear the roads behind the former German positions of debris and obstacles. In some areas the shelling and explosions had all but obliterated the roads; huge numbers of planks, logs and boards were brought forward and laid across filled shell holes and former trenches. The 16/Royal Irish Rifles for example, began work just after 0800 and had completed two tracks by early afternoon. The routes had been earlier marked out with stakes and when finished, snaked respectively for over 2,500 and 3,400 yards across the newly captured ground. As soon as the tracks were open two companies of the Rifles were put on digging new communication trenches to the crest of the ridge. During the course of the subsequent nights over 1,300 yards of trench, at least five feet deep, were opened for use. The battalion was then engaged on building a decauville track towards the ridge. Twenty-two days after the battle had begun, the battalion's War Diary simply recorded, 'REST!'

Second Army's success at Messines paved the way for the proposed offensive originally intended to drive the Germans from the Belgian Channel ports. Volumes have been written on the controversy surrounding Haig's plans and on the reasons for its ultimately limited success. This is not the place to reopen the debate on whether it is the politicians or generals who should bear the ultimate responsibility. To the troops involved in its execution, and largely unaware of the acrimony waging behind their burdened backs, it proved to be a battle of unremitting demands upon their powers of endurance. There were some initial successes, but in the subsequent weeks the weather and atrocious ground conditions combined to frustrate the British

126

efforts to secure what had become less ambitious objectives. By the middle of November the pummelled sea of mud, which represented what was left of the Passchendaele ridge, had been reached and taken. The early setbacks had convinced the generals that the only way to at least gain the higher ground was to organize and execute a series of set piece battles. These attacks, which stated their objectives in terms of scores rather than thousands of yards, were made across ground which swallowed men, guns and animals. When the battle was finally closed down, for a cost of perhaps 300,000 British casualties, the advance had secured five miles of poisoned ground and created a new salient which in places appeared more dangerous and exposed than the original. Having exhausted themselves in this titanic struggle, both sides settled down to endure the winter months in what had already become a zone of utter despair. The Pioneers shared the misfortunes alongside their comrades in the infantry and artillery. Their work was unceasing and their general discomfort exacerbated by the poor condition of their camps and the unrelenting misery of the weather. Unit morale and the ability to find working parties of reasonable size had been affected by huge drafts of men transferred from the R.E. The new arrivals were frequently hurled into the maelstrom *en masse*, having had little or no time to acquaint themselves with the work or nature of their new battalions. Nevertheless, the work that was asked of them was usually done. For a multitude of reasons there was little about Third Ypres which went according to plan, but what is certain, is that without the stoic and indefatigable labours of the Engineers and Pioneers on both sides of No Man's Land, the task of their respective infantry and artillery would have appeared that much more awesome.

It was the northern sector that witnessed the furthest advances on the first day of the battle. The 38th and 51st Divisions forced the Germans from the Pilckem ridge and back in the direction of Langemarck and St. Julien. Companies of the 19/Welch laid tracks across the former No Man's Land, while others carried forward the slabs and boarding. The 9/Gordon Highlanders cleared two cross-country tracks and in four days laid over 2,600 yards of trench board. During that time the battalion lost 61 men in addition to those who were evacuated sick. The action prompted the adjutant to note that in comparison with Arras, the shelling at Ypres was far more severe. In modest tone, the War Diary of the 22/DLI noted that the first two days of the battle, during which time it too laid tracks, called for 'no deeds of individual gallantry or endurance, but much scope for the exhibition of patience and determined coolness'. The 6/East Yorks showed such cool determination in August while laying tracks over former German trenches on the Pilckem ridge, losing 33 dead and 95 wounded in the process. The 18/Middlesex suffered a similar number of casualties, losing over 20 dead and almost 100 wounded when digging some 12,500 yards of trenches, flammenwerfer emplacements and erecting 800 coils of wire.

In general, Pioneers were used in the same way as they had been at Arras. Although there were to be exceptions, the experience of the Somme had taught that the strategy of attaching companies of Pioneers to attacking brigades should be largely abandoned. In future the infantry were expected to do their own consolidating, leaving the Pioneers to perform other duties. Ypres was also a different sort of battle to that fought on the Somme. The German defences in Flanders were not line upon line of front, support and switch trenches dug deep with underground passages and refuges. The shallow water table in the Ypres area meant that breastworks rather than trenches were the norm. These were supplemented by numerous strategically placed, and at times almost invisible, concrete pill boxes. As the battlefield deteriorated into the morass which has become synonymous with Third Ypres, the front lines were not lines, but merely shell holes containing a few, usually soaked infantrymen marooned within the festering marsh. It was not possible to 'consolidate' in the conventional meaning of the word, and besides, the advance was destined to continue until the Passchendaele ridge was taken. Apart from throwing out some coils of wire in front of the occupied shell holes, there was little that could profitably be done to make captured ground more secure. The restricted and confined area in which the battle was fought also made the construction of dugouts or more permanent positions an extremely dangerous undertaking. The infantry would take what little shelter they could in captured pill boxes or brimming holes and wait until relieved or ordered forward to continue the advance. The key to success lay in bringing forward the guns and sufficient ammunition over gained ground and pushing on towards the ridge. This, and the passage of burdened troops towards the front, could only be achieved if the bogs and bekes could be made, and kept, passable. Consequently, the principal task allotted to the Pioneers was to lay and maintain the roads and tracks, the arteries of the offensive, in the forward zones.

An essential element of the new strategy was to allow sufficient time between the stages to permit the guns to be brought forward and their new positions or pits prepared. The pressure on the artillery to move as quickly as practicable meant equal pressure upon the R.E. and Pioneers to extend the slab roads along which the guns would be hauled. The CRE of the 7th Division clearly believed that insufficient time and thought had gone into the staff's planning for the attacks of October:

> Five days only were allowed for preparation both before 4 and 26 October attacks. With a week's extra notice a tram line and a communication trench could have been provided which would have led to a reduction in casualties. The vital question of communications could have been vastly improved. Physical difficulties of bad ground, bad weather, also hostile shelling can be and were overcome by the energy and devotion of the troops concerned, but to give only days, when weeks may be required is perhaps chancing over-much. Physical difficulties and hostile fire are expected, but I respectfully submit that the uncalled for handicap of a precarious supply of necessary material, and an utterly unreliable system of transport, should be eliminated; the latter are subjects that demand reform.[9]

To the staff, time was of supreme importance. General Plumer wanted to forge ahead with the stage-by-stage programme to ensure that the army would on top of the ridge before the winter snows arrived. The autumn rain was bad enough, but the idea of spending another winter under the perpetual gaze of the enemy on the higher ground was fraught with additional dangers. Despite the apparent ability of the Germans to make it rain at will, the battles had to continue.

Under such intense pressure it is unsurprising that many Pioneer battalions used their War Diaries to record the difficulties and frustrations they faced during these weeks. The 7/DLI had to overcome tremendous problems when attempting to build a mule track up the Passchendaele ridge. Even with the help of 100 Belgian troops as additional labour, the Durhams were shelled off their work on several occasions. Similarly, the adjutant of the 24/Manchester complained that:

> Progress of work was very slow in consequence of having to carry planks such a long way from the dump to the job and also in consequence of hostile artillery barrages put up as a reply to practise barrages by our own troops.

Troops had to carry forward the intractable trench boards, the heavy sleepers, the awkward rolls of wire and the cumbersome fascines along treacherous tracks and in foul darkness lit only by the glare of flares and the flash of bursting shells.

Where there was still an existing stretch of *pavé*, the slab roads were sometimes laid alongside it. The 10/DCLI built such a track by laying 400 yards along the Wieltje – Gravenstafel road with the slabs butting against the *pavé* curb. It took almost eight days to lay the stretch, probably employing the usual ratio of one man laying to four men carrying. Service manuals described how field engineering *should* be completed but the realities of attempting to lay roads and tracks across the slough of Ypres was often very different. According to the prescribed method, mined craters or shell holes in roads had first to be pumped clear of water. They were then filled to within 18 inches of the rim with alternately laid courses of sandbags and finished off with rammed dry earth or chalk. Finally, the slab could be laid across. The slabs had pickets on the side to tie them in place and beneath, longtitudinal sleepers laid up to four feet apart. In the swamps of Flanders and in the heat of battle, the Germans did not always oblige by remaining as passive observers to these operations. If holes could not be avoided, they were normally filled with whatever sludge or debris was available, and the boards then laid across. The standard trench board was 6'5" long and 1'6" wide. It was covered with spaced 3" slats and sometimes with thick wire to help give grip. In heavily shelled areas tracks for the infantry were usually, although not invariably, laid directly on the ground with no attachment to transoms or trestles. To complicate the issue and make more demands on limited labour, pack mules could not be put over infantry tracks; as their hooves broke the 1" thick wooden slats, additional fascine tracks had to be laid. These involved more work than those for two-legged beasts because bulky fascines first had to be lugged forward – possibly as far as a mile from the end of a slab road or tramway – before then being covered with a thick layer of earth. Finally, wooden slabs were laid on longtitudinal runners. In order to avoid damage by animals to the rails of tramways and light railways, mule tracks were also often laid between the rails.[10]

Examples from two War Diaries will serve to illustrate the means by which such roads were laid and the conditions in which those who worked on them laboured. Following the attack by the 49th and 66th Divisions, the 19/L.F. struggled to build a plank road near Gravenstafel. The work was under the direct observation of the Germans, with the ground to be traversed cut to pieces by shell fire and rapidly disintegrating into a putrid bog. The shell holes were drained and filled with sandbags and the planks laid on top. It was decided that the work could not adequately be completed during darkness, so the whole process was finished off in daylight. The working parties were constantly shelled by guns of many calibres; this resulted in a casualty list of 12 killed and 64 wounded for the 14 days it took to build. In spite of the difficulties, the work was pushed through and completed in time for the Canadian Corps to use the track for its attack towards Passchendaele. The 11/King's too spent a considerable time working on tracks that were to be used during the Canadian attack. Recognition for the battalion's efforts on improving the Menin Road and Plumer's Drive arrived in the form of an exceptionally warm message of appreciation from Lt.Gen. Currie, commander of the Canadian Corps.

131

In the same area the 4/South Lancs had toiled to keep the St. Jean – Gravenstafel road open, especially in the sector where it crossed the original German front lines. This was:

> A very difficult job. The ground was very badly pock-marked by huge shell holes, 10 feet in diameter and 4 to 6 feet deep. These holes were filled in on the day of the action. At night the heavy rain settled the new earth. This, coupled with pack and artillery limber traffic, made the road a sea of mud. To repair it, the road was closed to all traffic and . . . fascines laid in the direction of the road, 2 feet apart, well bedded, and overlapping 2 feet at the joints. On these, again fascines were laid crossways to the direction of the road. The road was 20 feet wide. Tanks came back to our lines along the road and squeezed the lot flat, thus making a good hard foundation.

Having built or repaired the roads along which the animals would slither with their burdens and the infantry file to their jumping off points, the Pioneers had also to keep them open during the attacks. Platoons were normally spread along the tracks, with the greatest concentration being where the ground was wettest. Their task was to replace any length of board that might disappear into the swamp or be smashed by shelling. As he made his way towards his allocated position, each Pioneer carried a trench board besides his pick or shovel, rifle, wire cutters, notice boards and 120 rounds. The sections usually worked four hourly reliefs, sometimes spending days on these exposed duties.

On occasions, Pioneers went ahead of the infantry to prepare the ground over which the assault would take place. On one such operation the 22/DLI was ordered to lay bridges over the Hanebeke. In normal times this would not have been too difficult, but instead of being a mere four feet wide ditch, the months of shelling had converted the stream into a quagmire of oozing mud. It was decided that two six feet bridges should be placed on their four feet trestles end on end, thus making a twelve feet wide causeway. Two hundred mainly older privates were specially picked for the job. One hundred of them each carried a bridge, and the other 100 carried a pair of trestles; corporals and sergeants carried hammers, six inch spikes and axes. The party left their own lines three minutes before Zero, the noise of their hammering lost in the crescendo of the barrage screaming overhead. The infantry followed, traversed the bog, and went on to secure their objectives. The Pioneers stood by, some knee deep in the miasma, to repair the bridges and keep them passable. This required cold-blooded endurance of the highest order and, after spending several hours on the receiving end, some of the men sought and gained permission from the officers to follow the infantry and have a go at the Germans themselves.[11]

Constantly exposed to the elements and German shelling, which had the tracks the Pioneers repaired neatly registered, casualties from sickness, deaths and wounds rose remorselessly. A sample of battalions which served in the Salient shows that, as before on the Somme, the casualties were never dramatic, but none the less considerable. In October and November 1917 the 6/Welch lost 45 dead, the 14/Worcester 48, while the 7/Yorks & Lancs lost 36 in September and October. By contrast, the 18/N.F. had only eight deaths in two months and the 19/Welch, 19. The 13/Gloucester spent five months at the front, mainly working around Admiral's Road and Wieltje; during that period, which embraced both the drier periods of July and the autumn rains, it had two officers and 23 other ranks killed, five died of wounds, four missing, 135 wounded and 15 wounded at duty. These figures do not appear particularly severe, but it is important to remember that wounds and deaths were not the only reason why battalions might not be able to put as many men on working parties as official estimates might expect. In the month of July – that is during the preparatory stages rather than the period of infantry assaults, the 9/South Staffs had a total of 1,369 men report sick. Of these, 550 were given medicine and duty, 26 were evacuated to hospital and the remaining 992 either excused work completely or given light duty. When the average strength of Pioneer battalions at the time appears to have been about 780, including those details who would not normally be available for fatigue parties, this figure represents a significant proportion of working strength. One CRE reported that a Pioneer battalion might be able to put approximately 450 men to work when it first moved into the battle area, but 'after a few days', this figure would be reduced by about one half. Although he did not state his actual strength at the end of August, Lt.Col. Langham of the 5/Sussex wrote: 'Reinforcements badly needed as effective working strength getting very low'. His battalion had lost about 100 men to hospital suffering from the effects of gas in July and had been working almost continuously. However, the unit had sustained only 42 fatalities since its last recorded strength return of 41 officers and 1,085 other ranks in July.[12]

As they worked in the mud, amongst the rotting corpses and gas-soaked filth of poisoned ground, many Pioneers won awards for bravery. Sgt Carmichael of the 9/North Staffs covered a grenade thrown at his working party with his steel helmet; standing on the helmet when it exploded, he saved his section, but suffered a fractured ankle. Carmichael was subsequently awarded the Victoria Cross. Others won the Military Medal and the DCM, but most just tried to do their job and stay alive. Frequently shelled from their tasks, they could often do nothing until the fury passed on. The 5/Cheshire was supposed to be building shelters in Glencorse Wood when a German barrage crashed around them and forced the troops to cower for hours among the splintered boughs and shell holes. In September three companies of the 4/South Lancs were employed laying duckboards near the Schuler Galleries. An intense barrage of shells and machine gun fire erupted around them, but the men stuck to their task and won the praise of their colonel.

Other jobs were not quite so dangerous. The 7/DLI spent some time clearing captured pill boxes. The task was 'unpleasant but lucrative', owing to the considerable amount of German currency left by the dead or captured enemy.[13] The 10/DCLI spent much of October erecting Nissen huts and horse standings, while the Lewis gunners of the 5/SWB were congratulated for bringing down two enemy aircraft and breaking up another formation. Providing anti-aircraft cover, sometimes some distance to the rear, was a fairly common task for Pioneers and no doubt one that was appreciated. More mundane tasks in the Salient consisted of improving camps and building brigade and divisional HQs. The 19/Middlesex spent from October 1916 to mid-September of the following year working in and around the Ypres sector. It lost only 52 dead during the period but probably enjoyed its later sojourn at La Panne considerably more. The 16/RIR had arrived in Flanders before the Battle of Messines and only left in late September; its own division had gone to the Somme four weeks earlier. The Rifles were retained and attached to the 58th and 42nd Divisions because these two units had not yet been allocated their own Pioneer battalion. The 24/Manchester provide a good example of the time many Pioneers spent working in the front area. During September and October, the unit was officially at rest for only two days of the 37 it spent labouring in the area around Clapham Junction and Shrewsbury Forest. During that period of toiling in mud and rain, the War Diary makes no mention of the men having the opportunity to have a bath or a change of clothing.

After they were finally withdrawn from the Salient, the Irish Rifles and the Cheshires moved, with their divisions, to take part in the Battle of Cambrai. There were no new tactics or methods of using Pioneers in this battle, their principal function again being to keep communications as open as possible. Roads for tanks and cavalry were laid or extended and gun pits for the additional artillery dug. Carrying, wiring and support parties of the 12/Yorks earned the praise of its divisional commander for slogging their way into the inferno of Bourlon Wood. The 5/Northants made a stand at Revelon Farm when the Germans counter-attacked and subsequently remained in the front lines as infantry for four days. Near Bullecourt a few days earlier, the demands made upon the discipline, endurance and skill of the 11/Hants 'contributed appreciably'[14] to the retention of recently won positions.

In other, quieter, parts of the line, Pioneers continued to toil at their normal tasks and were occasionally called upon to do more. One company of the 19/N.F. was near the Birdcage when the enemy carried out a determined raid. One platoon helped the garrison to repel the Germans and lost a total of 12 killed or died of wounds and 23 wounded. In the adjoining Epéhy sector, the 4/South Lancs laboured at building dugouts and repairing trenches with far fewer losses. In October it had only two men wounded seriously enough to require evacuation and in December had but one man killed and 10 wounded. Even luckier were the men of the 12/Notts & Derby who worked on dugouts and galleries in Templeux Quarries. In October, only one man was recorded as having been wounded.[15] The 12/LNL sent 160 men to hospital that same month, only three of whom were wounded; the remainder were men who fell sick after the battalion had travelled from Macedonia to the Middle East. Contemporary opinion believed the sickness was the consequence of the troops over-indulging in the readily available supplies of fresh fruit. One battalion recorded that, 'so many oranges were eaten on the march that . . . drafts marching up from Gaza were known to have followed the trail of orange peel, and thus found their way across Palestine to Jerusalem'.[16]

Like the 1/12th Loyal North Lancs, the 5/Royal Irish Regiment was withdrawn from its division and left Salonika for the Egyptian desert. Eighty-eight of its members were admitted to hospital in the week it was due to leave and another 78 men went to hospital immediately the HMT *Briton* docked at Alexandria. The battalion re-equipped and within a few days was camped in the desert 'with no vegetation in sight'. It came under orders of the 60th Division, although some companies were working for the 53rd and 74th Divisions. After a few weeks training the battalion began digging wells, erecting water troughs and laying decauville track. By the time it rejoined its own division it had also been clearing mud and metalling the main road to Jerusalem. A major offensive began in December, taking place across a terrain 'absolutely roadless and with very few mule paths, extremely rocky and precipitous to an extent of which the map referred to gives no hint'. One company built a road which took a 6 inch howitzer and tractor 'where a mule could hardly go before'; progress of all companies was reported to HQ by means of a heliograph. Consolidating roads over such a barren landscape required not only donkeys, camels and native labour, but also a great deal of engineering expertise.

Other divisions and their Pioneers remained in the bleak winter of the Salonika front. The first impression of Salonika given to 2Lt. Simpson of the 26/Middlesex was 'indescribable . . .

more like a page from the Arabian Nights'; this opinion changed when he was sent up to the Lembert Plain. This, thought Simpson, was the 'most desolate, God-forsaken country one could ever wish to be dropped in'.[17] The battalion attempted to build roads and mine dugouts through solid rock, while flies, malaria, sudden storms, intense heat and poor food combined to make their lives as uncomfortable as possible. In recognition of the exacting conditions, in July hours of work were reduced to five a day. Nevertheless the battalion toiled away clearing a site for an aerodrome, building a slaughter house for the mobile veterinary section, a new divisional HQ, a swimming bath and, above all, maintaining roads. A major undertaking was to improve communications once the Struma river had been crossed. With the help of 800 infantry, the entire battalion spent nearly six weeks bridging the river and extending the decauville over and beyond its banks. The 8/Ox & Bucks performed similar tasks, again with the emphasis on improving communications. Ropeways and roads were blasted through rock and camps erected in the inhospitable terrain. Pte. Gray spent several miserable weeks of his early time with the battalion marooned and isolated by deep snow in a telephone relay station high in the mountains. His army career took a turn for the better when, as an accomplished pianist, he became a member of a concert party and consequently spent most of his time in the rear.[18]

Pioneers in the Balkans did not have to endure the same intensity of shelling as did their comrades on the Western Front. Life might also have been a little less frenetic, but the hardships were just as real. They were more likely to die from sickness rather than wounds, and even evacuation home was no guarantee that they were safe; a good proportion of them died from malaria in such unlikely places as Lancashire and Wales. The high percentage of those who died from sickness rather than battle injuries – for example 83% in the 23/Welch – demonstrates that although total fatalities were substantially fewer than in Europe and enemy activity less damaging, the risk of dying was still significant.[19]

On the Western Front the huge loss of life and the appalling physical hardships of Third Ypres clearly had a demoralizing effect on Major Cecil Hall, an officer of the 22/DLI. In a despondent letter to his sister in November 1917, Hall admitted:

> I am thoroughly tired with war and the great waste of lives and energy which are badly needed for greater things. It is very sad to see the numbers of men who have gone under. In good time I suppose it will all end, but it is a great trial of patience. I am sure though that it would be a great mistake to make an unsatisfactory peace now – the next generation, including your son, would probably have to fight it all over again.[20]

Major Hall was killed in May 1918; his nephew's generation did, of course, 'fight it all over again' twenty years later.

A Pioneer of the 9/North Staffs turned his venom on those at home who were escaping or evading call up. Having heard of the death of one brother, Percy Mellors wrote to his sister complaining of another brother, Horace, who 'walks about in freedom in England'. Mellors promised that, 'If I come through this safe and come home, I will insult him'. He closed the letter by declaring that he was 'fed up with it all. I will never grumble at home as long as I live.'[21] Captain Alfred Baer of the 18/Middlesex, who, in his letters at least, seems to have maintained a reasonably cheerful attitude, devised a cunning plan with the intention of securing him a temporary reprieve from the front. In a letter to his sister he asked:

> You might select a wife for me just for the duration; a married man has a much more sympathetic hearing on the leave question . . . besides, I've got that £50 tucked away in Projectiles . . . but get an heiress as it would save a lot of bother. I should not be very particular as to her looks as she is only going to be temporary and I could get a separation or a divorce when I get home on leave each time.[22]

Whether sister Elsie managed to secure a suitable partner for Baer is unknown, but he did survive the war. He wrote the letter from a hospital bed, no doubt enjoying the release from the dangers and fatigue of almost incessant work.

In addition to the usual jobs already described, Pioneers were expected to undertake a huge variety of tasks. They were often mundane and often relatively safe, but the frequent demands made upon their skills meant there was little opportunity for genuine rest. One source recorded that of the 19/L.F., 'some part of it was always at work, week after week, month after month, its War Diary consisting largely of a list of work carried out which provide no exciting stories, but which were essential to the safety and welfare of the troops'.[23] Another non-Pioneer chronicler described 'Pioneer work as always an unenviable task' and their life as a 'seemingly everlasting round of work'.[24] The work could often involve tasks connected with the several canals and rivers which traversed the rear areas. It could range from lowering the water level in La Basse Canal by means of pumping barges (the enemy were trying to *raise* the level to flood British positions), to unloading coal barges and building and camou-flaging temporary bridges across the Lys. Other slightly more unusual tasks which fell upon Pioneers included chasing escaped German POWs near St. Omer,[25] furnishing a 'church' in a dug out on Vimy,[26] ploughing and planting vegetables for French farmers and, perhaps the most bizarre, digging shell holes in a divisional practice ground.[27] It appears that on occasions Pioneers were also assumed to be responsible for keeping trenches in a reasonable state of hygiene. 2Lt. Croft of the 5/SWB complained bitterly to the O.C. 82nd Field Company, that it was not his fault that a platoon of North Staffordshires did not have latrines in its trench, and that he was certainly not about to 'accept responsibility for the nuisances committed by them'.[28] The 18/Middlesex had been detailed to perform sanitary duties and attempted to construct incinerators for faecal matter. After several experiments the men gave up and resorted to buckets. The Oldham Pals were similarly ordered to do something about the 'deplorable' sanitary condition of the trenches which could not 'altogether be attributed to troops of other nationalities', and to organize the sanitary arrangments for the train which brought the cadre of the 7th Division from Italy in 1919.

A diarist of the 9/Gordon Highlanders thought of all the jobs it was asked to do, the most 'agreeable' were tree cutting and timber shaping, the least being installing gas cylinders in the trenches and fusing Mills bombs.[29] Several battalions, for example the 5/Northants and the 14/N.F. had parties of men regularly working in saw mills or in the woods nearby. Concreting observation and machine gun posts was also a common task from 1917 onwards. In January 1918 the 19/L.F. was engaged on converting a series of former German pill boxes near Zonnebeke to form part of a new corps reserve line. The mebus, which had been battered by both British and later German artillery, were to be incorporated within a system of fire and communication trenches. Work was handicapped because there was disagreement among the engineers as to how the concrete should be laid. The 5/Northants also experienced problems when concreting machine gun posts to the west of Armentieres in the same month. In this instance, it was not so much a case of confusion about laying the stuff, but a lack of it. The canal along which the concrete was to be transported was flooded and barges could not get up. Shortages of materials is another frequent complaint in the War Diaries: the 12/Yorks was forced to build stables without roofs at Manancourt and one of the cavalry Pioneer battalions regularly noted that a shortage of sand bags was delaying its work.

Several battalion War Diaries note the difficulties caused by almost continual working of maintaining levels of skills among NCOs and specialists. The problem was exacerbated by regular demands for Pioneers to work in divisional workshops and schools of instruction. At times, the number of men involved could be significant. For example, in November 1917, at a time when it was already over stretched to find sufficient men for working parties, the 11/King's sent 50 men to form a corps workshop. This unit was clearly a battalion which intended to use the skills of its men to full advantage because within a month of arriving overseas, it had established three brigade workshops. These establishments absorbed three officers and 60 other ranks, most of whom are known to have been carpenters, blacksmiths, tinsmiths and fitters. Two months later the unit also set up a divisional armourer's shop. This fell under the control of the battalion rather than the R.E., whereas the brigade workshops were under the general supervision and regulation of the CRE. When it returned to the Salient in 1917, the battalion opened a small Pioneer school for infantry NCOs at Wulverghem. Here they were attached to the Pioneer companies for four days and received instruction in digging, draining, revetting and general trench maintenance. The 18/N.F. was forced to abandon its shift system of working in August 1917 – in which three companies worked in the forward area while the other rested – partly owing to pressure of work and partly because it was so short-handed. When it was brought back to strength the battalion introduced a new system in which four other ranks, one captain and two subalterns went back to the rear every five days and had four clear days of rest. This arrangement was 'much appreciated'.

Pioneer battalions did not take part in brigade training schemes, but frequently sent small groups of men to corps schools for instruction in infantry skills. However, the most usual way of trying to keep their men up to standard was to organize courses specifically for the battalion. The 19/L.F. ran its training programmes by allowing each of the companies to keep one of its platoons in camp at any one time. Other units appear to have instigated their programmes whenever pressure of work allowed. Such occasions also provided the opportunity to experiment with different methods of work. During one such occasion, the 2/Monmouth tried three alternative means of digging trenches: the first, called the 'intensive method' required teams of three, in which each man worked for two minutes on a three yards stretch of trench, and rested for four minutes. The 'semi-intensive' method had three men working for ten minutes on two men's tasks, with five minute's rest, while the 'ordinary' method had one man working on his allocation of five feet of trench, working and resting as he wished. The assessment concluded that this last method was the most productive. Similarly, the 19/N.F. decided that sand bagging should be done by teams of seven men; Number 1 should lay, 2 and 3 carry and the other four fill. At other and more frequent times, training was done on the job. In September 1916 the War Diary of the 20/KRRC noted that the battalion's work in the Hulloch-Loos sector was 'distinctly useful and the experience of mining and

141

making deep dugouts added greatly to the all-round value of the men from a Pioneering point of view'.

The 37th Division used the rare opportunity of having all its units out on rest at the same time and within a compact area to hold a divisional competition in the use of the Yukon pack. Two teams of 11 men from each of the three infantry brigades, as well as those from the R.E., Pioneers and machine gun battalion, competed to load and carry three full water tins, four picks, six shovels, one box of SAA, eight Stokes bombs, two coils of wire, two trench boards, three boxes of Mills bombs, ten large screw pickets, one case of rations and 14 filled Lewis gun magazines, over an obstacle course of about half a mile. The team of Pioneers came fourth, but the individual race, in which a man had to carry four picks and six shovels, was won easily by a Pioneer. The real significance of the event was to test and confirm the superiority of the Yukon pack over other means of carrying heavy, bulky equipment and stores to the front.

Nevertheless, the job with which Pioneers are most usually associated is digging. Given the original instruction by the War Office that at least 50% of a Pioneer battalion should have been used to such work, this is hardly surprising. It might seem inglorious but it was certainly dangerous and demanding. A War Diary might simply record that a certain yardage of trench had been excavated. What it does not so often mention is the circumstances in which that earth was dug: the consuming darkness, the energy-sapping mud, the loose tangled barbed wire which snagged and constricted movement, the marking tapes obliterated by shell fire, the shrieking arrival of splintering shells, the searching traverses of an enemy machine gun and the ever present horrors of insidious, seeping gas. One former Pioneer of the 7/DLI recalled:

> It is one thing to dig a trench through good, unbroken ground, but quite a different affair where the shell holes lie so thick that it is difficult to distinguish one crater from another, and the sides must be supported as one goes. And when after a barrage of such a nature as those which preceded the attacks on the Somme, a trench became an almost shapeless trace a little below the surface

of the ground and was filled for many yards with debris of the shattered parapet, splintered timber, tangled barbed wire and here and there, the dead. 'Clearing' was an even more difficult task than digging . . . But when, following on days of fighting, the infantry, ashen white, bearded, and slimed with mud, came after relief down a communication trench newly dug, thankful for its protection, one felt amply repaid for the days and nights of unceasing labour.[30]

Neither were the responsibilities of the officer in charge of the working party as straightforward as might be expected:

On these jobs, the subaltern's lot was not a happy one. The commander of each platoon first had to go out alone in No Man's Land to reconnoitre the ground and decide where the new trench should be dug. He has to ascertain such points as depth of existing trenches and how they were drained; commit to his memory any marked features on the ground and decide on the number of men he must take out to dig the required area. He has to organize the working party, arranging the rations, equipment, etc . . . find out the best route up to the area of operation, check on the nearest Dressing Station . . . and make sure that every man has his rifle and equipment by his side in case of surprise attack.[31]

On most occasions, the Pioneer subaltern in charge of a party striving to wire or dig amidst the darkness of a hostile night must have felt very alone. The responsibility of command, combined with a possible lack of confidence in his own technical ability, might have been sufficient for him to call down a torrent of abuse upon those who despatched him to the task. It is likely that his company commander or his C.O. had been directly responsible for sending him, but they were probably acting upon the orders of the CRE. The relationship between the Pioneers and the R.E. was of crucial importance to the completion of work coming under the aegis of field engineering and thus to the overall efficiency of a division. Aspects of this relationship have already been touched upon; it is appropriate now to consider more fully how the liaison between the two arms operated in the field.

143

NOTES

1. Unpublished history of 7/DLI. (DLI Museum) Unless otherwise stated, the detail comes from battalion War Diaries.
2. Ewing, J. *9th Division,* op.cit. Appendix VI
3. In September 1917, GHQ 7th Division thought it necessary to issue a memo to all its units refuting contemporary statements allegedly made by men returning to the Base. These troops apparently complained that their box respirators had proved to be useless. (Walsh papers in Oldham Local Studies Library)
4. *Extracts from Reports of Chief Engineers and CREs on Recent Operations (excluding those of 2nd Army), August 1917.* (Walsh papers, Oldham Local Studies Library)
5. Mellors papers. (Liddle Collection)
6. *History of the Northamptonshire Regiment,* op.cit. p.283
7. *Official History of the Great War, 1917,* Vol.2
8. Diary of H.G.Howes. (Dept. of Documents, IWM)
9. Report of the 7th Division's CRE attached to War Diary of 24/Manchester.
10. See Addison, op.cit for more technical information.
11. Davidson, op.cit. For an easily accessible official report on how communications were maintained during Third Ypres, see *Official History,* 1917 Vol.II p.213-218. (Report by CRE, Guards Division).
12. Langham might have believed in the principle that if you complain and request often enough, someone in authority will eventually respond. In February 1916, despite a strength of 31 officers and 747 other ranks, he complained that he needed another 250 men 'urgently' to continue with the work in hand. (W.D.)
13. Unpublished history of 7/DLI, op.cit.
14. Atkinson, A.T. *The Royal Hampshire Regiment,* (Maclehose & Co. 1950-52) Vol.2 p.257
15. The *Soldiers Died* roll for the battalion records one man who died of wounds in October.
16. Wylly, H.C. *The Loyal North Lancashire Regiment,* (R.U.S.I., 1933) p.352
17. Simpson, T. papers. (Liddle Collection)
18. Gray, G. papers. (Liddle Collection)
19. The 26/Middlesex lost 12 dead from malaria and pneumonia in October 1918.(W.D.)
20 Hall, C.C. papers. (Liddle Collection)
21. Mellors, op.cit.
22. Baer, A. papers, op.cit.

23. Latter, op.cit. p.279
24. Wyrall, E. *East Yorkshire Regiment,* op.cit. p.233
25. 10/DCLI.
26. Bickersteth, J.(ed). *The Bickersteth Diaries,* (Leo Cooper, 1995) p.223. The 5/Cheshire constructed this 'church' on Vimy Ridge.
27. A task performed by the 24/Manchester. Another rather unusual role was the appointment of the C.O. of the 9/Gordon Highlanders as Deputy Returning Officer for the Province of Alberta. (August 1917)
28. Croft, W.D. papers. (Liddle Collection)
29. Falls, C. *Gordon Highlanders,* op.cit. p.76
30. Unpublished history of 7/DLI, op.cit.
31. Lester, op.cit.

Chapter 8

WORKING IN PARTNERSHIP

It was noted earlier that when the idea of Pioneer battalions was first mooted neither the senior officers nor the Pioneers themselves were really sure of what the role of the new force should be. The units might have had the opportunity to practise certain engineering skills while in training at home and the skilled craftsmen amongst them might well have anticipated being called to use their trades to create specialized apparatus, but there was no agreed or even suggested procedure as to how the Pioneer units would be used when they reached the front. Technically Pioneers came under the authority of the CRE who, through his responsibility for allocating tasks, played the principal role in deciding their deployment. Because Pioneer units had not before existed in the British Army it was not surprising that there was a good deal of confusion as to how exactly they should be used and organized.

It is easy to blame the divisional commanders or the CRE for failing to utilize the services of their Pioneers in an efficient or optimum manner, but this is really merely to ignore the uniqueness of the situation. Divisional CRE were used to handling Field Companies amounting to about 300 men; now they had not only their traditional command to consider, but also an additional one thousand men with their own system of administration and a commander of probably equal rank to himself. The divisional commander for his part, could claim that his job was to control the wider operations of the division. After all, he did not take intimate decisions about where the division's guns should be

146

sited or what the day to day activities of the divisional cavalry should be, so he could argue that determining the tasks and the responsibilities of the Pioneers was not his direct obligation. This was certainly the case in most divisions, but in the regular 29th and several others, there are suggestions that an alternative arrangement did at least on occasions exist. A battalion history of the 2/Monmouth claims that the battalion took its orders not from the CRE but from the divisional staff. Working directly under the GOC it could 'conserve its energies for important tasks'.[1] Wiring seems to have been done under R.E. supervision, but trench construction was 'entirely in the hands of the C.O. once he had had instruction from the Staff'.[2] In July 1915 the War Diary of the 11/King's noted with a hint of relief that the disposal of working parties was now left to the C.O. and that they were to be detailed by him rather than the R.E. At Arras in 1917 the 5/Northants regularly worked under the direct orders of the GOC 35th Brigade. On less frequent occasions, C.O.s of Pioneer units rather than the CRE, could demand infantry for digging purposes directly from a brigade commander.[3]

The more usual delegation of authority meant that the relationship between the CRE and the Pioneers was the essential element in whether the best was to be had from the new attachments. In January 1917 the 22/DLI clearly thought that, 'On the whole . . . the system of the Pioneers working under the orders of the CRE . . . proved quite satisfactory'. Several War Diaries however reveal that sometimes the relationship was rather strained. Perhaps the most extreme was that of the C.O. of the 24/Manchester and the CRE of the 7th Division. The difficulties appear to have begun in the autumn of 1917 when the 24th was obliged to receive a large draft of former R.E. and despatch a similar number of men to other battalions. Lt.Col. Pountney seems to have apportioned the blame for the move to the CRE, rather than to the authorities at home. The vitriol in the correspondence which passed between them during the rest of the war illustrates at best a lack of cordiality, and at worst a relationship under severe strain. The real reason behind the problem between the two arms probably had more to do with the relationship between the staff and officers of a regular division, forced to accept a brigade and battalion of Pioneers from the New Armies, rather than with a genuinely difficult working relationship.[4]

Even in the 34th, one of the most famous of the locally raised New Army divisions, relations between the R.E. and the Pioneers could be difficult. Two of the division's brigades contained the Tyneside Irish and Tyneside Scottish brigades, all battalions of the Northumberland Fusiliers. These eight battalions of infantry had been raised amidst great popular enthusiasm from the areas around Newcastle. The Pioneer battalion was also a unit of Tynesiders and, like two thirds of the infantry, was a unit of the Northumberland Fusiliers. However, within a month of its arrival overseas the War Diary of the 18/N.F. shows that the battalion was far from content with its working relationship with the CRE. It was noted earlier that this attitude was perhaps in part the result of the battalion's disappointment at not having been allowed a period of instruction with an existing Pioneer battalion before going into the line. The dissatisfaction at being subordinated to the CRE is clear:

> The companies are under the orders of the CRE. The C.O. is thus entirely eliminated except for administrative purposes. This system does not seem advantageous in any way. It diminishes the C.O.'s authority and limits his sphere of usefulness and it stands to reason that an R.E. officer who knows nothing of the Battalion cannot get as good work out of it as its own C.O., at least if he can it is time to change the C.O.

This protest seems to have had an effect because the diary notes that for a few days afterwards the battalion was 'employed under its own C.O.' The more normal practice of working under the CRE was however soon resumed. The following order is typical of the type found in many War Diaries. It demonstrates how close the working relationship between the Engineers and the Pioneers was and how, at least in the early years of the war, the R.E. clearly dominated that relationship:

148

After tomorrow the Pioneers will only be employed on work along the Bois Grenier line and on defensive posts. The O.C. 209th Field Company will issue instructions to O.C. Pioneers as to what works he will undertake from time to time, and to furnish him with any general technical instructions necessary for him to carry out the work. The O.C. Pioneers will send in his own requisitions for materials and stores to the CRE direct and will arrange for drawing them as required from R.E. dumps and for the necessary transport.

Given this necessarily intimate relationship, and the belief among some Pioneer C.O.s that they should be allowed more independence and initiative, it is perhaps unsurprising that there were problems from time to time. Tucked inside several War Diaries are examples of acrimonious or acerbic notes passing between some Pioneer battalions and the divisional R.E. The most frequent complaint is of alleged failures by Pioneer working parties to meet with R.E. officers waiting to show the Pioneers where they should be working. Depending upon whether it was the R.E. or the C.O. of the Pioneers who had written the original complaint, the other party was usually held responsible for the failure to make the rendezvous. The conditions experienced on the way to the meeting point are usually mentioned as the chief contributory factor for the failure; shelling, mud, darkness, guides losing their way etc., are all blamed for delays in arriving or as the reason why the working party was marched back to camp without having made contact.

Problems could also arise when a Pioneer unit was detached from its own division and set to work under the command of another. The 20/KRRC thought that the ambition of the CRE of the 12th Division was to criss-cross the ground with as many communication trenches as the Pioneers could fit in. The Rifles' own CRE immediately ordered a halt to the cutting of new trenches, believing that the battalion already had enough to do looking after the existing ones.[5] The 12/Notts & Derby was similarly indignant when it was forced to lend one of its companies to the 4/South Lancs of the 55th Division. The Foresters were already aggrieved at having been left to work in the front

149

area when their own division had been withdrawn. Now they were unable to finish their own task because the South Lancs had fallen so far behind with their work. The adjutant of the Foresters, who from the lack of punctuation in the following note appears to have been as equally strained as his men, wrote:

> This is very rough on our men who have been under rationed by the 55th Division from the time the 24th Division left til the 41st Division relieved the 55th and also the men have been continuously at work since 31 August and owing to the extra work and being underfed the percentage of sickness has risen from 1% to 14%.

Another factor which sometimes caused friction between the two groups was the civilian background and experience of Pioneer officers. There are several pieces of evidence which suggest that some Pioneer officers considered they were better qualified or able to complete a task than the R.E. sent to instruct or supervise them. Many Pioneers were architects and engineers, with practical civil experience. They might come across a R.E. officer of considerably younger years than they and who possessed little or no previous engineering experience other than what he had learned at Woolwich. Major Davidson of the 22/DLI recalled that when he was ordered to dig two communication trenches, both of which would have to be tunnelled under the Menin Road, he left the job with complete confidence in the hands of a second lieutenant who only a few months earlier had been a mining engineer. Another of Davidson's subalterns was in charge of a party working alternate shifts with the R.E. on building an advanced dugout. This subaltern was also a mining engineer and complained to Davidson that when his party daily took over from the R.E., it had to spend a considerable time putting right what the Engineers had 'properly messed up'. The R.E. officer was told that if the Pioneers were not left alone to complete the work, the DLI would not accept responsibility. On another occasion, the corps C.E. proudly showed Davidson his magnificently designed and constructed assembly shelter. On

150

inspection, Davidson, who was a Fellow of the Society of Architects, suggested that the shelter was weak, over elaborate and badly designed. He then went on to show the increasingly disgruntled R.E. officer how he could have doubled the shelter's strength and used only half the work force employed by the Engineer. Davidson later excused the R.E. by noting, 'It is very hard for an R.E. to take civilian advice, even when it is professional, proffered by an older man'.[6]

There were times though, when the abilities of the Pioneers could be over-estimated by the Engineers. When C Company of the 17/N.F. was sent to work on a tunnel under No Man's Land near Annequin in September 1916 the officer of the tunnelling company assumed that being Pioneers, they would be able to take over the work from his men and carry on largely unsupervised. Unfortunately, the entire company of the Fusiliers claimed to be ignorant of tunnelling techniques. Similar ignorance was displayed by a young subaltern and former schoolmaster Harry Anderson when he was posted to the 9/South Staffs at the height of the Somme offensive. On his second night in the line he was sent into Death Valley with his platoon to lay a decauville track. Anderson did not know what a decauville *was*, let alone know anything about how to lay one.[7]

It is perhaps understandable that some R.E. officers were either a little doubtful or, alternatively, optimistic, about the skills or otherwise of the Pioneers in the early days of their existence. Regular infantry officers were unconvinced of the qualities of the officers and men of the New Armies, so it is hardly suprising that they should have been equally dubious about how the 'temporary' gentlemen of the Pioneers might perform. On occasions though, the R.E. perhaps took their suspicions a little too far. One day, a company of the 22/DLI composed almost exclusively of Durham pitmen, was delighted to discover that some R.E. had arrived to instruct them in the use of the pick and shovel![8]

A second lieutenant who had left his job as an apprentice engineer at Seaham Colliery to enlist in the 14/N.F., also felt that the Engineers did not accord the Pioneers sufficient respect for their civilian-acquired skills. Moreover he believed that the R.E.

treated them with less consideration than they gave to their own men. In a frequently vitriolic reminiscence, Dillon believed:

> That even if there were nothing for us to do, [they thought] we should be up and near and sharing the risks of others. This resulted in an unnecessary loss of life, and often jobs that could be done by a few involved a whole company, many of whom were standing around or taking what cover they could'.[9]

Another frequent cause of complaint was the continual request from the R.E. for the skilled men of the Pioneers. Plumbers, carpenters and smiths were in constant demand and Pioneer C.O.s complained that this continual drain of their skilled men greatly affected the efficiency of their own battalion. These men were often required by Field Companies or as artisans at R.E. workshops. Although they were usually only on temporary detachment, their absence from the battalion could cause problems. 2Lt. Tymms of the 4/South Lancs was so short of skilled men in his detachment of about 45 Pioneers, that he was forced to ask his adjutant for the services of a blacksmith to sharpen his men's picks. In view of the supposed composition of a Pioneer battalion, it is perhaps even more surprising to learn that, because a dugout was in danger of collapse, Tymms also asked for a 'skilled miner'.[10]

The almost incessant R.E. demands for Pioneer working parties was a further frequent cause of difficulty between the two commands. Dillon and other Pioneer officers thought that the CRE would sometimes use the Pioneers rather than expose his own men to the risks of working in dangerous areas. 2Lt. Croft of the 5/SWB pointed out to his own adjutant that the CRE frequently expected the Pioneers to work on successive nights during their periods both in and out of the line; of the division's three Field Companies, Croft explained, only two were ever expected to be in the front area at any one time. Furthermore he wrote, the CRE often requested that the Pioneers provide carrying parties. This he believed was a waste of skilled men as they would be better off employed on other tasks, leaving the infantry to do the carrying.[11] Another subaltern, Lester of

152

the 18/Middlesex, also believed the R.E. did not take as much responsibility for supervising work as they were expected to. He recalled that while building a light railway in Trones Wood, the R.E. captain who was supposedly in charge of the task appeared at the site for a mere five or ten minutes a day. The work was carried out by Lester and his men under extreme conditions, but it was the R.E. officer who received a Military Cross.[12]

It is clear that although individual officers might sometimes have felt the R.E. were not up to the task or did not sufficiently appreciate the work of the Pioneers, senior officers knew that among the ranks of the Pioneers were men of great ability and use. Large numbers of junior officers were detached or transferred to tunnelling companies and to the mine rescue school at Bethune. Senior officers too were occasionally transferred from the Pioneers to the R.E. Although there are others, perhaps the best known example of this traffic was the transfer of Major R. Lloyd George from the 19/Welch to 135th Army Troops Company R.E.[13] The expertise of those officers who remained with their battalions was also put to use by the Engineers. There are several examples of newly commissioned R.E. officers being attached to Pioneer battalions for instruction in field engineering. One such unit thought this practice was a 'remarkably eloquent tribute to the efficiency of the battalion'.[14]

War Diaries of Pioneer battalions contain many notes and telegrams congratulating them on the work achieved and expressing the gratitude of those for whom they worked. This one, sent by the O.C. of a Field Company R.E. to the C.O. of the 9/North Staffs is typical:

> On the departure of C Company from the work they have been employed on, I wish to express to you my appreciation of the good work they have done. They have borne a considerable share of the responsibility for keeping the trenches of the Right sector open, and officers and men have worked with great keenness and have shown considerable technical ability. I hope they may soon return.

However, despite the necessarily close working relationship which had to exist between the R.E. and the Pioneers, when the number of battalions and CRE are considered – as well as the length of time these relationships endured – there is a strange lack of documentary evidence to illustrate the administrative aspects of the cooperation. Mention has already been made of the inevitable social and professional links between officers of some Pioneer battalions and their divisions. This *concorde* would undoubtedly have assisted in forging a working relation between them. Yet a search through the relevant War Diaries of the individuals and units involved in working closely with Pioneers generally reveals an absence of anything but the most cursory references.

The highest echelon of the R.E. on overseas service were the Chief Engineers of the various armies. Of course, unless he had a battalion temporarily attached pending posting elsewhere, the C.E. of GHQ Troops need not have come across the daily workings of Pioneers. Not surprisingly therefore, he makes no references to them during his travels behind the lines or in his administrative work.[15] The C.E. of what eventually became the five armies of the BEF did have more to do with them. For example, in October 1915 Third Army's C.E. recorded where the Pioneer battalions in his army were working and on what general tasks, but without individually naming them.[16] He even wrote of the possibility of increasing the number of tunnelling companies by plundering miners from the Pioneer battalions of the 22nd and 27th Divisions. It was clearly not his responsibility to interfere too directly in the day to day work of the Engineers or the Pioneers within his army; his task was to take an overview of the engineering problems and tasks. He attended regular conferences with the army and corps commanders and might, on fairly rare occasions, make operational suggestions. For example, one C.E. recommended that because there were insufficient R.E. and Pioneers to do it for them, the infantry should create special 'dugout platoons' of about 20 men to dig their own accommodation. The C.E. of Fourth Army stated in simple language that he had not issued any operational orders for the opening of the Somme campaign as all R.E. units received their

154

orders from C.E. corps and CRE divisions.[17] He would only go so far as to insist that Field Companies and Pioneers should be capable of dealing with bridges to carry both field artillery and infantry and that CRE must arrange through their GOC division for early reconnaissance by Engineers and Pioneers of gaps to be bridged. He was certainly present at GHQ conferences attended by Pioneer colonels and so would be available to them for questions and advice.

The next level down on the R.E. chain of command was the C.E. corps and he, occasionally, might have a Pioneer battalion placed directly at his disposal. This again was usually only while a battalion was awaiting posting to a division just after arrival – as was the case with the 14/Worcester in June 1916 – or if a battalion had been detached from its division while out on rest. The task of corps C.E. was to tour his area, consult regularly with the CRE of divisions about work in progress, the state of dumps, etc, and generally ensure that the fundamental divisional requirements of water, power and so on, were being maintained.[18] The closest he normally got to a Pioneer battalion was sometimes to include the location of the various units as appendices in his War Diary. He clearly received reports from CRE which did from time to time include the work done by Pioneers and he did make recommendations which clearly affected the peformance of Pioneers. Two examples will illustrate the point.

In a report on operations of mid-1917 the C.E. corps and their divisional CRE decided that if the distribution of work was to be effective, Pioneers should be used for all work on communications which did not require skilled labour but which did need more physical effort than could be expected of the infantry.[19] The Engineers went on to recommend that Pioneers should really be of the class and physique of those who became Pioneers in the R.E. itself. Their training should be of a standard which would enable them to undertake most of what the Engineers called the 'less skilled work' currently done by Field Companies. They also requested that Pioneers should be thoroughly trained in building corduroy and other roads and in the rapid laying of decauville track. Although some Pioneers with access to the report might have disagreed with the R.E. thoughts on respective skill levels, as a token of the value in which the Pioneers were held the report went on to recommend that: 'From the point of view of the CRE, the strength of a Pioneer battalion should never be allowed to decline. Every man can usually be employed'.[20] A second example of how a C.E. could use his influence to suggest how the deployment of his own men and the Pioneers might be improved can be seen in a report by the C.E. of IV Corps following the Battle of Cambrai.[21] Acknowledging that the transport of R.E. stores would inevitably secure only third or fourth priority, he recommended that divisional dumps, then in the process of being centralized, should be re-established as close to the front as possible. This would make it easier for the Pioneers and Field Companies to draw tools and equipment and cut down the distance they would have to be carried. The C.E. corps also dealt regularly with army and corps Roads Officers. As Pioneers spent so much of their time trying to clear and repair roads in the forward areas, and because in late 1916 the system by which responsibility for roads devolved had changed, the C.E. would be keenly aware of the problems of finding sufficient labour. One C.E. suggested that the answer lay in placing a complete division at the disposal of each corps during operations for the sole purpose of providing labour for road maintenance. This, he believed, would then free Field Companies and Pioneers for more useful skilled work nearer the front.

It might be expected that War Diaries of the CRE divisions would make more regular references to Pioneers than his superiors. However, in the early months of a division's overseas history references are still often extremely patchy. The CRE's first responsibility was to ensure that the Field Companies were working efficiently. As the companies worked so closely with the Pioneers it could be assumed that there were regular meetings between their officers and those of the Pioneers. Yet before the opening of the Somme offensive there are few recorded meetings between a CRE and the C.O. of his division's Pioneer battalion. One of the rare exceptions to the norm is the diary of the CRE 37th Division. Within a few days of landing, the CRE and the C.O. Pioneers were inspecting the work to be taken over from another division. Regular joint visits to working sites followed, with the CRE occasionally superintending the tasks in progress. By contrast, the CRE of the 56th Division made only two references in his War Diary to the Pioneer battalion between February and July 1916.[22] The first was to record why he had been forced to borrow a clerk, four storeman and a number of carpenters from the Cheshires, while the second was to note the location of the Pioneer companies on 'Z' Day. This apparent lack of coordination is despite his visiting the front areas regularly and having frequent meetings with C.E. corps and divisional and brigade staffs. His main consideration was to attempt to get his Field Companies to complete their designated tasks at a time when they were one third short of their officer establishment. His counterpart in the 34th Division included a hint of criticism in his War Diary[23] when he explained that on 1 July his Field Companies were attached to the brigades and all orders were being given by the brigadiers directly to the companies. Although responsible for their work, he was 'powerless to act in any way'. He became almost jubilant later in the month when the Field Companies again went into action; on this occasion they came under his direct command. The inference in his subsequent report is that they achieved a lot more of what was asked of them this second time. He also made a rare reference to orders given specifically to his division's borrowed battalion of Pioneers, the 9/North Staffs. Without giving reasons – although we can probably assume he did not believe the Pioneers possessed the necessary skills – he decided that the battalion should grade the track of a new decauville line while his sappers laid it. The other mention he makes of the Pioneers is given in a later report on the operations, but the plaudits for the success go to his own units rather than the Pioneers. The CRE 19th Division made more references to his Pioneer battalion during the attack than most, but this was possibly a consequence of his having to use an unknown and untried unit in exchange for his normal battalion which was lent to another division.[24]

Recorded references to the orders given and the work done by Pioneers increase in the CRE's reports following the opening stages of the Somme. Lessons appear to have been learned from the confusion of the early days and references to meetings between CRE and Pioneer commanders appear more regularly. Verbal instructions were also undoubtedly given at such conferences and further changes and amendments were certainly discussed at subsequent meetings. By mid-1917, Pioneers are frequently included in R.E. move orders and much more specific detail of what work they were required to do and how it was to be accomplished is given. During Third Ypres, map references denoting the areas in which the Pioneers were to work appear and by the time of the March offensive the CRE diaries often, but by no means always, include numbers of tools to be supplied, name the R.E. subaltern responsible for ensuring the Pioneers knew what was to be done, rendezvous points, how many trench boards or bridges were available for use by them, and so on. Recorded evidence on the working relationship increases again during the counter-offensives of 1918. CRE can sometimes give quite detailed accounts of the combined work undertaken. He is necessarily concerned to record the relevant information with regard to his Field Companies but will also sometimes mention the cooperation and assistance given them by the Pioneers. He will also on occasions include this information when compiling his report for his C.E. corps. Nevertheless, and as we would expect, he saves the more lucid prose for the performance of his own men.

The area in which the closest recorded contact between the R.E. and Pioneers might be expected is that of the War Diaries of the Field Companies. Here again in general, references in the early years of the war are minimal. Like War Diaries of all arms, the quality and scope of these volumes vary enormously. To many adjutants or intelligence officers, completing the diary was just another of the many bureaucratic demands made upon their time by authority. They had far better things to do, and given the physical circumstances in which many diaries were compiled, it is perhaps surprising to discover how detailed some of them are; their extent depended very largely on the enthusiasm of the officer writing it and the other demands currently being made upon his time. Yet even in the most lengthy of the Field Company diaries, it is rare to come across recorded examples of liaison between the two complimentary arms. That of the 82nd Field

Company in July 1916 for example, notes in immense detail what was happening in other divisions up and down the line, but mentions its own division's Pioneer battalion only in the capture of Bazentin-le-Petit at the end of the month.[25] In contrast, the diary of another Field Company in the same division makes fairly regular mention of the work done by the 5/SWB. In the 56th Division the 416th Field Company's diary records extensive detail but, when discussing its notable success in one operation, makes only one passing mention of the fact that it had an attached platoon of Pioneers.[26]

It is known that before offensive operations, Pioneer subalterns were occasionally officially attached to Field Companies for periods which could extend to a week. The frequency of such attachments is unclear and probably depended upon the attitude and relationship of the CRE and the C.O. of the Pioneer battalion. When such liaisons did take place useful experience in understanding the working practices and problems of the other arm would undoubtedly assist overall efficiency and cooperation. It is also clear that as the war progressed commanders of Field Companies, who were at times only subalterns, were prepared to accept greater responsibility and themselves order forward Pioneer platoons or companies. Unfortunately however, there appears to be no written evidence to confirm that liaison meetings between Pioneer and R.E. officers increased at the same rate.[27]

In view of the huge amounts of paper work generated by battalions, divisions and corps, it is surprising to discover the relative paucity of extant sources which cover the working relations between the R.E. and Pioneers. What must be assumed is that contacts between the Field Companies and the Pioneers were more frequent than appears to have been the case from the surviving written evidence and that the majority of them tended to be informal. The very absence of them might suggest that the officers normally responsible for recording the units' activities thought it unnecessary to to do so because the cooperation was taken for granted. Field Companies and Pioneers tended to move together when going out on rest and were frequently billeted in the same villages or camps. Social ties between the respective messes could easily be developed in such surrounds and there would also be the professional attraction of men who came from similar engineering or mining backgrounds. When out of the line there are instances of combined training exercises where Pioneers practised the erection of shelters under the supervision of officers from the Field Companies. Furthermore, when in the field, the very nature of the work undertaken by the two arms would necessitate a frequent exchange of messages, opinions and men. Pioneer colonels and their company commanders are known to have made tours of inspection with O.C. Field Companies to consult on the work in hand and discuss future projects. Furthermore, when one Pioneer battalion relieved another, there was no need for officers from the Field Companies to be present. The Pioneers would be thought perfectly capable of informing the incoming battalion about work in progress. Pioneers were units in their own right, formed from battalions of Britain's line regiments; they did not need to be nurse-maided by the R.E. and would have felt insulted if the Engineers become more domineering than the necessities of command decreed. The apparent lack of adequate R.E. acknowledgement of the contribution made by Pioneers during operations can be explained by the fact that the Field Companies were primarily concerned to record what they had been doing and, where appropriate, applaud their own success. After all, Pioneer battalion War Diaries rarely acknowledge the assistance given them by the R.E. Just because the diaries are not overflowing with written evidence to provide documentary support for the relationship does not mean that the relationship was not close and, usually, successful.

However, appreciated and valued as the work of the Pioneers undoubtedly was in most divisions, it did not prevent the periodic sweep of rumours through the battalions as to what their future might be. In November 1916 John Jellicoe, a young officer in the 17/N.F., wrote excitedly to his father that 'we might be made into R.E.' This idea apparently appealed to Jellicoe because, 'it means more pay!'[28] Nothing came of this, but coinciding with the general reorganization of the BEF in early 1918, speculation throughout the Pioneer battalions reached a new

160

pitch. There was a widespread belief that as part of this rationalization the army was about to do away with them altogether. There was also a slighty less drastic, but almost equally unpopular rumour, reflecting Jellicoe's earlier belief that they were to be amalgamated with the R.E.

William Jaeger, serving with the 11/King's, believed the rumours began in December 1917 and that the unit's disbanding became an absolute certainty when the RSM and senior NCOs returned from a lecture on the subject delivered by the colonel. The regimental history of the King's agrees with the date given by Jaeger on the origins of the rumours. It goes on to state that the speculation was particularly 'unwelcome' because, 'after two and a half years of war, it was felt that Pioneers had made a place of their own in the Military Sun, which they were very loathe to relinquish'.[29] In contrast to Jaeger's assertion, the history of the 18/N.F. believed that the meeting of senior officers at Rouen was not to agree on the disbanding of the units, but actually to confirm their continued existence.[30] Similarly, the chronicler of the 5/Cheshire thought the Rouen meeting was concerned with a reorganization within individual battalions rather than with whether the whole concept of Pioneer units was to be abandoned.[31]

The contemporary belief that amalgamation was a possibility but that no final decision had yet been made, was fuelled by an instruction issued at the Rouen conference. The plan that all Pioneer battalions should be reduced to three companies was first discussed in January 1918; at Rouen, the C.O.s were informed that this had become policy and that they should reorganize their commands accordingly. Because the number of companies would then be identical to the number of R.E. Field Companies within a division, it seemed as if further preparatory work to amalgamation was in process. After all the disruption of the previous few months, this order came as another unwelcome development. To those battalions which had suffered heavy casualties and huge reinforcements from other regiments, it was merely a practical issue. But to those which had retained many of their original members it was both practical and emotive. Because the idea had been thought useful in developing

161

company and battalion *esprit*, several battalions had originally formed their different companies from men living in the same area. Nearly four years on, some companies had still managed to retain a very local identity. Nevertheless, decisions had to be made, and, for example in the 12/KOYLI, 'after weighty consideration, it fell to the lot of A Company to be disbanded'.[32] The axe fell upon this unfortunate group because, unlike the other three companies, it had been originally recruited from several rather than a single district. The C.O. of the Oldham Comrades was asked by Division whether he wanted to retain all four companies with only three platoons each, or have three at full strength. The battalion's original companies had not been formed from men of particular areas of the town, so the colonel simply decided to plump for the second option because he thought it was the 'most suitable for this unit'. Other battalions were unwilling to make the decision and prevaricated. The 22/DLI and the 2/5th LNL both stated that they would not disband a company immediately, but would wait for what they called 'natural attrition to take its course'. It is not clear from their respective diaries how the C.O.s decided when exactly attrition had indeed 'taken its course', or whether they were forced to reduce before they had intended, but both battalions were down to three companies within a matter of weeks.

Another interesting example of a battalion refusing to enforce the new stricture immediately is that of the 1/Monmouth. With a strength of well over 1,000 other ranks the battalion argued that with such a high establishment, it was impracticable to reduce to three companies. It agreed with Division that it would receive no further drafts until strength had been reduced by attrition to the new establishment of 23 officers and 734 other ranks. Despite the agreement, it did still receive drafts. At the time of the German offensive it was well over 1,100 strong and with no mention of it having received any other than A1 category men.

The great changes in the work and organization of Pioneers were to come after the war. For the remaining months they retained their separate identity and continued to work, albeit under the supervision of the R.E., as a distinct body. However, although battalions remained intact there were some among the

162

Pioneers who believed that it made little difference whether they retained this separate indentity or not. Ernest Wood, a company commander in the 24/Manchester believed that:

> Once we were converted to Pioneers we virtually ceased to be a battalion except for administration. Thereafter, only on remote and very brief occasions were operations conducted other than by individual companies which in action were isolated from each other to satisfy and comply with the needs of the fighting battalions in the line.[33]

After the war Wood argued that from their creation Pioneers should have been organized along the same lines as the divisional Engineers and artillery. This would have entailed allocating one company of Pioneers to each of the infantry brigades. The alternative was to have a theoretically centralized battalion but which, in practice, consisted of several virtually independent companies. The CRE of the 37th Division largely echoed these sentiments. In his War Diary he wrote an appreciation of the operations undertaken by the division between March and November 1918. He argued that the Field Companies needed more skilled and semi-skilled men, and that 'probably' the best way of securing this would be to amalgamate the R.E. and Pioneer companies into one unit under R.E. officers. This solution would also alleviate, he thought, the contemporary problem of the shortage of Pioneer officers with engineering experience.[34]

After the war another junior officer went a stage further than Wood by completely dismissing the whole idea of Pioneer units. To Dillon of the 14/N.F., the concept was 'a military nonsense, and only added more semi-combatants to the tail of an already encumbered division'. Furthermore, he believed, 'it also led to jealousy from the R.E., whose functions were intruded upon, and who were expert in such matters'.[35] How much weight should be put on Dillon's comments is open to some speculation. Although he later became a lieutenant colonel, his writing reveals a deep hostility towards the way the war was conducted and of the abilities of the High Command in general. He was by training a mining engineer and spent some time attached to tunnelling companies, for whom he had a thorough respect. He later left the Pioneers and transferred to the tanks.

Whatever the benefits or drawbacks of the Pioneers and R.E. maintaining separate identities, it must be stressed that in general the cooperation was close and effective. Whether the reduction to three Pioneer companies per division made this cooperation any better in the latter months of the war is unclear. What is clear is that the reorganization of 1918 merely added to the troubles and trauma of an already seemingly interminable winter of debilitating work. A stolid determination to see the job through was the essential requirement for Pioneers, infantry and artillery alike. They could expect little in the way of comfort and genuine rest, knowing instead that baths, recreation and proper billets were only for the lucky few. In the minds of men in many non-Pioneer units, there was a contemporary belief that Pioneers and their comrades in the R.E. were among this fortunate minority.

NOTES

1. Brett, op.cit. p.51
2. ibid.
3. In July 1916 the commander of 55th Brigade told the C.O. of the 8/Sussex that he could demand infantry labour when the Sussex were instructed to improve some defences near Bernafay Wood.
4. See Mitchinson & McInnes op.cit. for a longer discussion on this acrimonious correspondence.
5. Turbeville, op.cit. p.49
6. Davidson, op.cit.
7. Memoir of Harry Anderson. (Private Collection)
8. Davidson, op.cit.
9. Dillon, op.cit.
10. Tymms, F. papers. (Liddle Collection)
11. Croft, op.cit. At least one CRE was critical of the way some divisions worked their Pioneers. That of the 37th Division suggested: 'Perhaps some definite instructions might be given as to hours of work where troops of different divisions are placed alongside on the same work. A Pioneer battalion working 9 hours as a minimum might be found alongside another working 4 hours a day as a maximum. If they were

not maintained by *esprit de corps* and pride in their work, trouble might be caused'. (W.D.)

12. Lester, op.cit.
13. This was one of several postings of senior divisional officers following the alleged failure of the 38th Division at Mametz Wood.
14. Turbeville, A.S. op.cit. p.117
15. W.O.95.119
16. W.O.95.383
17. W.O.96.451
18. For example, W.D. of C.E. IV Corps. (W.O.95.736)
19. *Extracts from Reports of Chief Engineers and CRE on recent Operations (excluding those of Second Army) August 1917.* op.cit.
20. ibid.
21. W.O.95.736
22. W.O.95.2939
23. W.O.95.2444
24. W.O.95.2066
25. W.O.95.2069
26. W.O.95.2942
27. Before moving up, the usual rendezvous for the Field Companies and the Pioneers was the HQ of the latter. In mid-1917 it was recommended that if this was not the case, arrangements should be made beforehand to dispense, if necessary, with the C.O.'s authority. (*Extracts from Reports of C.E. and CRE.,* op.cit.)
28. Jellicoe, J. papers. (Dept. of Documents, IWM)
29. *The Record of the 11th Battalion of the King's (Liverpool) Regt. subsequently the 15th Battalion the Loyal North Lancashire.* Regimentally compiled. (Thomas & Co. 1920)
30. Shakespear, op.cit. p.74
31. Churton, op.cit. p.102
32. England, op.cit. p.80
33. Wood, E. letters. (In Walsh papers, Oldham Local Studies Library).
34. W.O.95.2519
35. Dillon, op.cit.

Chapter 9

A RACE APART?

One of the perceived advantages Pioneers had over the infantry, was the alleged comfort of their billets and camps.[1] There was a widespread belief that as the Pioneers contained a large proportion of skilled men and because they worked so closely with the R.E. (thus having access to their dumps), they constructed camps for themselves with greater care than they did for the less fortunate soldiery. Certainly the cooperation they had with the R.E. would do them no harm, and the number of carpenters, plumbers and masons within their ranks could supply a steady stream of skilled men when the comfort of the battalion was under consideration. Erecting huts either for themselves or for the use of other troops was a frequent occupation and required large numbers of skilled carpenters as well as a good deal of patience. On many occasions Pioneers also had the advantage of inhabiting the same camp or billets recently vacated by another Pioneer battalion. Thus, the work begun or completed by the previous unit could be appreciated or complemented by the incoming battalion. Furthermore, as Pioneers tended to be in the same area longer than their division, they had more time to adapt or construct amenities. Useful as this system of relief was, it was by no means a guarantee that all Pioneers were better housed or accommodated than the other arms.

A diarist of the 9/Gordon Highlanders acknowledged the compensations that being Pioneers could bring: 'Fewer losses, better quarters . . . and skills and materials to make them comfortable'.[2] Similarly, the 5/Cheshire recorded that it improved the living conditions 'at every place they visited . . . a matter of no difficulty owing to the number of skilled tradesmen in the battalion'.(3) These advantages were true for most battalions. Not far from Ypres in October 1917 the 7/York & Lancs built themselves a 'superb' camp, with each shelter boasting a fireplace, a good supply of wood and on one occasion even a substantial ration of coal.(4) Because their divisional baths were some distance away the 18/N.F. built their own spray baths from salved material, complete with attached drying room. The 24/Manchester was ordered to demolish surreptitiously an ironing hut near the Mailly-Maillet bath house while the camp commander was away on leave and re-erect it alongside its own bath house for the benefit of themselves and their division.(5) One man who appreciated the advantages being a Pioneer could bring was a company commander in a battalion of Northumberland Fusiliers. In a cheery letter home, Captain Watts, who had recently been transferred from the Tyneside Scottish to the 19/N.F., wrote that being divisional troops had 'a distinct advantage as we occupy comfortable quarters well to the rear'. He added that he was writing from 'a very comfortable billet with a real bed and mattress [with] plenty of pegs and stools for articles of clothing'.(6)

At another camp in the Salient in 1917, Jaeger of the 11/King's appreciated the big Nissen huts because they were warm and dry and the men could eat their food under cover. He was prepared to put up with being chatty, (believing that the colder and wetter it was the less lousy they were), in return for the comfort of the huts.(7) Another collection of huts and adapted farm buildings was known as Pioneer Camp. It was universally held to be the best in the area and was occupied mainly by Pioneer units. Turco Camp, a little to the east of Pioneer, was another one built largely of Nissen huts and was again thought by several Pioneer units to be one of the most comfortable. It was certainly an improvement, so the 18/N.F. believed, from the 'much-bombed' camp near Boesinghe in which the battalion had spent a miserable few weeks.(8) The disadvantage of putting in a great deal of work on a camp in expectation of a long stay was that the army frequently changed its mind. Many men thought that authority could be deliberately malicious in waiting until the camp and its facilities were completed before then ordering the battalion which had done the work to move on. The 5/Sussex suffered such frustration after labouring away erecting huts on a site at Bazentin-le-Grand. The finished collection of huts and facilities was christened Cinque Ports Camp and was roundly praised by III Corps for its planning and construction. Soon after completion, the battalion was posted elsewhere.

Even in the cramped and confined area of the Dardanelles, Pioneers did sometimes enjoy a slightly better existence than the infantry. Wyn Adams a subaltern in the 6/East Yorks, thought he was 'lucky' compared with the 'poor brutes up in the front line trenches [who] must be having an awful time of it'.[9] Similarly in Italy, where the 5/Sussex and the 24/Manchester were sent in late 1917. They built themselves camps which contained many luxuries and facilities constructed from local stone and timber and whatever materials could be salved or requisitioned. However, not all Pioneer battalions were quite as fortunate as those mentioned above. On many occasions they lived a miserable existence in shell holes, ruined trenches and bivvies. Furthermore, these periods of cold endurance were generally for a longer tour of duty than their comrades in the infantry were generally expected to perform.

During the depths of the Somme winter the 11/DLI spent several weeks in some appalling bivvies at Montauban. The working parties had to trudge long distances through the mud to their place of work and return in the dark to what amounted to shell holes covered with tarpaulins. The bivouacs had to be continually baled out and, to compound the misery, the site was a frequent target for the German guns. Breakfast and dinner were taken in the dark and after a long weary day at work some men were too tired to eat dinner or even turn out for the rum ration. The C.O. recorded that the men 'appear run down and are in need of a real rest'. On 30 December the C.O. of the 4/Coldstream Guards visited the site in preparation for relieving the Durhams. According to the DLI War Diary, the Guards were 'astonished at men being quartered in such a place and are not likely to take over the camp'. Another source claims that the

168

Guards simply refused to billet their men there and demanded an alternative site.[10] The Guards seem to have been very particular about their billeting arrangments. During a stay at the Bois du Warnimont the men were housed in huts while the officers were apparently relegated to tents. In late 1916 the 7/York & Lancs lived in a camp at Montauban not far from the pits occupied by the Durhams. Although it was accommodated in huts, the battalion had dozens of men, including the colonel, invalided out during this protracted winter.[11]

In the previous August, Captain Croft of the 5/SWB had recommended that a hutted camp somewhere in the Montauban region should be abandoned. It would take, he reported, such extensive repairs to the huts which had all been 'badly constructed', that it would not be practicable to occupy the camp during the winter months.[12] Whether this camp was in fact abandoned or not is unknown, but, even in reputedly more suitable ones, conditions might be not what the incoming unit expected. In May 1917 the 22/DLI moved into a camp in Vaulx Wood which was 'not too good . . . on account of it having been previously used for horse lines and left fouled'. Having spent months working in the front area, the 8/Royal Scots was withdrawn to St. Ricquier for a rest in January 1917. On arrival it took over billets previously occupied by the 8/Sussex. The Scots, rather disparagingly, thought the Sussex Pioneers had done too little to improve the facilities and the general accommodation. 'Only a few had beds and there was a considerable amount of work to be done before the billets were made really comfortable'. The 11/DLI moved into 'dirty billets' previously occupied by ANZAC troops at Picquigny, while in September 1917 the 9/South Staffs took over a camp at Dickebusch which another Pioneer battalion, the 12/Notts & Derby, had left in a 'very dirty state'.

Whether Pioneers, infantry or artillery, most units considered it to be a point of honour to leave billets in a clean and tidy condition. Battalions which did not put sufficient emphasis on the task of cleaning up before departure were not only cursed heartily by the incomers, but were also thought to be lacking in *esprit*. The 5/Cheshire for example, always placed 'the strictest attention' to

169

the condition of sanitation and cleanliness of billets,[13] and other units insisted that incoming battalions should hand chits to the out going company commanders agreeing that the billets were left in a satisfactory condition.[14] Sometimes a battalion could arrive at the rear areas expecting a period of rest and refitting in a comfortable camp, only to find that there was not even a camp ready for them. After a trying few weeks, the 10/DCLI left Kent Camp in the Salient in September 1917 expecting a rest of ten days at Conderkerke. It was informed that the arrangement was cancelled because there was no room at the camp; it was sent to another less salubrious one where, instead of resting, it spent the time training and digging. When the men of the 22/DLI arrived at Watou in a snow storm in December 1917, there was inadequate accommodation to greet them. Captain Davidson managed to requisition 55 bell tents, persuade local farmers to sell straw for bedding, find a supply of new uniforms and even discover a source to provide the men with beer.[15]

Officers such as Davidson could do a great deal to make the lives of their men more tolerable, to say nothing of the effect such practices would have on battalion morale. In contrast, the experience of the 18/Middlesex, a battalion which continued to attract more than its fair share of bad luck, would have done little to improve *esprit*. After spending a foul time working on the Somme, the battalion was withdrawn in September 1916 to discover that at bathing parade there was clean underclothing for only half the battalion. Despite this, a somewhat optimistic adjutant wrote that 'good work appears to have been done towards exterminating the Pediculi Vestamentorum'. There were probably very few men of the battalion who felt they could agree with him. The 24/Manchester was also clearly suffering from the effects of poor hygiene. After working in the mud of the Salient during the worst of Third Ypres, there were 40 reported cases of scabies. The battalion's M.O. claimed that 50% of the men had not had a clean shirt for nine weeks or fresh underclothes for over a month. The 'majority' of the battalion had not had a bath for five weeks.

Although many jobs in the rear areas could be done during daylight hours, a great deal of Pioneer work was of necessity done during darkness. Camps could be shelled or bombed at any time, and the Pioneers who were working near the front would often spend their sleeping hours in bivvies close to the lines of 18-pounders or 4.7" howitzers. Sleep was frequently disturbed by their own guns and made yet more uncomfortable by counter-battery fire from the Germans.[16] Nevertheless, the lot of the Pioneer could be substantially better than that of an infantryman. So much so that when the 11/King's was told that many of them were to be posted to the 12th Battalion, a line unit, William Jaeger looked to the future with some trepidation:

> After two and a half years in France with a Pioneer battalion and seeing all the horrors of war and participating in the pleasures that troops enjoyed while out . . . thoughts flew through my head that now I was to undergo the perils of staying for days in the trenches . . . firing shots into human beings and plunging cold steel into a man's body . . . Whilst working with Pioneers or Engineers we had always returned at dawn after our night's work to our dug outs or camp for rest and food: now that would all be done with . . . I had seen thousands of Very lights and heard machine guns and bombs in action so perhaps I would be called upon in the near future to handle these necessities of the front line. All these things I saw in my mind's eye[17]

Jaeger discussed the coming move with his comrades. Joe Hoyle from Oldham, who had served with the King's for as long as Jaeger, summed it up with a terse declaration that, 'It's a bloody bad job!'

There is no reason to believe that Pioneer units enjoyed better rations than the infantry despite the fact they spent a considerable time in other than the front trenches. The quality of a unit's rations depended a great deal upon the ingenuity of the quartermaster, the integrity of those detailed to deliver them to platoons and local trench conditions. Official rations could be supplemented by food parcels from a soldier's family or from regimental and local comforts committees. It was not because it happened to be a Pioneer battalion that the 16/Royal Irish Rifles was praised by Second Army's Inspector of Catering, but because its unit's organization and skills were apparently exceptional. Whether it was a true report on the battalion's arrangements, or merely an attempt by the authorities to show that it was itself functioning correctly for the benefit of the troops, many infantry and other Pioneer battalions would no doubt have been pleased to receive such a glowing tribute:

> Very good diet. Puddings almost daily. Clean cookhouse, very good stockpot in use. Good master cook. The messing of this battalion is above the average, and well supervised.

Besides the supposed superior billeting accommodation, another of the reasons why it was believed Pioneers were more fortunate than the infantry was the extra pay they drew. While this disparity was certainly the case in the early years of the war, the difference between the rates paid to the Pioneers and infantry narrowed as the war progressed.

The War Office decided that as the majority of soldiers in Pioneer battalions were in theory tradesmen or skilled men, they should receive higher pay than their comrades in the infantry. Their level of pay was not to be as great as that of the R.E., but the differentiation between Pioneers and infantry did, as we saw earlier, help to smooth away some of the disappointment when battalions were converted. There were however, several instances when the issue of respective rates of pay were raised in the House of Commons.

Questions were asked of War Office representatives when anomalies came to light in payments made to troops doing similar jobs. The extra 2d a day paid to a Pioneer still left him 8d a day worse off than his counterpart in the Engineers. This meant that when R.E. and Pioneers worked together on a job, the Pioneers received less. Generally, this differentiation was accepted, but periodically a M.P. would raise the matter in the House. In November 1915, for example, Mr Moore asked the Under-Secretary for War if he was aware that:

> Pioneer infantry battalions at the front are discharging similar duties in making roads and trenches to the Corps of Engineers and also to the labour battalions, yet the Pioneers only receive

pay at the rate of 1s.2d per day, while the Engineers receive 1s.10d, and the labour battalions 3s. a day for the same work; and if, having regard to the dissatisfaction which exists on this account, he will put the Pioneer battalions on an equality with the Engineers or labour battalions?[18]

For the War Office Mr. Forster replied that although these groups of men might be employed on similar work, because they had different qualifications and training, and because of 'the exigencies of war', he was not prepared to change the rates for which the men had enlisted.[19]

Awkward as situations such as these sometimes were, the real difficulty came when infantry were put to work alongside Pioneers. In July 1916 Sir William Pearce pointed out to Forster that infantry employed in carrying away the spoil Pioneers had dug were paid 2s a day, while the Pioneers drew only 1s.2d. Pearce wanted to know whether Forster was prepared to rectify this anomaly, which was, he said, 'keenly felt' by the Pioneers.[20] Such difficulties arose because infantry troops were paid extra money when used in this capacity, whereas the Pioneers, with their permanently higher rate, received no additional payments.

In view of this and other similar questions, in September 1916 the War Office despatched a memorandum to all Pioneer units. This asked whether the men were willing to accept their 2d a day extra and receive no additional working pay, or whether they wanted to revert to ordinary infantry rates and thus be eligible for occasional extra payments. The extant responses are few. One of them, recorded in the War Diary of the 12/KOYLI, merely mentions that the NCOs and men were presented with the options, but the men's answers were not recorded. The authorities decided that Pioneer and infantry pay should be identical but that Pioneers would be allowed to draw extra when undertaking specific tasts. There appear to be no references to the matter in any of the surviving reminiscences, but several histories refer to the differences between the rates received by the ex-Engineers who joined many Pioneer battalions in the autumn of 1917 and the Pioneers themselves. A diarist of the 7/York & Lancs noted that:

No-one grudged them their pay, but without the least ill-will in
the world, it is hardly surprising that some criticism arose of the
system whereby one man received three times the remuneration
of another working by his side on the common task.[21]

Pioneers had of course been used to working alongside Engineers
from the outset, and were therefore used to receiving less pay for
what was, on many occasions, the same work. The difference
now was instead of Engineers in the Field Companies being
members of a distinct arm, the former R.E., still drawing their
same rate of pay, were now wearing Pioneer collar dogs. These
newly appointed Pioneers often found themselves working
beside their former comrades in the Engineers, undertaking the
sort of task for which they had orginally been trained.

It might be assumed that given the pecuniary advantage
enjoyed by Pioneers in the early days of overseas travel and their
developing reputation for providing themselves with home
comforts, they might surreptiously or otherwise, have acquired
additional means of transporting their necessities from camp to
camp.

As unit War Diaries and published histories rarely give identical figures, there is some ambiguity over the number of carts,
wagons and horses which might comprise a Pioneer battalion's
transport. Some battalions specify riding horses among their
total, while others will include only draught animals. Similarly
with the wheeled transport. Some units appear to list only those
vehicles they were officially supposed to have, while others also
include those they acquired through sometimes nefarious
means.[22] Even among the 'official' figures, the proportion of
general service wagons to other limbers can vary quite substantially from battalion to battalion. This might be a legacy of a
unit's conversion from infantry to Pioneers or simply a semi-
official pragmatic solution to a Pioneer battalion's practice of
having to work its companies in dispersed parties.[23]

On mobilization the 21/West Yorks was provided with what
is, according to the available evidence, a fairly typical number of
horses and vehicles. It had 61 horses, 57 mules, eight G.S.
wagons, eight R.E. limbers, four cookers, two water carts, one

Maltese cart, one officers' cart and nine bicycles. Although the stated number of horses can vary from below 110 to 120, there are many examples of battalions embarking with similar establishments. In contrast to the West Yorks' total of 118 animals, the 5/Royal Irish Regiment left Liverpool in July 1915 with only 90 beasts. This substantial difference can perhaps be explained by the destination of the Irish Regiment. The battalion was off to the Dardanelles, and although at the time the offensive was intended to reopen the war of movement, it was perhaps thought that Pioneers on their way to Constantinople would require less transport than their counterparts on the Western Front. However, at least one battalion in France appears to have had an even lower establishment than the Royal Irish. In April 1916 the 14/N.F. claimed to have only 83 horses to service the battalion and its 20 four-wheeled and two two-wheeled vehicles. This is a very low number, especially as the battalion had only been in France for six months and had not recorded any significant numbers of casualties among its animals. When it became Pioneer battalion to the 46th Division, the 1/Monmouth recorded that it was eight draught horses short of establishment. If it had been up to strength it would mean the battalion expected to have 12 riding, 61 draught, nine heavy draught and 17 pack horses. It also stated that it was in possession of the required 23 four-wheeled and three two-wheeled carts. These figures are very close to the animals and vehicles the 6/East Yorks brought with it from Egypt in July 1916. Besides 12 riding horses, the battalion had 14 draught, 59 large and 16 small mules – a total of 89. It also brought 20 four-wheeled and four two-wheeled carts. However, if this establishment was meant to be typical of a Pioneer battalion in Egypt, it differs considerably from the number of animals the 5/Royal Irish Regiment possessed when it re-equipped in Egypt following its withdrawal from Salonika. It listed 13 officers' chargers, 143 mules, 27 G.S. limbers, four cookers and two water carts. When it later acquired 53 camels its mule establishment fell to 79 and by March 1918, shortly before it returned to Europe, its G.S. wagons had been reduced to 16. The 1st Cavalry Division's Pioneer battalion, which never had a strength in excess of 28 officers and 800 men, had a transport section of 34 men. The unit's animal establishment consisted of five riding horses and 65 mules, and the vehicles of four G.S. wagons, nine limbers, one water cart and three field kitchens. The battalion does record the possession of 33 light draught horses at one stage of its existence, but these seem later to have been replaced by mules.

Transport sections in all divisional arms had a deep affection for their animals, Troops worked hard to improve the welfare of the horses and mules by constructing hard standings and covered stabling. R.E. and infantry were often delegated to assist the transport drivers in this construction work, but the responsibility for grooming, feeding and looking after their general welfare fell upon the drivers. Casualties to the animals were often grieved as deeply by the troops as deaths and injuries among the men themselves. Furthermore, in the same way that a number of soldiers would always remain as a core of originals in a battalion during its time overseas, several units managed to retain a number of their mobilized animals.

Two years after it landed in France the 4/Coldstream Guards had 21 draught, 14 mules and five riding horses of those with which it had embarked. On the third anniversary of its arrival the battalion could still boast 17 draught, six mules and five officers' charges of its originals. As late as August 1918, the 17/N.F. bemoaned the loss in an air raid of some of the NER company's horses. These animals had joined the battalion as it trained at Hull in the far off days of 1914. The 18/N.F. lost 40 of its 'poor beasties' in an air raid on its transport lines near Ypres in September 1917, and recorded with obvious regret that the replacements were 'not as good as our old friends'. The 8/Royal Scots also suffered a major loss when two bombs fell on its camp in the same month. Twenty-nine of its horses were killed or had to be shot and another 16 wounded. The adjutant noted that all the pack animals which had joined the battalion on mobilization had now been killed. Bombs also accounted for 42 deaths and 16 wounded among the animals of the 4/Suffolk when its transport lines were attacked one night in September 1918, and shells landing in Siege Camp in October 1917 killed 47 of the 5/Sussex's horses. The 4/Coldstream thought themselves lucky that they lost only six horses killed and five wounded when a German plane raided Wellington Camp, but the 18/Middlesex claimed in December 1916 that there had been so many casualties among the animals that the transport was 'rendered immobile'. A proportion of these losses were probably a result of the weather rather than from hostile fire, but transport lines did frequently come under fire from enemy shells and gas bombardments. Sand bags around the hard standings could help to reduce the dangers from shrapnel, but the privations from the elements and the strain of active service affected animals as well as men.

In view of the apparent divergence in the establishments of animals in Pioneer battalions, it is difficult to be precise about how many vehicles a battalion might have on strength. The 5/DCLI considered that 'as a rule', most Pioneer units had a transport section of men and animals about twice the size of that possessed by a line battalion. That there was a substantial difference is suggested by the experience of the 19/L.F. When it was converted to a Pioneer unit in 1916, the battalion received an additional 42 light draught and eight heavy draught horses to bring it up to what was described as 'Pioneer' establishment. In the same year the 9/North Staffs, although an existing Pioneer battalion, was instructed to exchange four R.E. limbered wagons for four G.S. vehicles, which were larger, in order to bring its carrying capacity up to the required level. Changes in the type and number of vehicles probably went on, either officially or unofficially and recorded or unrecorded, from time to time in most battalions. The reduction from four to three companies in early 1918 meant that whether appreciated or not by the units concerned, officialdom acted in an effort to bring some sort of uniformity to transport sections.

A number of battalions recorded that they had to hand over surplus wagons and horses in order to conform to these new regulations. In February 1918 the 11/Leicestershire noted that it had 12 horses and four wagons above the official establishment; in due course, it handed over two G.S. wagons, six mules, two heavy draught and one riding horse to HQ of the 6th Division. What happened, if anything, to the two other wagons and the three extra animals, is not recorded. The 5/Northants simply noted 'all excess transport and equipment handed over', without specifying to whom, while the 12/KOYLI handed its surplus over to the 9/DLI which was in the process of being converted to Pioneers. This again suggests that transport establishments for Pioneers were generally higher than those of infantry battalions. In 1918, Pioneer units in Italy were officially required to possess 50 draught, seven heavy draught and 12 mules in addition to nine riding horses; these figures coincide exactly with those of Pioneer units on the Western Front following the reduction to three companies. The reorganization also compelled battalions to hand in excess tools. When the adjutant of the 12/KOYLI studied the list of tools which the 31st Division's Deputy Assistant Director of Ordnance Supplies insisted the battalion had been issued on mobilization, he realized that it was supposed to possess 250 shovels of a particular type. These shovels had apparently proved useless on active service and had long since been ditched. Upon enquiry, the R.E. said that they could provide the Pioneers with 80 of the tools. These subsequently arrived at the battalion's transport lines. Next day the quarter-master took the shovels to DADOS. He explained that he currently only had transport for that number and heard DADOS tell his staff to despatch them on to the R.E. dump. For the next two days the quartermaster kept drawing the same shovels from the dump and sending them to DADOS until the required '250' had been officially handed over.[24]

When it was reconverted to Pioneers from railway troops, the great regret among the 17/N.F. seems to have been the loss of several motor lorries. It does not specify how many of these had been in its temporary possession, but their departure was looked upon as signalling the end of profitable shopping trips to St. Pol.[25] Transport sections have traditionally enjoyed a reputa-tion for asserting an independence not always appreciated by their superiors. Drivers often viewed King's Regulations as an infringement of personal liberty, and were frequently dis-regarded in a manner so cavalier that even hardened transport officers blanched. The extra equipment and belongings which frequently appeared on wagons led to occasional purges. These usually only resulted in the surpluses being secreted away until the C.O.'s enthusiasm waned. It could be a little more difficult if one of the divisional staff or the general himself happened to view the transport when on a march. Generals had an unfortunate habit of appearing unexpectedly and often showed a more than cursory interest in the condition of the wagons and their contents. Once the column had passed under his watchful eye, battalion HQ might expect a communication from Division complaining of unexplained accoutrements seen dangling from limbers, of peculiar shaped wagons or carts nestled between the more regulation vehicles and of men and wagons resembling a convoy of brigands. Two examples of expressions of dissatisfaction on the part of divisional commanders will suffice to illustrate the point.

The first was a mild rebuke to the C.O. of the 18/Middlesex. The GOC had addressed the battalion, still only a few months into its active service overseas, expressing the hope that the transport 'would be brought to and kept at a higher state of efficiency'. The clear implication was that the section did not currently reach the expected standard. What passed between the C.O., his transport officer and subsequently the drivers is unrecorded, but we might assume that given the regular C.O.'s alleged dislike of his 'temporary gentlemen', his subordinates were left under no illusion of what in the future constituted an efficient section. The C.O. of the 24/Manchester also smarted from an unwelcome divisional admonishment in 1918. Lt. Col. Pountney had already issued a fierce directive to his transport, complaining about its unsatisfactory discipline and generally lax appearance. Four weeks later he was outraged to receive a missive from the general which complained of his having witnessed men wearing no equipment riding illegally on the battalion's vehicles. The fury with which Pountney turned upon his transport section no doubt reflected a sense of betrayal. The relationship between himself and his superiors was permanently strained and he was furious at his men for providing GHQ with ammunition to fire at him.[26]

A transport section's response to admonishments from above was a flurry of activity. Limbers would be cleaned up, harnesses

179

shined that little more brightly and excess baggage again discretely hidden. One reason why transport sections did not always appear to live quite to the letter of official regulations and were thus forced to undergo periods of correction, was the very nature of their work. Pioneer companies could be dispersed over a wide area and detachments of a single platoon or even of a group of specialists working on a particular job could make close supervision difficult. Some battalions had two transport officers in order to ease the practicalities and on occasions a number of limbers would be servicing the detachments and rarely visit the nominal transport lines. Working parties detached from the bulk of the battalion were usually under the command of a junior officer, which in itself could raise additional problems.

While Croft of the 5/SWB was working with a small detachment away from the battalion, he ran into several difficulties which might not have occurred in an ordinary infantry battalion. Criticized by his C.O. for not having fulfilled one particular demand from battalion HQ, Croft responded by claiming that he had never received the instruction. His one bicycle orderly, he explained, was 'continually at work', which made it very difficult for him to deal with despatches which arrived at short notice. A few days later he complained to the CRE and his own adjutant that he lacked the necessary authority to prevent men of other regiments from illegally cutting timber in the Vallee de Gorges. How could he, he asked, be expected to supply the number of pit props his unit was supposed to be cutting, when the resources were being stolen by others?[27]

Another junior officer, Tymms of the 4/South Lancs, also found himself in an awkward situation when commanding a small detachment. Desperate for advice, he wrote to his adjutant requesting help on what he should do with the unfortunate Cpl. Roberts. A passing brigadier had placed Roberts under open arrest for allegedly incorrectly supervising his working party. Inexperienced in the ways of army legal procedure, Tymms was at a loss as to what should happen next. He had already demonstrated a wish to cover himself from all angles by despatching a series of notes to the adjutant on a variety of issues. One such batch of correspondence concerned two broken hammers. The

180

handles of the tools had been broken 'while being used for their legitimate purpose', but Tymms was concerned that someone would inevitably be blamed. He complained that the handles were of 'poor quality' and that the men had been forced to use those tools because there 'did not seem to be any better' available. He sent the adjutant signed statements from two lance corporals who had used the tools and the affair seems to have died a natural death. However, three days later in what he called a 'Statement of Evidence', Tymms was again reporting to the adjutant that he had found one billhook, two spades and an entrenching tool lying around on a site under the supervision of L/Cpl. Carey. Carey had previously been warned, he wrote, that 'all tools should be returned to the divisional storeman every night'. He now sought advice on what should befall the careless NCO. It perhaps seems strange that amidst the detritus and waste of war a young officer was concerned about the consequences resulting from two broken hammers.[28]

When on detachment, young officers such as Croft and Tymms could often feel isolated and unsure of how to deal with disciplinary measures. None of the Territorial battalions which served as Pioneers were from units which operated a system of discipline akin to that employed in public schools. Both T.F. and New Army Pioneer units followed the more traditional army method. Although officers were encouraged and indeed expected, to be on good terms with their men, there was not the same *esprit* and understanding between officer and other rank as was evident in the more exclusive or long-standing T.F. battalions. As the war continued, the sometimes more reluctant and occasionally recalcitrant conscript replaced the generally more cooperative volunteer. This could be especially true if once trained, the man was posted to a battalion of another regiment. Many infantry battalions had to alter their normal means of command in order to accommodate the changed personnel. The young, often idealistic subaltern had to learn how to deal with his men – some of whom were possibly old enough to be his father – in a manner which both exercised the necessary discipline essential for the good efficiency of the battalion and, at the same time, showed care and concern for the men's welfare.

181

Until he had gathered sufficient experience in dealing with discipline and had won the trust or at least cooperation of his men, a junior officer might be inclined to cover his lack of confidence by bluster or excessive harshness. In preparation for his work on detachment Croft jotted down some notes and rules which he decided would serve him in good stead. Clearly understanding the necessity of relying upon the experienced NCOs, he was somewhat concerned about the apparent 'slack relations' he witnessed between some NCOs and the men. He noted that he should 'teach the NCOs to assert their authority', to stop all 'familiarity on the part of the men' and to instill 'smart and soldierly habits' by dint of their own example. This could be done, he decided, by laying stress on how NCOs gave orders to their sections, on the need for prompt obedience of their orders and by forbidding NCOs and other ranks from drinking in the same estaminets.[29]

Croft served in the battalion commanded by the tireless Colonel Trower. As an existing pre-war T.F. battalion, relations between men and officers had been established and the pattern set. In their civilian life its miners were used to obeying orders from men in authority whom they could trust. They were also used to working together in groups or gangs where a man of experience or physical or moral strength was the group leader. To these men discipline in the army was not a great deal different to the exercise of authority they experienced in the work place or trade union. The feeling of unit identity was easily fostered in a battalion such as this because men came from the same locality and from the same walk of life. Even when casualties had whittled away the originals, the replacements came from similar backgrounds. With continuity in command, the battalion's traditions and customs were maintained. The majority of Pioneer units did not enjoy that same sense of tradition and continuity. Indeed, the very nature of their work helped to accentuate the difficulties faced by the officers of these battalions. Even as a long-established T.F. unit, the 4/South Lancs thought that after conversion its very existence became something of a paradox:

On the one hand the daily routine of heavy manual labour in wet and muddy trenches, often under fire; the carrying parties, with men stumbling blindly forward over the shell-pocked ground; the wiring parties in No Man's Land, humping knife rests and crouching low every time the enemy's flares lit up the scene of desolation round about; all carried out in cold blood, the men frequently with none of the excitement of actual combat to stimulate their aching muscles. On the other hand, the discipline and devotion to duty required to overcome the laxness in turnout and soldierly bearing which was bound to develop under such conditions, and to maintain the cohesion and high military qualities demanded by the very nature of the work itself.[30]

Like any unit, Pioneer battalions had among their members men who for some deliberate, innocent or naive motive, either would not adhere to official regulations, or whose character or experience meant they could not withstand the strain of active service. It was noted earlier that recruits often took some time to become accustomed to army regulations; once overseas, their enforcement became even stronger. Any soldier who infringed them was subject to severe punishment. Several Pioneers suffered the ultimate penalty.[31]

Examples of lesser offences recorded in Pioneer War Diaries differ little from those sprinkled throughout those of any infantry or artillery unit. Corporal Shepherdson of the 19/N.F. was reduced to the ranks and given one month's Field Punishment No.2 for disobedience, while Pte. Hart, of the same battalion, was given 28 days No.1 for 'malingering'. The 6/East Yorks had a series of cases to deal with before it left Egypt for the Western Front: they included eight days Field Punishment No.2 for Pte. Maddison for drinking water from the Sweet Water Canal, four days No.2 for Pte. Andrews for (unspecified) 'irregular conduct on parade' and the loss of five day's pay for Pte. Gibson charged with 'neglect of duty when transport line Orderly'. Of a more serious nature were the 14 days No.1 given to Pte. Phillips for using obscene language to a NCO, a similar punishment for Pte. Finneran for 'reporting sick without a cause' and three months' hard labour awarded to Pte. Welsh by a Field General Court Martial for disobeying orders.

Pte. Stoker of the 22/DLI was also awarded hard labour – in his case six months – for wounding Pte. Dodds, who subsequently died from his injuries. In October 1916, Pte. Sherwin of the 12/Notts & Derby was given five years penal servitude for striking his superior officer. He was fortunate to have the sentence reduced to two years by the GOC 24th Division ten months later. Pte. Metcalf of the 9/Border Regiment was also fortunate to have his original sentence of three months Field Punishment No.1 for accidently shooting and killing his subaltern quashed by the GOC Third Army. In a rare example of a War Diary mentioning the trial of one of its men for desertion, the adjutant of the 5/DCLI recorded the sentence imposed upon Pte. Coster. This man had failed to answer his name at roll call on 13 June 1916 and had subsequently been arrested and sentenced to death. The verdict was confirmed and then commuted to five years in prison. Three days later General Monro, GOC First Army, suspended the sentence. A month later Coster was picked up by the Military Police at Locon. There is no further recorded mention of the matter until early November when Coster was among a group of men who were sent to the base as being permanently unfit for duty in the forward area. What happened to him after that is not recorded but he appears to have escaped execution. At the other extreme of the penal code, HQ of the 24/Manchester received a stern demand from the Town Major of Hazebrouck that men of the battalion refrain from climbing over a garden wall to steal fruit from the orchard within.

An excess of drink was the reason behind the appearance of many Pioneers before their C.O. and there must have been many such cases that do not figure in official or surviving documents. Many soldiers on leave or out on rest took solace and enjoyment in the bottle as a temporary release from the strain and perhaps disillusion with active service. Among several individuals mentioned in War Diaries are Pte. O'Connor of the 5/SWB, given 14 days No.1 for being found drunk in a French railway station, and CSM Bonsfield of the 11/DLI, who was found drunk on duty in October 1915. Sometimes groups of men would either decide to go on a binge, or simply happen upon circumstances which offered an opportunity which was too good to ignore. Private Howes of the 19/Middlesex remembered coming across a hoard of abandoned wine at Isola della Scala, with the result that his whole company ended up drunk.[32] While waiting for some long delayed buses on a cold night at Grouches, a party of the 18/Middlesex sloped off to some nearby estaminets. The 'regrettable result' of this expedition was that 23 men from two companies were gloriously drunk by the time the buses finally arrived. In the early hours, and with the temperature below freezing, they and the rest of the battalion ended up at the Citadel. Their blankets had been left behind with the transport and there were no tents to protect the men from the biting wind. The C.O., still outraged by the behaviour at Grouches, ordered the issue of a rum ration to the men in the two companies not affected by the earlier drinking bout. The C.O. also instructed Lt. Sifton, the O.C. of one of the companies concerned, to investigate and report upon the embarrassing incident. The colonel was so appalled by the young officer's 'quite inadequate' conclusions that he relieved him of his company and despatched him as a platoon commander to another company.

On at least one occasion all prisoners in one Pioneer battalion undergoing Field Punishment or under open arrest had their punishments commuted following a particularly fierce engagement. In October 1918 the 19/Lancashire Fusiliers made a frontal attack with other elements of its division near Naves. Three hundred and twenty men of two companies went over in four waves. In the face of overwhelming fire, none reached their objective and there were over 60 fatalities. As a token of the appreciation felt towards the Pioneers for taking on this unfamiliar role, the C.O. decided to cancel all sentences. The battalion took the opportunity of a few days' rest to collect the bodies and mourn its dead.[33]

Ordinary day to day offences by Pioneers and other troops were dealt with by their company commanders. If the matter was serious enough, or if the soldier wanted to take it to a higher authority, the C.O. would hear the case and pass judgement. To set an example to others who might wander from the straight and narrow, sometimes the punishment for a fairly minor

185

offence might be published in battalion orders. For example, L/Cpl. Turner of the 8/Sussex was fined 13/6d for 'damaging Government property'. Turner's crime was to alter some unspecified item of his clothing. Hardly the most heinous of crimes, the heavy fine of nearly two weeks' wages was probably awarded because the case coincided with an out-pouring of orders concerning, among other things, allegedly wanton wastage. These orders prohibited or warned against just about every conceivable offence known to the army. It was announced that men in a wide diversity of units had recently been discovered to be cutting the sleeves off their shirts; this 'unauthorized and wasteful practice' was ordered to cease immediately. Pay was to be deducted from men losing cap badges and as an increasing number of troops were returning from leave wearing non-issue boots, company commanders were instructed to demand to see the man's regulation boots; if they were not produced the soldier was to be fined for the cost of replacement. Other orders laid down the correct way of wearing braces, announced that the left hand salute was abolished, prohibited troops from passing through the officers' lines on their way to ablution benches, declared that marching in ranks of threes instead of fours was to be adopted on narrower roads and solemnly warned that any NCO or men who discovered a 'suspicious' rash on his skin should report sick. Sometimes having a rash could prove to be an advantage. When an outbreak of measles occurred in the 5/DCLI the Pioneers were allocated two estaminets and a coffee house for their sole use. Unlike their colleagues in other units, they would presumably not have to wait long to be served with their beer, wine and chips.

Minimising the risk of disease and infestation was a major concern of the army. Isolation was used for the more serious diseases and lesser measures for others. Orders for the 66th Division in 1918 announced that no man would be allowed to proceed on leave unless he had first obtained a chit from the M.O. declaring him to be vermin free. More severe punishments were reserved for men contacting what were considered to be avoidable serious diseases. Fourth Army's Standing Orders warned that starting from the date he was discharged from hospital, any NCO or man who contracted venereal disease would be deprived of leave for a year.

The consequences of offences committed while in training could follow the men across the Channel and cost them money when in the trenches. The men of W Company of the 19/N.F. were ordered to pay £2 0s 6d from their wages to cover half the cost of 12 ground sheets lost during manoeuvres in England. This was in addition to the £7 8s 8d they had to find as their share of the damage the battalion did to the barracks when leaving Perham Down. Furthermore, the battalion was warned that owing to continual claims for compensation made by local farmers, any soldier discovered cutting down trees near its camp would appear before the C.O.

Administering the daily routine of the battalion was principally the task of the adjutant. Because working parties were often dispersed over a wide area, many Pioneer battalions operated with two adjutants. One of them was sometimes called 'Assistant', but in practice this officer seems to have wielded as much power as his nominated superior. There is evidence to suggest that the assistant was in regular close contact with divisional HQ, without having to first seek approval from the official adjutant. The minutiae of battalion administration could result in prolonged correspondence with other agencies and if the work could be shared, so much the better.

A simple example of how much time might be involved in sorting out what was to the soldier an important consideration but to the machinery of the army as a whole of little significance, can be seen in the case of Sgt. North's kit. North, serving with the 4/Coldsteam Guards, was admitted to No.4 Field Ambulance on 1 July 1917.[34] He had his kit with him when admitted, and it went with him when he was transferred to No.47 Casualty Clearing Station two days later. Here it was handed in and the NCO was told it would be returned to him on discharge. When back with his unit North told his company commander that he was unable to retrieve his belongings. A substantial exchange of letters between the CCS, the divisional and later the corps medical services and the battalion's adjutant, Lt. Piggott, was the consequence of this administrative mix up. The issue was finally

187

settled in August when no less a personage than the Surgeon-General of XIV Corps was forced to admit that North's kit must have been broken up at the CCS. It was commonplace for kit and other possessions to disappear when men were admitted to hospitals, so it was probably with this in mind that the C.O. of the 9/Gloucester, Pioneers to the 66th Division, instructed that any man proceeding to hospital must take with him only leather equipment rather than the more functional, and thus more valuable, canvas webbing.

In all battalions a constant flow of men, arriving or departing, presented themselves at the transport lines; nominal rolls were constantly rewritten and personnel records logged. In normal times administrative demands upon orderly room staff were severe; during periods of intense work or fighting, they must have seemed intolerable. In 1917 many Pioneer battalions underwent drastic reconstitutions. It seems likely that in the affected battalions, while huge numbers of men left for fresh postings and new ones arrived, the adjutant's staff remained intact. They and the transport sections, which also appear to have been largely unaffected, became the few surviving original members of the proud battalions which, months or years before, had left the British Isles with such unity of purpose.

NOTES

1. The author Richard Aldington served as a private in the 11/Leicester. *In Death of a Hero*, infantrymen ask George Winterbourne several times if he has any candles. According to Aldington, Pioneers and R.E. were commonly supposed to be issued with large quantities of them. (Hogarth Press, 1984) p.278.
2. Falls, C. *Gordon Highlanders*, op.cit. p.75 In response to a letter from GOC 44th Bde. thanking the Gordons for helping the infantry to dig during exceptionally difficult circumstances, Colonel H.Gordon replied: 'We like to help the infantry whenever possible as it is the only way we can justify to ourselves the comparatively easy time we have'. (W.D.)
3. Churton, W.A. *The War Record of the 1/5th Cheshires*, (Chester, 1920) p.103.
4. Gilvary, op.cit. p.62

5. Mitchinson & McInnes, op.cit. p.87

6. Watts, Capt. C. papers. (Dept. of Documents, IWM)

7. Jaeger, op.cit. There were several different types of huts used by the BEF. The original Aylwin huts were not used after the summer of 1916, when the more common Armstrong and Nissen fabrications became available. The Armstrong huts were either 24' × 15' or 12' × 9'3" and the Nissen Bow Hut, 27' × 15'. Other portable varieties, such as the Tarrant and the Weblee were made in France by contractors. Although pre-fabricated, erecting them was no simple task. One Pioneer officer recalled: 'One of my most vivid memories, as the first company entrusted with this particular piece of meccano jigsaw [Nissen huts] is of one long cold day labouring for fruitless hours with nothing to show before we solved the vital point on which the instructions were silent. Unless the first few feet of interval board lining were fitted with the U piece externally, no lining could be put on at all! All else was clear to even a failed Eleven Plus save this one vital mystery. Did you not go into huts erected by other units with that cold gap of no interval lining boards for the first 18" from the floor?' (Captain E.Wood, 24/Manchester. Walsh papers, Oldham Local Studies Library)

8. Davson, H.M. *The History of the 35th Division in the Great War*, (Sifton, 1926) p.181

9. Adams, op.cit.

10. Unpublished diary of 11/DLI, attached to battalion W.D.

11. Atteridge, A.H. *The History of the 17th (Northern) Division*, (Glasgow, 1929) p.174

12. Croft, op.cit.

13. Churton, op.cit. p.103

14. Such orders were commonplace among both infantry and artillery units. For example, the 14/N.F. was instructed to ensure that all shelters and the cookhouse must be left 'scrupulously clean'.

15. Davidson, op.cit.

16. Pte.Harrison of the 22/DLI was run over and killed by a light railway locomotive used to supply guns sited in what was supposed to be a rest camp.

17. Jaeger, op.cit.

18. Hansard, 1915, 654. (31/11/15)

19. ibid.

20. Hansard, 1916, 998. (19/7/16)

21. Gilvary, op.cit. p.54

22. Animals too could sometimes be acquired by dubious means. A French interpreter was thrown from his horse and killed near to where a party

of the 5/DCLI was working. The Pioneers promptly seized the animal and put it on the battalion's ration strength.

23   See Appendix II
24. England, op.cit. p.81
25. For the benefit of the 24/Manchester, a subaltern in the R.E. noted the different carrying capacites for a three-ton lorry and a G.S. wagon:

	Lorry G.S.	Wagon
Decauville track	150 yds	50 yds
Barrels of cement	15	5
Trench gratings (6'× 18")	10	30
Pickets	600	200

(Walsh papers, op.cit.)

26. Mitchinson & McInnes, op.cit. p.148
27. Croft, op.cit.
28. Tymms, op.cit.
29. Croft, op.cit.
30. Whalley-Kelly, H. 'Ich Dien', The POW Volunteers (South Lancashire Regiment), 1914-34 (Gale & Polden, 1935) p.81
31. Five members of Pioneer battalions and one other man attached to the R.E. were executed. See Putkowski & Sykes, Shot at Dawn, (Pen & Sword, 1992)
32. Howes, H.G. papers. (Dept. of Documents, IWM)
33. Most of the battalion's dead were collected by the survivors a week later and were eventually concentrated into Haspres British Cemetery.
34. Piggott, J.C. papers. (Liddle Collection)

Chapter 10

IN SEARCH OF SKILLS

The heavy casualties suffered during the opening and subsequent days of the Somme necessitated an alteration in the way by which front line battalions were reinforced. No longer could a man expect to be sent automatically from his regimental training or reserve battalion, via the base camps in France, to his parent battalion serving abroad. The priority for officers at the base camps on the French coast was the despatch of reinforcements arriving from the U.K. to battalions needing a draft. Frequently men did remain within their own regiment, but many were forced to make the change from one to another. At the time, this procedure was heavily criticized both within the army and inside Parliament. Its opponents argued that all the work done in the training battalions to imbue the men with regimental *esprit de corps* would be lost if they were subsequently transferred to a regiment with different traditions and customs.

The War Office had not been deaf to the complaints of senior officers, Territorial Associations and M.P.s, and in August announced the creation of a Training Reserve.[1] The purpose of this new organization was an attempt to rationalize the whole training and drafting system and justify its practice of despatching men from home to other than their own overseas units. In its proposals the War Office acknowledged the importance of maintaining *esprit*, but also added that it was 'impossible to obtain in every case the drafts required for particular units from the reserve units which draw their recruits from the area affiliated to that unit'. Furthermore, the introduction of

191

the Military Service Act had largely removed the previous obligation of posting men in some units to a battalion of their choice.
It had tried, so it believed, to post men if not from battalion
reserves, at least by regimental reserves. The War Office now
warned that, 'in order to meet the urgent need of the moment, it
has been necessary to go further and pool by regimental
districts'. Hence the creation of the Training Reserve which, it
was hoped, would lessen the necessity of transferring men from
one regiment to another. In an effort to avoid or ward off further
criticism and discontent, the War Office finished the outline of
its proposals by appealing to the loyalty and patriotism of the
army. Commanders of all army, corps and divisions had their
attention drawn to the memo which finished with the assertion
that:

> The Army Council are confident that . . . the present situation
> will be recognized as unavoidable, and that all officers and men
> will loyally support a step which has been taken for the benefit
> of the Empire and of the Army . . . and will do their utmost to
> prevent any friction arising as a result of this decision.[2]

Although it still rankled, by 1917 this method of reinforcement
had become a fact of life in the BEF. The losses at Arras and then
in the opening stages of Third Ypres meant that the demands of
manpower would have to be met no matter what sentimentalities
or traditions might be impugned. Not surprisingly, Pioneer
battalions had also been affected by the system and had been
accepting drafts from many regiments and corps which had no
connection with their own area or regimental origins. For
example, the 19/L.F. received nearly 200 men from the 2nd and
3rd Battalions of the Monmouth Regiment in September 1916,
while the 22/DLI absorbed 50 men from the 11th Reserve
Cavalry Brigade in December 1916. This group of men was
described as 'partially trained',[3] a rather more polite expression
than that which described the 42 men of the Leicester Regiment
who arrived at the transport lines of their new battalion, the
8/Sussex. They were succinctly declared to be a 'very bad draft'.
The one hundred men of the KOYLI posted to the 22/DLI in June

1917 were accepted with alacrity as most of them had served in France before. Furthermore, a good number of them were former miners and thus used to pick and shovel work. Of another draft of 30 which arrived the following month, 'practically all' had previously served with an unstated Pioneer battalion. Other battalions received large numbers of men from unspecified units. They had simply been posted to the Pioneers in groups from the base depots. As records frequently do not give their unit of origin, it makes it particularly difficult to identify these drafts and their date of arrival with certainty.

Others are easier to pin-point. The 8/Ox & Bucks received a draft of 112 from the Royal Fusiliers in December 1916. These men were apparently kept in the rear area for a month's training between being posted and allocated to companies. Unfortunately it is not made clear whether they were receiving training in infantry or pioneering skills. The 11/DLI was pleased with a draft of 82 in January 1917, the NCOs among them being described as a 'good set' on account of the fact that they had all served for at least 12 months and had attended a month's course at Eastern Command's NCO school. This contrasted with an earlier group of 50 from the regiment's own 16th Battalion who, for some undisclosed reason, were said to be 'not suitable for a Pioneer battalion'. The 16/Royal Irish Rifles received an unlikely draft of Pioneers from the London Rifle Brigade in February 1917. Despite conscription, the LRB would still only accept men whom it considered would maintain its traditional character. Consequently these 90 men would have come from clerical rather than labouring backgrounds.

Several Pioneer units received men from Entrenching Battalions.[4] These organizations were really holding units in which men sometimes served between being posted from the base to their battalions at the front. These units usually only retained a colonel, an adjutant, a sergeant-major, a quarter-master-sergeant and one other sergeant. They often possessed no transport and frequently had to rely upon the courtesy and assistance of nearby units to borrow cookers or camp kettles. The battalions were occasionally a thousand or more strong and undertook work such as digging, pumping, wiring, trench boarding and so on. Men might spend three weeks or more in such a unit, normally posted to them in regimental batches and often with their own officers. They would usually be sent out in company strength to various locations, the company frequently comprised of men from the same regiment. After their period of service, or when their receiving battalion was out of the line or able to absorb a new draft, they were posted. They were frequently despatched together with those men with whom they had first arrived and, at least in 1915 and the first half of 1916, to battalions of their own regiment.

Those Pioneer battalions which did take drafts from Entrenching Battalions – such as the 19/L.F., which received 139 former DLI men *via* the 5th Entrenching Battalion, and the 18/N.F. which took 47 from the 2nd Entrenching Battalion – were generally greeted with some enthusiasm by their new units. The men from the 5th Entrenching Battalion were described as 'well disciplined, well trained and physically good'. The quality and standard of training of a later draft of 180 from the Yorkshire Regiment which came *via* the 10th Entrenching Battalion, was thought to be 'particularly good'. Even the Pioneer battalion of the Guards Division, the 4/Coldstream, had to wait for some of its drafts to serve time in the 7th Entrenching Battalion before they too were sent to their unit. Some of its reinforcements came direct from the Guards Division Reinforcement Battalion, but men continued to arrive from what became the 7th (Guards) Entrenching Battalion well into 1917.[5]

Some fortunate battalions were clearly unaffected by the changes in the reinforcement policy of the base camps and continued to receive men directly from their own depots. The 1/Monmouth received 42 'of good physique and turnout' from its own depot as late as September 1917 and the 22/DLI took 80 of a 'very useful type' from its own regiment in September 1916.[6] Clearly, on many occasions and despite intense pressure, the base could, in the view of the front line officers, get it right. Within only two months of overseas service, the 5/Northants took a draft of 'very good' men from its own regimental depot, many of whom had already previously served in France. The 5/Cheshire received large numbers of men from its own third line

194

battalion and its 6th(Reserve) Battalion in 1916. In fact, this battalion was to receive only one draft of non-Cheshire men during the entire war. Similarly, the 5/Border took a draft of 130 men in October 1916 from its own 3rd Battalion 'almost entirely made up of men who had served with other battalions of the Border Regiment'. The 8/Sussex was also delighted to take a draft of 50 men from its own regiment during the hectic days of July 1916 and the 8/Royal Scots received a huge draft of 306 in late 1916 from four of its own second line Territorial battalions. The C.O. of the 10/DCLI was however a little disconcerted to discover that after only two months overseas the battalion was sent a draft of men, 50% of whom had been rejected by the battalion as unsuitable just before it left for France. Perhaps by way of compensation, he did manage to retrieve another draft which was originally meant to have come to him, but was wrongly posted to the 1/Wiltshire.

On the frequent occasions when men might be posted from different regiments or from units which had little or no connection with pioneer work, it did not mean that their expertise or experience could not be utilized by their new battalions. Sgt. Wheeler for example, late of the 11/Hussars, was posted to the 4/South Lancs in March 1916 and was promptly promoted to CSM. In distant Salonika, the 26/Middlesex and the 8/Ox & Bucks received drafts of men from the Scottish Horse. The Ox & Bucks put them into the transport section to replace their own men who were perhaps not up to the job, while the Middlesex put its allocation into the machine gun section because they were 'such keen fighters'.[7]

However contentious and even annoying the arrival of some of the disparate drafts might have been at the time, it was nothing compared to two further problems that would confront battalion commanders in the autumn of 1917 and the early months of 1918.

The first of the two controversies arose as a result of the army's desire to make the Pioneer battalions more suited for the role for which they were designed. It was noted earlier that the Army Council Instruction which created the Pioneers and stipulated the proportion of men who were used to working with a spade had, of necessity and exigency, been largely ignored. There were exceptions. For example it is known that a fairly large draft of men from the Lowland R.E. Division were posted to the 9/North Staffs in April 1917, but such instances at that stage of the war were rare. By September 1917, changes in organizational structures and in enlistment policy meant that attempts could be made to rectify the consequent skill shortages within Pioneer units. The result of these changes was to allow the release of unskilled men then serving as Pioneers to conventional infantry battalions. To replace them, large numbers of R.E. were to be posted to Pioneer battalions.

Although some of the Pioneer battalions which received these R.E. noted that the new men did include carpenters, bricklayers and painters among their number, how skilled as field engineers and therefore suited to pioneer work these men were, is open to some dispute. In pre-war days, recruits to the R.E. underwent a trade test, but what evidence there is seems to suggest that during the war most recruits did not take a test. It is clearly admitted that in the early days of the war, when Woolwich and Chatham were besieged by new recruits, trade tests were dispensed with. Whether they were re-introduced when things had calmed down a little is unclear, (although there were several Army Instructions to the effect that they should be given to later recruits). Men with recognized skilled civilian trades, perhaps confirmed by production of a union membership card, could be posted to specialist units, repair shops etc., while many with mining experience ended up in tunnelling companies. The sheer explosion in the size of the corps undoubtedly meant that large numbers of men were simply trained in the basics of soldiering, instructed in the rudiments of field engineering – wiring, digging, bridging, etc. – and sent overseas. To cope with the hugely increased number of recruits, the R.E. created several reserve battalions. These usually numbered between 2,500 – 3,500 men and in theory provided five weeks' drill on the square, one week of musketry and six of field engineering.[8] As the quotation from the C.O. of the 24/Manchester below suggests, the incessant demands for men from the front meant that the period of training was frequently reduced. To compensate for the possible lack of skills among the men, it was expected that sufficient numbers of NCOs and officers would be adequately schooled in more advanced techniques to instruct and supervise the work being undertaken in the field. The more specialist apparatus could be made by craftsmen in the rear and transported forward as required.

That there were shortages in some trades required by the R.E. is evident from corps' records. It was not too serious until 1917 when, with munitions requiring an ever-increasing number of men, recruits with some specialist skills were becoming difficult to obtain. On call up those with certain trades, such as electricians, could be retained by the R.E., but if they were of A1 medical category, men with other skills could be posted to the infantry or artillery. This meant that blacksmiths, carpenters, plumbers and bricklayers, for example, could be made available for posting to any unit needing a draft.[9] Pioneer battalions would not of course mind receiving these men in the normal routine of reinforcement, but, as they were to discover, because their fitter counterparts were more likely to be retained by R.E. Field Companies or sent to the infantry, their physical ability to do the arduous work of the pioneer was open to question.

For the first two years of the war, R.E. reinforcements were sent to No.4 General Base Depot or No.2 Territorial Base Depot at Rouen. Men usually remained at the depots for some time, often employed as dock labour or on garrison guard duties and such like. Very little military or engineering training was apparently carried out. In February 1917 a new R.E. base depot was established and the classification of reinforcements by skill and degree of training was commenced. Shortly after it opened, this new depot began to receive men from the reserve battalions. The first to arrive were men of high or A1 medical category who had enlisted in 1914 and 1915 as home service Territorials. The passage of the Military Service Act now made these men liable for overseas duty and consequently they were combed out of the reserve battalions. In the first few months of the process some 5,000 of these Territorials were sent to France and posted to infantry battalions rather than R.E. Field Companies. They were replaced in the reserve battalions by men of a lower medical category. In the late summer of 1917, with demands for manpower increasing, these B1 men were also combed out and sent to France.

These changes meant that by August 1917 there were some 8,000 R.E. available for posting to Employment Companies, Artisan Companies, Labour battalions and Pioneer battalions. In the effort to increase the number of men with skills more suited to pioneer work within the battalions, many of these men were earmarked for despatch to Pioneer units. Consequently in September and October, Pioneer orderly rooms began to receive orders warning them to prepare to absorb large numbers of R.E. and to allocate a similar number of their own men for posting elsewhere. Several examples of the units affected will suffice to demonstrate the upheaval this entailed.

The 12/Yorks received 369 men from the 1st(Reserve) Battalion R.E. in September 1917 and was ordered in exchange to despatch 184 and 180 men to the 1/4th and 1/5th Territorial battalions of its own regiment. The 19/L.F. received 339 from the same R.E. battalion who, it was reported, were all tradesmen with 'technical (but little military) experience', and sent the identical number to its Territorial Force battalions of the 66th Division. The 6/East Yorks had to send 360 to three of its Service battalions in exchange for their allotment of R.E. The 11/Leicester lost 422 of its own men to T.F. and Service battalions of its regiment in return for 450 R.E. The 12/Notts & Derby despatched 256 to the 2/5 Notts & Derby, while the 7/York & Lancs received 384 from the Royal Anglesey Engineers in exchange for a similar number of their own sent elsewhere. The impact these changes made upon battalions could be huge – sometimes amounting to over 50% of their strength. Some units clearly tried to lessen the trauma by sending away men who had been posted to the battalion from other regiments in earlier drafts. Contriving to retain as many as possible of its original men, the 17/N.F. for example, exchanged men who had arrived from the Army Cyclist Corps some months earlier for its new R.E. For others, there was no alternative other than to despatch some of their original members. The diarist of the 19/N.F. thought it was 'heartbreaking' that its old hands had to go, to be replaced by men of dubious quality. He noted that the German offensive was likely to begin and that his fit men had been replaced by those with 'arms in slings, ruptured men and weaklings of many kinds'. The 7/York & Lancs recorded its unhappiness at the changes in personnel, albeit in fairly restrained tones. The battalion history described having to select from men, many of whom had served with it since its formation, as 'an invidious task'. It noted that the action 'naturally caused much indignation', but also accepted that it was a necessary part of the future re-organization of the BEF. The battalion's historian described the new men as volunteers of 1914 who had been 'kept at home against their will . . . all being skilled tradesmen, they were well fitted . . . and once acclimatized . . . pulled their weight with right good will'.[10]

Another battalion C.O. held a less charitable view of the men posted to his battalion. Lt.Col. Pountney had only recently taken command of the Oldham Comrades, the 24/Manchester. Having come from a Territorial battalion, the Hackney Rifles, he was well aware of the importance of battalion *esprit* and of the bond between locally recruited troops. He penned a stinging criticism of the R.E. arrivals:

> I desire to point out that carrying out these instructions will mean the complete destruction of the Battalion under my command for the following reasons:-The instructions are to send away to seven different units, belonging to three different Divisions, 378 of the men at present with my battalion. This draft together with the 80 casualties which have occurred since the unit came into the line would exhaust the whole working strength of the Battalion, leaving only a number of senior NCOs, the transport section and the specialists.
>
> The 378 men I am instructed to take in and are wholly untrained and undisciplined and their physical standard is low. None have seen war service. They are apparently low category men who have been left at home to do ordinary civilian work in the Army. They do not possess the rudiments of a military training, have no musketry instruction, and scarcely know how to salute. They are called 'Sappers' but certainly have no right to that name. I state this of my own knowledge, having personally

examined 113 men of this draft who have been sent on to me. The behaviour of these men under fire has been tested and was found to be very unsatisfactory.

I need scarcely lay stress on the very difficult nature of the work which the Pioneers of the 7th Division are being called upon to do at the present time. It is work that demands the very highest forms of discipline and of physical fitness. These qualities, the Battalion under my command has shown itself to possess. But if the old men are drafted out and the new ones taken in, the standard of the unit would be reduced to that of a Training Battalion at home. I put it quite bluntly I could not guarantee to do the work we are doing with such a battalion.[11]

Despite Pountney's letter, the die had been cast and the proposed transfer was ordered to proceed.

Pountney's task of selecting men to be transferred from his battalion was made more difficult by the fact that the 24th had been a very fortunate battalion. Between going into the line as ordinary infantry in February 1916 and its conversion to a Pioneer unit in May 1916, it had lost 46 men. Working as Pioneers it had suffered fewer than one hundred fatalities. Consequently there were still probably well over 300 original men in what had been a very locally-raised battalion. In order to make way for the R.E., Pountney now had the unenviable task of posting men who had specifically enlisted with workmates in the battalion, to other units. To emphasize further the radical change the transfers would make in the nature of the battalion, most of the new arrivals originated not from the cotton towns of Lancashire, but from the Medway towns of Kent.

Many other units underwent a similar, significant transition. The 392 ex-R.E. who arrived at the 9/North Staffs were Scottish, a fact which caused the battalion's diarist to regret that the battalion was 'very much less representative of the county of Staffordshire', while the 19/Welch took 197 men from the 1st and 2nd London Reserve Field Companies. Some battalions which had received drafts to replace losses taken on the Somme and at Arras absorbed them without having their character dramatically changed. For example both the 5th and 6/SWB had taken large numbers of Welshmen from the Monmouth

Regiment, while besides the Londoners, the 19/Welch absorbed a large draft from the Welch Fusiliers. The 11/South Lancs remained essentially a battalion of Lancastrians from around the St Helen's area despite considerable numbers of transfers, and the 11/King's Liverpool retained its identity as a West Lancashire battalion. Similarly, the 14/N.F. remained very much a battalion from Durham and Northumberland. Apart from a few fatalities of men posted from the Bedfordshire Regiment to the 9/Seaforth Highlanders, it is difficult to identify many English in either that battalion or in the 9/Gordon Highlanders and the 6/Argyll & Sutherland Highlanders. These battalions however tended to be the lucky ones. At the same time as it was sending men to the Seaforths, the Bedfordshire Regiment also supplied drafts to the 4/Royal Welch Fusiliers and the 16/Royal Irish Rifles. This last battalion, originally recruited from County Down, also took a large number of men from the 3/11 London Regiment, the Finsbury Rifles.

For those battalions which did receive large numbers of men from other regiments and regions of the country, communication and regimental traditions could cause difficulties. One company commander of a battalion from West Yorkshire received a draft of men from the Northumberland Fusiliers in mid-1916. One of these men was subsequently appointed CSM, but the officer claimed that for the final two years of the war he never understood a word his CSM addressed to him.[12] Men posted from rifle regiments to non-rifle battalions had to learn to march at a more leisurely pace and also adapt to different methods of discipline and procedure within their adoptive unit.

While the troops of the Pioneer battalions might not have liked the practice of being inundated by men whom the infantry had long believed to be 'mad, married or Methodist', they probably understood the theory behind the posting of the ex-R.E. to their unit. What they would have found more difficult to appreciate was why R.E. were also being posted to infantry battalions. In all, some 5,000 of these A1 men were distributed among infantry units. Among other battalions of the Northumberland Fusiliers, for example, the regular 1st Battalion took a large draft of men from the Lowland Division R.E. in April 1917, while in March the 25th (Service) Battalion took a substantial number from the Hants (Fortress) R.E. When many Pioneer battalions had been suffering from hugely depleted ranks and shortages of men with specific skills, it seemed to make no sense to fill them up with men of low medical category who might not even have ever taken a trade test, when suitable men were evidently available. Besides that of the Oldham Comrades, several War Diaries remark upon the quality of their new men in less than glowing terms. The 9/North Staffs thought its ex-R.E. were 'rather old' and that they did not possess the 'strength for carrying or the skills in digging of the Staffordshire miner', while the 9/South Staffs, although admitting that its 399 ex-R.E. were of good physique and intelligence, thought 'the average age was rather high'. This opinion is somewhat misleading because an analysis of the ages of fatalities among these and other ex-R.E. men shows that they were spread across the whole range of military service. The suggestion that the younger men went to the infantry and the older to the Pioneers is not sustainable.[13] Neither should we assume that all these men were absolute crocks. One man sent to the 12/KOYLI was far from being physically unfit. Colin Blythe was a professional cricketer for Kent and England who had joined the Kent Fortress Engineers in 1914. He was killed a few weeks after being drafted.[14]

Although many of the men were certainly of less than A1 category, whether all the R.E. drafts were made up of such poor *soldiers* as Pountney believed, is not known. No other War Diary speaks in such a deprecatory manner, but there are odd references from individuals. Major T.G.Davidson of the 22/DLI for example, reflected that the 'type of man and officer . . . has markedly deteriorated', and that although there were exceptions, he thought they were 'very unwilling individuals'. When it came to work, not only were the new men more reluctant, but also in his opinion, 'less handy'.[15] What is clear is that many units did lose at least a substantial proportion of their ex-R.E. men in a fairly short space of time. Reasons are not normally given – one of the few exceptions being contained in the War Diary of the 19/L.F. This unit sent 130 of its recent arrivals to the R.E. depot at Rouen for what was described as 'special work'. It might have been decided that if they were reasonably fit they would be better off returning to the R.E. and serving in Field Companies rather than remaining as Pioneers. This might suggest that they did possess the specialist skills which the R.E. were finding difficult to provide for their own units or it might simply have been the easiest administrative way for a battalion to lose a large number of men in preparation for the receipt of a draft of lower category men then being posted from home.

Some of the battalions who did lose their R.E. were the 19/L.F., the 12/KOYLI, the 6/East Yorks, the 11/King's Liverpool and the 22/DLI. The men did not usually go *en masse*, but more commonly over a period of weeks in batches of around 50. When the 10/DCLI was ordered to return 50 of them to Rouen it reported that it was 'impossible' to comply because it had only 19 such men.[16] These transfers coincided with the later unfounded contemporary speculation over the future of Pioneer battalions as a whole. The men knew that if their battalions were to continue to exist, the large numbers of the now disappearing former R.E. would have to be replaced by someone. The thoughtful among them would know that given the alleged manpower shortages, they would hardly have been brought up to strength by massive drafts of fit young men from home. What few of them would probably have anticipated was the extent to which they were about to be swamped by men of significantly lower medical status than even many of the ex-R.E. The quality and nature of the men and boys arriving in the early months of 1918 to replace the departed ex-R.E. were to cause a further headache for several battalion C.O.s.

Providing the new arrivals remained in a minority within their battalion, the majority of Pioneer units seem to have absorbed these latest drafts with relatively little difficulty and disruption. By this stage of the war battalions were used to accepting men of a wide range of ages, skills, physical condition and training. Indeed, nearly all infantry battalions were in the process of taking young boys or men whose call-up had been been deferred. The 31st Division posted a substantial number of 18 year olds to its Pioneers and, in the 18th Division, the 8/Sussex acquired 92 men 'most of whom were only 19 and out for the first time'.

The 6/SWB received young soldiers from Graduated Battalions which it described as 'good material but very immature', as well as some men who were over 35. These troops were 'combings' from protected industries or what was noted as 'departmental' corps. The War Diary of the 22/DLI complained that the physique of a draft, probably from the Lancashire Fusiliers, was 'much below average', while the 19/L.F. described their latest intake as men who had 'practically all been out before, but are not quite fit again'. The War Diary optimistically recorded: 'it is hoped however, that they will eventually become fit'. One undisclosed C.O. of a Pioneer battalion had been complaining in mid-1917 that neither the officers nor the men then being sent up to him were up to the task. He considered that because they were infantry reinforcements they lacked the engineering knowledge and capacity for manual labour. Consequently, he wrote, 'they break down easily'.[17] By late 1917 the 7/York & Lancs acknowledged that 'all fit men' were needed for the infantry and accepted that 'category men and others who were not considered fit for the firing line' ended up in Pioneer battalions. Its chronicler did add that the battalion was 'disappointed to find that few of them had any previous experience of technical or manual work'.[18] The 5/Cheshire was not quite as stoical in its acceptance of this practice. Having been ordered to post 100 of its A1 men to the regiment's 10th Battalion, it received 100 B1 men. 'All' these men were suffering from 'some complaint or weakness'. The writer went on to add that it was 'difficult to understand' why the changes were required 'as Pioneer work is very strenuous'.[19] Another aspect of the exchange which might also have rankled with the Cheshires was the order that 34 of their A1 men should be posted to the 5th Entrenching Battalion. They could probably not understand why A1 men should go to such a unit in preference to remaining with the Pioneers.

These battalions received substantial but not overwhelming numbers of B1 men. Yet even among these, the arrival of the drafts did cause some concern. Any battalion originals might look upon the poor physical condition of the B1 troops and reflect upon the work and sacrifices made in earlier years. Now, along with the disruption caused by the arrival of the ex-R.E. a few months earlier, many of the old soldiers feared for the future of their battalion. Sitting on his pack on a cold winter's morning, William Jaeger observed with some trepidation the arrival of these troops at the 11/King's. He later described the newcomers as a 'different class of men to our original chaps of August 1914',[20] believing that because more than half of them wore glasses, had round shoulders, suffered from numerous physical defects and were past middle age, they would never have passed the 1914 medical. He recalled that he did not expect them to be put to the same sort of work as 'healthy Pioneers' and assumed that in anticipation of their arrival the battalion had been doing little except road repairs for some weeks. If Jaeger and his comrades had witnessed the substantially larger numbers of such men arriving at various other Pioneer battalions, they might have felt inclined to question again what the War Office's intentions were for Pioneer units.

According to the army's classification, B1 men were fit enough to serve as garrison troops abroad. Many Pioneer battalions, the 5/SWB, 19/N.F., 11/King's and the 6/East Yorks, to cite only four, received large drafts of these men. A history of the 5/DCLI recalls how its draft of over over 400 men, mostly aged 19 or under[21] and 'entirely untrained for active service conditions', arrived at their new battalion. These boys came from the 4th (Reserve) Battalion then stationed at Larkhill. The draft left the base at Etaples with only a major, a CSM and a CQMS to march it to its new battalion. When they stopped for the night it was discovered the troops had no idea of how to cook in their mess tins. Fortunately, a nearby infantry unit lent the draft its cookers. The major managed to scrounge some tents and told off the boys in batches of 21. 'Pandemonium' broke out when he ordered the boys to bed, for they had regrouped themselves into tent parties with the result that unpopular members were left outside. Having already concluded that they draft were 'totally devoid of discipline and training', the major and his two NCOs viewed the prospect of the next day's 12 mile march with kit with some 'misgivings'. It was obvious that the troops were far from fit, and current regulations applying in Britain stated that B1 men should not march further than five miles. Nevertheless, the march had to be attempted and the boys were divided into parties of 40, each commanded by a 'committee consisting of the most insubordinate'. The fears of the major were soon realized. Within 30 minutes, 20 had fallen out and when the column reached the first hill, hordes of the boys collapsed on either side of the road. Eventually the last platoon, which was being whipped on from the rear, became the leading platoon. A passing officer of the War Graves Commission helped the major and his NCOs to get some semblance of order back into the column. When it resumed, the march was stopped by frequent shouts of 'Halt!' emanating not from the officer but from exhausted boys within the ranks. Attempts to identify the culprits were met by jeers from the column. On viewing a hairpin bend ahead, the troops broke ranks and careered across the fields to rejoin the road so avoiding needless exertion. Fortunately, a mounted officer and several more NCOs arrived from the battalion bringing with them two lorries. Kits were loaded on the lorries, but it still took eight hours to march 12 miles. The chronicler decided that this was 'no mean achievement' because only six of the youths failed to finish the march on their feet. Despite this less than auspicious start to their overseas service, within a week of their arrival the battalion was to hold ferocious German attacks upon Merville for over 48 hours and suffer over 450 casualties in the process.

Exceptional as this tale might have been, it is clear that many of the B1 men posted to battalions were returned very quickly to the base. Only 27 of a draft of 100 posted to the 10/DCLI actually joined it – the remaining 73 being so unfit they did not get further than the 2nd Division's Depot Battalion. So many of these newly posted B1 men were so patently unsuited to front line duties that even if they did arrive at the transport lines, battalion M.O.s had no alternative other than to send them back. To give just one example: 17 of the 99 who were sent to the 18/N.F. were back down at the base within three weeks of posting; many of those who were retained could not perform the same tasks or fulfil the same work schedules as the A1 men. As the demands made by the authorities upon the battalions were not proportionally reduced, this meant more work for the fitter men. The physical condition of some B1 men did apparently improve as time passed, but many more ended up in hospital. When possible the men with the greatest disabilities were put on administrative or light work, but as one battalion history candidly recalled: 'It must be admitted that their presence in the Battalion very considerably affected the work, and on marches of any length they were always a source of trouble and anxiety, a large number of them being unable to carry their packs for any distance'.[22]

Handicapped as these B1 men were in attempting many of the jobs ascribed to Pioneers, there were others who were in an even worse condition. Battalion commanders might have felt hard done by when such men were posted to them, but the divisional commander of the 59th Division must have felt particularly aggrieved when he reviewed his Pioneer battalion, the 25/KRRC. So many of the battalion, supposedly comprised of B1 men, were being reported as unfit for duty that the Inspector of Drafts arrived to have a look himself. On viewing the battalion the inspector immediately reclassified over 10% of its officers and other ranks as B2 or B3, and promptly sent them to the base. The battalion then remained well below strength for the rest of the war. Fortunately it was not called upon to do anything more strenuous than some fairly sedate, basic pioneering work.

Other battalions were more fortunate and avoided having a substantial part of the unit re-built by an influx of category men. They might have had to accept a number of such soldiers, but might at the same time also receive a draft of A1 men. In February 1918 the 6/East Yorks received five officers and 121 other ranks from its 12th Battalion. In September of the previous year the 6th had sent some of the 360 men it was required to lose in order to make room for its R.E. intake to, among others, the 12th Battalion. It is conceivable that some of the men arriving at the 6th in February were men who had originally been Pioneers, then became conventional infantry, and were now returning to their original battalion to become Pioneers once agin. Evidence from their army numbers suggests that this was certainly the case for several. The 11/Hants was happy to receive 100 fit men from its own 14th Battalion in February, the 5/SWB received 50 other ranks from its own disbanded 12th Battalion, the 5/DCLI nearly

200 from its 6th Battalion and the 11/King's absorbed 135 men from the disbanded 2/5th. By another strange quirk of fate, any surviving A1 men who had been posted to the 1/7th N.F. from the 17th Battalion in September 1917 became Pioneers again when the 7th was itself converted to a Pioneer unit in February 1918. Having been disappointed to lose some of its own men in the previous October, consolation of a sort came to the 19/N.F. in February. The 19th received a draft of men and officers from the regiment's disbanded 24/27th Battalion: 'That was a draft of men; they proved themselves time and time again'.[23]

The appearance of the category men coincided with another flurry of conversions. Despite having been overseas for up to three years, several regular and Territorial divisions of the BEF still did not have Pioneer units attached to them. In view of the ceasefire on the Eastern Front and the anticipated German offensive in the west, the War Office decided that the current process of reducing the number of infantry battalions in a division offered the opportunity to make the Pioneer establishment of those units complete. This meant that like their counterparts in 1915 and 1916, several more infantry battalions were about to lose their status as fighting units and become Pioneers.

An earlier burst of reorganization had taken place when the second line Territorial divisions went overseas in early 1917. Not all of these divisions received Pioneers immediately upon arrival – some had to wait as long as 12 months before having a battalion permanently attached. The new allocations necessitated the posting of both first and second line Territorial and New Army battalions to these divisions. As a mark of respect for the time spent together and the shared experiences of the Territorials with their regular and later New Army comrades, divisions usually put on some kind of show when the chosen battalions left for their new postings. The bands of the 1/Middlesex, 4/King's Liverpool and 2/Argyll and Sutherland Highlanders, for example, played out the 4/Suffolk as the Territorials reluctantly left to join the 58th Division. The Suffolks had served in several divisions since arriving in France and were in the process of leaving a New Army division for one composed of second line Territorial units of the London

Regiment. The bands of the 15th Division also played for the 6/7th Royal Scots Fusiliers when it left the division to join the 59th. Before departure the battalions were invariably addressed by the brigadier, thanked for the good work they had performed and told how much he regretted their loss. Although these speeches were routine and expected, there certainly was a feeling of widespread regret that many long-established relationships were in the process of dissolution.

The War Diaries of the early 1918 batch of conversions, like those of battalions converted earlier in the war, rarely express any note of emotion when recording their transition to Pioneers. That of the 1/7th N.F. notes simply, 'Move by motor lorry from Brandhoek to Fouquereul to take up duty with the 42nd Division as Pioneer Battalion', while that of the 9/DLI states, 'Battalion to become a Pioneer battalion'. The intelligence officer of the 16/HLI wrote: 'At 12 noon the 16/HLI was transferred from the 97th Brigade and posted as Divisional Pioneer battalion'. A rare example of emotion was displayed by the adjutant of the 5/Sussex in August 1915 during the first rush of conversions. The battalion had been warned that they were likely to be transferred from the regular 1st Division to the 48th, a division of Territorials. Two days later the divisional commander inspected the battalion, thanked it for 'always playing the game' and then, with a suggestion of incredulity, the adjutant recorded: 'Told we may be turned into Pioneers!'. The 2/5th Loyal North Lancs explained that, 'Owing to the re-organization of Brigades . . . the Battalion has been selected Pioneer Battalion to the Division'. Finally, the diary of the 6/7th Royal Scots Fusiliers simply says: 'This morning [21 February 1918] the Battalion leaves the 15th Division to go as Pioneer Battalion to the 59th Division. The brigadier expressed his sorrow at its departure'. Of course, the War Diary was not intended to be a repository of recorded emotions so it is understandable that most of them simply state that the conversion had taken place and then proceeded to get on with the job.

Rather more surprising is the absence of comments on feelings or reactions to conversion in the divisional and regimental histories published after the war. Neither do they go into much detail when discussing how and why battalions were selected for conversion. The most frequent comments usually claim that the reason for selection had been because the battalion had a proven record as diggers: the 5/Cheshire was chosen apparently 'in consequence of earning a high reputation as diggers and as constructors of field works',[24] while the 16/HLI was selected 'by reason of the uniformly high standard of working and fighting which it attained during twenty-seven months on the Western Front'.[25] The 4/Suffolk was 'disappointed' to learn of its conversion,[26] while the 8/Royal Scots, which had had the distinction of being the first Scottish T.F. battalion to be employed on active service, was said to have been chosen because it was 'composed principally of miners . . . [and] its work with pick and shovel had always been remarkably good'.[27] Several other unit and divisional histories make similar comments, but a more detailed discussion on how the experiences and work of Pioneer units were approached by writers after the war follows later

The departure of these battalions from divisions to take up a new role as Pioneers was repeated in other divisions up and down the British sector of the Western Front. Many battalions were completely disbanded and others became available for conversion to Pioneers. Famous and battle-tested battalions of both the Territorial Force and the New Armies were not exempt from the possibility of being removed from the brigades and divisions in which they had served abroad for perhaps three years. Most of these resented and disliked the scheme, but the demands of the army were paramount. Issues of sentimentality were not permitted to influence the decisions which would, it was intended, prepare the BEF to absorb and defeat the anticipated German offensive.

When the 1/7th Northumberland Fusiliers was ordered in February 1918 to leave the 50th (Northumbrian) Division and become Pioneers to the 42nd (East Lancashire) Division, its new division recorded that the Fusiliers did not 'conceal their chagrin' at having to leave their Northumbrian comrades.[28] The battalion had served overseas with the Northumbrian Division since May 1915, consequently the parting was resented. Its colonel wrote: 'Everybody is coming to see us and to say good-bye. Major-General Wilkinson comes nearly every day: he feels the loss of one of his best battalions keenly. The brigadier said good-bye two days ago . . . He told us we were leaving when we were at our best'.[29] One source suggests that its discontent did not last for long: 'The men soon threw themselves into the work and play of their new division with such zeal that they rapidly won popularity and a reputation for great courage and efficiency'.[30] However, an officer of the Fusiliers thought that although the staff of the 42nd Division treated their new Pioneers with 'kindness and consideration', there was at times friction between the Lancastrians and Northumbrians. Furthermore he insisted, the 'stock jests generally levelled at a Pioneer battalion were a little out of place' when addressed to a battalion with such a fine fighting record.[31] Unlike the Northumbrians, the troops of the 16/HLI at least had the satisfaction of being able to remain in their own division. The C.O. was asked if his battalion would supply the division's necessary Pioneer battalion and while the colonel replied that he would prefer to remain in command of a battalion which was devoted 'exclusively to fighting', he was prepared to take the larger view and do what was best for the division.[32]

The regimental history of the Loyal North Lancashire Regiment suggests that there was an element of democracy within the decision to convert. When the 57th Division, in which its 2/5th Battalion served, was ordered to select a battalion for conversion, the divisional commander who 'had always found the battalion in every way so satisfactory that he was very adverse to its being broken up or disbanded, and being aware that it contained an unusually large number of miners', decided that an option should be put to the men. They were apparently allowed to decide whether they wanted the battalion to be kept together as the divisional Pioneer battalion, 'when its fighting days would not be brought to a close' or that the battalion should go the way of others during that month of February 1918 and be disbanded. The men apparently unanimously accepted the first proposal and the battalion thus adopted its new role.[33]

There is no mention in any of the records discovered to suggest that C.O.s or adjutants of units that were disbanded in the 1918 reorganization of infantry brigades helped the Pioneers by taking any notice of a man's civilian occupation when they decided which of their men should be sent to which other battalions. In most units it was simply done by companies; one company went to one battalion, and another to another. Besides the sizeable drafts arriving in groups at their new unit, individuals too were also often sent up from the base. Some men arrived at a Pioneer unit's transport lines having undertaken a considerable perambulation through the regiments of the British army. Private John Hindelwood for example, joined the 9/Seaforth, having passed through the ranks of the KOSB, the Royal Scots Fusiliers and the Labour Corps. There are also examples of individuals coming from units which had a very tenuous connection with pioneering work. Hubert Parker, who was to die of wounds in April 1918, was posted to the 9/North Staffs from the Army Pay Corps.

In addition to sending drafts of former R.E. to Pioneer battalions, the War Office was by other means further attempting to improve the general levels of skills within such units. In 1915 a Pioneer depot was established at Gosport. By 1916 it had moved to Reading and functioned both as a depot and as a school of instruction.[34] Its purpose was to train both officers and men, thus providing a reservoir of personnel with some knowledge of pioneering work for overseas posting. The school ran three training companies for non-commissioned men and one for officers – each two hundred strong. When a man was discharged from hospital he went first to his reserve battalion and then, if space allowed, to the depot for the month-long course. If there were not enough candidates to fill a course by this means, men could be drawn from other reserve units; preference was given to men with engineering experience or from regiments which had a Pioneer battalion. On completion of the course officers had the special qualification 'Pioneer' written on their service sheets; the men had 'Trained in Pioneer School' put on theirs. Once qualified, both officers and men were drafted directly from the depot.

The arrival of such men from the depot was undoubtedly piecemeal and attracts little attention in the War Diaries. The

9/Seaforth Highlanders did receive a draft of 48 and a fairly regular supply of officers from the depot in 1916, but the great majority of diaries do not distinguish between those who came *via* the depot and those arriving through the more usual drafting channels. If they were posted in significant numbers to particular battalions, their presence might allow some reorganization of platoons along more specialist lines. Where this was possible it would be done in conjunction with the arrival of the large numbers of men from disbanded units. There is some evidence to suggest that at least one of the receiving divisions, and perhaps others, were taking the opportunity of this latest influx to shuffle men with particular skills from one platoon to another.

In a relatively quiet sector of the Italian front the 7th Division was attempting to post men with recognized trades to the 24/Manchester. When reinforcements arrived at the Divisional Reinforcement Camp, some were certainly selected specifically to be sent forward to the Oldham Comrades because they were former miners, carpenters etc. In the 32nd Division, the 17/N.F. exchanged 96 of its own men for 96 from the 12/13th Battalion. If they were former miners or tradesmen it is possible that the men coming from the 12/13th were considered to be more suited to Pioneer work than the 96 they replaced. Similarly, when a draft of men reached the 11/King's in January 1918, they were sorted out according to their trades and distributed into what appears to have been balanced working groups.

Some units had undergone similar reorganizations when converted earlier in the war. The extent of the internal adjustment to their new roles, and indeed the amount and quality of the training they received for it, probably depended to a significant degree upon the CRE of their division. As the new Pioneers came under the auspicies of the CRE, he could offer advice and see to its provision of tools and new equipment but he did not take on the responsibility of radically changing the way in which the battalion was run. Whether the CRE was prepared or able to help the converted battalions adjust to their new role possibly depended upon his relationship with the divisional commander. Having the opportunity to undergo a period of re-training could also depend upon whether the division was to be pulled out of the line. This was certainly the case for the newly converted 5/Sussex when it joined the 48th Division in August 1915. The division was so stretched that the Sussex had not only to maintain an estimated 12 miles of trenches but also on occasions to man strong points. The first time its War Diary actually mentions training with R.E. instructors was nearly nine months after conversion. The Sussex, like some other units, simply learned their skills on the job. This would also be the norm in divisions where Pioneers were regarded as being little more than digging or labouring units; in these divisions there was unlikely to be much effort put into training or helping them master new skills. The Field Companies would expect to provide the specialist knowledge and advice on the job, while the Pioneers did the labouring. Other divisions clearly took the training of Pioneers more seriously.

When it was converted in 1916 the 19/L.F. had been given training under special squads of R.E. NCOs, and in 1918 the 14/Warwick was reported to have enjoyed 'several excellent lectures' delivered by R.E. officers. Both the 6/Argyll & Sutherland Highlanders and the 8/Royal Scots had undergone two weeks of daily training with R.E. personnel and when the 5/Border joined the 66th Division in February 1918, each of its platoons spent a day on activities such as sand-bagging, revetting, erecting steel shelters, duckboarding, decauville tracks, wiring and slab road-making. The men also attended lectures on, among other subjects, 'The Role of the R.E.' and 'The Role of the Pioneer in Consolidation'. The lectures were usually either delivered by the CRE or his adjutant. When the 9/Gloucester replaced the Borderers in the 66th Division, a party of one officer and four other ranks from each of the division's Field Companies was sent to live with the newly converted battalion for training purposes. A similar number of Gloucesters replaced the sappers in the Field Companies – a practice which continued throughout the final months of the war.

The 5/Cheshire certainly did undergo some sort of readjustment and reorganization of men within its companies when it was converted. The battalion sorted out its troops to ensure that each company had its quota of skilled men. In each company a

214

'specialist' platoon of skilled men was created and into these were assembled a quota of bricklayers, joiners, carpenters, plumbers and other tradesmen. This meant that all of the companies were able to act independently; the disadvantage was that one shell landing in the middle of such a platoon could virtually wipe out that company's allocation of tradesmen. Because skilled men were becoming almost impossible to replace, towards the end of the war this became an increasingly serious consideration.[35]

Besides the 'specialist' platoons, the Cheshires also organized so-called 'sapper sections'. These sections were comprised of 'handymen' who were selected mainly for their civilian experience in mining and tunnelling work. The size and number of these units is unknown, but the fact that the Cheshires had to exchange two officers and 66 other ranks for experienced miners from the 1/Monmouth in August 1916 suggests that they were either limited in number or in constant demand. When it was converted the 5/Sussex created a scouts and snipers section, known more familiarly as 'Langham's Scouts' after their C.O. The personnel of this section spent much of the time after 1916 in manning observation and information posts[36]. These were duties not generally considered to be those of a Pioneer unit, although in the 42nd Division the 7/N.F. also provided the nucleus of a similar unit.[37] Whatever specialist engineering sections may or may not have been created in these converted battalions, the emphasis remained on training the men for fighting. Whenever time and circumstances allowed, battalions would practise bombing and musketry and run courses for Lewis gun teams, signallers and other specialists. Some battalions were certainly reluctant to accept that they had been converted, preferring instead to concentrate upon the skills which they had required as fighting infantry rather than those of what was now their primary occupation. In some cases, this was just as well. If the basic skills of soldiering had been neglected by the Pioneers, during the German offensives of March and April 1918 several divisions and corps might well have found themselves in considerably tighter spots than was ultimately to be the case.

The huge movements of troops between regiments and divisions were almost complete by the time the Germans began their series of hammer blows against the Allied line in March 1918. The role of the Pioneers in these desperate days is discussed below, but the ferocity of the attacks resulted in further reductions in the strength of British divisions. Some divisions were so badly mauled that they were withdrawn to England for rebuilding. Others went back to the rear areas to refit and train, usually taking their Pioneer battalions with them. Before looking at how they were re-constituted in preparation for the Allied counter-offensives, it is worth looking at the part some of the Pioneers played in stemming the German advance. For several battalions, especially those which had been converted to Pioneers from fighting units, it gave them the opportunity to show what they could do with rifle and Lewis gun rather than merely with pick and shovel.

NOTES

1. The proposals were formulated into ACI No.1528 of 1916.
2. ibid.
3. On Boxing Day 1916, the 6/East Yorks received 184 reinforcements from the 37th Infantry Brigade Depot which the adjutant described simply as 'untrained'. There was contemporary confusion as to what constituted a 'trained' man. An attempt was made to clarify the issue at a conference of senior officers, Fourth Army in May 1917. The officers claimed that a man on a draft described as 'untrained' could have in fact served previously at the front. They suggested that each man be given a chit explaining the extent of his training when drafted. (Report found in Davidson's papers, DLI Museum). Unless otherwise stated, the detail of drafts comes from battalion War Diaries.
4. The War Diaries for Entrenching battalions can be found in W.O.95. Although undoubtedly very useful, Entrenching battalions, by nature of their transitory nature, did have their faults. The CRE 37th Division complained that as the personnel of two such battalions he had working for him 'changed almost daily, neither the officers nor men have time to arouse the slightest interest in their work'. (W.D.)
5. The reserve battalion of the Coldstream Guards supplied 90 officers and 2275 other ranks to the 4th Battalion. This represents only 13.5%

of all drafts despatched to the overseas battalions. (Ross of Bladensburg, *The Coldstream Guards*, 1924)

6. The 22/DLI was also lucky to receive a further draft a few days later of men who came from the 12/KOYLI. This is a different draft from that mentioned earlier. Why these men, who had all apparently previously served with a Pioneer battalion, were not sent to their own unit perhaps indicates the pressure under which the base was operating.

7. Ox & Bucks Light Infantry Chronicles, 1916-17.

8. *History of the Corps of Royal Engineers*, Regimentally compiled. (IRE, 1952) Vol.5 p.134-5

9. ibid, p.358-9

10. Gilvary, p.53

11. War Diary.

12. Howcroft, G. *The First World War*, (Hurst, Kidd & Rennie, 1986)

13. There are certainly exceptions to this generalization. For example, when the 18/Middlesex moved camp in September 1917, five lorries were provided to carry the men aged 40 and over.

14. Blythe might have been kept in the U.K. not because he was physically unfit but because of his mental state. He was apparently an exceptionally nervous man.

15. Davidson, op.cit.

16. There are also occasional instances of transfers going in the opposite direction. For example, in the summer of 1917, eight other ranks of the 5/DCLI were transferred to the R.E.

17. *Extracts of Reports of C.E. & CRE on Recent Operations*, Aug.1917 op.cit.

18. Gilvary, p.66

19. Churton, op.cit. p.102

20. Jaeger, op.cit.

21. Matthews, op.cit. p.113-9

22. Churton, op.cit. p.103

23. Cooke, op.cit. p.65

24. Crookenden, A. *The History of the Cheshire Regiment in the Great War*, (Evans, 1938)

25. Chalmers, op.cit. p.114

26. Murphy, C.C. *The History of the Suffolk Regiment*, (Hutchinson, 1928) p.231

27. Ewing, op.cit. p.106

28. Gibbon, F. *The 42nd (East Lancashire) Division, 1914-18*, (Country Life, 1920)

29. Buckley, F. *The War History of the 7th Northumberland Fusiliers*, (Newcastle, 1926)

30. ibid.
31. Buckley, F. Q.6A and other places, (London, 1920)
32. Chalmers, op.cit. p.114
33. Wylly, *History of the LNL*, op.cit. p.220
34. The depot and school were established and organized under the provisions of several ACI, especially: 195 of 1915, 1175 of 1916, 487 of 1917 and 423 of 1918. 1175 of 1916 stated that drafts for Pioneer battalions would no longer necessarily receive pioneer training and announced that the depot would cease to be a draft finding unit. It was then converted to a school of instruction.
35. Churton, op.cit. p.47
36. Reed, P. *Stand To!*, No.33
37. Buckley, F. *Q6A*, op.cit.

Chapter 11

PIONEERING IN RETREAT

During the period March – May 1918 Pioneers were called upon to do other than their more normal duties. There had been occasions during the Battle of the Somme and at Arras when Pioneer battalions dropped their tools and picked up their rifles to ward off German counter-attacks. When the German brigades swarmed across No Man's Land in the various offensives that began on 21 March, many Pioneers were forced to man the trenches and take an active part in stemming the German advances. To those battalions which had only recently been converted from fighting infantry, nothing seemed to have changed; they had spent three years doing a similar job. But to those battalions which had been converted as long ago as 1916, or indeed those which had been raised and spent their entire existence as Pioneers, fighting as front line troops for a prolonged period was something novel.

Reflecting upon the battalion's part in the Battle of Loos, the historian of the 9/Gordon Highlanders believed that despite 'fear of ridicule, there are signs that many in the battalion hanker after a more martial role'.[1] The battalion had played an important part in the battle and if this was really the contemporary sentiment, its members would have again been disappointed in their role during the great German offensives 30 months later. The battalion was on Telegraph Hill, east of Arras when the attack was launched on 28 March and never came to close quarters. Despite this, it still suffered 57 casualties including 19 fatalities. If other battalions had felt a similar desire for action before the offensive began, their experience in March and April might well have made them yearn for a return to their earlier occupation.

Naturally some battalions were more fortunate than others. Their involvement depended upon where they were when the German blows fell and how soon they were moved towards the front or the front moved towards them. The 5/Northants was rushed up to Albert by motor bus and succeeded in holding up heavy attacks upon the Bouzincourt ridge. In the three days between the 25 – 28 March, it lost 34 dead and 45 wounded. The 8/Sussex, serving with the hard-fighting 18th Division, lost 20 dead and 93 wounded as it was caught up in the confusion of orders and counter-orders during its retreat towards the Somme crossings. Having spent five months in one area, the 12/Notts & Derby had just moved to the Maissemy district, where it began a fighting retreat to Domartin. It was then withdrawn and spent most of April refitting and re-equipping in the rear. The 19/N.F. was rushed down to the Somme just as the offensive began, reaching Maricourt Wood by 25 March. It was put at the disposal of 106th Brigade, temporarily attached to the 9th Division. Assaulted by shells and infantry, the battalion held its ground and two days later two companies supported a counter-attack made by the South African Brigade on the railway embankment at Dernancourt. It was involved again during April, sustaining a total of 67 killed and died of wounds in three weeks. Its sister battalion the 17th, also, in the words of its historian, 'reverted to soldiering'[2] in April when it was attached to the 1st Australian Division. Even so, it lost only 19 killed and 45 wounded during the period between January and May. The 10/DCLI suffered 31 killed on 25 March as the 2nd Division fell back towards Bapaume, while the 14/Worcester of the 63rd Division, which like the Cornwalls was in V Corps, fought a rearguard action near Martinpuich and lost 25 killed and over 300 wounded in three days. The War Diary of the Cornwalls was clearly written up some time after the events. After a long, detailed account of the battalion's actions the writer added some comments of his own. In an understandably proud and almost euphoric epilogue, he reflected upon what the battle had meant to the battalion. While at

Beaulencourt on 22 March he described the spirit of the officers and men as being 'most optimistic', and believed that most were 'longing to have a look-in to pay off old scores such as Passchendaele, Ypres and Langemarck'. Undaunted by their losses during the long retreat he concluded, 'the *esprit* was better, the will to win was more pronounced, the grim determination to conquer was far and away greater at the end than at the commencement of operations'.

The historian of the Severn Valley Pioneers also thought that his battalion had done more than might have been expected of mere Pioneers. The battalion spent much of early March working on new defensive positions near Ribecourt. On the night of 11-12 March the area held by the 63rd Division was deluged with mustard gas. So devastating was the onslaught that divisional strength was reduced by about one third. The writer believed that because the Pioneers were 'either better trained or more alert'[3] than the troops of the naval battalions, they did not suffer quite so severely. Nevertheless, between 12-20 March nine officers and 196 other ranks had to be evacuated from a ration strength of 34 and 560. The chronicler then wrote in substantial detail of how the remainder of the battalion made a fighting retreat across the old Somme battlefields until its three companies eventually reassembled at Englebelmer on 26 March. Its casualties for the month amounted to 25 officers and 354 men.

In comparison with other Pioneer units these and several other battalions escaped relatively lightly. Although called upon to man the line and fight, these attacks either tended to fall upon the infantry or upon Pioneers who were supported by other units. Other Pioneer battalions took the might of the German attacks on their own. Attached to brigades or simply thrown into the line to plug a gap, these units fought as well as their comrades in the infantry. Amidst the confusion of battle they could sometimes be almost forgotten. As German troops approached Holnon, no-one told the transport of the 5/DCLI that the division was retiring; it managed to get away from the encroaching Germans only with great difficulty. The battalion kept in touch with the brigades of the 61st Division as they retreated westwards. On 23 March its band, which had played many times for the division, was instructed to take up a position under cover of some banking near a hastily improvised front line. It was ordered to stay there and to commence playing when the 2/8th Worcestershire launched a counter-attack. As the troops went over the top, the DCLI crashed out the opening bars of the Worcestershire's regimental march. Thus inspired, the counter-attack threw the Germans back over 2,000 yards at the point of the bayonet.[4] During later ferocious German attacks near Hangard Wood, the Cornishmen lost 58 dead and 145 wounded. Pressure remained intense and the battalion was allowed no time to regroup. Three weeks later it lost just under another 90 fatalities while defending Bethune.

Well below strength at the beginning of March, the 8/Royal Scots had some desperate defensive digging to do near Boursies before the Germans attacked. At Morchies on 23 March they put up such a good display of musketry that one report later suggested that 'even veterans of the old regular army would have found it difficult to better the fire control shown by the Pioneers'.[5] The battalion fought hard to prevent itself from being surrounded and when relieved on the night of 25 March, sent in a casualty return of 35 killed, (including the C.O.), 137 wounded and 45 missing. The battalion was heavily engaged again during the early days of April, but was functioning again as Pioneers by the middle of the month. By this time it had lost another 35 dead and 56 missing.

One Pioneer battalion which won contemporary fame during April was the 12/KOYLI. It had come out of the line at the end of March substantially intact, but still received a large draft of young boys. On 11 April it went into action alongside a Guards Brigade at Couronne near Vieux Berquin. Here it fought with distinction, acquired the nickname of 'the Yorkshire Guards' and was acclaimed in a report of the action in *The Times*.[6] The battalion was declared to have 'held part of the line most deter-minedly, as well as the best fighting battalion could have done'. Its losses were considerable – amounting to 13 officers and 275 other ranks killed, wounded or missing. Until it was brought back to something resembling full strength, its three companies were each reduced to two understrength platoons. The 7/York

& Lancs also escaped fairly lightly in the opening stages, but as its division retreated, the battalion became front line troops. Supported by one 18-pounder field gun, the battalion fought in the wastes around Gueudecourt. It held the advance for a few hours before then falling back over the Ancre to Senlis. Owing to what the battalion record said was the 'abnormally'[7] low strength of the battalion when it went into action, its 25 dead and an unknown number of wounded, must have represented a significant proportion of its available men.

The 6/SWB was also understrength when the battle opened. It is difficult to be precise about establishments as each battalion was required to send in three different monthly strength returns – fighting, ration and effective. This makes assessing the numbers which might actually take part in a battle problematic. *In extremis* for example, HQ details might become involved and on other occasions one company of the battalion might be attached to a different division. The transport were normally kept away from front line fighting and there is evidence that even in the direst straits a battle nucleus might be kept in reserve. The available returns suggest that the average strength of Pioneer battalion at the beginning of March was 28 officers and 760 other ranks. In comparison to many infantry units this was a high figure. Of those 760, it might be expected that between 550 – 570 could man a trench and fire a rifle. The 6/SWB was a little below this average but despite the arrival of a draft of B1 men in December 1917, judging from the army numbers of the fatalities it was a battalion which still retained a considerable percentage of originals. When relieved at the end of the month a R.E. lieutenant-colonel submitted a report on the battalion's activities during the preceeding few days. From the morning of 21 March to the evening of 28th, A Company had marched 61 miles, C, 57 and D, 87. The transport covered 55 miles and had halted and unlimbered at 12 different camps. Each company had dug and manned at least 12 different positions and no man had had more than 18 hours sleep and the equivalent of three decent meals. On the evening of 28 March, the battalion marched into Pernois with the band playing and the men singing. The transport had not lost one animal through foot trouble and only 20 men had fallen out of the march.[8] The casualties had not been especially severe – 23 dead and 35 wounded – but the tragedy was that the battalion had to go through it all twice again within the next two months. It went into the line near Wippenhoek and between 9–15 April suffered 32 dead, 198 wounded and 154 missing. Sent down to the Chemin des Dames at the end of the month, it was again on the receiving end of a German attack in May when it lost over another 200 men.

The 6th's sister battalion, the 5/SWB, had a similarly trying time. Still commanded by the redoubtable Colonel Trower, it had suffered severely in March. Mid-way through the engagement it was made up to strength with a draft from the 11th Battalion; many of these were killed when the battalion went into the line again the following day. Major-General G. Jeffreys, GOC 19th Division, made 'special mention of the Pioneers who had not had the opportunity for training, but who had done exceedingly well in the fighting line'. Trower too declared that 'the newcomers vied with the old hands in worthily upholding the credit of the regiment and withstanding the tremendous advance of their Hun foes'. The battalion fought in the Messines area between 10-18 April before finally being relieved. In those four weeks it lost 137 killed and died of wounds. It too was sent with its division to recover on the Chemin, and was again mauled as the Germans advanced over the Aisne. It held the line with a French unit, established observation and stragglers posts and was only relieved on 17 June, after spending three weeks continuously in the line. Its losses had again been heavy with 37 dead. By dint of his own irrepressible personality, the C.O. began once more to rebuild battalion morale. Colonel Trower was well-known throughout the BEF as a man of unquenchable spirit. When meeting his counterparts of the 5/SWB, an officer of the 18/N.F. decided that despite being sixty, 'Trower was the liveliest of the lot of them'.[9] However, age and the strain of commanding the battalion since its formation had finally told on Trower's health and he returned home during the late summer.

The 11/Leicester and the 21/West Yorks were two other Pioneer battalions that fought and lost heavily during March and April. The former suffered during a rearguard action near

Fremicourt, while the West Yorks fought several actions in different locations, never being able to disengage for any length of time. Consequently, its losses were very heavy. It undertook a counter-attack with the 2/Duke of Wellington's and a battalion of the KOSBs of the 15th Division but, even when it was later withdrawn and moved to a different area, the battle seemed to follow it; five officers were severely gassed and evacuated when it was supposed to have been rebuilding in the relative quiet of St. Laurent-Blagny. The Territorial 4/South Lancs fought a stubborn and very bloody battle before Gorre Wood in April. Having suffered a total of six officer casualties and 138 other ranks in three days, it came out of the line with only four officers and 195 men. Another Territorial unit, the 4/RWF, suffered a very similar number of casualties when, as the only battalion in reserve, it was called upon to counter-attack at Aveluy. Two companies undertook the attack which, although largely unsuccessful, was later praised because: 'No troops could have deployed better or advanced more steadily under such intense fire, and the leadership of the officers could not have been excelled'.

The Territorials of the 7/DLI abandoned their work as a Pioneer unit and reverted to their former role as fighting infantry when the battalion covered the withdrawal of 149th Brigade on 26 March. It attempted a counter-attack with little success and heavy losses the following day, resisted the entreaties of a spy who arrived at HQ proclaiming that all troops had to leave at once, and was finally withdrawn on 1 April. It suffered a grievous blow a few days later when poor health forced the indomitable Colonel Vaux to relinquish his command. The battalion itself was allowed little respite and on 9 April was attached to its old brigade, the 151st. The following day HQ details were organized as a company and launched a counter-attack near Merville. When withdrawn, it concentrated at La Motte Chateau where it was targetted by British shells captured by the Germans from the fleeing Portuguese. It spent the next four days wiring, digging and sullenly witnessing the British destruction of an Expeditionary Force canteen in the Foret de Nieppe. The purpose was to prevent the goods falling into German hands, but the troops were disgusted to learn that if they wanted to obtain anything from the stores before it was burnt, they had to pay the usual prices. All three company commanders of the 7th were killed during this period, which was spent largely without any artillery support. Its persistence and stolidness won the praise of the divisional commander who expressed 'how proud [he was] to have such a Pioneer battalion in the division'. By 6 May the battalion had arrived at the Chemin des Dames where, in the words of its new commander Lt. Col. Birchall, they could 'lick their wounds and rest their jagged nerves'.[10]

Another DLI Pioneer battalion, the 22nd, also lost its C.O. during these tempestuous weeks. The battalion fell back with the rest of the 8th Division and within four days of the German offensive opening had lost an estimated 14 officers and 400 other ranks. On 26 March it launched a counter-attack north-east-wards from Harbonnieres in conjunction with the 2/Devon. The divisional history recalled that the attack, which took place despite a 'hurried march and the accumulated weariness of days of continuous fighting and retreating [was] delivered with a spirit which made light of their own fatigue and the enemy's opposition'.[11] According to one witness, Lt. Col. Cecil Morgan CMG, DSO, was wounded while carrying an 18-pounder shell under each arm; he died a few days later at Rouen.[12] The Durhams were pulled out of the line and reinforced with drafts from home before later being attached to 15th Australian Brigade for the operations around Villers-Bretonneaux.

For the next two weeks pioneering training, or indeed the anticipation that the battalion might be called upon to do any such work in the field, seems to have been forgotten. It practised schemes with the Australians before actually taking part in the mopping up tasks following the successful attack on the village. It suffered over another 50 dead during this operation, and was again reinforced. This time there was to be something of a respite for, along with several other battalions already noted – including the 7/DLI – it was sent down to the Chemin des Dames. In partnership with a French battalion, it spent a peaceful month forming part of the Gernicourt defences immediately south of the river Aisne. One officer who served with the battalion believed that when he rejoined it in early May, there were only

226

four officers and 60 other ranks of the old battalion of 1914. He also insisted that the battalion had been reconverted to infantry because, 'we had lost practically all our skilled tradesmen'.[13] There is no official acknowledgement that the battalion ceased to be Pioneers, but that it spent its time in May and early June fighting rather than performing pioneering duties is beyond doubt. Until the Germans poured over and around the Chemin, the battalion, like those of the other divisions which had been sent down to the sector to recuperate, enjoyed what one officer called their 'picnic interlude'. When the attack came the battalion discovered to its cost that its alignment was wrong; with the other survivors of those ill-fated divisions, it retreated towards the Marne. The remnant of the battalion was combined into one company which subsequently became part of a composite battalion. Within a month the battalion, one of those which had been specifically raised as Pioneers in the far off days of 1915, was absorbed by its own 7th Battalion.

During March, April and May the Pioneers of the 22nd had fought with distinction. Two DSOs, four M.C.s and 22 M.M.s were awarded for service and gallantry during those battles, but at an appalling cost. It lost five officers and 315 other ranks killed and an unknown number of wounded. Two officers and 84 NCOs and men are listed on the Soissons Memorial to the Missing. Among the names is that of Major C.Hall, DSO. Hall, who had earlier confided his disillusion with the war in a letter to his sister, had his head blown off as he led a bayonet charge against a force of Germans surrounding his position. Virtually all of the names of the non-commissioned men who died with Hall belong to boys aged 18 or 19. These were the youths who had been described on arrival as having a physique 'much below average'. They might have been small and slight, but they fought as well as any.

The losses taken by the 19/L.F. might also have made it a possible candidate for disbanding. As one of the battalions which had been converted to Pioneers having spent some time overseas as infantry, it continued to devote a lot of its time to normal training. The philosophy within the unit was said to be that it always considered Pioneers were as much fighting troops

227

as any other infantryman. Shortly before the German offensive began, over 400 of its men had passed a rapid fire test. Voluntary sessions were encouraged and members were assured: 'The GOC is taking great interest in the musketry of the battalion.' The rehearsals were put to good use in April when the battalion, detached from its division, manned the defences of Kemmel Hill. The Germans launched furious attacks upon this strategically important hill and eventually the British and the French forces were driven from the heights. Two DCMs and at least 12 M.M.s were later awarded, but the difficulty was finding a battalion to award them to. By the time it was withdrawn, 14 officers and 333 other ranks were listed as missing. Subsequent figures show it had 77 fatalities during the month. However, instead of being broken up – at one time battalion HQ consisted of only one officer and 17 men – it received drafts of men from another Lancastrian battalion then in the process of being disbanded, the 11/South Lancs.

By the end of March a week's hard fighting had reduced the 11/South Lancs to about 50% of its original strength. Notwithstanding a Victoria Cross awarded to Cpl. J.T.Jones, one DSO, four M.C.s, one DCM and nine M.M.s, the battalion was reduced to cadre. A later chronicler recorded the event stoically, acknowledging that it was 'a sad day . . . but unavoidable'[14]; total casualties for the week had been 418, including 59 fatalities. The majority of the survivors were posted to a battalion which had at least originated from the same county. Several other battalions also fought so hard that they virtually sealed their own fate. Having been little involved in March, at the beginning of April the 12/Yorks had an establishment of 40 officers and 847 other ranks. It was then called upon to fight a prolonged rearguard behind Armentieres and in two days during the Battle of the Lys lost 379 men. Its demise had clearly already been decided, for when it was pulled out of the line, four officers and 154 men were despatched to the 15/Yorks. It was not until early May that the unit was officially broken up and formed into a battalion training staff of ten officers and 51 other ranks. Ten other officers and 350 men, including a recently arrived draft, were sent down to the base for disposal. At the end of June, with

228

the absorption of the training staff by the 17/Worcester, the '12 (Service) Battalion, Yorkshire Regiment, (Pioneers)', in the words of its War Diary, 'ceased to exist'.

In the middle of March ten officers of the 11/King's were 'temporarily cross posted' to battalions of other regiments within the 14th Division. This did not spare them from the slaughter that was to follow as the division retreated for over two weeks, fighting just about every inch of the way. It was finally relieved by the 5th Australian Division near Villers-Bretonneaux and its three brigades were reorganized as one brigade of four battalions. With a sense of relish, the War Diary of the 11/King's noted 'the battalion is reorganized today as an Infantry Battalion'. No doubt to the later disappointment of the diarist, its new role was to be only short-lived. The battalion had marched and fought over 200 miles during the retreat and had lost at least 26 dead, 111 wounded and 167 missing. When it reached Villers-Bretonneaux its total strength was about 270. Despite receiving over 200 men from the 9/Rifle Brigade, the battalion, less a training staff of ten officers, 52 other ranks and the transport, was sent down to Etaples for posting elsewhere.

Two southern Pioneer battalions, the 13/Gloucester and the 11/Hants, also suffered a similar fate. The latter battalion fought a stout rearguard as its division fell back through its lines at St. Emile. According to the regimental history, 'they had the satisfaction of really using their rifles to good effect and, when driven back, they knew they had take a handsome toll of the enemy'.[15] In March alone it lost 68 other ranks killed and by the end of the month, when it was near Hamel, it was down to about 170 rifles. By mid-April it too was preparing to be reduced to a training cadre; the surplus, like that of the 11/King's, was sent to Etaples for disposal. The 13/Gloucester was also heavily engaged in March and at the end of the month was near Hangard Wood. On 10 April it arrived at St. Omer and was ordered to provide three companies, each of three officers and 150 other ranks as its contribution to No.2 Composite Battalion of the 39th Division's Composite Brigade. A further nine officers were to go to No.1 Composite Battalion, while battalion HQ was to form a cadre preparatory to training American troops. The composite battalions entrained on 11 April ('destinations unknown'), but both eventually ended up just to the south of Ypres. On 26 April the units near the Bluff spotted a huge body of Germans forming up to attack; communications broke down and few men escaped the onslaught. An exception was a small group of 17 men commanded by a young second lieutenant which, although surrounded, managed to fight its way through to safety. When No.2 Composite battalion was later withdrawn, the 13/Gloucester reported ten officers and 201 other ranks as missing. The survivors of the battalion were reunited a few days later and from them, the cadre and a demonstration platoon was selected. This latter organization was immediately deemed too large, the demands upon manpower then being so great, so the authorities insisted upon the retention of a demonstration 'section' rather than a 'platoon'. This unit remained with the 39th Division and the remnant of the battalion disappeared to the base. However, instead of being disbanded, and after having spent sometime training Americans, the cadre was despatched to the 66th Division. Later still, it was sent to line of communications duty with 197th Brigade.

A final example of a Pioneer unit which almost fought itself to destruction is the 18/N.F. Until the offensive began it had suffered relatively few casualties and when the Germans did attack, it had a fairly quiet time on Henin Hill. After a little fighting it was withdrawn and in April sent with the 34th Division to the Armentieres area. Here it occupied itself preparing bridges across the river Lys. When the German attack began, the companies were attached to the division's brigades and one company had a stiff fight defending the Erquinghem bridgehead. Some men did not get back to the British side before the bridge was blown and so fell into German hands. The activities of 13 April were described by one officer as resembling a 'field day'. He later recorded that he 'felt very proud of the Pioneers . . . for, by their cool behaviour, they not only kept brother Boche from being too curious, but encouraged others to follow their example'.[16] Four days later the battalion suffered from 'the heaviest barrage we were ever in'. It remained in the line for another three days, losing during the month 27 officers and well over 300 men. In May it was decided that the entire division would be reduced to a training establishment, so the Pioneers, in common with the other units, prepared themselves for disbanding. The diary of an original member noted, 'all the men and officers who joined the battalion in 1914 and 1915 took it badly with being in the battalion so long'.[17] Because it had not suffered too severely during its time overseas there were still something like 237 of the original members with the battalion. Even those who had been posted to it over the months tended to come from the training battalions of the Northumberland Fusiliers rather than those of other regiments. It was therefore still very much a battalion of men from the North-East. There was some compensation for these long-serving men as a good proportion of them were sent to the 14th Battalion and others went to the 19th. Both these units were of course existing Pioneer battalions. Furthermore, the colonel, two majors, four captains and eight subalterns were retained, along with an unknown number of other ranks to train first American, and later British, troops.

Some Pioneer battalions went through the tumultuous months of March and April almost unscathed. Quite remarkably, while the battalions of its 56th Division were being all but annihilated, the 5/Cheshire lost only 16 killed and 30 wounded during the German attacks around Gavrelle. The 6/East Yorks spent from March to July 1918 in the Loos area and were thus almost unaffected by the German attacks. At the end of March its strength was 35 officers and 818 men; at the end of April, it had just 72 fewer non-commissioned ranks. It lost only two men killed in April, a fact which perhaps inspired its historian to comment somewhat regretfully, that its 'fighting days as infantry were definitely over . . . [they] were not called upon to man the firing line'.[18] Similarly, although battles raged around them to the east, north and south, the 9/Seaforth Highlanders occupied a pocket of less hectic drama near Vierstraat. It spent most of its time digging and only on rare occasions was it called upon to support an action. The men of these battalions no doubt considered themselves fortunate, but there were others who seemed to relish the opportunity to fight. Those units mentioned above are only a selection, but attention should also be drawn to those battalions which had only been converted to Pioneers shortly before the German attacks. For these, the change was academic. They might have put in a few days pioneer training and spent more of their time in the rear than they had formerly, but when the German blows fell, they abandoned their new role and reverted to that which they knew best.

The 6/7th Royal Scots Fusiliers had been withdrawn from 45th Brigade and sent to the 59th Divsion as Pioneers in February 1918. They undertook some Pioneer training, but on the eve of the German offensive every officer and man, including the C.O. and adjutant, went out to dig the support line of the divisional front. The presence of the senior officers was apparently to set an example to the men and to underline the necessity of completing the work quickly. The battalion went into the line and fought a very hard battle near Vraucourt. According to a letter from the Historical Section of the Committee of Imperial Defence, because the Pioneers came under the command of 'several administrations, they did not get their due credit'.[19] This lack of recognition is a common complaint of Pioneer battalions and will be discussed more fully later. Severely mauled, the battalion was withdrawn and moved back to Locre. It became corps reserve and was ear-marked as a counter-attack battalion. On 17 April about 100 of its men were put at the disposal of 100th Brigade. These men were sent into the attack and: 'In the view of men who had served since Loos, the last two actions at Vraucourt and at Locre, were among the severest they had ever faced'.[20] Their reward for helping to stem the German thrusts was to be disbanded. A training cadre survived and was sent to supervise Chinese labourers near Mametz.

Another recently converted Scottish battalion was the 16/HLI. Its War Diary is a classic example of bureaucratic minimalism. The adjutant seems to have decided that listing work or training as a Pioneer unit was of little relevance and preferred instead to record either no detail at all or alternatively, to concentrate upon the activities of the battalion's band. There seems to have been a marked reluctance to admit that its role had changed, but by the same token it shows an equally indifferent attitude towards recording its fighting activities. It is from other sources that a picture of the ferocity with which the battalion fought can be sketched. Such a degree of modesty may be charming, but probably misplaced. When Major-General Shute relinquished the command of the 32nd Division to become commander of V Corps, he told the Pioneers: 'You have always been one of the best battalions in the division, but as Pioneers, you are absolutely at the top of the tree'. Similarly, the CRE inspected the battalion and complimented it on its 'excellent' work on the Reserve Line defences – a task about which the War Diary makes virtally no comment.

When the 5/Border was ordered to leave 151st Brigade of the 50th and become Pioneers to the 66th Division in March 1918, it marched through a blinding snow storm to relieve the 12/Notts & Derby. It took up residence in Templeux quarries and began its new role. The existing area defences were not particularly extensive, but facilities did include an officers' golf course. Two companies dug, wired and laid tramways, while the other began reclaiming the old French phosphate workings in the quarries. Two companies manned their battle positions in the quarries on 21 March, while the other remained at Roisel. Isolated posts in the quarries held out until mid-afternoon and only three officers and 80 men of the two companies escaped to rejoin the battalion. The remnant of the unit fell back with the rest of Fifth Army, launched an unsuccessful counter-attack at Aubercourt and was finally relieved on 31 March. Two weeks later the battalion was ordered to form a cadre and a demonstration platoon of ten officers and 48 other ranks. It then moved off to instruct some American units in basic skills. The remainder of the battalion began training as Vickers gunners but only 121 men were eventually transferred to the Machine Gun Corps. In May its future was secured when it amalgamated with the Lonsdale battalion and left to join the 32nd Division. With a tone of relief, its diarist recorded: 'The battalion once more takes its place amongst the fighting units after working a short time as Pioneer battalion'. During its 'short time' – which effectively amounted to 31 days – it won three M.C.s, 19 M.M.s and lost six officers and 94 other ranks killed or died of wounds.

233

Two battalions from the North-East with magnificent fighting records spreading back over three years also maintained their reputations as stalwart warriors. The 7/N.F. and the 9/DLI, both Territorial battalions and both only converted to Pioneers in February 1918, had also only recently left their own 50th Division and joined the first line Territorial East Lancashire and second line West Riding Division, the 42nd and 62nd respectively. The opening days of the offensive passed fairly quietly for the Fusiliers. They held the railway line near Achiet-le-Grand with two companies and two Field Companies of the R.E. The other company acted as escort to the guns. The 42nd Division put up a tremendous fight around Ervillers and Mory, before falling back in the face of overwhelming numbers. The tired defenders passed through the Pioneer and R.E. lines, the latter, according to one source, having never before been in the front line. At Fonquevillers they became front line troops, firing at close range into hordes of attacking Germans and even taking some prisoners. After days of frantic fighting the advance was halted and the Fusiliers, having even undertaken a trench raid, began to perform the function for which they had been converted. When withdrawn, their colonel looked upon the battalion with understandable pride: 'The old 7th has more than lived up to its past reputation . . . They look like the worst collection of tramps; but they are as cheery as ever, with not a single complaint'.[21] With the Germans contained, the battalion finally turned its attention to more mundane tasks. Colonel Liddell reported, for example, that he had established several workshops and was about to open a drawing office.

It will be remembered that the 9/DLI was one of the units nominated for conversion in 1915. It survived as fighting infantry on that occasion, but was finally converted 26 months later. Even then it nearly escaped the transition as there was a suggestion that it should be transfered to the 62nd Division as infantry. Like its North-Eastern comrades in the 7/N.F., it too took some time to acknowledge that its role had changed. Its C.O., Lt. Col. Crouch, had risen from the ranks and was a highly respected and very competent commander. On 26 March the battalion retired to a position behind the Bucquoy-Puisieux road in support to its division and as the infantry fell back through the Durhams' position, it became the front line. Assisted by a company of the 5/Dukes, the battalion fought off numerous German attacks during a torrid five days. Despite catching the Durhams in enfilade, the Germans were continually frustrated in their efforts to advance and nowhere managed to penetrate the line. One officer, in rather laconic vein, wrote: 'There was that morning [29 March] a great shooting of Germans'. The ferocity of the attacks was demonstrated when a party of about 25 Prussian Guards offered to surrender. As an officer and NCO of the 9th were about to accept it, one of the Germans shot them both. The covering party of the Durhams opened fire and only four prisoners were finally taken. During these engagements a stretcher bearer, Pte. Thomas Young, went out nine times under fire and in daylight to bring in wounded men. He survived and was subsequently awarded the Victoria Cross. Proud, although not surprised at what his men had achieved, Crouch lost no time in complaining to his superiors about his paucity of Lewis guns. When converted, the battalion's establishment was reduced to 12, a decision which Crouch found unacceptable.[22] A soothing, but inadequate reply to Crouch's indignant missive came from the divisional staff two days later. The divisional commander apparently confirmed that the shortage of Lewis guns during the recent fighting had put the battalion at 'a serious disadvantage' and agreed with Crouch that the unit had 'first rate personnel to handle a full complement.' He concluded with an assurance to the irate colonel that it was 'only in exceptional circumstances [that] a Pioneer battalion would take the line'. Furthermore he warned, as this was a matter which affected every division within the BEF, it would do no good to take it any further.[23]

Crouch remained unconvinced, but was forced to accept the decision of his superiors. He had to devote the next few days to assessing the state of training and abilities of a large draft of 18½ year old boys who had arrived to replace the losses. Nevertheless, it did not stop him from continuing to register his dislike of his battalion's new function. He penned another forthright letter on his lack of Lewis guns in September. Despite the GOC's assurance that Pioneers would be rarely used in the line, the battalion was used as assaulting infantry in both July and September. It was not, however, only the alleged inadequate number of Lewis guns which annoyed Crouch during the latter operation. He criticised the absence of Popham Panels – a signalling device – from Pioneers' equipment, a fact which he claimed, had prevented him from communicating with the support aircraft during the attack from Havrincourt Wood. A further object of his derision was the three company system in which Pioneer battalions had to be organized. This, he fumed, lacked sufficient elasticity for offensive operations and 'recommended' (probably a polite substitute for 'demanded') a return to the four company system. Unfortunately for Crouch, his vehemence fell upon deaf ears and none of his suggestions were adopted by the division.[24]

*   *   *

Although Crouch's own division was unreceptive to his proposals and complaints, in the spring of 1918 the War Office and the staffs at divisional, corps and army HQs were turning their collective minds as to how the BEF could be quickly and effectively rebuilt. By the end of May the German offensives had largely spent themselves. The British line had sagged and in places had been broken, but the German waves had washed against the retreating British and Dominion forces only to discover that, despite Ludendorff's optimism and expectation, their defence had remained resolute. The Channel ports had not been reached and the Anglo-French forces had remained in mutual contact. The German army had thrown in so many divisions and used so much of its diminishing reserves of resources that once they had halted, the outcome of the war was no longer in doubt. It might take another two years, but with the appearance of the inexhaustable supplies of American manpower and industrial resources, together with the ever-tightening stranglehold of the blockade, Germany would be beaten. However, to many soldiers of the British armies in France, in the spring of 1918 victory remained a very distant prospect.

During the course of the offensive thousands of young and not so young, reinforcements were sent across the Channel to France. Some battalions were rebuilt several times between

March and May and even those which had managed to retain some regional or regimental identity throughout former reconstitutions now ran the likelihood of being swamped by men from different areas or units. Many of the men despatched from training and reserve battalions at home were those whose call up had been deferred or whose state of health had formerly precluded them from overseas service. Young boys of 18 went across to replace their counterparts who had gone in January and February. Many of those young men, despite the misgivings expressed at the time, had fought and died in the efforts to stem the German onslaughts. Now a new influx of youngsters arrived to swell once more the depleted numbers of both the infantry and the Pioneers. Although the Pioneers were pleased to receive reinforcements, there were some complaints about the timing and the quality of the new arrivals. Much to the dismay of the battalion, 200 of these young lads reported to the 19/N.F. Its diarist could not understand why, with all the miners who were reputedly being sent out for active service, the battalion had to take on these 'immature boys . . . The material was good, but April 1918 was not the time to train unskilled youths on the actual work in the front line'.[25]

Once the line had stabilized the weary survivors of several British divisions were withdrawn to the rear areas for re-equipping. Much to the surprise of the Pioneers, whose past experience had warned them against expecting similar treatment, they went with them. Some divisions had been so badly cut up that they were be broken up and re-constituted with new troops and new battalions. The 11/King's learned on 27 April that it was to be disbanded and its personnel transferred elsewhere. Apart from a battalion training staff which believed it was to be used to train American troops, the remainder of this unit, which had served as Pioneer battalion to the 14th (Light) Division since January 1915, was sent to Etaples for re-posting. However, in July the cadre personnel of the battalion were officially transferred to the newly created 15/Loyal North Lancs. The embryo of this unit had been mobilized at Bullswater Camp in June, receiving men of just about every medical category. It was nominally a Category B battalion, which meant it accepted men posted to it straight from hospital, many of them still with walking sticks. The first drafts arrived on 18 June and on the following day the unit was officially designated the 15/LNL. By 22 June all surplus officers were sent away and its strength had reached 993. Travelling medical boards reduced the nominal roll by 254 and despite its original designation as a unit for home service only, it left Brookwood on 3 July and went to France. It was a totally hybrid battalion, composed of men from dozens of different regiments and different regions of the country; following further weeding out, its strength fell to 34 officers and 650 other ranks. It spent over five weeks training near the coast, while drafts of men regarded as sufficiently fit arrived to replace those whom the boards considered to be unsuitable. It retained its low medical status when it joined the 14th Division and there is no mention of the men having been specially selected for their civilian skills. As the officers had to attend a lecture on 'Pioneering' soon after their arrival, they too were also probably picked at random. Nevertheless, the battalion did some very useful work during the 'Advance to Victory' and suffered seven fatalities.

Two other Pioneer battalions which underwent even more extreme re-constitutions were the 12/Yorks and the 11/Hants. The former battalion, having served with the 40th Division, had suffered nearly 550 casualties during the German attacks of April. In early May it was broken up, with the battalion training staff of ten officers and 51 other ranks having been absorbed by the 17/Worcester. As we have seen, officially the 12/Yorks ceased to exist, but its C.O., Lt.Col. Becher, assumed command of the 17/Worcester.[26] Furthermore, the 12/Yorks supplied the RSM, the RQMS, three CSM, three CQMs, ten sergeants and five corporals. Their new battalion had originally been called the 1/Provisional Garrison Guard Battalion and had formed part of 176th Brigade in the 59th Division. It remained with the brigade for only one month, being redesignated the 17/Garrison Battalion during its short stay. It joined 121st Brigade for eleven days and then became Pioneer battalion to the 40th Division. The Garrison Guard battalions were, in the words of one writer, 'neither as smart nor as trustworthy as could be desired', and so with the intention of improving morale, were numbered as 'garrison' battalions of line regiments.[27] Despite the fact that no officer of the new unit had ever served in the Worcesters, the 1/Garrison Guard battalion became officially the 17/Worcester.

The battalion arrived in France in April and had apparently undergone some unspecified R.E. training. On 19 May it was ordered to march from Harbarcq to Hautevillers, a distance of just over four miles. This march was accomplished easily enough, but as one of the chief duties of the officers was to determine how well the men could perform under increasing physical strain, it was continued the following day. Owing to the excessive heat, 126 men fell out during the final mile. When it was about to be resumed on the 21st, 240 men were discovered to be unable to march; ten lorries transported these cases to the next scheduled stop. Having deposited their first loads, the lorries returned to the column, and picked up the remainder of the men in successive journeys. The result of this experiment was the M.O.'s report which judged that the great majority of the men would be unable to march for two consecutive days and would not be able to cover more than eight miles in any one day.

The M.O.'s report makes sober reading and illustrates how the tribunals at home were netting men whose health would have in ealier years precluded them from call-up. Twenty-five men of the new battalion were diagnosed as suffering from diseases of the heart, with a much larger proportion having irregular heart action. Forty had ruptures and 65 were affected by old wounds. Approximately 100 could be categorized as suffering from 'debility' resulting from poor physique, defective feet, age, chronic rheumatism and old tubercular trouble. Another 100 were unfit for service in the line owing to other physical disabilities. Some of the men had been categorized as B1 for ear trouble or defective sight; these, the doctor believed, would be suitable for digging and some limited marching. He warned against those with heart trouble doing any work and thought that the training was 'wearing them down'. The battalion was told that it could send away a certain number of the worst cases, but the doctor was unable to come to an immediate conclusion on how many this might be. He maintained that 20% to 30% were fit enough

239

to work near the line in a quiet sector in summer months, but that a number of the men with heart conditions and those who had suffered from shell shock, would be 'useless' in the forward areas. In his summing up the M.O. concluded that if travelling kitchens, two water carts and a motor ambulance followed the battalion and providing the march was no more than eight miles a day for two days, followed by a day's rest, the bulk of those who remained might be able to cope. During the next few months the battalion was never asked to undertake really strenuous work, and although it lost an average of over 40 a month sick – a far from excessive number – four of its men were awarded Military Medals.

An equally sorry tale of men who were barely fit enough to be wearing uniform, is that of the 11/Hants. Having been badly cut up during the March offensives, the battalion was disbanded in early May 1918. A training staff was retained and soon became engaged in instructing American troops. There were some difficulties in arranging mutually convenient times with the Americans on the firing ranges, and although it was thought that their 'organization leaves a lot to be desired', the training staff believed their charges showed 'marked intelligence'. Their period as instructors did not last long and by the middle of June the training staff was back in Lowestoft. Here it became the cadre of a new battalion.

The first draft of men, mostly B2 and unfit for much hard work, arrived from a home service labour company. Officially, B2 men were capable of working in labour units abroad but were not considered suitable for garrison duty. In early July the battalion, some 776 strong, moved to Aldershot and during the march from the station to camp 23 men fell out. On 6 July a first batch of 500 men went before the medical board; 400 were passed as unfit. The following day another 130 paraded before the board and only 29 were passed unfit. Three days later 392 of the battalion were despatched to a transfer centre, and another group of B2 men arrived to replace them. Of these 157, 19 were declared to be fit enough to stay. A draft of 72 men arrived from the 3/Hants and this was followed by a smaller group of Maltese and French extraction.[28] Apparently, only one of these men could speak any English. During the next few days men of a better medical category arrived and by 22 July, during a six mile march, only three men fell out. The following day the battalion left for France and although march discipline might have improved, the men were declared to be 'very ignorant of the correct way of digging etc'. In an effort to rectify the lack of more soldierly qualities – the pioneering ones would presumably be attempted later – a sergeant-major from the army gym school was temporarily attached to help with bayonet training and P.T. The battalion was next treated to a lecture on bayonet fighting by the fearsome Lt.Col. Campbell, then received a new C.O. – a major from the R.E. – and was despatched towards the front. There was some optimism that the battalion might be able to undertake some pioneer work as it was recorded that 'some' of the officers had had previous pioneer experience. While in the forward area the battalion was fortunate in having only two men killed; another two died from disease and several others were wounded. There is also a record of two Field Courts Martial but no mention of any awards.

The St. Helen's Pioneers, the 11/South Lancs, had also feared for its future when it was first withdrawn from the 30th Division in May 1918 and then attached to the 66th and later the 25th Divisions. Following these brief liaisons it returned to the U.K; here it absorbed the 18th Battalion and was reconstituted. In October, having been brought up to strength largely with B2 men who had had no Pioneer training of any description, it returned to France. Rejoining the 25th Division it suffered 46 casualties during its four weeks at the front.

The history of the 2nd Provisional Garrison Guard Battalion, like that of the 1st mentioned above, was also tied up with the 59th Division. The battalion was formed at Saulty in May 1918 with a strength of 13 officers and 847 other ranks. It was supposed to comprise B1 men and if required to fight, was intended to combine with two nearby labour companies. Its more likely role however, was thought to be manning stragglers' posts in the rear. Initially it led a fairly quiet existence, spending about six hours a day digging well behind the lines and one hour each day training. This scheme was reversed in mid-June when, following the departure in May of the 6/7th Royal Scots Fusiliers, the battalion was ordered to become Pioneers to the 59th Division. The six hours training and one of digging was in response to the order that the battalion should be prepared to line hold and fight. It was reorganized into a three company battalion and to make it sound more like a possible front line unit, the word 'Garrison' was eliminated from its title. In late July the title was changed completely, and the units became officially the 25/KRRC (Pioneers).[29] The battalion's subsequent efforts to post away its members who were clearly unsuited for work near the front has already been noted. Those who were retained remained reasonably safe as the battalion's somewhat sedentary life continued. It suffered only three wounded during the final months of the war.

Despite the severe manpower shortages not too many Pioneer battalions were obliged to fill up with such an overwhelming proportion of low category men. For those who were posted, life was often far from comfortable. With their sometimes substantial physical disabilities, they had to endure the privations of the autumn rains, the hardship of working and sleeping in the open and the prospect of forced marches with hard labour at the end. The advance was proceeding and the roads, no matter what the difficulties, had to be maintained.

NOTES

1. Falls, *Gordon Highlanders*, op.cit. p.76. Unless otherwise stated, detail is taken from battalion War Diaries. Fatalities are compiled from *Soldiers Died* lists, and other casualties from W.D., regimental and battalion histories.
2. Shakespear, op.cit. p.84
3. Stacke, op.cit. p.321
4. ibid, p.341
5. Ewing, op.cit. p.585
6. *Times*, 2 May 1918
7. Gilvary, op.cit. p.76
8. Quoted in battalion W.D.
9. Shakespear, op.cit. p.40
10. Unpublished history of 7/DLI, op.cit.

11. Boraston & Bax, op.cit. p.189
12. Davidson, op.cit.
13. ibid.
14. Whalley-Kelly, op.cit. p.258
15. Atkinson, op.cit. p.321-2
16. Shakespear, op.cit. p.89-90
17. ibid, p.95
18. Wyrall, op.cit. p.329
19. Quoted in battalion W.D.
20. Buchan, op.cit. p.427
21. Buckley, 7/N.F., op.cit. p.76
22. In April 1917 infantry battalions had 16 Lewis guns whereas a Pioneer unit had eight. In October 1918 the respective establishments were raised to 36 and 12. See Appendix 2
23. Correspondence in Crouch papers. (DLI Museum)
24. ibid.
25. When one of these young boys on guard duty was ticked off by his officer for some failure, the sentry apologized, saying: 'I'm sorry sir, but I'm new to this job'. Cooke, op.cit. p.75.
26. In July 1918, Lt.Col. Becher became the C.O. of the 12/North Staffs, an infantry battalion.
27. Stacke, op.cit. p.409-10
28. *The Soldiers Died* roll for the battalion does not have any Maltese or French names.
29. The regiment later claimed that the title was 'an honour which was greatly appreciated and which was worthily maintained'. (*KRRC Chronicle 1919*, p.92)

Chapter 12

CONVERTING AND COUNTERING

In the spring and summer of 1918 those Pioneer battalions which had served in France and Belgium for some years, as well as those that had either recently been created or converted, were joined by a number of units brought back to Europe from other theatres. Some of these had performed the duties of Pioneers in Gallipoli, Salonika and Egypt, while others had been used as conventional infantry. Soon after their arrival in France or Belgium, several of these battalions were informed that a new role and function had been devised for them.

In May 1918 the 2/4th Somerset Light Infantry left Port Said and 232nd Brigade of the 75th Division, arriving at Marseilles in early June. After spending the next five weeks constructing defences and having a fairly easy time around Proven, the battalion was inspected by Major-General Nicholson, GOC 34th Division, who informed it that it was now the Pioneer battalion to his division. The unit disbanded one of its four companies and set off to join its new division. The departure for its new attachment occurred at the same time as the 9/Gloucester was arriving by train from Salonika. This battalion had left the 26th Division unaware of its future and when it arrived at Serqueux it was put under the administration of the 50th Division. It resumed infantry training and shortly came under direct orders of 198th Brigade of the 66th Division. As the only non-Lancashire battalion in the division, and with the knowledge that the 10/DCLI which had served with the East Lancashires as Pioneers had long since departed, it probably discerned its fate.

The Gloucesters spent some time with their new division at Abancourt, adapting to the changed climate and environment. One of the most essential of their activities was the daily parade for 10 grains of quinine. Other Pioneer battalions were later to come across what the army called 'malaria reinforcements', but in the 9/Gloucester there was no distinction made in the sick returns between those suffering from malaria or any other ailment. A regular flow of men went each week to hospital, but in July and August the largest numbers leaving the battalion were those going on leave to the U.K. The battalion had left England nearly three years before, so this was the first opportunity for most of the surviving originals to go home. According to orders, each man departing on leave had to provide himself with a match box or other receptacle in which to put his quinine tablets and a chit from the M.O. declaring that he was vermin free. Boots had to be disinfected because cows that sometimes grazed on the nearby firing ranges were known to be carrying foot and mouth disease. Unfortunately this additional precaution was of little importance to the disappointed troops originating from the Gloucestershire parish of Stowell; owing to an outbreak of typhoid, this area was put out of bounds to leave men for five weeks. In late September the battalion was finally informed that it would become the division's Pioneer unit. Although there was some pioneering training undertaken, the War Diary chooses to record the sitting of a court of enquiry into how 'B' Company managed to lose four pairs of binoculars with rather more enthusiasm than it details its new work.

The 1/12th Loyal North Lancs arrived at Marseilles three weeks before the 2/4th Somerset L.I., but unlike the Somersets, came with its own division. There was a submarine scare *en route*, an alarm which would no doubt have been treated with great respect by a battalion which had lost 19 men on the *Ivernia* when she went down on 30 December 1917. The 12th was an existing Pioneer battalion, but like the 9/Gloucester spent much of its first weeks in France performing gas drills and fitting respirators. Officers and senior NCOs did have some instruction on field works under Major Glenn of the R.E., who also gave them a resume of what he called 'the several matters of interest' which he had observed during several tours of the front line. Leave opened in early June with parties departing weekly for a fortnight's stay in the U.K. The battalion had not been overseas quite as long as the Gloucesters, but the opportunity to return home would have been no less seized upon by the men. In one month alone, four officers and 345 other ranks were away on leave and by the middle of October, when the last party of three officers and 140 other ranks departed, all members of the unit had received their allocation of fourteen days. With so many men away on leave at any one time, as well as up to 200 suffering from 'flu, training and working were undoubtedly handicapped. Nevertheless, sufficient men were found to lay a decauville line and to assist the 250th Tunnelling Company in making concrete emplacements.

The final Pioneer battalion to arrive at Marseilles in the spring of 1918 was the 5/Royal Irish Regiment. It had served with the 10th and 52nd Divisions and on disembarkation was sent first to the 53rd Division. It spent some time on line of communication duties at Tardinghem and was subsequently attached to the 50th Division. Unlike the 9/Gloucester, the Royal Irish was to stay with the Northumbrian Division for the remainder of the war.[1]

One of the last units to reorganize its forces following the German offensives was the regular 5th Division. The division had successfully contrived for some months to evade the stipulated reduction of its infantry brigades to the required nine battalions. Eventually the authorities demanded that prevarication should cease and the specified changes be executed. The division was thus obliged to lose three of its existing twelve battalions. As it was unthinkable that the staff would allow the disbanding of one of the regular battalions, the axe had to fall on some of the division's five non-regular battalions. The existing Pioneers were the 6/Argyll and Sutherland Highlanders. It was promptly returned to its old division, the 51st. Next, the 15/Warwick and 12/Gloucester were disbanded, the 16/Warwick went into 13th Brigade and the 14/Warwick became the Pioneers. It is difficult to see what qualification this battalion had over the others for becoming Pioneers. Originally the unit had recruited from non-manual workers and although the composition had gone through several transitions, there is no indication that it now contained a higher proportion of skilled men than the others. The decision to retain it rather than one of the other two battalions was probably on the grounds of its seniority among the city of Birmingham battalions. There was some compensation for eight officers and 197 men of the disbanded 2nd City battalion for they were posted to the new Pioneer battalion. According to the War Diary of the 14th, these men requested that they be allowed to join the Pioneers, but whether they and the four officers and D Company of the 12/Gloucester who also joined, possessed any specific pioneering skills is unknown.

In the final months of the war Pioneer battalions, both old and new played a significant part in some of the most decisive and heaviest fighting. Although the majority of the units were to do little more than follow the advance, some continued to fulfil the role of front line fighters they had performed during the March and April offensives. Two Scottish battalions received much praise for their activities in July. The 9/Gordon Highlanders took part in the open warfare near Buzancy – there being no entrenching or pioneering work for them to do – while the 8/Royal Scots, who marched over 60 miles in full kit in four days, also took part in an attack along the Ardre valley. Praise was subsequently heaped upon its 'B' Company for being the only unit of 154th Brigade to reach its objective near the Bois de Coutron. Having suffered 109 casualties, the battalion returned to northern France at the end of July, musing that its sojourn in Champagne had been 'full of interest'.[2]

The Territorials of the 9/DLI, who had won much fame in March 1918, also fought along the Ardre and were again later singled out for praise. The nature of the fighting was such that the Durhams were not required as a pioneer battalion and, like the Gordons and the Royal Scots, were used as fighting infantry. On 21 July the battalion debouched from a wood and attacked downhill towards the German positions. The attack was completely held up by scores of German machine guns hidden in the dense undergrowth of the next wood. After sustaining over

30 fatalities the battalion consolidated the few hundred yards won and two days later attacked again. Despite losing a considerable number of men while still forming up – 'C' Company taking 60 casualties before it went over the top – the attack successfully captured 85 Germans, nine machine guns and retook eight French 75s. In recognition of the vital part played by the battalion, Major-General Braithwaite, GOC 62nd Division, wrote a congratulatory letter to the Durham Territorial Association:

> It was necessary to employ the battalion as a fighting battalion . . . [it] fought magnificently . . . Their assault and capture of Cuitron was one of the finest incidents in the long battle, and throughout the engagement their gallantry and devotion to duty are beyond praise. I am very proud to have so distinguished a battalion in the 62nd Division.[3]

In September the battalion attacked Vaulx Wood and Havrincourt. This second attack cost it nearly 30 dead and again won specific praise from the divisional commander. However, a later report on the assault was not quite as complimentary as the general's missive of July. Platoon officers in the right forward company had become early casualties and the sergeants were blamed for not showing 'sufficient energy' in pushing forward through the scrub which, it was acknowledged, also hindered progress.[4] On the left flank, the company involved kept up with the barrage and despite considerable opposition captured 60 prisoners and ten machine guns. It then repulsed a counter-attack, but as there were only about 16 survivors it withdrew when another German attack was seen to be forming. It might be that the commanders were seeking scapegoats for the failure of the right company and blamed the sergeants because they were available. Yet despite the criticism the battalion's work in July and September demonstrated that it had lost none of its original fighting spirit. It might have become a Pioneer unit but by continuing to train as infantry it could still be used, if required, as a potent attacking force.

Another of the recently converted battalions, the 2/4th

Somerset L.I., was also supposed to take part in a direct assault. The battalion was ordered to attack in cooperation with the 7/Cheshire, but it arrived late at the start line and missed the barrage. The Somersets were still prepared to go over, but as the Cheshires were not considered to be 'in a fit condition to take part', the attack was aborted. Even so, the battalion still lost three dead and 15 missing. The British Empire Pioneers, or more correctly the 20/KRRC, also had an unfortunate time in July. On occasions the battalion was caught between trying to perform pioneering duties and acting as line holding infantry. As their chronicler remembered: 'While most honest members of a Pioneer unit would acknowledge that our lot was preferable to that of the ordinary infantry as a general rule, it may well be doubted whether on the Hinges – Locon front the Pioneers had not the more trying and dangerous time'.[5] Similarly, the 19/N.F. had to help out the infantry at Aveluy Wood in June. An attack failed and instead of consolidation, two platoons of the Fusiliers went forward and captured two machine guns and 20 prisoners.

The detail recorded in the War Diary of the 8/Sussex is fairly typical of the planning and preparation undertaken by battalions for these operations. The battalion received sheaves of orders from divisional HQ, detailing how and when it was to move, bivouac positions, dress to be worn and what rations to be carried. These were supplemented by the CRE's orders which were more specifically concerned with its technical role in the forthcoming attack. One company was instructed to mark out and cut a dry weather track for use by horse transport south of the Bray – Corbie road and to erect notice boards giving directions of roads, the names of captured trenches, woods and any other feature that should fall into British hands. Another platoon was to repair the Bray – Corbie road as far as the brickfield near Heilly so that it could be used by ambulances. Other platoons were employed constructing 50 infantry trench bridges and once the R.E. had delivered the required paint and Jeyes Fluid, they were to complete and locate them ready for use. The battalion was also warned that in the event of an enemy withdrawal, it should send forward a small party to reconnoitre roads and report back. Suspected booby traps at cross roads and elsewhere were to be clearly marked 'Dangerous'.

The depth of detail listed in this War Diary can be contrasted with the paucity evident in at least two others. The 16/HLI contrived to keep its fighting activities hidden beneath a cover of terse, abrupt entries seemingly designed to reveal nothing of its feats. It concentrates instead upon the reputation earned by the battalion for its smartness. In similar vein, the entries of the 19/Middlesex reveal virtually nothing of its quite substantial role in the fighting of September.

Rather than refuse to commit their activities to the bureaucracy of the War Diary, some accounts take a phlegmatic or stoical approach to the work carried out during the final hundred days. A chronicler of the 8/Royal Scots thought that taking part in a battle, 'meant little more than that it had to perform its work under more violent shell fire and under more disagreeable conditions than usual'.[6] Having received several 'thanks' messages for its work in bridging the Ancre and keeping the advancing troops supplied with ammunition and rations, the 19/Welch was then used as a fighting reserve. One company was employed in an attack and then the battalion returned to its more familiar role. A diarist noted rather dryly that this 'holiday work', although welcome, did not later hinder its more usual work of consolidation.[7] In October, the 6/East Yorks also appeared to have revelled in the opportunity to display once again its fighting qualities. The regimental historian wrote that during August and September its part in the operations, although 'unrecorded', was 'very real' and performed 'most gallantly . . . The call for their assistance was insistent, and they answered that call with a devotion to duty of which it is impossible to write too highly'.[8] Appreciated as this work obviously was, when the battalion was instructed to do some trench holding, the order caused a 'thrill of excitement . . . it was like old times again'.[9] In a cheery note, albeit one which smacks a little of hollowness, Colonel Liddell of the hard-fighting and recently converted 7/N.F., informed his men that their orders were simply to follow the advance and keep the roads clear: 'So start off and go straight ahead till we hear that the Boche are in the next village. Then we just pick out the first convenient bankside and push up some bivvies for the night'.[10] The 5/Cheshire was also in the forefront of the offensive in September 1918 when the 56th Division and the Canadians stormed the Canal du Nord near Sauchy-Lestree. Loaded down with extra picks and shovels, the Pioneers moved through the infantry and engaged the enemy machine guns on the canal bank. The Germans were driven off by the Pioneers' Lewis guns and rifle fire before the Cheshires began the task of assisting the R.E. Field Companies to bridge the canal. According to the O.C. First Army's Advanced Heavy Bridging Depot, the work of throwing over a bridge with a 90 foot span was done in record time. Once they had done their heavy ramping, platoons of Cheshires were engaged in reconnoitring roads in the captured area and in assisting the R.E. dismantle booby traps.

One young officer who was sent out for the first time during the offensives expressed himself rather surprised to be sent to a battalion, which according to his diary, 'spent its time doing pioneering work'.[11] Roderick Jamieson was posted from the 3/SWB to the 4/RWF and his diary entries suggest that he did not initially understand that his new battalion was a Pioneer unit. The monotony of pioneering duties was relieved for Jamieson in early September when the battalion was called upon to clear St. Pierre Vaast Wood. The obviously bucked subaltern recorded that the operation 'might have been sticky, but [we] were very lucky'. Someone who knew all about the activities and duties of Pioneers was the apparently inexhaustible Colonel Trower of the 5/SWB. The open warfare of the summer thrilled Trower and gave him the opportunity to pen another of his famous orders of the day. On 4 September he told his men:

> The record of the past few weeks is most cheering . . . the sun is shining . . . and we may all look forward to the time now coming when our brutal and dishonourable foe shall be for ever humbled.

In July, on the third anniversary of the battalion's arrival in France, Trower had composed another equally inspiring exhortation for his troops:

251

Colonel Trower rejoices to think he has still around him many of those who have stood this long period of active service in the cause of Right and Justice . . . Brother officers and soldiers let us spare no effort in the future to cement the bonds of strict discipline, combined with true comradeship in the time that is before us, until a brutal and degraded enemy, who murders women and children, and is proud of it, is at last rendered powerless for evil.

If Pioneers were to be in the forefront of what was expected to be a particularly difficult attack, battalions would create a battle surplus. These were never particularly large – for example, in July the 14/N.F. sent 40 men classified as 'administration' and 43 as the 'nucleus' to the transport lines – but they do indicate that Pioneers were expected to sustain casualties. And sometimes they could be substantial. In its operation at Epéhy on 18 September, the 5/Northants had 128 casualties, while in the very nasty action near Naves in October, 260 of the 320 19/L.F. who took part became casualties. Fortunately, these considerable casualties were not universally reflected in the rolls of all Pioneer units. The 14/Worcester lost only one dead and seven wounded during the nine days of the Battle of Albert and just another two wounded during the storming of the Drocourt-Queant Line. The regimental historian later admitted that the working parties, which were spread all over the battlefield, were 'blessed by good fortune'. Perhaps the Worcesters were particularly fortunate, as even the 11/South Lancs, which had returned to France in October following its re-constitution as a Category B unit, lost seven dead and 38 wounded when crossing the Sambre-et-Oise Canal.

Pioneers in other theatres also lost men as they struggled to keep the roads clear and the front areas serviced. In far away Mesopotamia the 8/Welch laboured to cut gun and wagon tracks through the barren rocks and wastes of the desert. In the extremes of climate and terrain the battalion continued to lose more men through disease and heatstroke than enemy fire. Similarly, the 9/Border in Salonkia lost well over 50% of its fatalities from disease despite its active part in the September operations against the Bulgars. As they cut through rock and laid acres of wire on the Asiago plateau, the 5/Sussex and 24/Manchester had taken relatively few casualties. In the final offensives against the Austrians the Oldham Comrades lost only a handful of members but were obliged to develop new skills of bridge builders and ferrymen.

Although these and other units were often actively engaged in the storming of enemy positions, other battalions worked away at the more traditional jobs demanded of Pioneers and at the more mundane aspects of army life. When not actually involved in fighting, the 16/HLI continued to make its parade appearance something of a fetish. An obviously delighted officer noted that: 'People in authority began to sit up and take notice of the fastidiously groomed and well-disciplined battalion'.[12] Following a medal parade Lieutenant-General Haldane apparently stopped his car to tell the 16th's C.O. that his battalion was 'the finest unit on parade' that day. Among other battalions who prided themselves on their soldierly appearance was the 7/N.F. Although it is difficult to be exact, what evidence there is tends to suggest that those units which had been raised as Pioneers or converted early in their history, were less fussy about their general appearance and march discipline than those which had spent most of their time as infantry. There are of course exceptions to this generalization, perhaps most notably the older T.F. units and the 4/Coldstream Guards.

Having spent many weeks following its conversion in February not as Pioneers but fighting infantry, in May the 7/N.F. eventually found time to practise its new trade. Each of its three companies established a mining platoon and these were soon engaged in digging and constructing deep dugouts. The remaining platoons, not surprisingly given the battalion's acknowledged distaste at becoming Pioneers, spent their time training on the ranges and in gas drills. The former miners of the 5/Cheshire were also engaged in digging – sinking wells in the bed of the Cojeul near Arras. A few weeks later, when the 56th Division crossed the Honnelle, the Cheshires again displayed their penchant for bridging when they speedily cleared the debris of a demolished viaduct and erected up a new crossing.

Railway work continued to be an important aspect of Pioneers' duties, but as we have seen, the 17/N.F. were converted back to Pioneers having spent some months as Railway Construction Troops. When it rejoined its division, only to find the other units were about to be withdrawn from the line, one of its officers gloomily noted that 'rest and refitting were never required by Pioneers, [so] the battalion plugged away'.[13] Another battalion which had spent a great deal of its time building or running railways was the 7/York & Lancs. However, the subsequent changes in its personnel and the loss of so many of its originals handicapped the unit when it was ordered to lay tracks near Honnecourt. One of its officers recorded that 'nearly all' the recent arrivals were ignorant of the techniques of building or running a railway. This meant that the first attempts at laying the track were 'not a bit professional'.[14] Fortunately there were sufficient survivors of the time spent at Ypres in 1917 to be made gang leaders and supervise the work until a detachment of Canadian Railway Engineers arrived to assist.

In early March the 2/5th Loyals underwent a bloody introduction to its new role as Pioneers when the billets of 'C' Company at Estaires were shelled. During the rest of March and April it had little else to do than dig and wire in the rear, although it did spend some time maintaining its infantry skills. In early May it relieved the 7/N.F. around Gommecourt Park and continued to fulfil the sort of tasks expected of Pioneers. For the next two months it performed unspectacular but essential work. An indication of what a battalion could achieve is evident from the work detailed in its War Diary. It completed 2,480 yards of new trenches, reconstructed 2,870 yards of old, completed the construction of two deep dugouts, began the excavation for another two, erected 75 small elephant shelters and laid 2,930 yards of wire. The troops worked mainly at night and suffered from intermittent shell fire and gas discharges. The men seem not to have fired any shots in anger, but lost five dead and at least five wounded. It was unglamorous work but it meant that at least the infantry did not have to do it. Another new Pioneer battalion, the recently established 17/Worcester, performed similarly undramatic work around Steenwerck. It lost only one dead and two wounded, all from long distance shell fire, while it dug, wired and repaired roads.

Road building and repair continued to be a major task for most units during these final months. The 9/Gordon Highlanders performed this vital job near the Haute Deule Canal in October. The troops worked from before dawn until after dark, clearing the roads of felled trees, telegraph poles and filling in craters. The 7/N.F. was actually assisted by a crowd of French civilians to clear away the blocked approaches to a bridge over the Sambre at Hautmont, while a company of the 8/Royal Scots successfully completed a task of road repair near Iwuy in three, rather than the nine days corps had estimated the job would take. Rarely sharing the glory or the accolades showered upon the infantry in these tumultuous days, the Pioneers persevered in their uninspiring work. Yet even though the people at home might not read of the part played by the Pioneers in the advance through France and Belgium, the Pioneers themselves knew how vital their role was. With obvious pride, Davidson of the 22/DLI recalled:

> It must be made clear that often it was the work of a Pioneer battalion which enabled an attack to be developed or supported . . . yet when the task was ended, the labour and the sweat were forgotten as the guns came slithering down the bank, crossed, strained up the far side and with a lurch vanished beyond its crest.[15]

One great advantage the Pioneers had over most of the infantry battalions was their fighting strength. In the last two months of the war, many brigades went into the attack with what in 1916 would have amounted only to battalion strength; in contrast, during these final months most Pioneer units remained near to the official establishment of 24 officers and 859 men. The medical category of the men was certainly lower than it had been, but the units could generally muster about 200 men more than an ordinary infantry battalion. Possibly the lowest strength of any Pioneer unit in the summer of 1918 was the 30 officers and 517 men of the 21/West Yorks. At the other end of the scale, when hostilities ended the 14/Warwick assembled 35 officers and 963 men. In April the 5/Northants mustered 1,000 other ranks, and even in Macedonia the 9/Border boasted 30 officers and 928 men. This was a little under the official Salonika establishment which in March 1918 became 1051 all ranks. There is evidence to suggest that the totals were regularly exceeded, but the official establishment for Pioneer units in the Italian theatre was 26 officers and 831. In Egypt, the 5/Royal Irish Regiment usually maintained a non-commissioned ranks strength of over 800 in early 1918.

Like those of infantry battalions, effective strengths of Pioneer units on the Western Front were reduced in June with the appearance of 'pyrexia unknown origin' or 'flu. This 'four day fever' as it was also known, more than decimated many units and put in jeopardy some of the operations planned for June. For example, the 21/West Yorks had ten officers and 180 men down with it in June; this reduced its fighting strength to 443 other ranks. The 17/N.F. had a worse rate, with 514 recorded cases, involving 300 at any one time. The 12/KOYLI had an average of 90 cases a day in addition to the 80 men whose condition warranted hospital treatment. Despite the numbers of men preoccupied with the 'flu, the 17/N.F. still managed to raise £1,970 on War Loans day – a sum the battalion claimed was the highest achieved by any unit in France. In an equal display of patriotism, the 7/York & Lancs raised £2,523 in September from the sale of War Savings certificates. This was despite the cynical suspicion in the minds of many that the contribution was 'little else than a gratuity to Mr Lloyd George'.[16]

While the ordinary work of the battalions had to continue through the summer and autumn, other units found themselves in unexpected roles and with insecure futures. The 6/7th Royal Scots was reduced to a training cadre in May, with the bulk of the battalion being despatched to Calais for disposal. The cadre wandered around the front for four weeks seeking a role, until it was sent back to the U.K. and attached to the 16th Division. Here, the survivors were eventually absorbed by the 18/Scottish Rifles. This battalion went out to France as part of the re-constituted 16th Division, so the former members of the 6/7th once again became infantry. The 13/Gloucester was another unit which in May was reduced to cadre. The battalion had fought to virtual destruction in April and from the survivors a demonstration section was selected. The remnant of the battalion was sent to Etaples while the demonstration section joined the 39th Division's demonstration platoon. This platoon trained American troops in infantry and engineering techniques until August when it was transferred to the 66th Division. A few days later it continued its odyssey, ending up on the coast at Haudricourt where it began preparing a camp for the reception of 'malaria reinforcements'.

Companies of the 18/N.F. had served with infantry battalions during the April battles and in May it too was destined to be reduced to a training establishment. The personnel of the battalion's rump consisted of the colonel, two majors, four captains, eight subalterns and an undisclosed number of other ranks. They were engaged in training American machine gun battalions in musketry, P.T., bayonet and gas drills; these troops were later joined by some of their colleagues in the Engineer units of the 28th(U.S.)Division. Their work was then extended to include teaching the Americans to wire and construct trenches. In August the Fusiliers were instructed to prepare a camp at Abancourt for the reception of 'malaria reinforcements' from England. Preparing the camp posed no difficulties for the Northumbrians, but they might have considered that this second period as infantry instructors was testing the skills of Pioneers to the limit. The reinforcements were a thorough mixture of men. Some of them had been evacuated from Eastern theatres of operations and returned to the U.K. for convalescence, while others were arriving as complete battalions from Palestine and Salonika. The first draft of 331 reinforcements arrived in mid-September. They were scheduled for light training and treatment, consisting of P.T., musketry, close order and gas drill. This was timetabled to last for three hours in the morning, with the afternoons devoted to recreational training. While undergoing this training, each man was to receive 15 grains of quinine per day. The Fusiliers' role was to supervise the troops' rehabilitation before sending them on to the 50th and 66th Divisions, both of which had earlier been reduced to cadre and were then in the process of re-constitution. The former Pioneers continued to perform these tasks until December when the cadre was moved to Le Havre in preparation to receive the first batches of demobilized soldiers.

Contemporary reports on how the armistice was received by front line troops vary. Some units declared their men showed no emotion and continued with their work, while others acknowledged scenes of excited revelry. The 4/Coldstream became involved in 'scenes of great enthusiasm' in Maubeuge, but had little time to enjoy them as almost immediately the battalion began to prepare for the march into Germany.[17] The 11/Hampshire did not think itself quite as fortunate as the Guards. Its historian gloomily reflected that the armistice meant 'less to Pioneers than to other units'.[18] This is something of an overstatement, as most infantry battalions were to be engaged on road clearing and repairs in the often long, boring months before demobilization. Nevertheless, the Hampshires' chronicler insisted that apart from the occasional references to education and demobilization, entries in the War Diary 'would hardly indicate that anything special had happened on 11 November'.[19] By contrast, the regimental historian of the Suffolk regiment wrote that 'very shortly' after the armistice its 4th Battalion abandoned the pioneering jobs it had been doing on road and bridge repairs. Instead, the battalion spent its time on vocational training and education classes. 'Even the most conscientious soldier' during this tedious time it was admitted, 'did his duty perfunctorily'.[20]

As most units continued to labour at the jobs they had been doing for the bulk of their existence, the recorded post-armistice experiences of the 4/Suffolk are at variance with those of the majority of Pioneer battalions. Some gave help to French and Belgian civilians returning to their devastated lands and homes. The Pioneers and other divisional troops of the 14th Division formed an Agricultural Company to assist local farmers, while the 17/Worcester helped with the reconstruction of civilian housing. However, because most Pioneer battalions still contained a large proportion of erstwhile miners, demobilization was to take away significant numbers by the end of the year.

The first parties of miners began to leave their units by the end of November. Initially the numbers tended to be low, but as the process moved into top gear, larger parties were despatched. Only 11 men left the 14/N.F. on 29 November as its first group; within five days another 200 had gone. Two hundred miners left the 7/York & Lancs in early December and the 12/KOYLI which, it will be recalled had been raised by the West Yorkshire Coal Owners Association, began returning its men to England in mid-December. The 5/SWB still had over 800 men in early January, but by the end of February over 600 miners had left it to return to the Valleys. The demobilization process continued to accelerate into the New Year, and by March many units were returning their cadre to the U.K. In the meantime, and in view of the contemporary unrest that was evident in several units serving both at home and abroad, the men had to be kept occupied.

Apart from the inevitable and seemingly never ending demands on their labour for clearing snow and mud from roads, the Pioneers were called upon to perform some new tasks. Throughout the BEF there was an explosion in the number of football fixtures played. Amongst others, the 7/N.F., the 24/Manchester and the 14/Royal Warwicks – who scored 37 goals with only four against – all won their respective divisional football cups. But it was not only the games themselves that required man hours. Pioneers were employed building grand-stands for the spectators and laying out pitches. Viewing areas were also constructed for divisional racecourses and boxing arenas, as were new hutted camps for the troops and reception areas for returning refugees. The expertise and skills of the Pioneers were in demand up and down the line. They were the ready source of carpenters, plumbers, mechanics and navvies; with the R.E., they became the odd-job men of the rapidly disappearing army. A trawl of regimental museums and local archives has unfortunately produced only one almost complete demobilization book and nominal role of a battalion as it was when hostilties ended. Others will undoubtedly come to light but at present their absence makes it difficult to be precise

259

about the proportion of skilled men to labourers in the various units. What evidence does exist suggests that although there was a huge variety of skills within a battalion, they probably did not fulfil the stipulated proportion laid down for Pioneer units by the War Office.

The demobilization roll of the 24/Manchester has survived and from its pages a detailed analysis of its men's civilian occupations can be attempted.[21] Of the first 625 men to enlist in the battalion in late 1914, 35% had worked in the textile industry, 10% were described as 'labourer' and 8% were white collar workers – insurance agents and shop workers. Nine per cent were skilled men from the local foundries, but only 3% were skilled men from the building trades and less than 1% were miners. When the battalion was demobilized, after having been almost completely rebuilt in 1917 by former R.E.s, it presented a different, but by no means dramatically altered composition. The occupation of 73% of the 925 other ranks is recorded. The textile industry still contributed the largest number of members, but the figure had dropped to 27% Those described as 'labourer' had fallen slightly to 9%, the percentage of white collar workers remained exactly the same, the number of men employed in the metal trades rose to 15% and that of skilled men in the building trades to 20%. If the 674 men whose civilian occupations are known reflect a true cross-section of the complete battalion, the unit clearly failed to fulfil the requirements for Pioneer battalions laid down in 1914. Instead of the specified 50% of men used to working with pick and shovel, a maximum of only 11% could be so described. It was probably assumed that the erstwhile cotton spinners, florists, tram drivers, shop assistants, asylum attendants and watch repairers would soon enough acquire sufficient expertise at what the army called 'earth excavation'. As 35% of its members possessed a recognized trade, it did at least get nearer to achieving the required 50% of skilled men. What is surprising is the apparent lack of miners. There is a vague possibility that the demobilization roll was written after the battalion's miners had already gone – that could explain why the occupation of 27% of the men is not listed. However, another orderly room source shows that the battalion put only 13 'miners' on the first two demobilization trains. Both trains left Italy in late December. The demobilization book was certainly completed by the middle of January, by when 65 men had been despatched home. Even if these had all been former miners, and there is nothing to suggest they were, they would still only represent 7% of strength.[22] This small proportion is probably not typical of most battalions – details above suggest that other units had a significantly higher proportion – yet it might not be unique. What is clear is that despite the huge number of ex-R.E. and the deliberate posting of small groups of men with the required trades from within its own division, the Oldham battalion did not fit the official bill for a Pioneer unit. It was clearly easier for the War Office to specify what the ideal should be than it was for commanders in the field to secure it.[23]

Some Pioneer battalions became in essence holding units. Men were posted to them either on their way down the line for demobilization, or on their way through to the army of occupation. Others actually became part of the Army of the Rhine and although they might undergo a rapid turnover of personnel, could grow to unprecedented sizes. When the 20/KRRC was required to find 200 men to guard Weisweiler power station against the possibility of civil unrest, its historian noted that the troops were all recent recruits and were commanded by regular officers who a few weeks previously had commanded brigades.[24] By the end of March 1919 the 12/Loyal North Lancashire, which had arrived at Bonn in February with 11 officers and 131 men, had an establishment of 68 officers and 1,265 other ranks. This was unusual, but other units did reach sizes far in excess of that enjoyed during hostilities. While their battalion remained in existence, whether growing or reducing in size, the Pioneers remained active. Several units, for example the 6/East Yorks and 12/Notts & Derby, had men posted away to prisoner of war companies. Inside the huge coastal depots Pioneers were engaged in many types of work: these included salvaging and demolishing camps and sending the de-loused and re-clothed demobilization parties home. Some of the tasks were not without dangers. Three members of the 18/Middlesex were killed by an explosion when salvaging ammunition at Malincourt. Perhaps one of the most unlikely tasks fell to a party of the 17/Worcester who were detached from the rest of the battalion currently guarding stores at Harfleur and ordered to escort a group of German prisoners home by sea.

When not working or playing, Pioneers, like all other units still in France, attended education classes. The quality and variety of the talks given – usually by junior officers press-ganged into the job – depended on the attitude of the C.O. Some battalions listened to or endured lectures on the 'Rise and Fall of the Roman Empire', 'France and its People' and 'Airships'. While some talks might have been of ostensible educational value, or at least a diversion from working outside in the cold, it is difficult to imagine what benefits the members of the 19/Middlesex might have derived from a lecture by a Mr. J.C. Bee-Mason on 'The Craft of the Bee-Hunter'.[25] Nevertheless, time passed and provided a man had not re-enlisted or had been only recently posted from home, there was a good chance that he would be out of uniform and back home by the summer. Some would clearly return having benefited from their newly-acquired education. In January 1919 the adjutant of the 12/Royal Irish Rifles claimed: 'The outstanding feature of the month's work is the continued progress made by the Illiterate class'. Its members had succeeded in reaching the equivalent of an elementary school's 3rd Standard. The officers too were taking advantage of the peaceful conditions by paying for a civilian to give them lessons in Spanish.

Because casualties among Pioneer units were fewer than those of the infantry, it is tempting to think that a substantial proportion of men who enlisted in a battalion when it was mobilized or created would still be serving with it when hostilities ended. Yet this is to ignore the huge personnel changes which occurred in the autumn of 1917. In addition to natural attrition and postings of men from other regiments, the influx of the R.E. meant that most battalions were barely recognizable to those which had left for France. As no staff at any base would have possessed the temerity to attempt to draft other than Guardsmen to the battalion, a notable exception to this was the 4/Coldstream.

After two years at the front, the battalion could still muster seven officers and 504 men of its original composition. Of these, three officers and 240 other ranks remained when the Prince of Wales presented its colour in January 1919.[26] Another battalion which appears to have retained a large proportion of its originals was the 18/N.F. Only 12% of the battalion's fatalities were men who had been transferred in from other regiments.[27] Furthermore, judging from the army numbers of the other fatalities the majority were either original members of the battalion or men who had come from the reserve battalions of the Northumberland Fusiliers. When it was reduced to cadre in May 1918, there were still some 237 original members serving with it.

Once the demobilization system moved into gear, most battalions would have tried to get their longest serving members despatched home before their more recent arrivals. If the former were miners, railmen or agricultural workers there was not much of a difficulty, but other originals, particularly those of the orderly room staff, might have been deliberately retained or even have volunteered to remain until the cadre returned to the U.K. There were certainly eight originals with the cadre of the 24/Manchester and 13 who returned with the 5/Cheshire. Other battalions no doubt also came back with a handful of originals, although it is difficult to do more than speculate. When the cadre did return, the usual practice was for its home town to hold some sort of civic reception. This could take the form of the torch light procession given to the 4/Suffolk at Ipswich, or a special parade of already demobilized former members such as that held by the North-Eastern Railway for the 17/N.F. The cadre would then usually lay up the colours at a local church or the town hall. Civic dignitaries and colonels, past or present, would deliver speeches of appreciation and thanks, followed normally by a celebratory meal. After that its future depended upon whether the unit was a Territorial or New Army battalion. If it was the former it might anticipate a return to infantry status; if the latter, it would be disbanded and struck off the list of serving units. That was to be the fate of the great majority. Pioneer battalions had been created for the duration, had performed their duty and were now, like most other wartime creations, no longer required.

NOTES

1. Between May and October 1919 the battalion was attached to the 2nd Division.
2. Ewing, op.cit. p.651
3. Correspondence in Crouch papers. (DLI Museum)
4. ibid.
5. Turbeville, op.cit. p.116
6. Ewing, op.cit. p.677
7. The battalion lost only one man dead during this period.
8. Wyrall, *The East Yorkshire Regiment*, op.cit. p.357. Although the battalion apparently enjoyed its temporary duty as fighting infantry, it was not quite so enthusiastic about its new accommodation. Before the Allied counter-offensives, the unit had spent months in one sector making itself as comfortable as circumstances allowed. During the advance, the War Diary notes several times that the accommodation was 'poor'.
9. ibid.
10. Buckley, *7/Northumberland Fusiliers*, p.80
11. Jamieson, R. papers. (Liddle Collection)
12. Chalmers, op.cit. p.118
13. Shakespear, op.cit. p.94
14. Gilvary, op.cit. p.85
15. Davidson, op.cit.
16. In January 1918 the 1/Monmouth claimed that 61.4% of the battalion subscribed to War Savings Certificates.
17. The 4/Coldstream covered the 214 miles from Maubeuge to Cologne in 20 marching days.
18. Atkinson, op.cit. p.437. The W.D. of the 15/LNL recorded the armistice and added: 'This however, did not affect the Battalion's work'.
19. Atkinson, op.cit. p.437
20. Murphy, op.cit. p.396. At 1055 on 11 November, a shell, fortunately a dud, landed in the garden of the house which functioned as the orderly room of the 25/KRRC. The crash startled the transport officer just as he was giving a retiring salute to the adjutant. (*KRRC Chronicle, 1919*, p.92)
21. In Oldham Local Studies Library.
22. The 15/LNL had despatched 'the last' of its miners by 18 December. This brought the battalion's total of demobilized colliers to only 44.
23. Of the 39 men listed in a platoon nominal roll of the 9/South Staffs, there are only two labourers and three clerks. The remainder,

including six miners, are all skilled men. Thirteen come from what could be called the building trades and five from the metal industries. Not all of them had their civilian skills utilized by the army: former masons, miners and bricklayers were described as 'cooks'. It is not known when this roll was compiled, or whether this distribution of skilled to non-skilled men was typical of the battalion. It was probably written fairly late in 1918. (Private collection, David Baldwin).

24. Turbeville, op.cit. p.140
25. Other unlikely topics included, 'The Czechs and Slovaks' and 'Colonial Governments'.
26. Letter to the Prince of Wales dated 14 Jan.1919. Piggott's papers. (Liddle Collection. Many Pioneer battalions were presented with a King's Colour before the cadre returned home.
27. See Appendix I.

Chapter 13

PIONEERING THROUGH OTHERS' EYES

Reference has already been made to the relationships forged between Pioneer battalions and the CRE during the course of the war. Generally speaking the arrangement of Pioneers working under the authority and supervision of the Engineers seems to have worked satisfactorily or better. What is less clear is how the Pioneers were regarded by the men for whom they laboured – the infantry and the artillery. In extant sources it is rare to find in the personal reminiscences of individual soldiers, whether officers or other ranks, discussion, appreciation or comments about the usefulness or otherwise of the Pioneers. This is perhaps not altogether surprising, as in general men remember and record the experiences which were of immediate concern or importance to their own activities. They rarely pass comment upon the quality of the revetting, the siting of the sumps or the craftsmanship of the dugout supports and interiors. Understandably, the infantry were more concerned with the depth of the trench they were occupying and whether the sandbags around the dugout would absorb the blast of a 5.9 inch shell or disintegrate on impact. They would also be concerned about how deep and effective were the belts of wire in front of the parapet but probably gave little thought to the men who might have erected them. Furthermore, when out at rest, few men recorded their appreciation of the quality of the latrines or ablution benches in the camps. Instead, they were more likely to recall whether there was fresh straw in the billet and whether there was an estaminet nearby from where they could buy eggs and chips.

This is not to suggest that the troops did not appreciate the work or construction done on their behalf. Memoirs frequently mention the relief expressed by weary men when they flopped to rest out of range of German guns. In their quiet satisfaction at being away at least temporarily from danger, many troops would possibly have thought that other infantry had done the work of erecting the camps and providing the facilities. Throughout the war the shortages of labour demanded that troops supposedly on rest had to labour and carry in the front as well as the rear areas. Whether the trenches had been dug or the camps constructed by Pioneers or front line infantry posed merely an academic question. Furthermore most troops, certainly in the first three years of the war, probably acknowledged little distinction between themselves and the divisional troops and R.E. Field Companies. They all served at the front and were exposed to the same dangers.

Although the troops themselves only infrequently mention the work of the Pioneers in preparing the ground or supporting the offensives, generals tended to be a little more forthcoming in their praise. It is easy to understand why the CRE felt either obliged or inspired to send messages of thanks to the Pioneer colonel for the work done by his men; they worked in close cooperation and it was in everyone's interest that whatever job was required to be completed should be done as effectively as possible. Neither is there any difficulty in understanding why divisional commanders frequently sent telegrams of appreciation to the Pioneers. They had the morale of the division to consider. The consensus among senior officers was that troops would be bucked if they knew the staff was taking notice of their work. After the Somme the troops became increasingly cynical about these protestations of appreciation. Widely known as 'thanks parades', a battalion would parade before the divisional commander or one of his subordinates to hear how well it had done in the preceding action and how satisfied the authorities were with its performance. However, frequent and regular as these parades were for the infantry, it is difficult before 1918 to identify recorded parades of a Pioneer battalion being addressed by a divisional commander. A rare exception was the public recognition by the GOC 37th Division of the work done by the 9/North Staffs in digging communication trenches near Arras in May 1917.

One reason for this could be that Pioneers were seldom assembled as battalions. The regularity with which companies and platoons were detached from the main body meant that battalion parades were often only possible when the unit had been withdrawn completely from the line and reassembled far to the rear. By contrast, infantry battalions were normally withdrawn as a unit and even as a brigade. It was a relatively easy task to pass on the congratulations of the commander to them. Pioneers, on the other hand, often received their congratulations from the officers who commanded the detachments and instead of a battalion parade, heard them as they prepared for work in their dispersed platoons. Some of the men might have appreciated the thought, others would have merely shrugged their shoulders, muttered some sardonic remark about the race of generals and trudged away to their labours.

It is difficult to decide whether all the cynicism towards the various staffs, evident in the last years of the war, was justified. This is not the place to attempt an analysis of the merits or demerits of how staff operated or of the relations with their subordinates. What is pertinent to this study is an investigation into whether messages emanating from divisional headquarters to Pioneer battalions were sent as a perfunctory obligation or as the result of a genuine desire to record the staff's appreciation of work undertaken by the Pioneers.

The majority of congratulatory messages received at Pioneer battalion HQ demonstrate a similar, and at times identical, format. The following, sent by the GOC 36th Division is typical of the genre:

> Officers and men have worked with a will and with skill and intelligence at all work that has been given them to do and the results are most creditable to the Battalion and worthy of praise.[1]

Examples such as this can be found in just about every Pioneer battalion's War Diary. They suggest that the work was appreciated and although there are not too many ways of varying the format of a 'thank you' note, there was not perhaps too much thought put in by the staff as to how the messages could be made to sound genuinely and uniquely sincere. The staff would claim, justifiably, that the *thought* was the essential thing and turn their attention to more pressing matters. Despite the frequency of the notes, there is evidence to demonstrate that the messages were received with pride and pleasure by at least the C.O. of the Pioneer unit. He would sometimes despatch a message in reply. Lt. Col. Glasgow of the 8/Sussex responded to his divisional commander's wire with the following note:

> Thank you very much for your letter, the contents of which I shall have the greatest pleasure in conveying to all ranks . . . The knowledge that our work is appreciated by our Divisional Commander is a great incentive to us all and you may be sure that the whole Battalion will, by its work, strive to maintain your good opinion.

On other occasions the Pioneers were included in the message sent to the entire division or corps. In these instances individual units are not specifically identified, nor is the work undertaken. Instead, all arms are congratulated on the action taken by the corps or division, with stress laid on the fact that units had worked together as a team and so no particular unit should be singled out. This message from the commander of VIII Corps to all units under his command in December 1917 is similar to many:

> You are selected troops holding one of the most difficult, muddy and unpleasant parts of the line . . . [you have] shown fine spirit . . . [and are] imperturbably cheery. The responsibility of holding this part of the line is great and the honour in the successful accomplishment of our task is correspondingly great . . . [our defences] will enable us to wish for nothing better than that the enemy may attack us so that we may have the opportunity of

mowing them down with our rifles, Lewis guns, machine guns and artillery as we did in the glorious days of the first Battle of Ypres . . . My message to you therefore is: Resolute determination and unconquerable grit leading to certain and complete victory.

As a way of expressing appreciation of the work done by a battalion over a period of time, its C.O. might be given an award. The citation would include praise for the colonel and for the men under his command, acknowledging that again, it was team work which mattered. Colonel Trower, the long-serving and seemingly indestructable C.O. of the 5/SWB was awarded the Order of St. Anne, Third Class in September 1916. When conferring the honour Major-General Tom Bridges declared that it was for:

> Distinguished service and training and for commanding his battalion since its formation in October 1914 and for gallantly leading it in the field . . . Only thoroughly well-disciplined men could have carried out the tasks allotted to this Battalion.

Many references have already been made to the regular practice of loaning Pioneer battalions to host divisions and corps. This might entail moving a unit a substantial distance from its usual division – a separation which could last for some time. A more regular practice was for the Pioneers to stay working in the front area while the remainder of their division went out on rest. The battalion would work loosely in conjunction with the Pioneer unit of the incoming division. This cooperation need not have been particularly close. The two battalions were likely to work together only if detached companies happened to be in the rear areas on specific jobs. More often the loaned battalion would work in one part of the divisional sector, while the division's own battalion worked in another. When the loaned unit returned to its own division, the host commander or CRE usually despatched a message of thanks along with it. Sometimes this was more than just mere courtesy. After the 24/Manchester had spent an exhausting and dangerous time working for the 58th

Division around Bullecourt, General Fanshaw, the O.C. of the London Division, did more than just send the customary message of appreciation. He concluded his note with the comment that, 'the greatest test of the efficiency of a battalion is when it works well for a formation other than its own'. To underline how well Fanshaw thought the Oldham Comrades had performed for his division, he rode over to present personally the prizes to the winners at the battalion's sports day. Such messages were also sometimes included in subsequent divisional histories. For example that of the 6th Division, which overall gives fairly minimal accounts of the work of the 11/Leicestershire, states that when the Pioneers left to undertake some railway work, 'their absence was much felt by the Division'; when the battalion returned, it was 'welcomed back bringing with it a letter from GOC II Corps congratulating them on their excellent work'.[2]

On at least one occasion a general went somewhat overboard in his enthusiasm to praise the work of his divisional Pioneers. So appreciative was he of the tasks undertaken by the 19/N.F. that the O.C. of the 35th Division declared: 'Pioneers do not require working parties, carrying parties or unloading parties to be detailed from the infantry, thus robbing Peter to pay Paul, and destroying the fighting efficiency of the infantry'.[3] Had any infantry private, who had sweated and toiled as a member of some working party attached to a section of Pioneers, read that eulogy, he would conclude that his pre-conceived opinion about the sanity of generals was fully vindicated.

In the years following the war, divisional histories were written for 38 of the 61 divisions which served overseas and which had Pioneer battalions attached to them. It is difficult to draw emphatic conclusions from these volumes as the extent and scope of their coverage of a division's work varies considerably. However, several common features by which these studies dealt with the contribution of their Pioneer battalions can be identified.

The majority of the histories give fairly detailed accounts of the work done by the Pioneers. Although they rarely discuss the activities of the Pioneers in the same depth as they cover those of the infantry brigades, there are reasonably regular references to them. Typical of these are the histories of the 17th, 23rd, 19th and 20th Divisions. These give frequent, often one sentence references to the Pioneers, stating where they were working and the tasks undertaken. Their activities are generally worked into the context of what the rest of the division was doing, and also explain the contribution of the Pioneers to the outcome of a particular action. The language used is generally complimentary and will sometimes mention individuals by name. Statements such as 'very creditable work', 'without their help', 'their energy and skill', 'worked magnificently as always' and 'did fine work' are very common. The authors of these volumes certainly understood the worth and value of the Pioneers, but are not particularly effusive in their praise. They perhaps make adequate references to the Pioneers in the same way as they will mention the work of the divisional artillery and some of the other supporting arms.

Other histories go somewhat further and praise the Pioneers in more flamboyant vein. One of the most prolific writers of divisional and regimental histories in the post-war years was E. Wyrall. Given the number of volumes he wrote, it is not surprising to discover the use of similar statements and sentences. Other writers probably learned from Wyrall's work and also used what turn out to be familiar lines. In several of his volumes Wyrall describes the Pioneers as 'gallant fellows' who 'gave their all' and 'worked splendidly'. He writes in glowing, and what might even be interpreted as patronising terms when looking at the overall, rather than specific, contribution of the battalions. For example, he declares that the 7/DLI was 'regarded by their divisional commander with that affection which all divisions gave to their Pioneers',[4] and that the 10/DCLI was 'looked upon with affection by all ranks and units of the Division'.[5] The chronicler of the 9th Division praised the 'imperturbable manner in which the . . . Pioneers worked under the heaviest fire', in an action which 'aroused the sincere admiration of the infantry; they seemed to be men without nerves'.[6]

While the Pioneers of these and other divisions might read with satisfaction of their work described in such appreciative style, those who served with several other divisions might have felt some disappointment when scanning their respective divisional histories. Many of these volumes acknowledge the existence of the Pioneers, but tend to mention them only briefly and occasionally as if the comment was something of an afterthought. Their experiences are set in the context of those of the other divisional troops, stressing that 'team work [was] an essential feature' of a division's activities and that 'the assiduous though less showy efforts of the Sappers, Pioneers . . . [meant that their] very work was freely given by each branch and was necessary for the common success'.[7] Despite this general acknowledgement, specific references to the battalions can be minimal. The first significant mention of the 22/DLI in the 8th Division's history is of its digging prowess in March 1917, while in that of the 47th Division the 4/RWF is barely mentioned until April 1918. In the 42nd Division's volume, while it is admitted that the battalion's work was of the 'greatest value',[8] the 7/N.F. do not get a specific mention during the final months of the war until late October. Even then, rather than detailing some of its fighting or pioneering activities, the reference is concerned with the battalion's victory in the divisional football cup. One volume gives its praise in a somewhat back-handed manner. The writer of the 25th Division's history bemoaned the fact that following the departure of the 6/SWB the division had no Pioneer battalion until the 11/South Lancs joined some three months later. 'This was unfortunate as the infantry units . . . were unable to spare the large working parties required for the repair of roads and bridges'.[9] At least their absence had been noticed.

This style of volume covers the non-infantry arms in separate sections at the end of each chapter. Two such volumes are those describing the activities of the Guards and the 40th Division. The former makes fairly regular references to the 4/Coldstream, while the latter work is one of the more miserly in its mentions of the division's Pioneers. When dealing with the formation of the division, it covers each arm in turn except the Pioneers. Even the ambulance units are mentioned, but it is not until the next chapter that Whitton remembered, 'there was a Pioneer battalion'.[10] Another volume writes off its Pioneers a little too early. It mentions them regularly until the offensives of March 1918 and then, after describing the battalion as a 'remnant', ignored them for the next eight months of the war. The writer of the 51st Division's chronicle does not even refer to the Pioneers when the division underwent a major reorganization in January 1916 and throughout the remainder of the work, there is a paucity of references. Similarly, there is no mention in the 52nd Division's narrative of the arrival or the subsequent departure of the 5/Royal Irish Regiment. These less than generous mentions could be compared with the history of the 59th Division. This unit was officially a 'B' category division, composed of battalions whose men were of low medical status. Although the division played a fairly limited role in the final offensives of 1918, its historian thought it worthwhile to mention not only the arrival and departure of the 6/7th Royal Scottish Fusiliers, but also of the 25/KRRC which replaced them.[11]

Even the renowned historian and military writer Cyril Falls makes only infrequent mention of the 16/Royal Irish Rifles in his work on the 36th Division. Wyrall claimed in his study of the 50th Division that 'to everyone's regret, the 7/DLI were ordered to be transferred to the 21st Division'.[12] In fact, the battalion was transferred, not to the 21st, but to the 8th Division. Here it absorbed what was left of the 22/DLI. However, the writers of the 8th Division's history clearly thought that the 22nd was not absorbed but sent elsewhere. They wrote that after having performed 'splendid service . . . their departure was universally regretted'.[13] The failure of these writers to record correctly the postings of the battalions might be a reflection of how the Pioneers were regarded with respect to the other divisional units. Perhaps the saddest but most predictable lack of discernible appreciation of its Pioneer battalion is that of the 33rd Division. The 18/Middlesex underwent some unfortunate experiences during its time overseas and to be almost ignored by its divisional history seems unnecessarily harsh. The narrative was written by the former C.O. of the 33rd Battalion MGC, so it might be assumed he would understand the desire of the supporting arms for a reasonably full account of their activities. In his appreciation of the work done by such units, the Middlesex did not warrant a mention even in the section which dealt with the R.E. Field Companies.[14]

If some Pioneer battalions felt that their respective divisional histories had not done them full justice, they might have hoped their own regimental history would put the record straight. Here again however, there is a rather mixed bag as they tend to record the work of the Pioneers in language and styles similar to those used in the divisional accounts. The fact that several authors of regimental histories also wrote divisional ones would be a simple explanation as to why this is the case.

The bulk of such works, perhaps predictably, regard the activities of the Pioneers as of less importance than their other battalions. The amount of space allocated to the Pioneers is always substantially less than that given to the seemingly more glamorous infantry. The authors of several of these studies offer something of an apology for the lack of detailed, extensive coverage. The explanation in the Yorkshire Regiment's volume that its 12th Battalion's 'history is not easy to trace', has already been cited[15] and this preface was used to excuse the subsequent lack of space allotted to the battalion in comparison to the regular and other service units. Most regimentally produced works follow a similar line. While there is not a complete dismissal of the work of Pioneers, there is a reluctance to devote much more than the requisite courtesy in acknowledgement that they existed, that they served overseas and that they made a valuable contribution to victory.

The nature of the work they did would not generally offer itself to descriptions of their experiences in dramatic or heroic manner, but the writers can summon up sufficient enthusiasm to make some appreciation of their work. The Middlesex's history noted that the 'records [of the 18th Battalion] show how these brave Pioneers . . . did so well under extraordinary difficulties with indomitable pluck',[16] while that of the Worcesters, one of the more fulsome in its praise, said of its 17th Battalion, 'their work had been of the greatest assistance to the attacking troops', and they did 'much good useful work until the end of hostilities'.[17] The chronicler of the South Lancashire Regiment thought that the work of its 4th and 11th Battalions ' . . . provided ample proof that the rare combination of qualities called for by the difficulties inherent in their roles had been attained by all ranks'.[18] Similarly, the writer of the East Yorkshire Regiment's history explained that in August 1917 its 6th Battalion 'carried out its duties splendidly and with a tenacity which won praise from everyone'.[19] While also acknowledging the grit required to keep the battalion at work, the Suffolk Regiment's historian empathized with the men of its 4th Battalion who, 'had no peace by night or day and could not move back to bathe or change their clothes. Brigades came in and went out; but there the 4th Battalion remained to their discomfort and the dismay of others'.[20] When talking of its 14th Battalion the historian of the Worcesters wrote that its work was 'uneventful' but, like that of the 4/Suffolk, thought that the battalion had 'laboured valiantly in bitter cold and drizzling rain'.[21] The 19/L.F. was reported to have carried out its 'arduous and often thankless tasks'[22] despite the dreadful conditions, while the writer of the activities of the Gordon Highlanders believed the 9th Battalion were 'first class Pioneers who always worked well and never better than when a battle was in progress'.[23] Statements like these and the repeated use of such words as 'tenacious', 'valiant' and 'magnificent' are commonplace throughout the regimental accounts. When writing the story of the Highland Light Infantry, Chalmers was concerned that the image and integrity of its 16th Battalion might have been harmed when it was converted to Pioneers. To put the record straight he insisted that 'its new status was not lower than its old, (and it had to make its sacrifices without some of the glory)'.[24] The volumes of regiments which had one or more of its battalions converted rarely go as far as that, contenting themselves instead to acknowledging their new roles and then restricting themselves to the more usual comments and references.

As a means of demonstrating that other arms appreciated the work of their Pioneer battalions, some regimental histories include a selection of congratulatory messages sent to battalion HQ. The 12/Yorks' specific mention in the C-in-C's statement of gratitude following the 40th Division's action at Bourlon

Wood was later reproduced in the history. Major-General F.J. Duncan, commanding the 61st Division, congratulated the 5/DCLI for its work in August 1918. The Cornwalls' historian thought it worthwhile to record the glowing tribute:

> The Pioneer is one of the most valuable men in the Service . . . Without him it would be well-nigh impossible to hold ground won. He must remember that he is also a fighting man. I have noticed with much pleasure the good spirit in your battalion.[25]

Referring to a different theatre of war, and perhaps bemoaning the circumstances which had sent its 12th Battalion to a London division, the historian of the Loyal North Lancashire Regiment clearly believed this message from the GOC XX Corps was worthy of inclusion:

> Will you thank your troops for the splendid work they have put in on the laborious and uncongenial task of road-making in your area, which has not only rendered possible further offensive operations, but in the event of the enemy ever being in a position to attack Jerusalem, has quadrupled our powers of defence by permitting the free movement of troops in the mountains.[26]

These examples are typical of the many reproduced in the regimental histories. Clearly, they are included with the object of inducing pride in the battalions and of convincing the reader that the Pioneers' contribution was as valuable in its own way as that of any other unit. However, at times, some volumes struggle to sound enthusiastic when describing the activities of their Pioneers. After a long narration covering the activities of its 7th, 8th and 23rd Battalions, and despite the fact that this particular work had been done for long periods under shell fire and in atrocious conditions, the historian of the Middlesex Regiment could only say of the 19th Battalion that, 'little can be told excepting that the Battalion was at work on the roads or digging cable trenches in the neighbourhood of Delville Wood'.[27] In similarly grudging tone, another volume explained that, 'It is not possible to make a thrilling story out of the drab monotony of the daily round of work carried out by a battalion employed as Pioneers'.[28] Having described the work of the 6/East Yorks at Ypres, the regimental historian admitted that his narrative of the Pioneers' activities was 'brief and apparently uninteresting'.[29] Perhaps there is a limit to the number of ways in which laying tracks across a rain and shell swept landscape can be made to sound interesting, but the writer does at least concede that the experience was 'pregnant with memory'[30] for those who served in that evil place.

Perhaps the worst example of a lack of acknowledgment for its own battalions is seen in the *Annals* and *Chronicles* of the KRRC. Apart from mentioning its creation, the next reference to the British Empire Pioneers in the former volume is only a cursory mention during the Battle of the Somme – three months into its overseas service. The 1918 *Chronicles* do not even acknowledge the creation or actual existence of its 25th Battalion. It was perhaps never the most active or glory-seeking of the KRRs, but it seems especially niggardly that its own regiment could not devote some space to offer a tribute in its year of creation. Perhaps even more damning was the 20th Battalion's entry in the 1918 *Chronicles*. In order to blow its own trumpet to sister battalions, each of the regiment's battalions submitted a *resumé* of its activities. Unfortunately, the adjutant or intelligence officer of the 20th clearly felt his battalion could not live up to the reputation or successes won by the other units. In blatently apologetic style he wrote, 'The chronicler of the history of a Pioneer battalion has very little material on which to base an interesting narrative. Ours is not the showy part of the great war machine; we dig and delve, wire and revet'.[31]

This self-deprecation sufficiently angered one officer of the 20/KRRC to set in train what was to become the first published battalion history of a Pioneer unit. In post-war publications A.S.Turberville believed that Pioneers had had less than justice done them and laid out the purpose of his book:

> This brief history was undertaken because it was felt that the few pages relating to the 20th Battalion, which were contributed to the different volumes of the KRRC Chronicles, were scarcely

adequate as a permanent record of this unit, and that the suggestions that the doings of the Pioneer Battalion did not provide material for an interesting narrative was hardly fair to those who served in it.[32]

Turberville's work was complemented by published battalion accounts of, among others, the Northumberland Fusilier battalions, the 7/York & Lancs and the 12/KOYLI. These works do not claim quite the same motive behind their conception, being more intended simply to record the work done by the battalions and the sacrifices made. Unsurprisingly, they dwell upon the successes and achievements of the units and are written in a slightly amused, tongue in cheek style. Like several of the regimental histories they praise their men and their work by printing messages sent by generals. For example: Major-General Ingouville-Williams' telegram to the 18/N.F. which informed its colonel that 'no better Pioneer battalion' existed in the army and that he would always remember 'their gallant and faithful service'. In self- congratulatory tone, the colonel himself later recorded how on one occasion he felt 'very proud of the Pioneers . . . for by their cool behaviour they . . . encouraged others to follow their example'.[33] The volumes detailing the experiences of the 17/N.F. and the 12/KOYLI note similar examples of how others viewed their work. Written in a lighter vein, neither hesitates to poke fun at itself when the situation offered the opportunity.

Other accounts of Pioneer battalions were written after the war and either privately published or were eventually deposited in museum archives. Their lengths vary, as do their worth as accurate records of the experiences of their battalions. One unit's work is even embodied within an unpublished novel. Frequent references have been made to these throughout the course of this study, but two of the most readily accessible and worthwhile of these are a book by Francis Buckley detailing the work of the 7/N.F., and a reminiscence by Major Davidson of the 22/DLI. The former had served with the Fusiliers while it was still an infantry battalion and remained with it following its conversion, while Davidson had joined the DLI shortly before it left for France. Both writers had easy access to the War Diaries of their

279

respective battalions and leaned heavily upon them for material. The styles of their works are very different – Buckley's is pedantic and tedious in its relating of detail, while Davidson's is coherent, articulate and expansive. Yet he does not allow himself any false pretences, preferring instead to follow a line of disarming honesty in declaring:

> These operations of Pioneers have not the glamour of those charging with bayonets fixed, nor do they engender that hot bloodied mixture of funk and fierceness which an assault upon the enemy position calls out.[34]

Another officer of his battalion wrote of its activities at Third Ypres in a similar modest way: 'There were no deeds of individual gallantry or endurance, but much scope for the exhibition of patience and determined coolness'.[35] Colonel Charlesworth of the 12/KOYLI was equally prepared to praise the nerve and determination shown by his men, but in a more sardonic tone thought that in return for their display of courage, 'the 'reward' in the army for good work was to be put immediately on to another task rather more fierce than the first'.[36]

The idea that Pioneers regretted not having the satisfaction of getting to close quarters with the enemy and thus being in the position to gain what they might have believed to be their share of gallantry awards, is a recurrent theme in several volumes. The 19/L.F. was praised for maintaining its morale despite suffering casualties 'without the satisfaction of retaliation'.[37] Davidson also thought that 'the endurance and cold determination to remain for long periods under fire, without retaliation, takes a deal of supporting'. After one such experience he recalled, 'no one received any award, though the battalion was thanked'.[38]

There is little evidence to prove whether Pioneer battalions did actually receive a disproportionately lower numbers of awards than other units, but at least one battalion did feel that it was not receiving its fair share. Arthur Walsh served with the 24/Manchester as adjutant from 1916 until the end of the war. While completing a reminiscence of his career, he noted that

280

from 1 July 1916 until 1 July 1917 the 7th Division made 988 awards. Of these, 265 went to the divisional troops and ancillary arms, while 692 were distributed among the 12 infantry battalions. On average each of these battalions thus received 57 awards, but the Oldham Comrades, who had often spent longer periods working in the front sector than had the infantry, received only 31.[39] If this picture was repeated throughout other divisions of the BEF, Pioneers might have wondered why the messages of thanks were not more frequently accompanied by confirmation of recommendations for awards passed upwards from their own colonels.

Because the evidence is not always complete it is difficult to prove whether recommendations for awards for Pioneers were less likely to be converted to actual awards than was the case for the infantry. Although inconclusive, two examples might suggest that Pioneers did not do particularly well once the recommendations had been submitted. In October 1916 the colonel of the 6/Argyll & Sutherland Highlanders recommended that 13 of his officers should receive the M.C. or a mention in despatches and that 30 other ranks should get the DCM or M.M. Eventually, it was decided that five officers should have the M.C., two should receive a MID, while 13 of the men should be awarded the DCM or M.M. This means that of those recommended, 54% of the officers and 47% of the men received an award. The 8/Sussex did somewhat better than the Argylls. Following its work on 1 July, the colonel recommended that two of his officers should receive the M.C., three men should get the DCM and seven the M.M. In September 1916 it was confirmed that both officers would receive the M.C., while all ten of the men would receive the M.M.[40] The 9/North Staffs only had one DCM and 16 M.M.s awarded for the entire year of 1917, a particularly nasty one for the battalion, although Sgt. Carmichael did win the Victoria Cross and 11 men received a MID.

Awards to Pioneers were more plentiful in the last year of the war, especially those earned during the German offensive. It is unlikely that this was a consequence of a sudden recognition that medals were being unfairly distributed; rather that the Pioneers' fighting abilities had been more obvious to divisional commanders between March and May than had their digging activities in earlier months.

In recent times acknowledgement of the work performed by Pioneers has continued to be rather patchy. In many works on specific battles or general accounts of the Great War published in the last twenty years, their role is frequently underplayed. It is understandable in some respects because, as we have seen, they do not feature prominently in many of the basic secondary works which are usually the starting point for many researchers. Battles are often simply recorded as assaults by particular brigades, supported by particular artillery units. The work of the ambulances, the divisional train, the R.E. and the other divisional arms are generally less well considered. Besides the regimental and divisional histories, many writers might turn initially to the *Official History* in order to set their researches in context. If they are not made aware of a division's supporting arms from these volumes, only the most diligent and thorough will deliberately attempt to weave in the Pioneers' contribution as they unfold their stories. The volumes of the *Official History* do mention the Pioneer battalions, but usually only in a lone sentence or frequently as a footnote. Naturally, the flow of the narrative describing the sequence and features of the attacks is the essential aspect of the work, and the inclusion of supporting units for the sake of equality would disrupt that object. Adding their contribution in footnotes was not intended as a slur, but simply to assist in recalling the primary events.

Nevertheless, it might have been assumed that in the most recent research the work of the supporting arms might have been more fully developed. In several modern books written about particular battles, Pioneers have retained their almost Cinderella-like role. Three examples will serve to illustrate the point. In his book on the Welsh Division at Mametz,[41] Colin Hughes fails to include the fighting and digging done by the 19/Welch during the attack on the wood. The battalion did not play an insignificant role in the battle and suffered 34 dead. Similarly, Martin Middlebrook in his eminently thorough work on 21 March[42] does not find room to include other than the most cursory references to the several Pioneer battalions which fought on that day. The work performed by Pioneer units in the taking of High Wood is also given fairly scant treatment in Terry Norman's book.[43] Neither is it only recent authors who have neglected the Pioneers. When a commemorative plaque recording the attack on Mametz by the Manchester Pals battalions of the 7th Division was being prepared in 1993, the committee almost failed to include the name of the 24/Manchester alongside those of the city battalions. In like manner, the adjunct to the 14/Worcester was very much an after-thought to the 63rd Division's memorial at Gavrelle.

This lack of recognition might be a legacy of contemporary views of Pioneers. Although the evidence is sketchy, there are odd references which suggest that Pioneers themselves were concerned that they were not getting the coverage or the acknowledgement they deserved. During the summer of 1916 there were rumours circulating within Oldham which suggested that the Comrades were not pulling their weight. The *Oldham Standard* printed a rebuttal to the accusations:

> There has been a great deal of discussion in the town recently as to the position of the Old Pals and some very unfair remarks have been circulated which reflect little credit on those who have given utterance to them. The Pals are taking an active and foremost part in the 'great push' . . . The Old Pals are bearing thir part nobly and well, and Oldham has every reason to be proud of their conduct in the field.[44]

A few days later, a robust refutal of the Comrades' alleged lack of activity was made by one of its members:

> I do not know who it was that put it in the Oldham papers about the Pals carrying ammunition up to the trenches but he certainly did not know anything about what we are doing. Our lads had to work in more danger sometimes than the troops in the trenches. Many a time we had to follow the attack up and clear roads out in the open while other troops round about were in the trenches where it was safer.[45]

Shortly afterwards, one of the local papers printed the bold headline – 'Bravo 24th. Position held under Murderous Fire: A reply to the Critics'. The paper then published the complete letter from a NCO of the battalion which described the action the Pioneers had fought at Bazentin-le-Petit on 14 July:

> I see according to the *Oldham Standard* which I received there have been some rumours going around about our battalion whether as far as I can make out it has done its work and all that sort of thing. I expect some of the armchair critics have been chattering again . . . I don't know about us not being capable as a fighting unit and all that sort of clap-trap, you would perhaps be surprised to know that on one occasion, two of our companies were called out at a second's notice to help another regiment who were hard pressed at the time. They immediately downed their tools and got into the Germans straight away and held the position under murderous fire . . . Believe me, officers and men of other regiments were calling out to our lads as they passed them, 'Good old 24th', 'bravo' and other complimentary remarks. We have been congratulated on all hands for our good work. Although we don't fight only in case of emergency, our work . . . is considered very important consolidating positions etc . . . These people who are so fond of talking ought to have been around this quarter since 1 July with our lads and they would have lost their grip.[46]

This flurry of letters and editorials seems to have stopped any griping that might have been going on in the town, but it is perhaps indicative of a contemporary and subsequent notion that Pioneers were not proper soldiers. Engineers and the artillery do not appear to have suffered from similar sniping, and the infantry of course, were praised as regularly as the official *communiques* allowed. The Pioneers, perceived as ageing, partially disabled, unskilled beasts of burden, have not been accorded the acknowledgement their essential work deserves. Perhaps the final word should thus be left to a Pioneer. A battalion Christmas card of the Wool Textile Pioneers sums up in their own words how they regarded themselves and their purpose:

Fill the shell holes on life's way,
Duckboards down its trenches lay.
Just help those who bear the brunt,
Make jumping-off points for the stunt.
Build their dugouts, make their roads,
Lay their tramways, bear their loads.
Get on top – put back your fear -
Push on through life – a Pioneer.[47]

NOTES

1. W.D. of 16/Royal Irish Rifles. Unless otherwise stated, the examples are taken from battalion War Diaries.
2. Marden, T. *A Short History of the 6th Division*, (London, 1920) p.34
3. Major-General A. Marindin. Quoted in Shakespear, op.cit. 'Foreword'.
4. Wyrall, E. *The History of the 50th Division*, (Lund, 1939) p.145
5. Wyrall, E. *The History of the Second Division*, (Nelson, 1922) p.520
6. Ewing, J. 9th Division, op.cit. p.137
7. ibid. p.381
8. Gibbon, *42nd Division*, op.cit. p.122
9. Marden, T. *The History of the 25th Division*, p.342
10. Whitton, F. *The History of the 40th Division*.
11. Unfortunately, the divisional memorial tablets laid up in churches in Leicester, Stafford, Derby and Chesterfield remember all the divisional units, including the RAVC, except the two Pioneer battalions. In defence of those who designed the tablets, all the other units originated from the North Midlands.
12. Wyrall, *50th Division*, op.cit. p.351
13. Borasyon & Bax, op.cit. p.242
14. Hutchinson, G. *The Thirty-Third Division in France & Flanders*, (Waterlow, 1921)
15. See Chapter II
16. Wyrall, E. *The Diehards in the Great War*, (London, 1926-30) p.288
17. Stacke, op.cit. p.485
18. Whalley-Kelly, op.cit. p.250
19. Wyrall, *East Yorks*, op.cit. p.233
20. Murphy, op.cit. p.270
21. Stacke, op.cit. p.485
22. Latter, op.cit. p.261
23. Falls, *Gordon Highlanders*, op.cit. p.139

24. Chalmers, op.cit. p.115
25. Matthews, op.cit. p.139
26. Wylly, *The Loyal North Lancs.* op.cit. p.353
27. Wyrall, *Diehards*, op.cit. p.307
28. Whalley-Kelly, op.cit. p.81
29. Wyrall, *East Yorks*, op.cit. p.234
30. ibid.
31. *KRRC Chronicles*, 1918, p.258
32. Turbeville, op.cit. p.vii
33. Shakespear, op.cit. p.48 & p.89-90
34. Davidson, op.cit.
35. Captain A. Perkins. Quoted in W.D.
36. England, op.cit. p.75
37. Latter, op.cit. p.261
38. Davidson, op.cit.
39. Mitchinson & McInnes, op.cit. p.100
40. A DCM was also awarded but this appears to have dated from an earlier engagement.
41. Hughes, C. Mametz, (Orion Press, 1982)
42. Middlebrook, M. The Kaiser's Battle, (Penguin, 1983)
43. Norman, T. *The Hell They Called High Wood*, (Kimber, 1984)
44. *Oldham Standard*, 19/7/1916
45. *Oldham Standard*, 5/8/1916
46. *Oldham Standard*, 9/8/1916
47. Christmas card, 1918 from 21/West Yorks (Wool Textile Pioneers) In Moore, C. papers. (Liddle Collection)

POSTSCRIPT

When the armistice came into effect, every British division serving on the Western, Southern and Balkan Fronts was serviced by a Pioneer battalion. In addition, all five Australian and the New Zealand division each had a battalion of Pioneers; the Canadian Army Corps employed four Infantry Works Companies which fulfilled a similar function. This meant that nearly 80,000 men, or the equivalent establishment of almost five divisions, were serving as Pioneers. Yet although the concept of Pioneer battalions had survived the army reorganization of 1918, their long term future was, in effect, already determined.

A Royal Warrant of 21 February 1917[1] allowed the creation of the Labour Corps. This new organization also adopted a badge very similar in design to that used by divisional Pioneer units.[2] The idea of the corps was to introduce a greater degree of flexibility to the means by which essential communications and labouring could be performed in the rear areas. The corps expanded rapidly, employing men on the myriad tasks which ranged from unloading ships to building gun emplacements. By 1918 there were 88 Labour Corps HQ units and 241 Labour Companies in France. Besides these units there were eight Indian and 195 Chinese labour companies. Demand for work in the rear and front areas was so great that beside these companies of the Labour Corps and the Pioneer battalions, the five armies of the BEF were serviced by 259 Area Employment Companies, 58 Divisional Employment Companies,[3] 38 Artisan Works

Companies (R.E.), seven Agricultural Companies and a huge number of, among others, Field Companies, Army Troops Companies and Land Drainage Companies.[4] All these organizations were capable of providing skilled and non-skilled labour. As well as men conscripted directly into the Labour Corps, many of the men serving in the companies were medically downgraded former Pioneers.

With the war over, the Labour Corps and the Pioneer battalions were disbanded. When the Territorial Force gave way to the Territorial Army in 1920, T.F. battalions which had served as Pioneer units during the war reverted to infantry. All the first line T.F. units which had been converted were reformed in 1920, although by the time the Second World War broke out some had combined with other battalions or had again been converted – this time to armoured or anti-aircraft units. In a period of severe financial restraint, the War Office decided that the much reduced regular and Territorial Armies no longer required labour other than that which could be supplied by the R.E. This was widely recognized as a short-sighted policy and when war clouds again gathered, provision was made for a special labour force to be formed from reservists. By the end of September 1939, twenty-six of these Labour Companies were in France.[5] With no personal weapons, insufficient equipment and inadequate clothing, they gave the impression of being little better than Fred Karno's Army. In an attempt to improve both their status and efficiency, the name was changed first to the Auxiliary Military Pioneer Corps and then in November 1940, simply to the Pioneer Corps.

Enlisting not only British citizens but also about 1.5 million foreign nationals, members of the corps performed a variety of jobs in every theatre of war. The image of aged men from a distinctly lower military caste, engaged in labouring rather than combat activities, is sustained in the minds of most. Worthy and essential as these troops and civilians were, they bore little resemblance to the fine battalions of fit young men who, for the majority of the Great War, were both fighters and workers. Whether the battalions had been converted from infantry or raised specifically as skilled labour, their expertise, resolution

288

and general contribution to the Allied victory, has been largely unrecognized.[6]

NOTES

1. ACI 611 of 1917.
2. The badge consisted of a rifle, pick and shovel, with a laurel wreath and crown.
3. This included nine companies of the Canadian Expeditionary Force.
4. The figures are taken from *Order of Battle of British Armies in France*, November 1918.
5. Elliot, Major E.R., *The Royal Pioneer Corps*, 1945-93, (SPA 1993) p.16
6. The title 'Pioneer' lives on in the modern British Army. Infantry battalions retain a Pioneer section and 23 Pioneer Regiment is a distinct unit. It comprises four squadrons, totalling about 500 men. Its soldiers are trained in artisanal skills and as fighting infantry. Its main role is to provide skilled labour for the Royal Engineers.

Appendix I

FATALITIES AMONG PIONEER BATTALIONS

Compared to the losses sustained by the infantry, total fatalities among Pioneer battalions were small. Apart from the final year of the war Pioneers, as we have seen, were not normally required to undertake large scale offensive action; consequently, they escaped the wholesale slaughter experienced by many battalions during Allied offensives. Pioneers themselves realized their chance of survival was greater than that of their comrades in the infantry. In addition to enjoying a lower casualty rate overall, several battalions also considered themselves to be 'lucky'. Soon after its arrival overseas, the 5/Northants considered that the 'feeling grew that the 5th was a "lucky" battalion',[1] but it took until late 1917 before members of the 18/N.F. began to 'think of ourselves as a lucky battalion'.[2] Having finished a period of work at Ypres in October 1917 with only eight dead and 33 wounded, the historian of the 12/KOYLI thought that the battalion was under 'the special protection of Providence'; he later noted that it was 'very noticeable all through the war that we always appeared to come off lightly even when other units in the vicinity suffered severely'.[3]

In general terms those units which served in more distant theatres, suffered fewer fatalities than those which spent the war on the Western Front. There are exceptions to this generalization; for example, the 6/East Yorks lost 56% of its dead during its relatively short period in Gallipoli, and the 8/Welch lost the fifth largest number of other ranks of all Pioneer battalions despite spending the war in Gallipoli and Mesopotamia. In contrast, the 26/Middlesex, 8/Ox & Bucks and 23/Welch, all of which served in Salonika, are among those units which lost very few men. The units with the highest casualties were those which were most heavily involved in the March and May offensives of 1918. They were frequently used as fighting infantry and suffered accordingly. It was noted earlier that the 5/Border lost almost 100 dead during its three month stint as a Pioneer unit in early 1918.

Several of those Pioneer units which were caught on the Chemin des Dames in May 1918 have a very high percentage of their men with no known grave. The names of 94% of the 14/N.F.'s dead and 95% of the 22/DLI's are on the Soissons Memorial to the Missing. However, the 5/SWB, which was also very much in the thick of the action, has only 42% of its fatalities listed on the memorial. This figure is closer to the percentage of unknown graves for Pioneers killed during the Somme campaign, but is still considerably higher than the percentage of those who died at Arras in 1917. Figures for the missing of those units involved in the German attacks of 21 March and the subsequent retreat are also, in general, higher than those for Arras and Third Ypres. The 12/KOYLI has 72% of its fatalities of April 1918 on the Tyne Cot Memorial, while the 11/Hants has 58% of its March dead on the Pozieres Memorial.

Considering the distances over which the Germans advanced in March and April 1918 and the overwhelming force they brought to bear on certain sectors of the British line, it is not surprising to discover that the majority of Pioneers killed during those months have no known grave. Similarly, given the calamity that was the opening day of the Somme offensive, it is perhaps equally predictable to find that the majority of Pioneers who were killed on 1 July also have no known grave. Like those of the infantry, R.E. and artillery who were killed that day, their names were later engraved on the Thiepval Memorial to the Missing. The highest percentage of casualties who were not later recovered or identified is usually found in those areas where the advance made the least headway and where the lines at the end of the day remained much as they had at the beginning. In some areas the bodies of the fallen lay out in No

Man's Land, exposed to shell fire and the elements, for several months.

Over 50% of the fatalities among the 12/KOYLI, the 1st and 2/Monmouth, the 5/Cheshire, the 14th and 18/Northumberland Fusiliers were not later identified, yet even in an area where the advance was most successful the names of 64% of the 8/Sussex's losses were also later carved on the Thiepval memorial. The fact that a certain percentage of deaths do not have a known grave does not, of course, imply that a battalion had been particularly brave or foolhardy. Neither does it mean that just because the graves are now unknown, they were not identified at the time of their first burial. Even graves behind the lines might have been obliterated by shell fire and remains unidentifiable if exhumed and reburied after the war. Nevertheless, the evidence might suggest that because Pioneers were taking such an active part in the fighting in exposed or forward positions, they were unable to recover a majority of their men.

What is perhaps surprising is that the percentage of unidentified men remained high throughout the campaign. It might be assumed that because Pioneers often returned to camp at daylight or worked in areas behind the lines, they would bring the bodies of their fallen comrades back with them for proper burial. If the local circumstances allowed it, and if the men were not already too burdened with tools or spoil, it is probable that some companies and platoons did do this. The 11/Leicester has only 14% of its fatalities of July – December listed on Thiepval, the 7/York & Lancs, 20% and the 11/South Lancs, even including its dead of 1 July, has only 30%. The 22/DLI has 39%, but hidden within that figure, 62% of its 21 dead of 23 October were not later identified. In comparison, over 70% of the dead of the 8/Sussex, 9/South Staffs and the 11/Hants, and over 80% of the 19/Welch and 14/Worcester who were killed as the campaign ground on into the autumn and winter of 1916, were not later identified. The change in the way that Pioneers were used during the Arras offensive is reflected in the lower casualty figures. Because most Pioneer battalions were not sent over with the attacking brigades but largely kept behind the front lines improving the roads and tracks, most units lost under 20 men killed during April and May. Even those which did work on communication and fire trenches in the forward zones, and those which were kept at work long after their division had been withdrawn, suffered fewer casualties at Arras than for a similar working period on the Somme. It is difficult to come to any sort of conclusion when dealing with such low figures, but only two of the 16 most heavily involved battalions have a total of over one third of their fatalities as 'unknowns'.

A similar set of figures unfolds for Third Ypres. Again, because the fighting was compressed into such a small area and the advances were spread over such a long period of time, bodies appear to have been recovered fairly consistently. Even during the rains of October and November and the consequent deterioration of the battlefield, two thirds of the fatalities among most battalions were recovered and buried in graves which were later identified; the 7/York & Lancs, which spent much of September and October building a railway towards the contested area, lost 25 killed but none of their names are listed on the Menin Gate or Tyne Cot. This battalion also lost a further 11 who died of wounds during the same period. In many Pioneer units the proportion of those killed to those who died of wounds is very close to two to one. The proportion of those who died of wounds is considerably lower during the Somme offensive – several units recorded over 85% of their fatalities as killed in action. This is probably a consequence of several factors. A man might be wounded but shelling frequently prevented his evacuation. Furthermore, by the end of the Somme campaign a wounded man would often have to be carried a considerable distance across ground which hampered the struggle of the bearers and thus the chances of his own survival. Despite these difficulties, the 5/SWB clearly either managed to evacuate a high percentage of its wounded – 45% of its total Somme fatalities – or recorded men as having 'died of wounds' when other battalions might have described them as 'killed in action'. In later campaigns, except for the very few days in March and May 1918 when battalions were all but annihilated, the proportion remains remarkably consistent at one third. At times when they were working behind the lines a wounded Pioneer

293

would have been much closer to immediate treatment at the aid posts or even the CCS. The wound might well have proved fatal, but because he died when undergoing attention he would have been listed as 'died of wounds'; in the front area, the same wound might have eventually caused him to bleed to death, but because he was not evacuated, for official purposes he was 'killed in action'.

The process by which many Pioneer battalions were forced to accept men from different regiments and from the Royal Engineers was discussed in Chapter 10. In their final fatality rolls not all regiments have reliable information about the former regiments of men who died while serving with their battalions. There are certainly omissions in the Pioneer rolls, not only of men who were posted from other line regiments, but also those who arrived from the R.E. The following table is therefore necessarily incomplete, but it is a worth noting the significant number of men in Pioneer battalions who were transferred in from other regiments. Only those battalions which are known to have received significant numbers of Royal Engineers are detailed.

Battalion	Transfers in as a % of total deaths	R.E. deaths as % of fatalities among all transfers in	R.E. deaths as % of total battn. deaths
19/L.F.	56%	22%	13%
12/Yorks	39%	44%	17%
11/Leics	32%	55%	17%
7/DLI	22%	31%	7%
7/York & Lancs	22%	50%	11%
13/Gloucs	21%	41%	9%
9/S.Staffs	20%	60%	12%
11/King's	18%	37%	18%
24/Manchester	12%	43%	5%
12/Notts & Derby	10%	68%	7%

These figures show that at least in these battalions, fatalities among the former R.E. represent a generally high proportion of those men who were transferred into a unit. As most of them appear to have served in these battalions only from September 1917 to January 1918, it demonstrates how huge the influx of these men must have been and, more importantly as far as the number of men with presumed recognized trades were concerned, how far the authorities were going to improve the level of skills within Pioneer units. However, they also suggest that because the ex-R.E. only amount to a relatively small overall percentage of a battalion's deaths and unless the men already serving possessed the necessary skills, for most of the war these units would not have contained men with recognized trades in the proportion required by the ACI of 1914.

The table below lists the fatalities sustained by battalions which served as Pioneers. For battalions which were converted from infantry to Pioneers, the figures are those of the men who were killed or died only while their battalion was actually serving as Pioneers. It is possible that some men were wounded while the battalion was still fighting as infantry, but did not die until after the unit had been converted. Some units have a variety of dates for when they were converted so for the purposes of this table, the dates taken are those given in James. It is impossible to give a figure for the 4/Coldstream as its roll is not separate from the other Coldstream battalions. In view of the many different fatality totals given in War Diaries, battalion and regimental histories, these figures are taken from the *Soldiers Died* lists published in the early 1920s. The number of dead officers in the table is very incomplete. These figures are taken largely from the *Officers Died* rolls, but as officers were frequently attached rather than transferred to battalions, they are certainly an under-estimation.

FATALITIES WHILE SERVING AS PIONEERS

BATTALION	DIVISION	TOTAL O.R.	OFFICERS	ORIGIN
22/DLI	8th	526	12	N.A.
6/East Yorks	11th *	432	19	N.A.
5/SWB	19th	432	10	N.A.
7/DLI	50th & 8th	430	35	T.F.
8/Welch	13th *	420	11	N.A.
6/SW	25th	392	8	N.A.
1/Monmouth	46th	352	23	T.F.
2/Monmouth	29th	351	11	T.F.
9/Gordon H.	15th	342	11	N.A.
5/Northants	12th	337	7	N.A.
14/ N.F.	21st	325	17	N.A.
9/Seaforth H.	9th	323	12	N.A.
6/A & S.H.	5th	323	31	T.F.
4/South Lancs	55th	304	32	T.F.
13/Gloucester	39th	292	9	N.A.
8/Royal Scots	51st	292	32	T.F.
11/DLI	20th	288	5	N.A.
18/Middlesex	33rd	279	10	N.A.
11/King's	14th	277	9	N.A.
4/R. Welch Fus.	47th	273	28	T.F.
9/N. Staffs	37th	272	12	N.A.
20/KRRC	3rd	269	5	N.A.
5/DCLI	61st	266	17	T.F.
19/Lancs Fusiliers	49th	261	5	N.A.
11/South Lancs	30th	256	5	N.A.
11/Leicester	6th	258	13	N.A.
19/N.F.	35th	252	9	N.A.
10/DCLI	2nd	251	9	N.A.
7/York & Lancs	17th	238	6	N.A.
14/Worcester	63rd	225	6	N.A.
12/KOYLI	31st	219	1	N.A.

5/Cheshire	56th	218	23	T.F.
8/R. Sussex	18th	215	15	N.A.
21/West Yorks	4th	215	6	N.A.
12/Notts & Derby	24th	211	4	N.A.
11/Hants	16th	204	16	N.A.
6/Welch	1st	188	0	N.A.
18/N.F.	34th	182	6	N.A.
5/R. Sussex	48th *	173	18	T.F.
19/Welch	38th	169	2	N.A.
9/S. Staffs	23rd	164	4	N.A.
16/R. Irish Rifles	36th	158	7	N.A.
9/DLI	62nd	155	6	N.A.
19/Middlesex	41st &	148	2	N.A.
12/Yorks	40th	133	9	N.A.
5/R.Irish Regt.	10th *			
	52nd,			
	53rd			
	& 50th	123	9	N.A.
24/Manchester	7th *	118	7	N.A.
17/N.F.	32nd	117	4	N.A.
5/Border	66th	94		T.F.
3/Monmouth	49th	71	4	T.F.
9/Border	22nd *	58	2	N.A.
12/Loyal N. Lancs	60th *	58	4	N.A.
6/7 R. Scots Fus.	59th	56	1	N.A.
26/Middlesex	27th *	51	0	N.A.
16/HLI	32nd	43	1	N.A.
2/5 Loyal N. Lancs	57th	41	1	T.F.
8/Ox & Bucks	26th *	41	0	N.A.
4/Suffolk	58th	39	8	T.F.
23/Welch	28th *	30	0	N.A.
7/N.F.	42nd	29	7	T.F.
2/4 Somerset L.I.	34th	17		T.F.
9/Gloucester	66th	15		N.A.
25/KRRC	59th	9		N.A.
15/Loyal N. Lancs	14th	7	0	N.A.
14/R. Warwick	5th	3	0	N.A.

| 17/Worcester | 40th | 2 | | N.A. |
| 5/Black Watch | 8th | 0 | | T.F. |

* denotes spent some or all of its time as Pioneers away from the Western Front

NOTES

1. *The Northamptonshire Regiment*, (Regimental Comm.) op.cit. p.276
2. Shakespear, op.cit. p.70
3. England, op.cit. p.76

Appendix II

There is an enormous degree of confusion and contradiction over the official strength and composition of Pioneer battalions. Different War Office documents record a variety of establishments for men, animals and vehicles. There is strong evidence to suggest that battalions sought to maintain whatever levels of men and equipment they believed they could get away with.

When Pioneer battalions were created in 1914 their official mobilized strength was declared to be 30 officers and 1,034 other ranks. (This included three attached RAMC personnel). Each battalion was to have the usual HQ details found in any infantry unit. The machine gun section had four guns and 35 men, the Pioneer section 11, the signal section 17 and the transport 46. Each battalion was intended to possess 14 riding, 60 draught, 9 heavy draught horses, 35 vehicles and nine bicycles. Among the vehicles there were supposed to be 18 G.S. and four R.E. four-wheeled limbers.

From the figures available, no battalion which left the U.K as a Pioneer unit succeeded in embarking with the specified number of soldiers. Most battalions went abroad with a full complement of officers but with less than 1,000 men. The highest recorded number of other ranks is 1,007 (21/West Yorks), with the lowest 811 (9/Border). The 4/Coldstream left with only 22 officers, while the 5/DCLI embarked with 34.

According to some sources, the offical establishment was reduced in 1918 to 27 officers and 734 other ranks. These figures are contradicted by other evidence. For example, the War Diary of the 22/DLI gives the establishment as 24 and 859 (including 6 attached personnel), with each company comprising six officers and 235 men. Another document (121/France/1588/OB/2155) gives 27 officers and 714 men, with each of the three companies consisting of six officers and 232 other ranks.*

There is greater uniformity with figures for the transport details. A reorganized battalion was supposed to have 6 riding, 50 draught, 7 heavy draught and 12 pack horses. These animals were to service 21 vehicles, with the number of G.S. or R.E. limbers having been reduced to 13. (In January 1916 battalions were ordered to substitute four G.S. wagons for four R.E. limbers. This necessitated an increase of four drivers and eight draft horses.) However, Chapter 9 notes that many battalions clearly contrived to retain more than their prescribed number of limbers and horses.

When battalions were reduced to three companies, the size of a unit's HQ company certainly increased. The number of stretcher bearers decreased but the increase in the number of instructors and signallers more than made up for the loss.

The machine gun section had also disappeared by 1918. Battalions had four machine guns in 1915 and eight Lewis guns in 1916. Many Pioneer machine gun sections spent a great deal of their time on detachment, often forming the anti-aircraft defence for divisional HQ. In 1918 establishment was increased to 12 Lewis guns; these were generally divided between the companies.

* see also page 256.

300

Appendix III

PIONEER BATTALIONS

The following is a list of battalions which served as Pioneers for some part or all of their history. Temporary attachments to divisions other than their own for work when overseas, are not generally noted. The detail has been taken from James, War Diaries and unit histories. Battalions are listed alphabetically rather than by seniority and the titles of those which were raised specifically as Pioneer units are printed in italics.

6th Bn. Argyll & Sutherland Highlanders, (T.F.) WO.95.1538

Based at Paisley. A.& S.H. Bde. Highland Division. To 1st Highland Bde. April 1915. To France May 1915 and became part of 152nd Bde. 51st Division. Coverted to Pioneers and to the 5th Division June 1916. To Italy in December 1917. Returned to France April 1918. Reconverted to infantry and to 153rd Bde. 51st Division in October 1918.

1/5th Bn. Black Watch, (T.F.)   **W.O.95.1719**

Based at Arbroath. Black Watch Bde. To France November 1914 and to 24th Bde. 8th Division. Converted to Pioneers in the 8th Division, 18 Oct.1915. Reconverted to infantry and to 154th Bde. 51st Division on 6 Jan.1916. To 118 Bde. 39th Division in Feb.1916. Amalgamated with 1/4th Bn. in March 1916 to form 4/5th Bn. To 46th Bde. 15th Division in May 1918.

5th Bn. Border Regiment, (T.F.)   W.O.95.2402

Based at Workington. To France as L.of C. Oct.1914 until May 1915 when it went to 149th Bde. 50th Division. Dec.1915 to 151st Bde. Converted to Pioneers 12 Feb.1918 and joined the 66th Division. Reconverted to infantry 7 May 1918 and to 97th Bde. 32nd Division.

9th (Service) Bn. Border Regiment, (K3 New Army)
                                             W.O.95.4847

Formed at Carlisle in Sept.1914. 66th Bde. 22nd Division. Converted to Pioneers in Feb.1915. To France with the 22nd Division in Sept.1915. It left for Salonika in Oct.1915, with its division, and remained there for the duration.

5th Bn. Cheshire Regiment, (T.F.)   W.O.95.2943

Based at Chester. Cheshire Bde. Welsh Division. Feb.1915, left Welsh Division and to France. Joined 14th Bde. 5th Division. Converted to Pioneers 29 Nov.1915. Left 5th Division 13 Feb.1916 and joined the 56th Division as Pioneers.

4th Bn. Coldstream Guards   W.O.95.1206

Formed at Windsor in July 1915 as Guards Pioneer Bn, but was soon renamed the 4th Bn. To France 15 Aug.1915 and joined the Guards Division.

1/5th Bn. Duke of Cornwall's Light Infantry, (T.F.)
                                             W.O.95.3050

Based at Bodmin as part of the Devon & Cornwall Bde, Wessex Division. Left the division and converted to become Pioneers to the 61st Division in April 1916. To France with the division May 1916.

10th (Service) Bn. Duke of Cornwall's Light Infantry,
W.O.95.1335

Raised at Truro as Pioneers in March 1915. Taken over by War Office in Aug.1915 and to France in June 1916. Joined the 2nd Division as Pioneers. Between Aug. and Nov. 1917 it was attached to the 66th Division as Pioneers. Rejoined the 2nd Division.

7th Bn. Durham Light Infantry, (T.F.)   W.O.95.2823

Based at Sunderland as part of the DLI Bde. Northumbrian Division. To France in April 1915 and became part of 151st Bde. 50th Division. Converted to Pioneers in Nov.1915 and stayed with the 50th Division. June 1918 moved to the 8th Division as Pioneers and absorbed the 22nd Bn. Remained with the 8th Division.

1/9th Bn. Durham Light Infantry, (T.F.)   W.O.95.3077

Based at Gateshead as part of the DLI Bde. Northumbrian Division. To France in April 1915 and became part of 151st Bde. 50th Division. Converted to Pioneers in Feb.1918 and joined the 62nd Division.

11th (Service) Bn. Durham Light Infantry, (K2 New Army)
W.O.95.2108

Formed at Newcastle in Sept.1914. Became part of 61st Bde. 20th Division. Converted to Pioneers in Jan.1915 and to France with the 20th Division in July 1915.

22nd (Service) Bn. Durham Light Infantry, 3rd County, (New Army)
W.O.95.1702

Raised as Pioneers by Durham Recruiting Committee in Oct.1915. Taken over by the War Office in March 1916. To

France 17 June 1916 and attached to the 19th Division. Joined the 8th Division as Pioneers on 2 July 1916. Absorbed by the 1/7th Bn. in July 1918.

6th (Service) Bn. East Yorkshire Regiment, (K1 New Army)

W.O.95.1804

Formed at Beverley in Aug.1914. Became part of 32nd Bde. 11th Division. Converted to Pioneers in Dec.1914 and landed at Suvla Bay 7 Aug.1915. To Alexandria in Feb.1916 and to Marseilles, with its division, in July 1916.

9th (Service) Bn. Gloucestershire Regiment, (K3 New Army)

W.O.95.3130

Formed at Bristol in Sept.1914 and became part of 78th Bde. 26th Division. To France in Sept.1915 and to Salonika in Nov.1915. July 1918 it left the 26th Division and returned to France. It joined 198th Bde. 66th Division and was converted to Pioneers. Remained with the 66th Division.

13th (Service) Bn. Gloucestershire Regiment, Forest of Dean Pioneers

W.O.95.2577

Raised at Malvern by Lt. Col.H.Webb, M.P. as Pioneers in Dec.1914. Taken over by War Office in July 1915 and joined the 39th Division. To France with the division in March 1916. It was reduced to cadre in May 1918. The cadre joined the 66th Division. In Sept.1918 to L. of C. with 197th Bde.

9th (Service) Bn. Gordon Highlanders, (K2 New Army)

W.O.95.1929
W.O.95.1930

Formed at Aberdeen in Sept.1914 and became part of 44th Bde. 15th Division. Converted to Pioneers in Jan.1915 and to France with its division in July 1915.

11th (Service) Bn. Hampshire Regiment, (K2 New Army)
W.O.95.1966

Formed at Winchester in Sept.1914 and went to Dublin as army troops attached to the 16th Division. Converted to Pioneers in Dec.1914 and to France with division in Dec.1915. In May 1918 it was reduced to cadre and returned to U.K. Reconstituted with the 13th Bn. Border Regt. and returned to France with the 16th Division in Aug.1918

16th (Service) Bn. Highland Light Infantry, (New Army)
W.O.95.2385

Raised in Glasgow in Sept.1914 and became part of 97th Bde. 32nd Division. To France in Nov.1915. Converted to Pioneers in Feb.1918 and remained with the 32nd Division.

11th (Service) Bn. The King's (Liverpool Regiment), (K1 New Army)
W.O.95.1890

Formed at Liverpool in Aug.1914 and as army troops to the 14th Division. Converted to Pioneers in Jan.1915. To France with its division in May 1915. In April 1918 it was reduced to cadre. The cadre returned to U.K. in June 1918 and absorbed in the 15th Loyal North Lancs.

12th (Service) Bn. King's Own Yorkshire Light Infantry, Miners, (New Army)
W.O.95.2353

Raised at Leeds by the West Yorkshire Coalowners Association in Sept.1914. Converted to Pioneers in early (probably May) 1915, with the 31st Division. Taken over by War Office in Aug.1915 and to Egypt with division in Dec.1915. To France with division in March 1916. Between July and November 1917, it was attached to Fifth Army for Light Railway work. Rejoined the 31st Division.

20th (Service) Bn. KRRC, British Empire League Pioneers, (New Army)

W.O.95.1405

Raised as Pioneers by the British Empire League in Aug.1915. To France in March 1916. In April or May it joined the 3rd Division as Pioneers.

25th (Service) Bn. KRRC

W.O.95.3017

In May 1918, the 2nd Provisional Garrison Guard Bn. which had just been formed in France, joined the 59th Division. It was renamed the 25th (Garrison) Bn. and was converted to Pioneers in June 1918. It remained with the 59th Division and in July, the title 'Garrison' was dropped.

19th (Service) Bn. Lancashire Fusiliers, 3rd Salford, (New Army)

W.O.95.2786

Raised at Salford in Jan.1915 and became part of 96th Bde. 32nd Division. To France in Nov.1915 and in Jan.1916 joined 14th Bde. 32nd Division. In July 1916 it became GHQ Troops, and was converted to Pioneers. Joined the 49th Division as Pioneers on 7 Aug.1916.

11th (Service) Bn. Leicestershire Regiment, Midland Pioneers, (New Army)

W.O.95.1601

Raised as Pioneers at Leicester in Oct.1915. To France in March 1916 and joined the 6th Division as Pioneers in April 1916.

2/5th Bn. Loyal North Lancashire, (T.F.)

W.O.95.2974

Formed at Bolton in October 1914 and became part of 170th Bde. 57th Division. To France in Feb.1917 and was converted to Pioneers in Feb.1918. Remained with the 57th Division.

1/12 Bn. Loyal North Lancashire, (T.F.) W.O.95.3150

Probably raised as Pioneers at Lytham in Aug.1915. Until June 1916 it was attached to the 69th Division. Joined the 60th Division as Pioneers in June 1916 and went to France with the division later that month In Nov.1916 it joined the 32nd Division as Pioneers and remained with the division until the battalion rejoined the 60th Division in Salonika in Jan.1917. In June 1917 it went to Egypt, and in April 1918 joined the 74th Division. It left Egypt for France with the division in May 1918. In March 1919, it rejoined the 32nd Division and became part of the Army of Occupation.

15th (Service) Bn. Loyal North Lancashire, (New Army)
W.O.95.1890

Formed at Cromer in June 1918. It became a Pioneer battalion and absorbed the 11th King's (Liverpool) Regt. In July, it joined the 14th Division and went to France with the division as Pioneers.

24th (Service) Bn. Manchester Regiment, Oldham Comrades, (New Army)
W.O.95.1163
W.O.95.1646
W.O.95.4222

Raised at Oldham in Oct.1914 and became part of 91st Bde. 30th Division. Taken over by the War Office in Aug.1915. To France in Nov.1915 and moved with its Bde. to the 7th Division in Jan.1916. Converted to Pioneers in May 1916 and remained with the 7th Division. To Italy in Nov.1917.

18th (Service) Bn. Middlesex Regiment, 1st Public Works, (New Army)
W.O.95.2417

Raised as Pioneers in London in Jan.1915 by Lt.Col.John Ward,

M.P. Became Pioneers to the 33rd Division in July 1915 and went with the division to France in Nov.1915.

19th (Service) Bn. Middlesex Regiment, 2nd Public Works, (New Army)

W.O.95.2627

Raised at Hornsey as Pioneers in April 1915 by Lt.Col.John Ward, M.P. In Oct.1915 it joined the 41st Division as Pioneers and went to France with the division in May 1916. To Italy in Nov.1917 and returned to France with the division in March 1918.

26th (Service) Bn. Middlesex Regiment, 3rd Public Works, (New Army)

W.O.95.4885
W.O.95.4890

Raised as Pioneers in London by Lt.Col.John Ward, M.P. in Aug.1915. In June 1916 it was attached to the 69th Division, and during July and August, to the 62nd Division. It left the 62nd Division in Aug. and went to Salonika to join the 27th Division. After the armistice, it went to Batoum in S.Russia and became embroiled in the Civil War and War of Intervention.

1/1st Bn. Monmouthshire Regiment, (T.F.)   W.O.95.2679

Based at Newport as part of the Welsh Border Bde. Welsh Division. Left the Welsh Division and to France in Feb.1915 where it joined 84th Bde. 28th Division. Converted to Pioneers in Sept.1915 and joined the 46th Division.

1/2nd Bn. Monmouthshire Regiment, (T.F.)   W.O.95.2295

Based at Pontypool as part of the Welsh Border Bde. Welsh Division. Left the Welsh Division in Nov.1914 and to France where it joined 12th Bde. 4th Division. After a spell of amalgamation in the 28th Division with the other two Monmouth battalions then overseas, it rejoined 12th Bde. 4th Division. In Jan.1916 it became L. of C. and was converted to Pioneers in May 1916. It then joined the 29th Division.

1/3rd Bn. Monmouthshire Regiment, (T.F.)   W.O.95.2787*

Based at Abergavenny as part of the Welsh Border Bde. Welsh Division. Left the Welsh Division and to France in Feb.1915 where it joined 83rd Bde. 28th Division. After it resumed its own identity in Aug.1915, it left 84th Bde. and returned to 83rd Bde. In Sept.1915 it was converted to Pioneers and joined the 49th Division. In Aug.1916 it became GHQ Troops and was then broken up.

(Although catalogued, the W.D. has disappeared)

5th (Service) Bn. Northamptonshire Regiment, (K1 New Army)
W.O.95.1842

Formed in August 1914 and attached to the 12th Division as army troops. Converted to Pioneers in Jan.1915 and went with the 12th Division to France in May 1915.

9th (Service) Bn. North Staffordshire Regiment, (K3 New Army)
W.O.95.2524

Formed at Lichfield in Sept.1914 and attached to the 22nd Division as army troops. Converted to Pioneers in April 1915 and joined the 37th Division. To France with the division in July 1915.

1/7th Northumberland Fusiliers, (T.F.)   W.O.95.2650

Based at Alnwick as part of Northumberland Bde of Northumbrian Division. To France in May 1915 and became part of 149th Bde. 50th Division. Converted to Pioneers in Feb.1918 and joined the 42nd Division.

14th (Service) Bn. Northumberland Fusiliers, (K3 New Army)
W.O.95.2146

Formed at Newcastle in Sept.1914 and attached to the 21st Division as army troops. Converted to Pioneers in Jan.1915 and went with the 21st Division to France in Sept.1915.

17th (Service) Bn. Northumberland Fusiliers, N.E.R. Pioneers, (New Army)
W.O.95.2385
W.O.95.2893

Raised by North Eastern Railway at Hull in Sept.1914. Converted to Pioneers in Jan.1915 and joined the 32nd Division in June 1915. To France with its division in Nov.1915. Attached as GHQ Railway Construction Troops from Oct.1916 until Sept.1917 when it rejoined the 32nd Division. From Nov.1917 to May 1918 it became GHQ Railway Construction again. At the end of May 1918, it joined the 52nd Division as Pioneers.

18th (Service) Bn. Northumberland Fusiliers, 1st Tyneside Pioneers, (New Army)
W.O.95.2451

Raised at Newcastle in Oct.1914. Converted to Pioneers in Feb.1915 and joined the 34th Division in Aug.1915. To France with its division in Jan.1916. Reduced to cadre in May 1918, ceased to be Pioneers and joined 116th Bde. 39th Division in June. A month later it moved to 118th Bde. and in Aug. to the 66th Division. In Sept.1918 it became L. of C. with 197 Bde.

19th (Service) Bn. Northumberland Fusiliers, 2nd Tyneside Pioneers, (New Army)
W.O.95.2477

Raised at Newcastle in Nov.1914. Converted to Pioneers in Feb.1915 and joined the 35th Division in June 1915. To France with its division in Jan.1916.

12th (Service) Bn. The Sherwood Foresters, (K3 New Army)
W.O.95.2201

Formed at Derby in Oct.1914. Became army troops attached to the 24th Division, and in April 1915 was converted to Pioneers. To France with the 24th Division in Aug.1915.

8th (Service) Bn. Ox. & Bucks Light Infantry, (K3 New Army)
W.O.95.2252
W.O.95.4866
W.O.4909

Formed in Oct.1914 at Oxford. Became army troops and attached to the 26th Division. Converted to Pioneers in Jan.1915 and to France with its division in Sept.1915. To Salonika with the 26th Division in Nov.1915.

5th (Service) Bn. Royal Irish Regiment, (K1 New Army)
W.O.95.4295
W.O.95.4832
W.O.95.4575
W.O.95.2823

Formed at Clonmel in Aug.1914 and became part of 29th Bde. 10th Division. Converted to Pioneers in June 1915 and landed at Suvla Bay 7 Aug.1915. To Salonika in Oct.1915 and in Sept.1917 to Alexandria. April 1918 it joined the 52nd Division and moved to France. In May 1918 it became L. of C. and in July went to 50th Division as Pioneers. In May 1919 it went to the 2nd Division.

16th (Service) Bn. Royal Irish Rifles, 2nd Co. Down, (New Army)
W.O.95.2498

Raised in Sept.1914 from the Co. Down Volunteers at Lurgan. Converted to Pioneers in Jan.1915. To France with the 36th Division in Oct.1915.

311

8th Bn. Royal Scots, (T.F.)   W.O.95.2857

Based at Haddington as part of Lothian Bde. To France in Nov.1914 and joined 22nd Bde. 7th Division. Converted to Pioneers in Aug.1915 and joined the 51st Division.

6/7th (Service) Bn. Royal Scots Fusiliers, (New Army)
W.O.95.3017

In May 1916, the 6th and 7th Bns. amalgamated to form the 6/7th Bn. It remained in 45th Bde. 15th Division until Feb.1918. It was converted to Pioneers and joined the 59th Division. In May 1918 it was reduced to training cadre and joined 47th Bde. 16th Division in June. It returned to U.K. and in July was absorbed by the 18th Scottish Rifles.

5th Bn. Royal Sussex Regiment, (T.F.)   W.O.95.1269

Based at Hastings and attached as army troops to Home Counties Division. To France Jan. or Feb.1915 and joined 2nd Bde. 1st Division. Converted to Pioneers in Aug.1915 and joined the 48th Division. To Italy with its division in Nov.1917.

8th (Service) Bn. Royal Sussex Regiment, (K2 New Army)
W.O.95.2029

Formed at Chichester in Sept.1914 and became 54th Bde. 18th Division. Converted to Pioneers in Feb.1915 and went to France with the 18th Division in July 1915.

14th (Service) Bn. Royal Warwickshire Regiment, 1st Birmingham, (New Army)
W.O.95.1538

Raised in Sept.1914 and became part of 95th Bde. 32nd Division. To France in Nov.1915 and to 13th Bde. 5th Division in Dec.1915. To Italy in Nov.1917 and returned to France with the 5th Division in April 1918. Converted to Pioneers in Oct.1918 and remained with the 5th Division.

1/4th Bn. Royal Welch Fusiliers, (T.F.)   W.O.95.2721

Based at Wrexham as part of North Wales Bde. Welsh Division. To France in Nov.1914 and joined 3rd Bde. 1st Division. Converted to Pioneers in Sept.1915 and joined the 47th Division.

9th (Service) Bn. Seaforth Highlanders, (New Army)
                                                     W.O.95.1757

According to one source, the battalion was formed on 1 Sept.1914. Others claim it was Oct. Attached to the 9th Division and was converted to Pioneers in Feb.1915. To France with its division in May 1915.

2/4th Bn. Somerset Light Infantry, (T.F.)   W.O.95.2451

Raised at Bath in Sept.1914 and became part of 135th Bde. 45th Division. To India in Dec.1914 and then to Andaman Is. Back to India in Sept.1917 and then to Suez as part of 232nd Bde. 75th Division. Arrived in France in June 1918 and joined the 34th Division. Converted to Pioneers in July 1918 and remained with the 34th Division.

4th Bn. South Lancashire Regiment, (T.F.) W.O.95.2917

Based at Warrington as part of the South Lancs. Bde. West Lancs. Division. Left division and to France in Feb.1915. Joined 7th Bde. 3rd Division and converted to Pioneers in Oct.1915 In Jan.1916 it became Pioneer bn. to the 55th Division.

11th (Service) Bn. South Lancashire Regiment, St.Helen's Pioneers, (New Army)   W.O.95.2323

Raised at St.Helen's as infantry in Sept.1914. Converted to

Pioneers early in 1915 and joined the 30th Division as Pioneers in May 1915. To France with its division in Nov.1915. In May 1918 it was reduced to training cadre and joined the 66th Division. In June 1918 it joined the 25th Division and returned to U.K. In July it absorbed the 18th Bn. and as a reconstituted unit went back to France in Oct.1918. It rejoined the 25th Division as Pioneers.

9th (Service) Bn. South Staffordshire Regiment, (K3 New Army)
W.O.95.2178

Formed at Lichfield in Sept.1914 and became army troops attached to the 23rd Division. Converted to Pioneers in Jan.1915 and to France with the 23rd Division in Aug.1915. To Italy with its division in Nov.1917.

5th (Service) Bn. South Wales Borderers, (K2 New Army)
W.O.95.2071

Raised at Brecon in Sept.1914 and became part of 58th Bde. 19th Division. Converted to Pioneers in Jan.1915 and to France with the 19th Division in July 1915.

6th (Service) Bn. South Wales Borderers, (K3 New Army)
W.O.95.2238

Formed at Brecon as part of 76th Bde. 25th Division. Converted to Pioneers in Feb.1915 and to France with the 25th Division in Sept.1915. In July 1918 it joined the 30th Division as Pioneers.

4th Bn. Suffolk Regiment, (T.F.)   W.O.95.2996

Based at Ipswich as part of Norfolk & Suffolk Bde. East Anglian Division. Left the division and to France in Nov.1914 where it joined the Jullundur Bde. Lahore Division. After a few days, joined 46th Bde. 15th Division and then in Feb.1916 to 98th Bde. 33rd Division. Converted to Pioneers in Feb.1918 and joined the 58th Division.

1/6th Bn. Welch Regiment, (T.F.)   W.O.95.1256

Based at Swansea as part of South Wales Bde. To France in Oct. 1914 as army troops and to L. of C. Joined 84th Bde. 28th Division in July 1915 and in Oct. to 3rd Bde. 1st Division. Converted to Pioneers in May 1916 and remained with the 1st Division.

8th (Service) Bn. Welch Regiment, (K1 New Army)
W.O.95.5153

Raised at Cardiff in Aug.1914 and became part of 40th Bde. 13th Division. Converted to Pioneers in Feb.1915 and landed at Anzac in Aug.1915. To Egypt in Jan.1916 and then to Mesopotamia in Feb. Remained with the 13th Division.

19th (Service) Bn. Welch Regiment, Glamorgan Pioneers, (New Army)
W.O.95.2548

Formed at Colwyn Bay in Feb.1915 and was probably the first battalion to be specifically raised as a Pioneer bn. Became Pioneers to the 43rd Division and then to the 38th Division when the Welsh Division was redesignated. To France with its division in Dec.1915.

23rd (Service) Bn. Welch Regiment, Welsh Pioneers, (New Army)
W.O.95.4909

Formed as a Pioneer unit at Porthcawl in Sept.1915. In May and June 1916 it was attached to the 69th Division and then sailed for Salonika. Arrived in Aug.1916 and joined the 28th Division as Pioneers.

21st (Service) Bn. West Yorkshire Regiment, Wool Textile Pioneers, (New Army)   W.O.95.1472

Raised in the West Riding as a Pioneer unit in Sept.1915. To France in June 1916 and joined the 4th Division.

14th (Service) Bn. Worcestershire Regiment, Severn Valley Pioneers, (New Army)   W.O.95.3105

Raised as a Pioneer unit in Sept.1915 at Worcester by Lt.Col.H.Webb, M.P. Taken over by War Office in March 1916. To France in June 1916 and joined the 63rd Division as Pioneers.

17th (Service) Bn. Worcestershire Regiment, (New Army)
        W.O.95.2601

Formed in France in June 1918 from the 17th (Garrison) Bn., which was formerly the 1st Garrison Guard Bn. Absorbed cadres of 12th Yorks and 10th Worcester. Converted to Pioneers and joined the 40th Division.

12th (Service) Bn. Yorkshire Regiment, Teeside Pioneers, (New Army)
        W.O.95.2601
Raised at Middlesborough in Dec.1914. Taken over by the War Office in Aug.1915 and joined the 40th Division as Pioneers in Sept.1915. To France with its division in June 1916. Reduced to cadre in May 1918 and the cadre was absorbed by the 17th Worcester.

7th (Service) Bn. York & Lancaster Regiment, (K2 New Army)
        W.O.95.1995

Formed at Pontefract in Aug.1914 and became part of 50th Bde. 17th Division. Converted to Pioneers in March 1915 and went with its division to France in July 1915.

N.B. Several Pioneer battalions formed Depot Companies before they left for France. As they were later absorbed into Reserve Brigades and not retained specifically as Reserve Pioneer battalions, they are not included in this list.

Appendix IV

Examples of Work undertaken by Pioneers

TYPE A
STANDARD DUG-OUT
Scale:- One Inch – 12 Feet

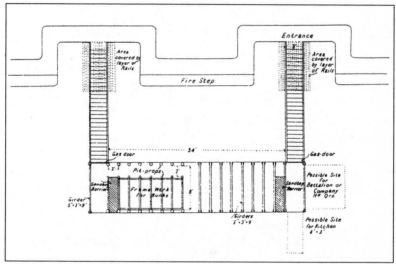

A standard platoon dugout. It had two entrances, a shell proof cover of up to twenty feet and bunking accomodation for thirty men. It was meant to take over 200 RE and attached men, with up to another 800 to carry the spoil, working in four shifts, eleven days to complete. Pioneer companies could be attached to Tunnelling Companies to observe and learn the work. After a period of such instruction, the Pioneers were then supposed to take over the construction, under the supervision of a Tunnelling officer.

317

Cruciform Post

These became a standard form of defensive post. Pioneer battalions were frequently involved in their construction, often assisted by the infantry. The posts were designed to house two Vickers and two or four Lewis guns, manned by a garrison of up to thirty men. The posts contained dugouts for telephones, company HQ, bomb and SAA stores. They could be used as isolated posts or, if the arms were extended to form parallels and the stems lengthened into communication trenches, they could be linked to other systems.

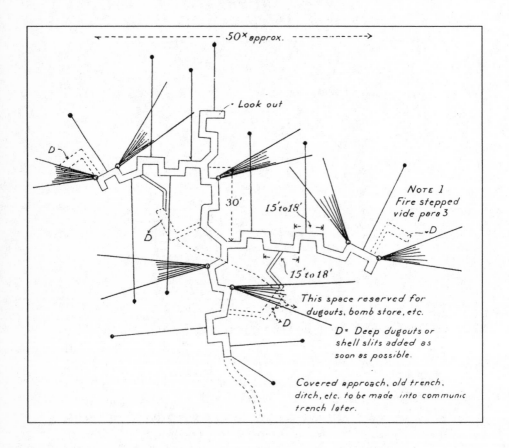

Trench and Dugout Construction

Apart from road maintenance, Pioneers spent most of their working time digging. Often, but not necessarily always, working under the supervision of the RE, Pioneers excavated, revetted, trench boarded and constructed dugouts. The following diagrams show how Pioneers were instructed to approach a variety of their many tasks.

CONSTRUCTION & REPAIRS OF TRENCHES

1st Corps — August 1917.
Scale:- 1 in – 3ft

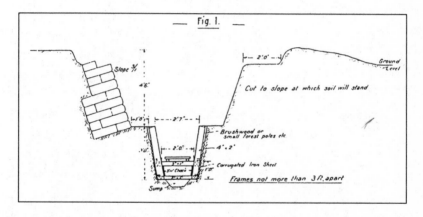

Alternative Method with Pickets in Hand Ground when Frames are not Available

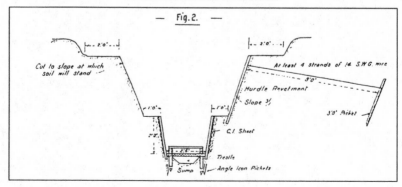

319

COMMON REPAIRS TO TRENCHES
THE RIGHT AND WRONG WAY TO DO THEM

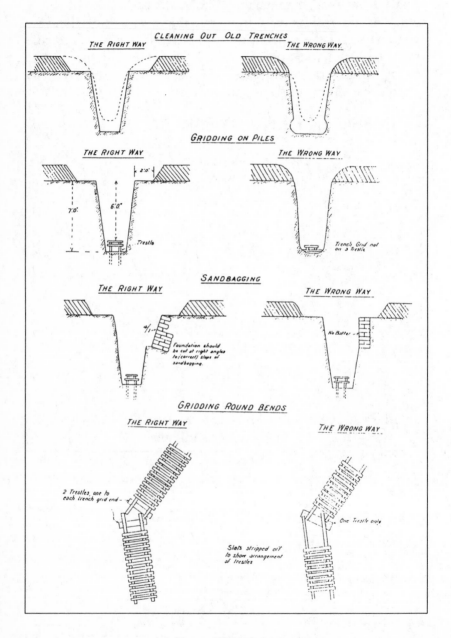

Nº 1. ENTRANCE FRAME

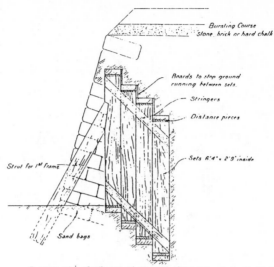

Bursting Course
Stone, brick or hard chalk.

Boards to stop ground running between sets.

Stringers

Distance pieces

Sets 6'4" x 2'9" inside

Strut for 1st frame

Sand bags

To prevent bulging, Sandbags should always be bedded at right angles to angle of batter.

Nº 2. ENTRANCE FRAME

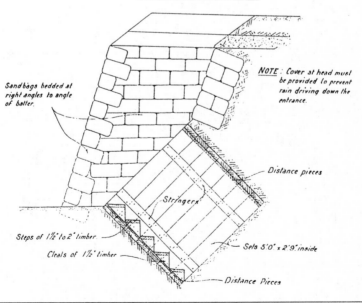

Sandbags bedded at right angles to angle of batter.

NOTE : *Cover at head must be provided to prevent rain driving down the entrance.*

Distance pieces

Stringers

Steps of 1½" to 2" timber.

Cleats of 1½" timber

Sets 5'0" x 2'9" inside

Distance Pieces

321

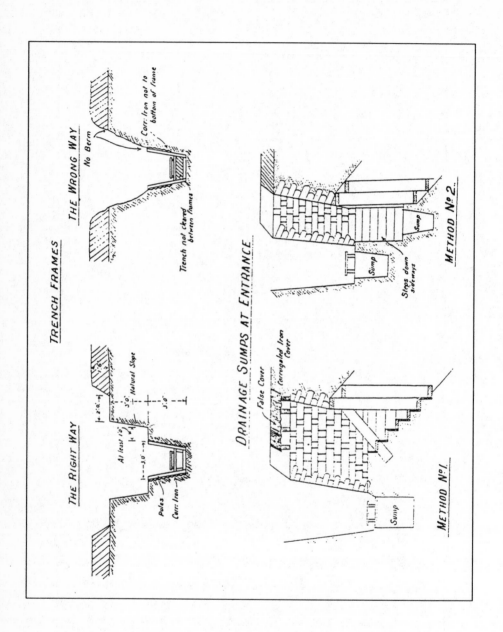

TRENCH FRAMES

THE RIGHT WAY

THE WRONG WAY

No Berm

Corr: Iron not to bottom of frame

Trench not cleared between frames

At least 1'0"

2'0"

6'

3'0" Natural Slope

3'0" — 3'0"

Poles

Corr: Iron

DRAINAGE SUMPS AT ENTRANCE

False Cover

Corrugated Iron Cover

Sump

METHOD Nº 1.

Sump

Steps down sideways

Sump

METHOD Nº 2.

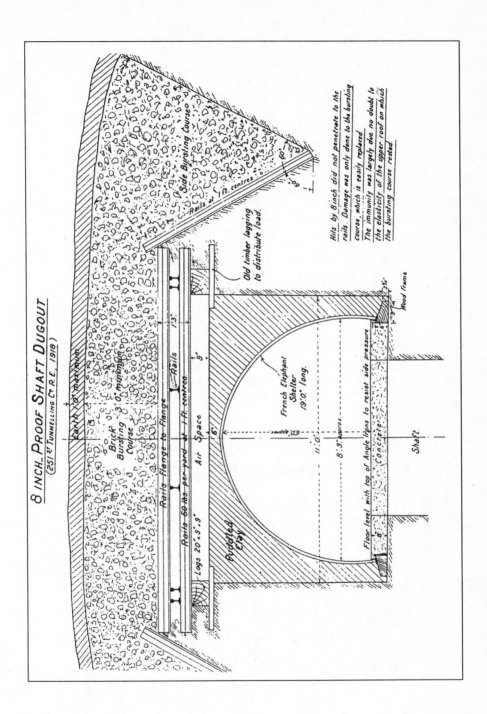

8 INCH. PROOF SHAFT DUGOUT
(251 ST TUNNELLING Cº R.E, 1918)

Earth of maximum

Side Bursting Course

Rails at 1 ft. centres

60°

6′ 0″

Brick Bursting Course 3′ 0″ minimum

Rails flange to Flange

Rails 1′ 3″

Rails 60 lbs per yard at 1 ft. centres

Logs 20′ × 9′. 9″

Air Space

9″

6′

11′ 0″

6′ 0″ approx.

French Elephant Shelter 19′0″ long.

Puddled Clay

Old timber lagging to distribute load.

Floor level with top of Angle Irons to resist side pressure

(Concrete)

6′

8′. 9″ approx.

Shaft.

1′. 9″

9″

Wood Frame

Hits by 8inch did not penetrate to the
rails. Damage was only done to the bursting
course, which is easily replaced
The immunity was largely due no doubt to
the elasticity of the upper roof on which
the bursting course rested.

323

SOURCES

Only primary and secondary sources used in this study are included in the following lists.

Unpublished Official Sources:

War Diaries: Public Record Office references for Pioneer battalion W.D. can be found in Appendix II: Those for other units as footnotes at the end of each chapter.

Other Unpublished Sources:

1. Papers held by the Department of Documents, Imperial War Museum:

Baer, A., Garvie, Capt., Howes, H., Jellicoe, J., Lester, R.M., Watts, C.

2. Papers held by the Liddle Collection, University of Leeds:

Adams, W., Bevington, R., Capper, D., Croft, W., Davey, R., Dillon, N., Gray, G., Hall, C., Jaeger, W., Jamieson, R., Kershaw, K., Marriot, S., Mellers, P., Moore, C., Piggot, J., Simpson, T., Sutton, G., Travers, S., Tymms, F., Vaux, E.,

3. Other collections:

Anderson, H. Private collection.
Baldwin, D. Private collection.
Cooper, M. Durham Light Infantry Museum.
Crouch, Lt.Col. Durham Light Infantry Museum.
Davidson, T. Durham Light Infantry Museum.
Kitchener Papers. Public Record Office. PRO 30/57/50.
Laing, W. Durham Light Infantry Museum.
Townsend, W. Papers, Light Infantry archive, Pontefract. Unpublished history of the 7/DLI, Durham Light Infantry Museum.
Walsh, St.G. Oldham Local Studies Library.

Published Sources:

Official Publications:

Army Council Instructions. (HMSO, 1914–19)
Hansard, 1914 -1918
Officers Died in the Great War, (HMSO, 1919)
Official History of the Great War, (HMSO, 1935–45)
Order of Battle of Divisions, (HMSO, 1920)
Registers of the Commonweath War Graves Commission.
Soldiers Died in the Great War, (HMSO, 1920–22)

Secondary Sources:

Addison, G. *The Work of the R.E. in the European War,* (Mackay, 1926)
Aldington, R. *Death of a Hero,* (Hogarth Press, 1984 edition).
Atkinson, A. *The Royal Hampshire Regiment,* (Maclehose, 1950-52)
Atkinson, C.T. *The Seventh Division, 1914–18,* (Murray, 1927)
Atkinson, C.T. *The History of the South Wales Borderers,* (London, 1931)

Atteridge, A. *History of the 17th (Northern) Division,* (Maclehose, 1929)

Bewsher, F.W. *The History of the 51st (Highland) Division, 1914–18,* (Blackwood, 1921)

Bickersteth, J *The Bickersteth Diaries,* (Leo Cooper, 1995)

Boraston & Bax, *The Eigth Division in war, 1914–18,* (London, 1926)

Brett, G.A. *The War History of the 1/2 Monmouth,* (Pontypool, 1933)

Buchan, J. *The History of the Royal Scots Fusiliers,* (Nelson, 1925)

Buckley, F. *Q.6A and other places,* (London, 1920)

Buckley, F. *The War History of the 7th Northumberland Fusiliers,* (Newcastle, 1926)

Chalmers, T. *History of the 16th Battalion HLI,* (M'Callum, n.d.)

Churton, W. *The War Record of the 1/5th Cheshires,* (Chester, 1920)

Cooke, C.H. *Historical Records of the 19th (S) Bn. N.F. (P),* (Newcastle, 1920)

Coop, J.O. *The Story of the 55th (West Lancashire) Division, 1916–18,* (Liverpool, 1919)

Cooper, B. *The 10th (Irish) Division in Gallipoli,* (Jenkins, 1918)

Crookenden, A. *The History of the Cheshire Regiment in the Great War,* (Evans, 1938)

Dalbiac, P.H. *The History of the 60th Division,* (Allen & Unwin, 1927)

Davson, H. *The History of the 35th Division in the Great War,* (Sifton, 1926)

Elliott, E.R. *The Royal Pioneers, 1945–1993,* (SPA, 1993)

England, R.E. *A Brief History of the 12/KOYLI,* (Wakefield, n.d.)

Ewing, J. *The Royal Scots, 1914–19,*

Ewing, J. *The History of the 9th (Scottish) Division,* (Murray, 1920)

Falls, C. *The Gordon Highlanders in the First World War,* (AUP n.d.)

Falls, C. *The History of the 36th (Ulster) Division,* (Belfast, 1922)

Gibbon, F. *The 42nd (East Lancashire) Division,* (Country Life, 1920)

Gillon, S. *The Story of the 29th Division,* (Nelson, 1925)

Gilvary, M.T. *The History of the 7th (S) Battalion, the York & Lancs (P)* (Talbot Press, 1925)

Headlam, C. *History of the Guards Division in the Great War,* (Murray, 1924)

Howcroft, G. *The First World War,* (Hurst, Kidd & Rennie, 1986)

Hughes, C. *Mametz,* (Orion Press, 1982)

Hutchinson, G.S. *The Thirty-Third Division in France and Flanders,* (Waterlow, 1921)

Inglefield, V.E. *The History of the Twentieth (Light) Division,* (Nisbet, 1921)

James, E.A. *British Regiments, 1914–18, (Samson, 1978)*

Jerrold, D. *The Royal Naval Division,* (Hutchinson, 1923)
 KKRC Chronicles, 1915–19. (Regimentally compiled)

Latter, J.C. *The Lancashire Fusiliers,* (Gale & Polden, 1949)

Marden, T.O. *The History of the Welch Regiment,* (Cardiff, 1932)

Marden, T.O, *A Short History of the 6th Division,* (London, 1920)

Marden. T.O. *The History of the 25th Division,*

Matthews, E.C. *With the Cornwall Territorials on the Western Front. Being the History of the 5th Battalion DCLI in the Great War,* (Cambridge, 1921)

Maude, A.H. *The 47th (London) Division, 1914-19,* (Amalgamated Press 1922)

Middlebrook, M. *The Kaiser's Battle,* (Penguin, 1983)

Mitchinson, K.W. *Gentlemen and Officers,* (IWM, 1995)

Mitchinson, K.W. & McInnes, I. *Cotton Town Comrades,* (Bayonet Press, 1993)

Munby, J.E. *The 38th Division in the Great War,* (1920)

Murphy, C. *The History of the Suffolk Regiment,* (Hutchinson, 1928)

Nichols, G.H. *The 18th Division in the Great War,* (Blackwood, 1922)

Norman, T. *The Hell They Called High Wood*, (Kimber, 1984)
On the Western Front with the 1/3rd Monmouth, (no name or date)
Ox & Bucks Light Infantry Chronicles, 1916–17.
The Record of the 11th Bn. King's (Liverpool) Regiment, subsequently the 15th Bn the Loyal North Lancashire, Regimentally compiled. (Thomas & Co. 1920)
History of the Corps of Royal Engineers, Regimentally compiled. (IRE, 1952)
Ross of Bladensburg. *The Coldstream Guards*, (1924)
Sandilands, H.R *The 23rd Division, 1914–18*, (Blackwood, 1925)
Shakespear, J. *Historical Records of the 18th (S) Battalion, N.F.(P)*, (Newcastle, 1920)
Shakespear, J. *Historical Records of the 17th (S) Battalion, N.F.(P)*, (Newcastle, 1922)
Shakespear, J. *The Thirty-Fourth Division, 1915-18*, (Witherby, 1921)
Stacke, H.F. *The Worcestershire Regiment in the Great War*, (Cheshire & Sons, 1929)
Thompson, R.R. *The Fifty-Second (Lowland) Division, 1914–18*, (Maclehose, 1923)
Turbeville, A. *A Short History of the 20th Bn KRRC*, (Hull, 1923)
Ward, C.H. *The 56th Division*, (Murray, 1921)
Ward, S.G. *The Story of the Durham Light Infantry.*
Whalley- Kelly, H. *'Ich Dien', The POW Volunteers (South Lancashire Regiment) 1914–34*, (Gale & Polden, 1935)
Whitton, F. *The History of the 40th Division*,
Wylly, H.C. *The Yorkshire Regiment*, (no publisher. n.d.)
Wylly, H.C. *The Loyal North Lancashire Regiment*, (RUSI, 1933)
Wyrall, E. *The Diehards in the Great War, 1914–19*, (London, 1926–30)
Wyrall, E. *The West Yorkshire Regiment in the Great War*, (Bodley Head, n.d.)
Wyrall, E. *The East Yorkshire Regiment*,
Wyrall, E. *The History of the 19th Division, 1914–18)*, (Arnold, 1932)

Wyrall, E. *The History of the 50th Division,* (Lund, 1939)

Wyrall, E. *The History of the 62nd (W.R.) Division, 1914–19,* (Lane, 1924)

Wyrall, E. *The History of the Second Division,* (Nelson, 1922)

INDEX

Adams, 2Lt. W., 45, 168
Aldington, R, 188
Alexandria, 45, 136
Allenby, Gen., Sir E., 56
American troops, 229, 230, 231, 233, 240, 257
Anderson, 2Lt. H., 151
Ardre, 247
Armentieres, 31, 228, 230
Arras, Battle of: 121–4, 292–3
Aveluy, 86, 113, 225, 249

Baer, Capt. A., 107, 138
Baghdad, 119
Bapaume, 220
Basra, 46
Bazentin, 92, 168
Beale-Brown, Gen., 66
Beaumont Hamel, 76, 91
Becordel, 74
Becourt, 121
Bevington, R., 20
Bourlon Wood, 135, 276–7
Braithwaite, Gen., 248
Bridges, Gen, G. T., 270
Buckley, Capt. F., 279–80
Bulfin, Gen. E., 8, 61, 62
Bullecourt, 124–5, 135
Burton, Lt-Col., 27
Butte de Warlincourt, 105
Buzancy, 247

Cambrai, Battle of: 156
Campbell, Lt-Col., 241
Candas, 111
Capper, Lt. D., 6, 29, 30, 71
Carmichael, Sgt. VC., 134, 281
Charlesworth, *family*, 3, 16, 280
Chemin des Dames, 224, 226
Citadel, 41, 96, 185
Combles, 105
Cooke, Lt-Col., 46
Courcelette, 66, 99
Croft, 2Lt. W., 139, 152, 169, 180
Crouch, Lt-Col., 234–6

Currie, Gen. A., 131

Davidson, Maj. T., 51, 78, 150, 151, 170, 202, 255, 279
Delville Wood, 93, 95, 99, 100, 101, 277
Derby Scheme, 8
Dillon, 2Lt. N., 5, 13, 48, 78, 152, 163
Double Crassier, 47

Fanshaw, Gen. R., 271
Fergusson, Gen., 57, 59
Foncquevillers, 76, 86
French, Field Marshal Sir, J., 55, 68
Fricourt, 82, 94

Gallipoli, 44, 45, 46, 175, 290
Glasgow, Lt-Col., 269
Gavrelle, 231, 283
Glory Hole, 50, 85
Gommecourt, 75, 76, 78, 79, 81, 82, 90, 254
Gorre Wood, 225
Gough, Gen, Sir H., 98
Gray, G., 137
Great Midland Railway, 116–7
Guillemont, 98
Guinchy, 98, 101

Haig, Field Marshal Sir D., 32
Haldane, Gen. J., 253
Hall, Maj. C., 16, 138, 227
Hanebeke, 132
Hangard Wood, 222, 229
Hazebrouck, 35, 184
Heale, Lt-Col., 14
Heilly, 97, 249
Heligoland, 85
High Wood, 92, 282
Hindenburg Line, 124
Hohenzollern Redoubt, 46, 48
Howes, H., 144, 185
Huts, 167, 189

Jaeger, W., 6, 13, 161, 167, 171, 205
Jamieson, 2Lt. R., 251

Jeffreys, Gen. G., 224
Jellicoe, 2Lt., 160
Jones, Cpl. J. VC., 228

Kavanagh, Gen. C., 57
Keir, Gen., 57, 60
Kershaw, 2Lt. K., 16, 21, 48
Kitchener, Field Marshal Earl, xii, 55, 67

La Boiselle, 87, 90, 94
Lancashire Dump, 80
Langemarck, 127, 128
Langham, Lt-Col., 134, 144, 215
Lester, 2Lt. R., 17, 143, 153
Le Transloy, 105
Lloyd-George, Maj. R., 153
Lochnagar, 80, 84
Longueval, 93, 94, 98
Loos, Battle of: 46–8, 141, 219
Ludendorff, Gen., 236
Lys, Battle of: 228

Mametz, 77, 82, 87, 92, 232, 282
Mailly-Maillet, 167
Marriot, S, 63
Marseilles, 45, 244, 245, 246
Mash Valley, 85
Maurepas, 106, 109
Meaulte, 74, 102
Mellors, P., 138
Merville, 225
Mesopotamia, 46, 119, 290
Messines, Battle of: 115, 118, 125, 126, 224
Middle East, 136, 175, 256
Military Service Act, 192, 197
Montauban, 83, 91, 103, 168, 169
Moore, C., 286
Monro, Gen., 184
Morchies, 222
Morgan, Lt-Col. C., 226
Morley, Lt-Col., 14
Mouquet Farm, 101, 113
Murray, Freeman, 8

Naves, 185, 252
North-Eastern Railway, 4, 6, 10, 112, 263

Passchendaele, 127, 130
Pay, 160, 172–3
Pioneer depot, 212–3, 218
Ploegsteert, 116
Plumer, Gen. Sir H., 55, 58, 59, 61, 129
Poperinghe, 116

Pountney, Lt-Col., 147, 179, 199–200, 202
Pozieres, 88

Rawlinson, Gen. Sir H., 98
Rhine, 261
Ribecourt, 221
Roclincourt, 66
Roisel, 233
Rouen, 121, 161

Salonika, 44, 45, 136, 137, 175, 195, 252
Sauchy-Lestree, 251
Schwaben, Redoubt, 76, 86, 100, 102
Serre, 80–1, 104
Shute, Gen., 223
Simplex, 114
Simpson, 2Lt. T., 17, 136
Somme, Battle of: *Chapters 4, & 5*, 221, 292, *Film of*, 97, 109
Struma, 137
Sutton, Col., 14

Templeux, 136
Thiepval, 76, 84, 85, 86, 88, 101
Townsend, W., 81
Trower, Col., 14, 90, 182, 224, 251, 252, 270
Tymms, 2Lt. F., 152, 180–1

Vaulx Wood, 169, 248
Vaux, Col., 38, 225
Vieux-Berquin, 222
Vimy, 122, 139
Vraucourt, 232

Walsh, Capt. St., G., 280
Ward, J. MP., 7
War savings, 256
Waterlot Farm, 101
Watts, Capt. C., 167
Webb, Col. Sir H., 8
West Yorkshire Coal Owners' Assoc., 3, 10, 81
Wolff, Capt. C., 17
Wood, Lt. E., 163, 189
Wulverghem, 141

Young, T. VC., 235
Ypres, 49, 2nd Battle of: 60, 61, 63, 72, 3rd Battle of; 115, 127 to 135 *passim*, 137, 158, 293
Yukon pack, 142

332

INDEX TO ARMS, FORMATIONS AND UNITS

Armies –
First – 62–65, 251
Second – 55–62, 171
Third – 108, 121
Fourth – 114, 186–7

Army Cyclist Corps – 198
Army Pay Corps – 212
Army Works Corps – xii

British Empire League Pioneers – *see*
    20/KRRC

Cavalry –
1st Division – 66, 122, 175
Dehra Dun Brigade – 37
9th Brigade Pioneer Bn – 66
11th Reserve Brigade – 192
Regiments – 11th Hussars – 66, 195;
    North Irish Horse – 39; Scottish Horse
    – 195; 2nd Dragoon Gds – 66; 5th
    Dragoon Gds – 66

Corps –
II – 56, 57, 59
V – 56, 57
VI – 56, 60
VIII – 269–70
XIII – 111
XIV – 106
XVII – 111
XVIII – 115
Canadian – 122, 131
Railway Engineers – 254
2nd Bn Railway Troops – 116
8th Bn Railway Troops – 116, 118
7th Labour Company – 116
New Zealand – 287

Depot Companies – 23

Divisions –
Guards – 2, 22, 273

1st – 209
2nd – 93, 206, 220
3rd – 56, 98, 99
4th – 57, 64, 99
5th – 57, 64, 94, 99, 246
6th – 57, 271
7th – 44, 64, 65, 82, 92, 97, 122, 139,
    144, 21, 280–1, 283
8th – 85, 87, 106, 273, 274
9th – 48, 56, 93, 220, 272
10th – 3, 44, 246
11th – 44
12th – 15, 56, 86
13th – 12
14th – 56, 237–8, 258
15th – 3, 209
16th – 4, 30, 256
17th – 19, 272
18th – 83, 100, 203, 220
19th – 85, 224, 272
20th – 272
21st – 84, 91, 274
22nd – 4, 154
23rd – 2, 5, 42, 272
24th – 47
25th – 86, 241, 273
26th – 244
27th – 154
28th – 58
29th – 62, 72, 76, 80, 91, 147
30th – 65, 83
31st – 73, 80, 81, 203
32nd – 233
33rd – 17, 274
34th – 79, 84, 87, 91, 94, 95, 148, 230,
    244
35th – 271
36th – 268, 274
37th – 142, 268
38th – 7, 92, 127
39th – 229, 257
40th – 49, 238, 273
42nd – 135, 209, 210, 211, 215, 234,

273
43rd – 2
44th – 2
45th – 2
46th – 56, 57, 59, 61, 75, 78, 82, 106
47th – 47, 62, 93, 273
48th – 76, 81, 91, 209, 214
49th – 1, 57, 59–62, 66, 86, 131
50th – 59, 65, 105, 210, 234, 244, 246, 257, 274
51st – 39, 127, 246, 274
52nd – 246, 274
53rd – 2
54th – 2
55th – 68, 149
56th – 64, 68, 72, 75, 159, 231, 251, 253
57th – 211
58th – 135, 208, 270–1
59th – 2, 107, 207, 209, 232, 238, 241, 274
60th – 2, 8, 136
61st – 47, 221, 277
62nd – 234, 248
63rd – 1, 220, 221, 283
66th – 131, 186, 188, 198, 214, 230, 233, 244, 257
74th – 1, 136
75th – 1, 244
1st Australian – 220, 287
Lahore, 37
Meerut, 37

Engineers –
C.E. Armies & Corps – (see Chapter 8)
GHQ – 154; Third – 154; Fourth – 154; IV – 156; IX – 115, XVII – 112
CRE Divisions –
7th – 129, 147; 12th – 149; 19th – 157; 34th – 157; 37th – 52, 156, 163–4, 216; 56th – 82, 157
Field Companies (R.E.) –
11th – 103; 82nd – 139, 158, 159; 123rd – 12, 20; 151st – 12, 20; 209th – 149; 416th – 159; 1st London Reserve – 200; 2/2nd Highland – 104
Hants (Fortress) R.E. – 202
Light Railway Troops – 118
Lowland Division R.E. – 201
Railway Construction Troops – 254
Railway/Tramway Companies – 111, 112, 114

Reserve Battalions – 196–8
Royal Anglesey Engineers – 198
Tunnelling Companies (R.E.) –
183rd – 66; 250th – 246

Entrenching Battalions – 193, 216
Guards – 194; 2nd – 194; 5th – 194, 204; 7th – 194; 9th – 68; 10th – 194

Forest of Dean Pioneers – see 13/Glouc.

Garrison Guard Battalions – 238–242
Glamorgan Pioneers – see 19/Welch
Graduated Battalions – 204

Infantry Brigades –
South African – 93, 220

Infantry Regiments –
Coldstream Guards, 4th Bn – 12, 13, 32, 24, 37, 40, 43, 47, 101, 102, 120, 168, 169, 176, 177, 187, 194, 216, 253, 258, 262–3, 273, 299, 302
Argyll & Sutherland Highlanders, 6th Bn – 41, 94, 99, 124, 201, 214, 246, 281, 301; 7th Bn – 57
Bedfordshire Regt – 201
Black Watch, 1/5th Bn – 40, 41, 52, 65, 301
Border Regt, 5th Bn – 59, 194, 214, 233, 291, 302; 9th Bn – 4, 30, 45, 184, 252, 256, 299, 302; 11th Bn – 233
Cheshire, 5th Bn – 64, 72, 75, 79, 81, 82, 101, 134, 145, 161, 166, 169, 194, 204, 210, 214, 215, 231, 251, 253, 263, 302
Devonshire, 2nd Bn – 226
Duke of Cornwall's L.I., 1/5th Bn – 3, 20, 33, 47, 177, 184, 186, 205, 207, 217, 221–2, 277, 302; 6th Bn – 208; 10th Bn – 25, 33, 39, 93, 104, 130, 134, 170, 195, 203, 206, 220–1, 244, 272, 303
Duke of Wellington's, 2nd Bn – 225; 5th Bn – 235; 6th Bn – 59, 60
Durham L.I., 6th Bn – 59; 7th Bn – 38, 59, 105, 107, 122, 124, 130, 134, 142, 225–6, 272, 303; 8th Bn – 57, 58, 59; 9th Bn – 43, 59, 178, 209, 234–6, 247–8, 303; 11th Bn – 3, 29, 34, 41, 48, 105, 168, 169, 184, 193, 303; 22nd Bn – 8, 16, 32, 73, 78, 85, 86,

91, 102, 106, 115, 128, 132, 147, 150, 151, 162, 169, 170, 183, 189, 192, 193, 194, 202, 203, 204, 217, 226–7, 255, 273, 274, 279, 291, 292, 300, 303

East Surrey, 2nd Bn – 48; 8th Bn – 83

East Yorkshire, 6th Bn – 4, 44, 45, 46, 101, 115, 119, 128, 168, 175, 183, 198, 203, 205, 207, 216, 231, 250, 261, 276, 278, 290, 304; 12th Bn – 207

Gloucestershire, 9th Bn – 188, 214, 244–5, 246, 304; 12 Bn – 246; 13th Bn – 57, 102, 104, 115, 133, 229–30, 257, 304

Gordon Highlanders, 4th Bn – 60; 9th Bn – 3, 10, 12, 16, 19, 21, 24, 48, 51, 94, 127, 139, 145, 166, 201, 219, 247, 255, 304

Hampshire, 11th Bn – 4, 30, 41, 47, 100, 135, 207, 229, 238, 240–1, 258, 291, 292, 305; 14th Bn – 207

Highland L.I., 16th Bn – 11, 209, 211, 232–3, 250, 253, 276, 305

Honourable Artillery Company – 16, 20, 56, 104

King's (Liverpool), 2/5th Bn – 208; 7th Bn – 63, 64; 10th Bn – 56; 11th Bn – 3, 6, 39, 52, 131, 140, 147, 161, 167, 171, 201, 203, 205, 208, 213, 229, 237, 305

King's Own Yorkshire L.I., 12th Bn – 3, 10, 13, 16, 20, 72, 73, 80, 81, 104, 116, 119, 123, 162, 173, 178, 202, 203, 222, 256, 259, 279, 280, 290, 291, 292, 305

King's Royal Rifle Corps, 13th Bn – 104; 20th Bn – 7, 8, 16, 18, 30, 37, 43, 49, 98, 118, 141, 149, 249, 261, 278–9, 306; 25th Bn – 207, 242, 264, 274, 278, 306

Lancashire Fusiliers, 19th Bn – 10, 65, 67, 116, 131, 139, 140, 141, 177, 185, 192, 194, 198, 202, 203, 204, 214, 227–8, 252, 276, 280, 306

Leicestershire, 192; 11th Bn – 26–29, 177, 198, 224–5, 271, 292, 306; 12th Bn – 27

Lincolnshire, 10th Bn – 85

London Regt., 5th Bn – 62, 64, 193; 10th Bn – 199; 3/11th Bn – 201; 14th Bn – 82, 90; 16th Bn – 60

Loyal North Lancashire, 1/5th Bn – 60; 2/5th Bn – 162, 209, 211, 254, 306; 1/12th Bn – 8, 136, 245–6, 261, 277, 306; 15th Bn – 237–8, 264, 306

Manchester, 24th Bn – 11, 37, 44, 65, 77, 82, 87, 92, 97, 98, 106, 109, 123, 125, 126, 130, 135, 139, 145, 147, 162, 163, 167, 168, 170, 179, 184, 196, 199–200, 213, 253, 259, 260–1, 263, 270, 280, 283–4, 307

Middlesex, 18th Bn – 7, 17, 33, 35, 43, 47, 51, 93, 102, 103, 104, 111, 128, 138, 139, 153, 170, 177, 179, 185, 217, 261–2, 274, 275, 307; 19th Bn – 7, 100, 126, 134, 185, 250, 262, 277, 308; 25th Bn – 17; 26th Bn – 7, 17, 136, 137, 195, 291, 308

Monmouth – 192, 201; 1st Bn – 11, 57, 60, 61, 75, 78, 79, 82, 86, 106, 162, 175, 194, 215, 264, 308; 2nd Bn – 57, 61, 62, 72, 76, 80, 105, 114, 141, 147, 308; 3rd Bn – 57, 60, 66, 67, 86, 309

Newfoundland Regt., 79

Northamptonshire, 5th Bn – 25, 31, 34, 45, 51, 91, 102, 111, 124, 135, 140, 147, 178, 194, 220, 252, 256, 290, 309; 6th Bn – 71

North Staffordshire, 5th Bn – 9th Bn – 32, 43, 86, 87, 90, 123, 124, 134, 138, 153, 157, 177, 196, 200, 202, 212, 268, 281, 309

Northumberland Fusiliers, 1st Bn – 201; 7th Bn – 37, 208, 209, 210, 215, 234, 250, 253, 254–5, 259, 273, 279, 309; 12/13th Bn – 213; 14th Bn – 5, 10, 14, 15, 18, 19, 32, 33, 48, 74, 75, 78, 84, 95, 99, 140, 151, 160, 175, 231, 252, 259, 291, 310; 17th Bn – 3, 6, 10, 11, 16, 34, 35, 41, 75, 85, 86, 87, 111, 112, 113, 115, 117, 118, 120, 151, 160, 176, 178, 189, 198, 213, 254, 256, 263, 279, 310; 18th Bn – 6, 10, 18, 20, 33, 35, 39–40, 50, 72, 74, 79, 84, 95, 115, 121, 123, 133, 141, 148, 161, 167, 176, 194, 206, 224, 230–1, 257, 263, 279, 290, 310; 19th Bn – 9, 37, 91, 135, 187, 198, 205, 208, 220, 231, 237, 249, 271, 310; 24/27th Bn – 208; 25th Bn – 202; 32nd Bn – 112

Notts & Derby, 2/5th Bn – 198; 8th Bn – 59, 60; 12th Bn – 47, 96, 97, 136, 149, 150, 169, 184, 198, 220, 233, 261, 311

Rifle Brigade, 9th Bn – 229; 13th Bn – 124

Royal Irish Regt., 5th Bn – 3, 7, 44, 136, 175, 246, 256, 274, 311

Royal Irish Rifles, 16th Bn – 35, 36, 76, 80, 86, 111, 115, 126, 135, 171, 193, 201, 262, 274, 311

Royal Scots, 8th Bn – 36, 39, 41, 47, 64, 65, 66, 93, 104, 114, 115, 116, 169, 176, 195, 210, 214, 222, 247, 250, 255, 312; 15th Bn – 84

Royal Scots Fusiliers, 6/7th Bn – 209, 232, 242, 256–7, 274, 312

Scottish Rifles, 1/6th Bn – 63; 18th Bn – 256

Seaforth Highlanders, 9th Bn – 1, 32, 35, 48, 51, 93, 111, 122, 201, 212, 213, 231, 313

Somerset L.I., 2/4th Bn – 244, 248–9, 313

South Lancashire, 4th Bn – 37, 56, 132, 134, 135, 149, 152, 180, 182–3, 195, 225, 276, 313; 11th Bn – 3, 83, 201, 228, 241, 252, 273, 276, 292, 313; 18th Bn – 241

South Staffordshire, 2nd Bn – 93; 9th Bn – 5, 29, 31, 34, 37, 40, 42, 43, 94, 133, 151, 169, 264–5, 292, 313

South Wales Borderers, 5th Bn – 3, 15, 18, 33, 34, 37, 85, 87, 90, 97, 104, 134, 139, 152, 159, 169, 180, 184, 200–1, 205, 207, 224, 251, 259, 291, 293, 314; 6th Bn – 3, 33, 87, 200–1, 204, 223–4, 273, 314; 11th Bn – 224; 12th Bn – 297

Suffolk, 4th Bn – 176, 208, 210, 258, 263, 276, 314

Sussex, Royal, 5th Bn – 76, 115, 134, 168, 209, 214, 215, 253, 312; 8th Bn – 14, 29, 38, 71, 78, 80, 81, 83, 84, 87, 100, 169, 186, 192, 195, 203, 220, 249–50, 269, 281, 292, 312

Warwickshire, Royal, 14th Bn – 214, 246–7, 256, 259, 312; 15th Bn – 246; 16th Bn – 246

Welch Fusiliers, 4th Bn – 201

Welch Regt., 6th Bn – 315; 8th Bn – 9, 11, 46, 51, 119, 133, 290, 315; 14th Bn – 92; 19th Bn – 7, 12, 20, 37, 92, 127, 133, 153, 200, 201, 250, 250, 282, 292, 315; 23rd Bn – 7, 137, 291, 315

West Yorkshire, 11th Bn – 5; 21st Bn – 73, 90, 99, 174, 224–5, 255, 256, 284–5, 299, 315

Wiltshire, 1st Bn – 195

Worcestershire, 2/8th Bn – 222; 14th Bn – 8, 133, 155, 220, 221, 252, 276, 283, 292, 316; 17th Bn – 229, 238–40, 254, 258, 262, 275, 316

Yorkshire Regt., 1/4th, 1/5th Bn – 198; 12th Bn – 10, 12, 49, 52, 53, 135, 140, 198, 228, 238, 275, 276–7, 316; 15th Bn – 228

York & Lancaster, 7th Bn – 3, 10, 15, 19, 34, 48, 97, 105, 116, 118, 124, 133, 167, 169, 173–4, 199, 204, 222–3, 254, 256, 259, 279, 292, 293, 316

121st Indian Pioneers – 14

Labour Companies – 115, 287
Labour Corps – 287

Midland Pioneers – see 11/Leicester

New Army – xi, 1, 2, 21, 54, 55, 58, 210
North-Eastern Railway Pioneers – see 17/Northumberland Fusiliers

Oldham Comrades – see 24/Manchester

Pioneer Corps – xii, 288
Pioneer Regiment – 289
Public Works Pioneers – see 18th, 19th & 26th Middlesex

Severn Valley Pioneers – see 14/Worcester
St. Helen's Pioneers – see 11/S. Lancs

Teeside Pioneers – see 12/Yorks
Training Reserve – 191, 192
Tyneside Pioneers – see 18th and 19th N.F.

Welsh Pioneers – see 23/Welch
Wool Textile Pioneers – see 21/West Yorks